POPULAR RELIGION, LIBERATION AND CONTEXTUAL THEOLOGY

This publication is no. 8 in the series KTC (KERK EN THEOLOGIE IN CONTEXT - CHURCH AND THEOLOGY IN CONTEXT) of the Faculty of Theology of the Catholic University of Nijmegen, the Netherlands.
Editorial staff of the series:
prof.dr. P.H.J.M. Camps
drs. B.A. Endedijk
dr. H.S.M. Groenen
prof.dr. H. Häring
prof.dr. J. Van Nieuwenhove

POPULAR RELIGION,
LIBERATION AND CONTEXTUAL THEOLOGY

Papers from a congress
(January 3-7, 1990, Nijmegen, the Netherlands)
dedicated to Arnulf Camps OFM

Edited by
Jacques Van Nieuwenhove
and
Berma Klein Goldewijk

UITGEVERSMAATSCHAPPIJ J.H. KOK – KAMPEN 1991

Translation, interpretation and correction: Irene Bouman-Smith
Translation of the text of S. Semporé by Jan Hoeberichts and of A. Máté-Tóth by Othmar Noggler

© Copyright 1991 by the Faculty of Theology, Catholic University of Nijmegen, the Netherlands
Licensed edition, published by Uitgeversmaatschappij J.H. Kok b.v., P.O.Box 130, 8260 AC Kampen,
the Netherlands
Cover design: Dik Hendriks
Desk editing: Universitair Publikatiebureau KUN
Lay-out: Infobever, Nijmegen
ISBN 90 242 3499 9/CIP/NUGI 631

Contents

Popular religion, liberation and contextual theology
Exploring some questions

Jacques Van Nieuwenhove and Berma Klein Goldewijk, the Netherlands

The initiative to organize a congress and dedicate the report to Professor Arnulf Camps OFM was born from the desire to celebrate an event which marks not only his professional life, but also the future of the Department of Missiology in the Faculty of Theology in Nijmegen, a Department whose president he has been since 1963. That event is his retirement. Rather than publish a Liber Amicorum devoted to the contribution which he has made to missiology, we preferred to review actual problems that are part of liberating practices and that ask for pertinent missiological reflection. We opted for the complex subject of popular religion, its liberative significance and its relevance for contextual theology. The results of our efforts are published in this book which we dedicate to Arnulf Camps as a sign of our gratitude and esteem.[1]

The wholeness and the ambiguity of popular religion

The more immediate motives for choosing the theme of popular religion and liberation resulted both from the second general assembly of the EATWOT in Oaxtepec, Mexico (1986)[2] and the EATWOT consultation on religion and liberation, New Delhi, India (1987)[3]. In Oaxtepec, the question of popular religion and its liberating impact was dealt with explicitly. It was recommended that in-depth research be started on popular religion. In making this recommendation the Association not only indicated a theme to be studied, but also proposed a hermeneutical perspective and some methodological principles for its implementation. Starting from the increasing evidence that religion is a part of liberation struggles in the third world today,[4] and that traditional religions have become

1 At the end of the book we reproduce a bibliography which illustrates Arnulf Camps' constant concern to re-think the major questions confronting the christian conscience and missionary action. A 'tabula gratulatorum' provides evidence of the international breadth of his activities.
2 'Commonalities, differences and cross-fertilization among third world theologies. A document based on the Seventh International Conference of the Ecumenical Association of Third World Theologians – EATWOT, Oaxtepec, Mexico, December 7-14, 1986', in: *Voices from the Third World*, 11(1988), n.1, 121-151.
3 'The EATWOT consultation on religion and liberation, New Delhi, India, 1-5 December 1987', in: *Voices from the Third World*, 11(1988), n.1, 152-171.
4 Aloysius Pieris expressed this in his statement: "A true revolution cannot go against religion in its totality. If a revolution succeeds, it does so normally as a cathartic renewal of religion itself... No *true* liberation is possible unless persons are 'religiously motivated' toward it. To be religiously motivated is to be drawn from the depths of one's being." (A. Pieris, *An Asian theology of liberation*, Maryknoll, Orbis Books, 1988, 100).

1

centres of popular resistance and a source of inspiration to sustained struggle, the EATWOT decided to identify the liberating elements of religion and to strengthen reflection on popular religion on the basis of concrete liberation practices in the third world.

In 1987, in New Delhi, the first results of this recommendation were to be seen. Twenty-two participants coming from the three continents of the third world came together. On that occasion a fundamental thesis was elaborated which stated that the liberating character of religion can be found in its search for wholeness. This search for wholeness, so the EATWOT consultation affirmed, throws into sharp relief the brokenness not just of our personal lives but also of our social world.[5] It does not, however, automatically generate liberating practices. The EATWOT consultation was very explicit in describing the limitations of popular religion: it often tranquilizes its followers and fosters passivity; it promotes dependence on religious agents; it can be used as a convenient means of keeping people resigned to their situation of oppression, interpreted as "God's will", or as the fruit of their unexpiated sin (karma). Against this background, the EATWOT drew attention to the ambiguity of popular religion: sometimes its vision of wholeness arouses movements of socio-political resistance and protest; at other times it revitalizes fundamentalism, sharpening ethnic divisions and promoting escapism and submission to oppressive power structures.[6]

In this sense we should like to draw attention to the identities of popular religions and to the diversity of the roles played by popular religion in different historical contexts. In the seventies and eighties in Latin America urban religious movements experienced a new expansion; they included not only base ecclesial communities and pentecostal,[7] charismatic and spiritist movements of all kinds, but also – in the case of Brazil – the expansion of umbanda, one of the Afro-Brazilian religions. Brazilian social scientists explain the rapid expansion of Afro-Brazilian religions by arguing that popular religion plays an important role in the social integration of the impoverished masses in an increasingly anonymous urban society.[8] The question is whether this explanation is sufficient. How does this explanation relate to the historical fact that Afro-Brazilian religions, especially the candomblé, are for centuries a source of socio-cultural identity within a

---

5 EATWOT underlines the critical role of the "search for wholeness". Other authors – for example Virgil Elizondo – stress more specifically its significance as a source of plenitude and harmony. In this line, Elizondo argued that religious symbols – symbols which are in fact the result of an assimilation of those of Iberian christianity into a genuine pre-Colombian culture – enable Mexican minorities in the USA to synthesis contradictory life forces into a harmonious tension, experiencing joy and giving meaning to life no matter the circumstances (see V. Elizondo, 'Popular religion as support of identity: A pastoral-psychological case-study based on the Mexican American experience in the USA, in: Concilium, 1986, n.186, 38.
6 See 'The EATWOT consultation....', a.c., 152-153.
7 See F. Rolim, Pentecostais no Brasil. Uma interpretação socio-religiosa, Petrópolis, Vozes, 1985.
8 See R. Ortiz, A morte branca do feiticeiro negro, Petrópolis 1978; and idem, 'A morte branca do feiticeiro negro. Umbanda: integração de uma religião numa sociedade de classes', in: Religião e sociedade, 1977, n.1, 43-50.

dominant society?[9] On the other hand, in Afro-religious studies, umbanda is interpreted as a religion perfectly attuned to a new period of socio-urban development in Brazil. In umbanda, people from the middle classes and some sections of the upper classes appropriated elements of Afro-Brazilian culture and reinterpreted these within a completely different socio-cultural universe. One of the implications of this was that umbanda was capable of adapting to the accepted values and ideologies of modern, urban society.[10]

In Eastern-Europe, in Poland in particular, popular catholicism appeared to be an important factor in the resistance to an authoritarian regime. Pilgrimages developed into impressive demonstrations. Moreover, in the changes taking place today, catholicism has played a certain role in building up and defending a national identity. As Wladyslaw Piwowarski said: catholicism became the faith of a nation, guaranteeing national identity and giving sense to the sufferings of individuals. At the political level, it was both conservative (in relation to the nation) and critical (in relation to the state).[11] The question here is whether popular catholicism in Eastern Europe has not emerged out of the shadow of the last forty years with a surprising new content and meaning.

On the other hand, in Western Europe – and to some extent also in the South of Europe – we observe a process of the gradual disappearance of popular religion. Moreover, the West often considers popular catholicism as a closed chapter and it rejects it in terms of a static and traditionalist form of religiosity. Here, popular religion, on occasion, turns out to be an irrelevant residue from the past.

From these different developments it appears that the cultural and socio-political identities and functions of popular religion differ depending on the specific context. Sometimes it functions as an explicit or implicit form of symbolic protest of a minority against an officially imposed pattern of society, religion or culture. At other times, popular religion appears as an element of massive resistance and the forming of a national identity. In both cases, however, it is decisive for survival, for overcoming all kinds of suffering and for the coherence, wholeness and continuity of life.[12] In addition, we know that in some cases popular religion is manipulated by religious leaders or the state, sometimes provoking fanatical reactions as, for example, book burning.[13] However ambiguous popular religion,

---

9 See C. Brandão, 'Creencia e identidad: campo religioso y cambio cultural', in: *Cristanismo y sociedad*, 1987, n.93, 65-106; and also C. Geertz, *The interpretation of cultures*, New York, 1973.
10 See D. Brown, *Politics of an urban religious movement*, Thesis Ph.D., University of Columbia, 1974.
11 See W. Piwowarski, 'The guarantor of national identity: Polish catholicism', in: *Concilium*, 1986, n.186, 22-23. In the same vein, religious symbols would appear to be a key-factor in the survival of (the identity of) a minority group in the USA – a legitimatizing of a "people" – and a resource for resistance against the dominating culture (see V. Elizondo, *a.c.*, 36-38).
12 See A. Opazo Bernales, *Hacia una comprensión teórica de la religión de los oprimidos*, San José, CSUCA, 1982; S. Judd, 'Fashioning a vital synthesis: Popular religion and the evangelization project in Southern Peru', in: *Concilium*, 1986, n.186, 113-121.
13 See P. Fry, 'Feijoada e soul food: notas sobre a manipulação de símbolos étnicos e nacionas', in: *Ensaios de opinião*, 1977, n.4; E. Dussel, 'Popular religion as oppression and liberation: Hypotheses on its past and present in Latin America', in: *Concilium*, 1986, n.186, 91. With

3

the first question thus is not whether popular religion exercises a socio-political function, but rather which function it does exercise and how this relates to changes in its identity. All this convinced us that intercontextual dialogue is necessary if we are to discuss the subject.

AN INTERCONTEXTUAL DIALOGUE

In order to launch such a dialogue we invited participants representing the very many backgrounds against which we see popular religion. Of the 70 people who took part – coming from 24 different countries – 22 came from countries of the third world.[14] The preponderance of males was obvious. Nevertheless, 18 women from different continents were present, expressing feminine points of view of the issues under discussion.

Special mention should be made of the participation of theologians from Eastern Europe. Who would have been able to predict, at the beginning of 1989, that christians from Eastern Europe would be able to leave their country quite freely to take part in a theological congress? A few months before the congress took place, peoples have overthrown the totalitarian regimes which oppressed them for decades. We are witnessing a liberation movement at the very heart of historical socialism which for too long had been the victim of the supremacy of the single party. This is a revolutionary movement: the "wall" came down. It has overturned the history of Europe and it raises new questions: The danger of seeing Europe concentrating on its internal relationships and of abdicating its responsibilities towards the third world is all too real. It does, however, create new space for dialogue. In welcoming participants from Hungary and Czechoslovakia, we committed ourselves to discover both their long history of resistance to a totalitarian ideology and system and the role which the gospel has played in their struggle for liberation.

Towards an interpretation of popular religion

The congress aimed to identify further the liberating and oppressive elements of popular religiosity. The first challenges, as EATWOT demonstrated, consists of deepening insights into the real practices and forms of consciousness of popular religion. In making these observations, we open a complex debate with regard to the socio-scientific and theological interpretation of popular religion.

---

regard to the destruction of the Aymara religious system in Northern Chile, readers can consult J. van Kessel, A. Droogers, 'De kerk en de indianen in Chili en Brazilië. Over negatieve resultaten en positieve voornemens', in: J. Tennekes, H.H. Vroom (eds), *Contextualiteit en christelijk geloof*, Kampen, Kok, 1989, 151-157.

14 Participants came from Africa (Burkina Faso, Cameroon, Benin, Zaire, Rwanda, South Africa); from Latin America (Brazil, Colombia, Uruguay, Costa Rica, Nicaragua); from Asia (India, the Philippines, Sri Lanka, Indonesia, Hong Kong); from Europe (Hungary, Czechoslovakia, Germany, Great Britain, Belgium, France, the Netherlands, Portugal).

THE CONCEPT OF POPULAR RELIGION

There is indeed a complex debate concerning the interpretation of popular religion. The difficulties in constructing an adequate interpretation begin already with the definitions of "people" and "popular religion" or "popular religiosity".[15] The fundamental question is: to what extent can particular forms of religion or religiosity be characterized as "popular"? What is the meaning of "people" or "popular"? Sometimes, "people" stands for the oppressed classes or the poorer strata of the population,[16] as opposed to groups possessing more knowledge and power. At other times, "people" is identical to "nation", or a minority within a nation, thus considering popular religiosity as the religious culture of a collective subject with a proper historical experience and cultural tradition. Also we see that many theologians do use a vague and very broad definition of 'people'. This is the case when, for example, Samuel Rayan defines third world-theology as a theology of the people which constitutes itself in "the struggle of ethnic groups against racism; of women against sexist oppression and patriarchy; of Africans against cultural oppression which they have named anthropological pauperization...; and of all the ex-colonies against socio-economic and political oppression littered by imperialist policies".[17]

A clarification and discussion of the concept used would seem inevitable. One suggestion might be to give serious consideration to the approach of EATWOT when it affirms that popular religiosity receives its "popular" identity because it contains a "cosmic" element. This cosmic element of popular religion enables us to go beyond the vigorous oppositions between "politics" and "culture". It also admits an understanding of popular religion in terms of the symbolic universe and the wisdom of the majority of the world population, living in situations of utter poverty, generating their own religious practices and forms of consciousness. Such a broader interpretation might even be an important element in understanding why popular religion plays such a dynamic role in Eastern Europe. There we do indeed find a context with new forms of poverty and struggle for survival as the consequence of the massive poisoning of the soil and pollution of the air resulting from the uncontrolled emission of pollutants by heavy industry. Could this ecological catastrophe perhaps sharpen a cosmic form of consciousness in both East and West Europe? It is an open question.

---

15 Does it make any sense to declare that popular religiosity is a popular 'religion'? According to Enrique Dussel, popular catholicism and official catholicity are two different religions (see E. Dussel, *a.c.*, 83). Osmar Erwin Gogolok defines it as the "religion of the people" rather than popular religiosity (see 'Pastoral aspects of popular religion in Brazil', in: *Concilium*, 1986, n.186, 105-112).

16 Medellín understood 'people' to be the peasants and the marginalized urban workers deprived of property. Thus 'people' is understood in opposition to a quantitative and qualitative minority (see L. Maldonado, 'Popular religion: its dimensions, levels and types', in: *Concilium*, 1986, n.186, 3-11. This seems to be very similar to Engelbert Mveng's use of the term 'people' (see E. Mveng, 'African liberation theology', in: *Concilium*, 1988, n.199, 9.

17 See S. Rayan, 'Third world theology: where do we go from here', in: *Concilium*, 1988, n.199, 125-129. We could ask Enrique Dussel to what extent the base ecclesial communities are not only rooted in the people, but – as he said – the people itself (see E. Dussel, *a.c.*, 92).

THE CRITICAL A-PRIORI

Influenced by a-priori criteria inherent in a dogmatic marxist- or Enlightenment-approach to religion, theological reflection and pastoral action seem to have preferred a negative approach to popular forms of religion. That which is "popular" falls victim to the masters of suspicion and modern criticism of religion, rooted in liberal or marxist secularism.[18] It was treated as an unorthodox, alienated and alienating or inferior form of culture and religion.

There is in the third world a growing reaction against these unilateral approaches. As EATWOT stated, "it is no longer possible to write (religions) off as merely the ideological legitimatizing of oppressive systems".[19] There is also a growing consensus which regards popular religion as a way – often the only way – for many hundreds of millions of human beings living in conditions of stark deprivation and neglect to find meaning and hope in a situation of anonymity and death, to strengthen their identity and their will to survive. Popular religion is considered "a reservoir of the wisdom, the aspirations and the hopes of the poor",[20] or an essential dimension of the cultural and religious identity of a people which has the right to be a creative subject of culture and religion.[21]

CONSTRUCTING AN INSTRUMENT OF ANALYSIS

Liberation theologians in Latin America made a remarkable contribution to the analysis of popular religion. In a first period, early in the seventies, they emphasized in particular its alienating elements and its ideological distortions. At that time, two fundamental insights were crucial. First, the awareness that people also integrated structures and mechanisms of domination into their own religious practices and imaginations. Moreover, it was thought that popular religion functions as an element of resignation and acceptance, leading to fatalism when confronted by domination. In short, popular religion was considered a socio-cultural factor in need of basic correction.

These positions were criticized from various sides. In the first place, from inside the popular movements, struggling with ethnic, racist and sexist forms of domination. They also provoked sharp critical reactions from Africa and Asia. Whereas the Latin Americans placed the emphasis on the construction of a critical class-consciousness, African theologians, on the contrary, stressed the importance of constructing a cultural identity.[22] From the Asian point of view too, attention was

---

18 See C. Parker, 'Popular religion and protest against oppression: the Chilean example', in: *Concilium*, 1986, n.186, 28. See also Aloysius Pieris' polemic against "the polarization of the church into a Christ-against-religions theology and a Christ-of-religions theology" and his analysis of the Western and colonialist character of the criticism of religion to which we refer (see A. Pieris, *o.c.*, 88-93).

19 See 'The EATWOT consultation....' *a.c.*, 152.

20 See idem, 157.

21 See, for example, Gustavo Gutiérrez' argument for "the right of the poor to think" in his *La fuerza histórica de los pobres; Selección de trabajos*, Lima, CEP, 1979, 156-181 (translation in: *The power of the poor in history*, Maryknoll, N.Y., Orbis Books, 1983, 90-107).

22 See, for example, E. Mveng, *a.c.*, 17-34.

given to the minority position of christianity and the direct relationship which existed between massive poverty and religion.[23]

Stimulated by internal and external criticism, Latin American theologians recognized that the building up of a critical consciousness of mass poverty and unjust racist and sexist relations proceeds not only from class-consciousness but also grows in the struggle for specific cultural, religious and ethnic identities.[24] They also observed a notable cultural and religious potential in popular religiosity.[25]
The issue at stake is which starting point would be the most adequate for an analysis of popular religion. Some interpreters emphasize the anti-racist factor, as well as the ethnic and cultural identity of a minority.[26] Others choose as their starting-point the struggle against sexist domination and try to discover in which way this pervades popular religion. Still others focus on the way in which class-relationships influence popular religion.[27] The danger of each interpretation is that it restricts and narrows the specific character of popular religion, integrating it according to certain theoretical or political premises. The interrelation of these different perspectives, however, remains an open question.
In this regard, we must face the current challenges to patterns of marxist analysis. Various interpretations of the process of change in Eastern Europe would seem to suggest that the bankruptcy of the totalitarian regimes in that part of Europe also means the end of all marxist instruments of analysis. We might well ask if these recent developments do indeed place us on the horns of the dilemma of simply rejecting or accepting marxist analysis. Rather, these challenges are the result of concrete processes of historical change. The key question to be asked is whether the marxist instruments of historical analysis will be able to cope with current national, ethnic, cultural, religious and sex-specific issues.[28]

Maybe we can take still another step. The changes that occurred within the religious universe of popular religion still require to be interpreted. From anthropological and sociological studies of candomblé and umbanda in Brazil it is indeed obvious that Afro-Brazilian religions do assimilate social conflicts within

---

23 See, for example, A. Pieris, o.c., 87-110.
24 See J. de Santa Ana, 'The situation of Latin American theology (1982-1987)', in: Concilium, 1988, n.199, 49-50.
25 See the well-known thesis of G. Gutiérrez with regard to the religious-revolutionary potential of organized and committed poor in Latin America, in: G. Gutiérrez, o.c., 96-99.
26 See Q. Duncan et al. (eds), Cultura negra y teología, San José, DEI, 1986, esp. 'Parte I (Relatorio de la consulta)', 13-44; and 'Parte II: Agenda para la consulta "Cultura negra y teología"', 45-70.
27 See O. Maduro, Religião e luta de classes. Quadro teórico para a análise de suas inter-relações na América Latina, Petrópolis, 1981 (or. cast. 1980); F. C. Rolim, Religião e classes populares, Petrópolis, Vozes, 1980.
28 With regard to the Latin American debate on this subject, see S. Torres, J. Eagleson (eds), The challenge of basic christian communities, Maryknoll, N.Y., Orbis Books, 1981 (especially 13-76). For a reflection on 'functionalistic', 'essentialistic' and 'marxist' approaches to religion, see G. Baum, 'Definities van godsdienst in de sociologie', in: Concilium, 16(1980), n.6, 31-40.

their own religious universe and do rework them.[29] This brings up the question of what kind of changes occurred in the religious contents of popular religion.[30] It has been discovered in Brazil nowadays, that giving pre-eminence to the socio-political functions of popular religiosity makes the religious universe itself appear as a mere static, unchangeable element. Thanks to this approach, the extent to which religious contents do change and how they themselves have been influenced by socio-political and cultural changes throughout history became clear. One of the consequences of this approach is a deeper insight into the capacity of Afro-Brazilian religions to respond over and over again to the concrete problems of life. That may help to explain why these religions appear to be so attractive. These socio-scientific interpretations are, however, new to Latin American theologians and so far they have not really been worked out.

Popular religion and contextual theologies

We have made observations and asked questions here concerning the need for a) an intercontextual dialogue on popular religion which exposes its socio-political and cultural identity and functions; b) an instrument of analysis that will permit anti-racist, anti-sexist and class options; c) an interpretation of changes in practices and forms of consciousness of the subject of popular religion, thus gaining a deeper insight into modifications in the symbolic universes. A theological approach to popular religion, however, also presupposes specific criteria and critical contextual hermeneutics which, in turn, call for inter-disciplinary cooperation. For the time being, however, the theological interpretation of popular religion remains a controversial issue, even within the EATWOT dialogue.[31] In the following paragraph we shall limit ourselves merely to some observations concerning the question of how contextual theologies are dealing with popular religion.

Latin American liberation theologians tend to see the bible as the centre of the religiosity of the people. According to Gustavo Gutiérrez, a liberation theology must be a theology that goes with and comes from the people, and in doing so it of necessity becomes a spiritual theology, integrating biblical symbols which are constitutive of people's religious and social consciousness. On this basis, he and others encourage the formation of a critical approach of people's faith which, in

---

29 See Furuya Yoshiaki, 'Entre "Nagoização" e "Umbandização". Uma síntese no culto Mina-Nagô de Belem, Brasil', in: *Annals*, Japan Association for Latin American Studies, 1986, n.6, 13-35; id. 'Caboclos as possessing-spirits. A review of two models in Afro-Brazilian religious studies', in: *The Japanese journal of ethnology*, 51(1986), n.3, 248-274.
30 See C. Brandão, *Os deuses do povo. Um estudo sobre a religião popular*, São Paulo, Ed. Brasiliense, 1986; id., *Memória do sagrado. Estudos de religião e ritual*, São Paulo, Ed. Paulinas, 1985.
31 In an evaluation of the results of EATWOT's theological research, Samuel Rayan barely mentions the issue of popular religion (see, *a.c.*).

turn, orientates liberating changes.[32] The question here is to what extent the christian inspired consciousness to which Gutiérrez refers is representative of Latin American popular religiosity. The same basic question can be asked with regard to theological reflections coming from the "independent churches" in Africa,[33] or from Asian "small human communities".

With regard to the base ecclesial communities, the theologians mentioned laid heavy emphasis on their ecclesial identity. They also provided a legitimation of the way in which these communities, through a new sacramental practice, including new ministries, contribute to a new model of the church of the poor. They paid less attention, however, to the different dimensions of popular religious consciousness and the changes in devotional practices within the base ecclesial communities.[34] We ask ourselves if and how African or Asian liberation theologians are equipped to face these challenges.

With regard to the inculturation of theology in Africa, Sidbe Semporé observed that the christianity of the masses represents an authentically African and potentially evangelical response to the gospel message. Africanization or inculturation, he concluded, should be accomplished starting from the experiences of the base.[35] Here the question arises: why and in what sense is the christianity of the masses only potentially evangelical? The purpose of inculturation is often defined in a dialectic way: the positive values of non-christian religions or non-Western cultures should be assumed by church and theology but at the same time be purified, elevated and transformed by the christian tradition. Problems arise, as Felix Wilfred argued, when established theological norms are criticized in the name of apparently non-orthodox religious practices and convictions.[36]

An additional question has to do with the rationality of theological language. More than the rest, Asian theologians take distance with regard to a rationality which gives a privileged position to logical analysis, which tends to harden the dialectical opposition between truth and error and shows a clear preference for tangible and controllable results. Felix Wilfred sought to demonstrate that Asian thought is typified by an approach to reality and to the sacred characterized by a perception of order and internal harmony which re-links all the specific situations

---

32 See, for example, G. Gutiérrez, *We drink from our own wells. The spiritual journey of a people*, Maryknoll, N.Y., Orbis Books, 1984.
33 See, for example, M. Schoffeleers, 'Afrikaanse theologie en zwarte theologie. Twee contextualiteiten in conflict', in: J. Tennekes, H.H. Vroom (eds), *Contextualiteit, o.c.*, 86-104.
34 See B. Klein Goldewijk, 'Nationaal consolideringsproces van kerkelijke basisgemeenschappen (1975-1988)', in: *Lotgenoten-Bondgenoten. Solidariteit in Brazilië*, Nijmegen/'s-Hertogenbosch, KSC/SGM, 1990, 51-86, here 80-83.
35 See S. Semporé, 'Popular religion in Africa: Benin as a typical instance', in: *Concilium*, 1986, n.186, 50-51, and id. 'Afro-christianisme, un courant irreversible', in: *Spiritus*, 30(1989), n.115, 193-205.
36 See F. Wilfred, 'World religions and christian inculturation', in: *Indian theological studies*, 25(1988), n.1, 5-26.

to a totality which is experienced as mystery.[37] In the Asian context, in the author's opinion, inculturation raises a radical question for the hermeneutical models prevailing in theology. Does this search for the characteristics of Asian thought imply a basic criticism of any form of rationality linked to liberating practice?

A final question concerns the partnership of the poor in doing theology. It is generally recognized that the theological reflection of a large number of third world-theologians is supported by a mystique of the poor. In their theology the poor person is seen as the accusation of the established order, the privileged recipient of the gospel and of the Kingdom or even the privileged hearer of the message. It is in the poor person that the sacramental presence of God in history manifests itself and is a key which grants access to the deepest meaning of the scriptures. According to Samuel Rayan, to all this must be added the fact that – because of their political struggle and consciousness of their own oppression – the poor are becoming partners in the field of doing theology, and even subjects of theologizing.[38] We may well ask what this partnership means for our way of reflecting theologically on popular religion.

The church's official position with regard to popular religiosity and popular catholicism raises a number of questions. In saying this, we know that since Vatican II and the meetings of the Latin American Bishops' Conference in Medellín (1968) and Puebla (1979), churches have taken an increasingly open stand with respect to popular religion.
Nevertheless, popular catholicism developed to some extent within and to some extent parallel or opposed to the legally imposed official catholicism forced on the third world in the colonial period.[39] These facts lead us to the question of the extent to which official catholicism has remained foreign to the religious universe of broader sectors of the population, even after the period of romanization.[40]

---

37 "In Asia religion is viewed mainly an anubhava. It is the inner experience in which the dichotomy between subject and object is overcome, and a deep communion with the entire reality – cosmic, divine and human – is maintained." (see F. Wilfred, 'Inculturation as a hermeneutical question. Reflections in the Asian context', in: *Vidyayoti*, sept. 1988, 425). See also F. Wilfred (ed.), *Verlaß den Tempel. Antyodaya – indischer Weg zur Befreiung*, Freiburg i.B., Herder, 1988, 7-17.
38 See, S. Rayan, *a.c.*, 128 and 138.
39 See R. Azzi, *O catolicismo popular no Brasil*, Petrópolis, Vozes, 1978. With regard to Latin America, L. Maldonado concludes that ecclesial authority has always moved around between four attitudes which the author summarizes as follows: proposition, prescription, tolerance and proscription. In reply, the people's attitude to the church varied from one of voluntary acceptance, forced submission and syncretism, to rejection and repudiation (see. L. Maldonado, *a.c.*, 10).
40 See R. Azzi, 'Formação histórica do catolicismo popular Brasileira', in: B. Beni dos Santos et.al. (eds), *A religião do povo*, São Paulo, Ed. Paulinas, 1978, 44-71; E. Hoornaert, *Formação do catolicismo Brasileiro 1500-1800. Ensaio de interpretação a partir dos oprimidos*, Petrópolis, Vozes, 1978; P. A. Ribeiro de Oliveira, 'O catolicismo do povo', in: *A religião do povo, o.c.*, 72-80; id., *Religião e dominação de classes. Gênese, estrutura e função do catolicismo romanizado no Brasil*, Petrópolis, Vozes, 1985.

Whether this open ecclesial approach – formulated in terms of "evangelization of the culture" – will perhaps once again use popular religion as an instrument for its own purposes remains to be seen. After all, christian theology still bears traces of superiority in the name of the gospel and the eschatological salvation in Christ. This way the openness to the redeeming and liberating meaning of non-christian popular religions can be restricted.[41] To what extent?

TO CONCLUDE

All of these considerations convinced us that an inter-contextual dialogue is necessary to bring the subject up for discussion. We hope that our publication, with the contributions of eminent social scientists and theologians, will contribute to the further identification of the liberative and oppressive elements of popular religiosity. The present book is not a mere discussion about theories, or a stifling academic debate. The first challenge, as EATWOT demonstrated, does indeed consist of analyzing the significance and the functions of popular religions within the framework of present historical tensions and conflicts. The EATWOT also showed the need to deepen insights into real practices and forms of consciousness of popular religion. These insights are also needed for the further completion or correction of the socio-political and theological understanding of liberation and culture within these developments. Finally, we hope that these contributions will help overcome the well-known impasse in the dialogue between theologians of the third and the first world and will at least launch the urgently-needed dialogue with the second world.[42]

All that remains is for us to express our gratitude towards all the members of the organizing committee, and we do so with all our heart. Thank you therefore to Andreas Müller, Othmar Noggler, Jan Heijke and Jan van Lin for their cooperation. Particularly thanks to Jan van Lin for having created possibilities for the publication of this book. To the members of the secretariat: Jan Wouda, Benedict Laval, Helma Hurkens, Marinus Huybreghts and W. Coenen. To them we express our gratitude for their help in welcoming the participants and in organizing the congress.

The whole team helped create a climate which encouraged reflection and an intercontinental encounter. We gratefully acknowledge Irene Bouman-Smith, who did most of the translations from the french and the correction work for the whole book. Special thanks also to Jan Hoeberichts and Othman Noggler for

41 See, for example, F. Rehbein (S.Sp.S), *Candomblé e salvação. A salvação na religião nagô à luz da teologia cristã*, São Paulo, Ed. Loyola, Col. Fé e realidade XVIII, 1985.
42 See B. Klein Goldewijk, E. Borgman, F. van Iersel (eds), *Bevrijdingstheologie in West-Europa*, Kampen, Kok, 1988. For a feminine perspective, L. Lagerwerf, 'South Africa. Women's struggle in theology, church and society', in: *Exchange*, 17(1987), n.48, 33-51; ibid., 'African women doing theology', in: *Exchange*, 19(1990), n.1, 1-60; A.G. Honig, 'Asian women theology', in: *Exchange* 17(1987), n.47, 1-48; N. Nauta, B. Klein Goldewijk, 'Latin American women doing theology', in: *Exchange*, 17(1987), n.48, 1-31; E. Borgman, B. Klein Goldewijk, 'Feministische theologie in de context van de eerste en de derde wereld', in: *Bevrijdingstheologie in West-Europa*, o.c., 127-140.

their translation work. Of course we could never have held this congress without the generous financial assistance of 21 religious and missionary congregations from the Netherlands, or without the substantial aid which we received from the aid agencies AMA; the Bisschoppelijke Vastenaktie; the Missionswissenschaftliches Institut – Aachen; Missio – Munich; the Missionszentrale der Franciskaner – Bonn; Novib; and the Stichting Katholieke Noden. Nor must we forget the Catholic University of Nijmegen and, in particular, the Faculty of Theology, which provided so much assistance to the secretariat.

PART I

AFRICA

The issue of paganism in the post-colonial era
African perspectives

Achille Mbembe, Cameroon

The prodigious advance of popular piety in post-colonial Africa forces us to bring back to their correct proportions those elements which play a role in the encounter between christianity and indigenous forms of religion.[1] Such a task, indeed, requires us to take our distance from those ethnological theories which, until now, have dominated the study of African religions.[2] Indeed, for a number of reasons which I cannot set out in detail here, such approaches lead nowhere.[3] I should, however, emphasise the a-historical character of their method. The latter is based on the idea, and an idea of which it is difficult to conceive, that not only African societies were outside time and duration, but, moreover, that there was one sole tradition. It was this one sole tradition which, at all times and in all places, organized the methods of defining identities, legitimacies and meanings.[4] This tradition was fixed, unprepared to change and closed in upon itself. It was only the arrival of the religions of the Book which were able to get the better of it, because their advent created a major crisis of relevance.

Yet today, no one, at least no historian, doubts that there existed a plurality of symbolic and institutional constructs within pre-colonial Africa.[5] Here we should probably make the necessary distinction between the various "popular" (or otherwise) forms of religious practice: the rites linked to the needs of daily life, village cults, ceremonies of initiation, royal worship... On the other hand, it is now generally accepted that the fields of African religion were never homogeneous, and were still less stable. At no time in history were they determined once and

1 For a formalistic approach to this matter, and some of the debates which have arisen from it, see R. Houston, 'African conversion', in: *Africa*, 41(1971), n.2; 'On the rationality of conversion', in: *Africa*, 45(1975), n.3-4; H. Fisher, 'Conversion reconsidered', in: *Africa*, 43(1973), n.1.
2 As we see from the impressive bibliography collected by Ntedika Konde, 'La théologie africaine. Bibliographie sélective (1925-1975)', in: *Revue Africaine de Théologie*, 1(1977), n.2, 149-266; 2(1978), n.3, 141-156 and n.4, 283-305; 3(1979), n.5, 121-131; 4(1980), n.6, 257-265 and n.7, 105-131.
3 See, in particular, A. Mbembe, *Afriques indociles. Christianisme, pouvoir et état en société postcoloniale*, Paris, Karthala, 1988, ch. 3.
4 For an overview of the discussions on the subject of "tradition", readers should turn, in particular, to F. Eboussi Boulaga, *La crise du muntu. Authenticité africaine et philosophie*, Paris, Présence africaine, 1977; and *Christianisme sans fétiche*. Révélation et domination, Paris, Présence africaine, 1981.
5 See, for example, T.O. Ranger and I. N. Kimambo (eds), *The historical study of african religion*, Berkeley, University of California Press, 1976; Y. Person, 'Pour une histoire des religions africaines', in: *Archives des sciences sociales des religions*, 36(1973), 91-101.

for all to the point of becoming closed to innovation. The "circulation" or the exchange of worship and rites (as a result of wars of conquest, migrations, the process of political centralisation, ecological changes as often occurred at times of drought or famine, demographic and technological rhythms) is therefore a constituent element of African history.

More seriously, the constitution of the fields of religions themselves was almost always something more than merely a religious matter. To the extent that among the native peoples, just as in other historic societies, there can be neither religion nor symbol without reference to that which is different, without the extraction and the allocation of resources and services, without regulation of conduct, without more or less legitimate representations of the social order, then we can see that the very principle of the constitution of these said fields was, by its nature, a political problem. Indeed, it constantly raised the issue of "government" in the widest sense of the term (government of domestic units, of lineages, of clans, of the environment, of the space and of the climate, of human beings, of wealth and of symbols, of knowledge and of things in general....). It is this inherent conflict in the work of defining the general aims and the fundamental principles of a society, and the laying down of norms of behaviour, which the naivety of the ethnological approach tends to obscure. In doing so, it becomes confused in thinking out, in a consequent manner, the modalities of the passages to christian monotheism in Africa. This sprang not from a differentiation or a clean break with native religions (because, from the outset, it rejected any form of "relationship" with them) but from an imperial desire (for conquest, for domination) which, itself, was founded on the specific form of the "truth".

Since, however, I am speaking of monotheism, I must say what that means. I shall then demonstrate how its historic paths have been conditioned, not so much by the issue of atheism (as people often claimed to believe in the West) but by what we must call "the pagan question".[6] Thereafter I shall go on to prove that the clear opposition between "monotheism" and "paganism" is erroneous, to the extent that there is a greater relationship between these two orders than anyone has been prepared to admit. In the African context, it is this which enables the native largely to de-dramatise what is called his "conversion" to the narratives of the Book. Finally, I shall set out what, in the post-colonial era, is the political efficacity inherent in popular modes of religious expression which borrow from pagan meditation (here paganism is understood in the most flexible sense, i.e. alas, the most approximate sense).

---

6 Our reading will be very different from the phenomenological one provided by M. Augé in *Génie du paganisme*, Paris, Gallimard, 1982. In deciding to explain paganism by demonstrating what it is not, Marc Augé believes that "first and foremost it is the opposite of christianity" in that 1) it is not dualist and sees no opposition between spirit and body, nor between faith and knowledge; 2) it does not conceive morality as a principle exterior to the relationships of power and of meaning; 3) it postulates a continuity between the biological and the social orders; 4) it postulates that every event is a sign and every sign has a meaning; 5) it has never been involved in mission.

Forms of the divine and forms of power

Here we shall not retrace the origins of the concept of monotheism. They are more than a little obscure.[7] What is important are the realities which it proposes and the manner in which these realities fit into an economy of power in a given historical situation.

Thus the monotheist paradigm suggests at least two cross-references. The first is that of "totalization". In principle, any monotheistic regime is based on the concept of exclusivity and of concentration, as opposed to a situation which is typified by a plurality of gods, and their dispersion among various different figures. The second cross-reference is that of "monopoly". Indeed, the belief in a single and distinct God of the world is only possible if it is accompanied by the suppression of all other forms of worship. As a result, monotheistic practice is presumed to be incompatible with the worship of other gods. It is this radicalness which gives it part of its unconditional and absolute nature. It assumes that the unique God, precisely because of that uniqueness, cannot be equalled. Because of his completeness, the worship offered him, is, in principle, incompatible with any other worship rendered to any other god. Much more than this, however, the revelation of the unique takes place within the history of a specific people, the object of special consideration and care, and endowed with a unique mission. And it is through the mediation of this specific people that God integrates himself into the history of humanity as a whole. In other words, henceforth it is no longer possible to see this people merely as one of the innumerable peoples who inhabit the earth. Thus, for example, because Israel took upon itself the role of divine election, it was expected to play a anti-idolatry role, particularly towards other nations declared to be pagan. As a result, the latter had to

---

7 Some claim that it dates back to Ancient Egypt. The conquests of the XVIIIth dynasty resulted in this country becoming an empire. At the level of religion, this new imperialism resulted in the development of new ideas, at least among the intellectual and political elites. They achieved their most sophisticated form under Pharaoh Amenhotep IV (later known as Akhenaton). Akhenaton elevated the worship of Aton into the official religion and declared the latter the one and only God. But his attempt was short-lived, for by the end of his reign, the worship of individual gods was reinstated, and polytheist tendencies reigned anew. For further information see S. Morenz, *Egyptian religion* (tr. A.E. Keep), Ithaca, Cornell University Press, 1973, 137-150; and S. Freud, *Moses and monotheism* (tr. K. Jones), New York, Vintage Books, 72-73. What is, moreover, evident, is that the bible borrowed a certain number of its facts from the Egypt of the pharaohs. The most obvious case are the borrowings from the hymn to Aton to be found in Psalm 104. The elements borrowed from the Egypt of the pharaohs was, in most cases, "reworked" in the light of the theological and political interests of the receiving culture. See, for example, the study by P. Auffret, *Hymnes d'Egypte et d'Israel. Etude de structures littéraires*, Vandenhoek & Ruprecht Göttingen, 1981. For more systematic developments going beyond the Egyptian framework alone, see, B. Lang (ed.), *Monotheism and the prophetic minority. An essay in biblical history and sociology*, Almond, Sheffield, 1983. See principally the following works in German: O. Keel (ed.), *Monotheismus im Alten Israel und seiner Umwelt*, Fribourg, 1980; B. Lang, 'Neues über theologische Geschichte des Monotheismus', *Theologische Quartalschrift*, 163, 1983; E. Peterson, *Der Monotheismus als politisches Problem*, Leipzig, 1935. For the follow-up to the debate begun by Peterson, see K. Hungar, A. Schindler, *Monotheismus als politisches Problem? Erik Peterson und die Kritik der politischen Theologie*, Gütersloh, 1978.

17

"convert" to the "true" God who, in the last resort, was none other than the God of Israel.[8]

But we must go beyond this characterization and deal with the specific question of the production of meaning. For the idea of monotheism also refers back to the concept of the "ultimate", i.e. the first and last principle of everything. In this respect we see that there can be no monotheism except in relation to a process of producing a "truth" which not only determines the foundations and the finalities of the world but, moreover, is the origin of all meaning. Indeed, any monotheistic system presupposes the "work" of identifying the precise field of meaning, of the reproduction of spaces and the transmission of meaning. To this extent we can affirm that monotheism is a specific form of the shaping of knowledge about the "ultimate". It is an historic form of annexation and thereafter of appropriation of the concept of "truth" and its final forming into an exclusive image of the divine. Now, the problem of the identification of final ends is the very prototype of a political question. By clearly stating its rejection of any idea of the relativity of "truth", monotheism postulates the existence of a universe of sole meaning.

In such a universe, the margin allowed for dissent is very limited. Eventual disputes cannot, in fact, have anything to do with the manner in which this meaning is constituted because, just as much as the meaning itself, the forms in which it is constituted belong to that system of undebated issues which no form of contestation is supposed to call into question. Hence the dramatic importance given to "heresy". Now, to the extent to which it is a question of integrating a specific ideo-normative profile into the human situation, we are no longer confronted merely by a religious problem. Since there can be no monotheism without the organization of some kind of arrangement, prescribed as legitimate, by means of which the conflicts between a plurality of divinities can be resolved in such a way that one of them is endowed with the monopoly of the "truth", the method of producing this arrangement does indeed constitute an act of a political order. The "truth" which has thus been annexed and monopolised to the benefit of a specific figure of that which is divine can, if needed, be converted into a source of coercion and used against one's enemies or those who are deemed to be such. The result of such an "act" is also essentially of an historical order, because through the effect of institutional mechanisms of subordination or adherence, and through the effect of a violence which is not only symbolic, the primacy of "One God" is assured and then imposed as legitimate by those in

---

8 Later, in the christian interpretation of "divine election", the coming of Jesus of Nazareth and his violent death on the cross resulted if not in the abolition of the "Old Covenant" , at least in it being overtaken, and the church took to itself the mission at one time given to the jewish people of becoming the "elect" people of God.

authority.[9] As a result, it is difficult to see how this supremacy could express itself other than as a figure of domination, but one which is historically situated.[10] Let us look at this in concrete terms on the basis of the example of biblical mono-theism.[11]

Biblical monotheism is incomprehensible unless its birth and its development are linked to the violent process of the crystallization and disintegration of the Israelite state.[12] In ancient Israel, human language with regard to the uniqueness of God is born at that point where internal and external factors flow together. The principal issue which underlies this development is the secular destiny of a nation confronted by a series of events of historical discontinuity.[13] Indeed, we know that since the 9th century vast changes had taken place in Israel's manner of integrating into local geopolitics. The two kingdoms of the North and the South had been caught up within the sphere of influence of the regional powers who were battling for hegemony in the Near East. This process of turning them into satellites took place in several stages. Prior to 722, the role of the two kingdoms in the region was that of dependencies of Assyria, to whom they paid tribute. After 722, the kingdom of the North became purely and simply an administrative district of Assyria. The same thing happened to the kingdom of the South after 586. Such upheavals promptly raised the problem of the political existence and the permanence of the identity of a country and a society crushed by the omnipotence of its neighbours.[14] Human language about the uniqueness of God thus had a clear political status. If it is risky to claim that it was but the product of an

---

9 This is the only approach which is capable of overcoming the criticisms of religion as developed by marxism, rationalism or even the German catholicism of the first half of the 19th century. I would remind readers that the majority of these criticisms were limited to the – over hasty – observation that monotheistic religions were responsible for the alliance between belief in God and political despotism. For a concrete and belated example, see E. Peterson, *Der Monotheismus als politisches Problem*, Leipzig, 1935.

10 While perhaps abusing somewhat the author's intentions, it is in this light that we can interpret the work by F. Eboussi Boulaga, *Christianisme sans fétiche. Révélation et domination*, Paris, Présence africaine, 1981.

11 We shall not try, here, to present a history of the concept of biblical monotheism. To do so would involve taking into account too many variables: the cultures of the ancient Near East and the mutual borrowings among such cultures; the history of the writing and the dating of the Old Testament texts; the combination of the different ethnic and cultural "stocks" (nomad societies, rural, pastoral urban societies, sedentary and bedouin cultures), the power shifts among the groups; the network of alliances; a periodization of jewish history itself... An attempt at synthesis is to be found in F. Smyth Florentin, 'Du monothéisme biblique: émergence et alentours', in: *Archives des sciences sociales des religions*, 59(1985), n.1, 5-16. In order to appreciate the difficulty of such a task and the intertwining of things political, religious and mythical resulting – among the jews in particular – in a sacralized fable, see G. Garbini, *History and ideology in Ancient Israel*, New York, Crossroad, 1988.

12 For a general view of this history see M. Grant, A *History of Ancient Israel*, London, 1984.

13 See T.H. Robinson, *The Decline and fall of the hebrew kingdoms. Israel in the eighth and seventh centuries B.C.*, Oxford, Clarendon Press, 1926.

14 It is to this extent that B. Lang, in his article 'No God but Yahweh! The origin and the character of biblical monotheism', in: *Concilium*, n.177, 1985, p. 48 can affirm that the need to adore a national and unique God developed as a reaction to "political crisis" and that therefore "nothing can be expected of diplomacy and foreign military aid any longer".

unhappy and vulnerable conscience, it cannot be denied that it developed against a background of crisis. What was, in fact, at stake was not only a vision of society and of its government, but, in addition, the problem of the historical interactions of power in a context of the unequal interchange between the "elect of God" and their neighbours.

It would, however, be a pity to take such a mechanistic view of a problem which is scarcely unilinear. The worship of Yahweh as the only God to be adored in the Temple in Jerusalem was never introduced in a single move. On the contrary, for long the idea met with firm resistance within a culture which itself was tradition-ally polytheistic.[15] These religious struggles, and the violence which accompanied them, should not merely be interpreted as epiphenomena of the imperatives of foreign policy. They can also be explained in terms of the domestic conflicts which divided Israel itself.[16] And in this sense, they had their own autonomy. What was at stake in these conflicts had just as much to do with the control of positions of power as with the allocation of material and symbolic resources. We should not, in any case, underestimate the close relationship which existed between the worship activities and the accumulation procedures.[17] The temples were not simply places of worship, they were also "financial market places". Each cult was founded upon a "social base" which, itself, enjoyed mobile relationships with those holding royal power.[18] Moreover, the latter held leading positions in the network of material and political interests fighting for their favour or seeking to assert themselves to the detriment of competing networks. When necessary, the disputes between these various interest groups borrowed the idioms of religion. Such idioms took away nothing of their material nature.

Having expressed these reservations, we can then emphasise the very real fact that Israel's extraordinary vulnerability and the precariousness of its position on the regional chess-board helped structure these struggles. It also had a major impact on the religious policy of its sovereigns.[19] The problem of knowing how to

---

15 As is proved by the various borrowings from "pagan" models, the importance of sacrifices to Baal, to the sun, to the moon or to the stars, and the importance of the prophets' pleas on behalf of "No God but Yahweh". On some of these issues, see R. de Vaux, *Histoire ancienne d'Israel*, 2 vols., Paris, 1973; and W. Kornfeld, *Religion und Offenbarung in der Geschichte Israels*, Innsbruck, 1970.

16 With regard to the encounter between Yahweh and Baal, and the violence which followed, as well as the impact of these variables on the birth of the state, some information is to be found in D. Baly, *God and history in the Old Testament. The encounter with the absolutely other in Ancient Israel*, New York, Harper and Row, 1976, 39-67.

17 On this aspect of the question, readers would learn much from studying M. Silver, *Prophets and markets. The political economy of Ancient Israel*, Boston, Kluwer-Nijhoff Publishing, 1983.

18 Thus the "No God but Yahweh" movement could count upon its "organic intellectuals" – the prophets and the members of the priestly families. Moreover, we need only think, for example, of the stormy relationship between King Ahab and Elijah. With regard to the divine landscape in general and Yahweh's relationship to the other gods of the period see, W.F. Albright, *Yahweh and the gods of Canaan*, London, 1968.

19 For example, it is public knowledge that King Ahab (874-853) supported the worshippers of Baal against whom the prophets fought. Joram (852-834) limited himself to imposing restrictions

integrate successfully into the regional power game (the problem of war, military inferiority, defeat, exile, prosperity and the building up of their own identity in the face of the surrounding imperialism) heightened the drama of the violence of the intrigues which grew up around issues whose religious significance was but one aspect among others.[20] Be that as it may, the essence of our argument is that biblical monotheism must be understood, first and foremost, as a rule of "truth". But it is a rule of "truth" which is imbedded in the permanent compromises with the secular destinies of a given people. In other words, the biblical language about the uniqueness of God is, of necessity, at some point involved in the act of interpreting the historical vulnerability of this people. This interpretation nevertheless endeavoured to be "significant", because it claimed to link this vulnerability to an area of sovereignty whose essence was inherently divine. It is this divine sovereignty which was to explain it and to invest it with a meaning whose bearing was universal. Thus we see that the monotheistic idea implicitly raises and resolves the problem of "government". The importance given to the idea of divine sovereignty is revealing in this respect, as is the manner in which responses were found to the conflicts arising from Israel's borrowing of an institution of pagan origin: royalty.[21]

The issue of a strong, centralised power had haunted Israel throughout its history (the passage from nomadism to a sedentary life, tensions brought about by the assimilation of foreign elements, external pressures and threats).[22] It was a question which was raised with ever increasing intensity as the successive defeats and the identity crises were laid at the door, at least to some extent, of the lack

---

upon them. Jehu (941-813) set out to do away with them altogether. He had Jezebel, the widow of Ahab, executed, and massacred the Baal worshippers. Hezekiah (723-699) introduced reforms with the aim of destroying all their shrines and their idols, and of purifying the Temple in Jerusalem of all so-called pagan ornaments.

20 In this respect, it is significant to note that when the Jews of Babylon returned to Jerusalem after the edict of Cyrus in 538, Ezra (of priestly lineage), his brothers, Aharonides and Nehemiah, brought with them out of Babylon not only men, women, male and female servants, camels, asses, gold and silver; they also brought with them the Torah of Moses. In order to emphasize his investiture by the divinity, and in order to impose new laws on all those who were members of Israel, Ezra turned for support to the power of Artaxerxes, one of whose rescripts elevated the Torah to the rank of an obligatory code not only for the jews returning from exile, but also for the local people. Thus the Torah, as a legal code, gained a pre-eminent position not because of its "plausibility" alone, but by an administrative act of Persian power, despite the fact that it claimed to draw its authority from another source. On this issue, see R. Goetschel, 'Pouvoir et vérité dans la période formative du judaisme palestinien', in M. Michel (dir.), *Pouvoir et vérité*, Paris, Cerf, 1989, 122-143.

21 With regard to this study, I shall rely to a large extent on the contribution by B. Renaud, 'Pouvoir royal et théocratie', in: M. Michel (dir.), *Pouvoir et verité*, Paris, Cerf. 1981, 77-97, which I shall, from time to time, paraphrase.

22 See the survey provided by M. Weinfeld, 'The transition from tribal republic to monarchy in Ancient Israel and its impression on jewish political history', in D. J. Elazar (ed.), *Kinship and consent. The jewish political tradition and its contemporary uses*, Boston, University Press of America, 1983, 151-168. In order to appreciate the importance attached to the problem of political centralization, we must take into account the socio-economic structures in operation at the time and the central role given to the structures of the family, the clan, the tribe, and patriarchy in general. See the information given in C. H. J. De Geus, *The tribes of Israel*, Amsterdam, Van Gorcum, 1976, 120-181.

of political centralization. These crises, however secular they might have been, were translated into religious language. The issue of the national god and his areas of competence was, as a result, projected into the field of tensions. To put it another way, however unspoken they might have been, the doubts about Yahweh's ability to guide his people effectively, to protect them against their external enemies, to lead them to victory in war, and to guarantee their prosperity began to be expressed openly, even if, in the long run, they preferred to exonerate Him by asserting that it was a lack of fidelity to the covenant which was responsible for the defeats and the tribulations.[23] Whatever the answer given to this "doubt", the problem remained: that of reconciling a measure of political centralisation resulting in the institution of kingship with the concept of the sovereignty of Yahweh as the sole king of Israel.

This question was far from superfluous, because in a pagan regime kingship was rooted in the very sacredness of the cosmos. Hence the central position occupied by the king in the religious order. Indeed, he assumed an intermediary function between the world of the gods and that of nature. But in view of the fact that he also administered the rites of intercession and propitiation, he also filled a priestly role. It was this which placed him at the heart of a ritual apparatus which was itself fed by its own theological representations. This was how the process of divinization of the "pagan" kings took root, the human institution participating, in a functional manner, in the sovereignty of the gods.[24]

We can appreciate the difficulties created by such borrowing within a universe in which the only sovereignty recognised was the sovereignty of Yahweh. To the extent that faith in Yahweh alone constituted the dominant rule of "truth", it was a question of knowing how to institute a new position of power (the kingship) which would, however, not arrogate to itself the same powers as under a "pagan" rule – i.e. which would no longer function as an alternative to God – and whose inherent sovereignty would not be in competition with the only sovereignty recognised, that of Yahweh. The problem was a serious one, given the fact that in the so-called pagan model, the king's powers also covered the domain of worship. As such, they had both ritual and theological implications. Now, under a monotheistic system such a claim would not only have borne within it the seeds of political absolutism, it would also have resulted in the re-introduction of a pagan dynamic into an order which specifically defined itself as the very antithesis of idolatry.[25]

---

23 On the concept of the "covenant" itself, see D. J. Elazar, 'Covenant as the basis of the jewish political tradition', in: *Kinship and consent...* pp. 1-58. On the same issue, but covering a more specific period, see A. Jaubert, *La notion d'alliance dans le judaisme aux abords de l'ère chrétienne*, Paris, 1963. A more recent work is that by J. Jackson Flanders, Jr, (et al.), *People of the covenant. An introduction to the Old Testament*, 3rd ed., Oxford, Oxford University Press, 1988.
24 For greater detail readers should consult C. J. Gadd, *Ideas of divine rule in the Ancient Near East*, London, 1948.
25 In fact, as B. Renaud reminds us, the kings of the bible made little effort to resist the temptation to arrogate to themselves priestly powers, or at the least they played a role of patronage, transferring the Ark to Sion, building the temple...

This is one of the reasons why biblical monotheism played a decisive role in the regulation of royal power, and, when necessary, provided radical criticism of it.[26] The refusal to allow kingship to participate directly in the sovereignty of God opened the way for criticism of royal power, and this was the task assumed by the prophets. The basis of this monotheistic criticism of royal power was the concept that only God is God. Royal power, on the contrary, was seen as bringing with it the virtual danger of a lack of faithfulness to the covenant between God and "His" people. The criticism of the prophets, exercised in the name of the sovereignty of Yahweh and the "contract" between Yahweh and "His" people sought to prevent royal power from usurping the divine status and the attributes of God. In so doing, this criticism not only prevented the royal power from setting itself up in absolute terms, it also established limits which made it impossible for it to harness the values of the covenant for its own benefit. As a result, Yahweh became not a state divinity, but the God of the covenant with a people. It is the people, and not the king, who are the privileged partner in such an alliance.

I have just demonstrated how, to a large extent, the biblical language with regard to the uniqueness of God disguises a political language linked to the concept of kingship and divine sovereignty, i.e. the issue of "government". I have also pointed out that the discussion with regard to the relationship between divine sovereignty (Yahweh is the one king and Israel His chosen people)[27] and the monarchy was decided in favour of God. I should emphasise that the invention of biblical monotheism was far from being a spontaneous act. Biblical monotheism must be seen as an historical construction. And, as an historical construction, it is the outcome of struggles among those groups which sought hegemony in the kingdoms of the North and of the South. But it is also a response to a political situation marked by the destruction of a small state which thereafter became dependant upon the powers which held sway at the time. Monotheism, as an idiom, could not, however, solve Israel's political problem. Given the way in which it was formulated and experienced by the Jews, the only serious claim which it might have was an ethnic one. There are several reasons for this setback. We need only mention one. Paradoxically is originates in the fact that, unlike the so-called pagan gods, one of the distinctive characteristics of the biblical God is his relative isolation. He has no family. He is neither the son nor the cousin of any other god. He has no wife; He has no progeny. Thus His claim to power is total because it cannot be disputed by any member of a possible lineage. This exclusivity is to some extent linked to the way in which religious identity in Israel was

---

26 In order to understand some of the non-religious bases of the prophetic criticism of power, see M. Silver, *Prophets and markets. The political economy of Ancient Israel*, Boston, Kluwer-Nijhoff, 1983, 121-188. With regard to the prophetic tradition in general, and the prophets' stands against Israel, cf. A. Künen, *The prophets and prophecy in Israel. An historical and critical enquiry*, Amsterdam, Philo Press, 1969, 148-185.
27 With regard to the supposed election of Israel significant information is to be found in D. Jacobson, *The story of the stories. The chosen people and its god*, London, 1982.

enlisted to help the Israelites overcome the tribal identity. In this respect, the contribution of the prophetic tradition was decisive (cf. Is. 13-21; Jr. 46-51; Ez, 25-32; and the first two chapters of Amos). It is in the light of this exclusivity that we must understand the laws with regard to ritual purity[28], and the outward observance of those laws which were supposed to distinguish the Jew from the gentile. It is also in the light of this logic of closing in upon oneself that we must understand the dissolution of mixed marriages at the time of the reforms of Esdras and Nehemiah: the major distinction between those who were Jews by birth, those who were not, and those who could never become so... Such prescriptions were unlikely to propel judaism into a universalist path, given the fact that the cultural taboos and the specific traditions into which it was locked lacked "plausibility" for non-Jews.[29] This is one of the reasons why jewish monotheism should be regarded as an enclosed monotheism.[30]

Monopolising historic mediation

It is precisely this closing off which christianity sought to overcome when, theoretically at least, it did away with the distinction between the Jews and the Greeks, it relativized the importance of the prescriptions with regard to food and ritual observances, and it declared of no matter any form of exclusion based on ethnic origin; thereafter it affirmed the community of humanity which bound master and slave, the uncircumcised and the circumcised.[31] One order, universalist in its claims, gradually replaced another order which was ethnic in character. In the paragraphs which follow, I shall leave aside the search for factors which might explain this passage from judaism to christianity, as well as the reasons for the victory of christianity in the West. First of all I shall examine some of the political outcomes of biblical monotheism, thereafter I shall deal with the same questions, but this time by applying them to the specific form of monotheism represented by christianity.

I shall waste no time on the obvious, or what has until now held the attention of students, i.e. the relationship between the church and the state, particularly since

---

28 See J. Neusner, *The idea of purity in ancient judaism. Studies in judaism in Late Antiquity I*, Leiden, 1973.
29 This does not mean that it did not become involved in proselytism. With regard to its "missionary" activities, see W.A. Braude, *Jewish proselytism in the first five centuries of the common era*, Providence, 1940.
30 In order to appreciate the nuances of the "exclusiveness" of this tradition, see R. Murphy, 'Nation dans l'Ancien Testament', in: *Concilium*, n.121, 1977, 103-105.
31 In actual fact, practice was far removed from theory. But at least a new fiction was opened up. For greater detail, and from the point of view of marxist analysis, see D. Kyrtatas, *The social structure of the early christian communities*, London, Verso, 1987. With regard to the "passage" from judaism to christianity, we cannot mention all the sources here. Readers should, however, see e.g.: A. Harnack, *The mission and expansion of christianity in the first three centuries*, vol. 1, 2nd ed., New York, G. Putnam's Sons, 1908. As for the discussions with regard to Jesus' relationships with judaism, readers might find it useful to consult E. Nammel and C. F. D. Moule (eds), *Jesus and the politics of his day*, Cambridge, Cambridge University Press, 1984.

the 11th century.[32] As we know, the classic argument is that in the West, one of the characteristics of the political culture inherited from the various historic forms of christianity is the separation of church and state, the separation of the political and the religious spheres, and the dissociation of the temporal and the spiritual, each of which is endowed with its own legitimacy.[33] This separation of power does not mean that the so-called christian cultures had no impact on the building up of the state or on the edification of such concepts as authority, submission or obedience[34], or even on the very idea of sovereignty. On the contrary, the contribution of the various forms of christianity was such that the so-called modern states owe to them not only their bureaucratic and hierarchical forms but also their techniques of government[35], as well as their theories of sovereignty.[36] At last the religious sphere acknowledged the right of things temporal to a monopoly of political functions, while politics was freed from religious tutelage. In return, one of the effects – among others – of the implosion of the roman empire and its replacement by a conglomeration of fragile and small political units was to set free, to the benefit of the christian religion, an area of self-constitution and an autonomous apparatus, "endowed with its own resources and functioning independently of princes or lords".[37] In short, christian monotheism served as a "cultural code" whose importance lay, on the one hand, in its ability to contribute to the development of politics as a distinctive category, endowed with an autonomous legitimacy, and, on the other, its manner of conceiving things religious as mediation par excellence in the administration of divine grace.[38]

---

32 I have explained in *Afriques indociles...*, 22-29 the extent to which this dichotomy bears little fruit, at least as far as the African historical experience is concerned.

33 According to some authors it is this which marks the difference between the polities of the West, (endowed with "autonomous" areas, governed by systematic considerations of legitimacy and legality, and by individual role players) and the muslim polities (within which the political community and the umma are one). With regard to this kind of contrast see, B. Badie, *Les Deux Etats. Pouvoir et société en Occident et en terre d'islam*, Paris, Fayard, 1987, pp. 129-182. While it is not entirely a criticism of Badie's views, readers might nevertheless care to consult M. Arkoun, 'The concept of authority in islamic thought', in: K. Ferdinand and M. Mozaffari (eds), *Islam, state and society*, London, Curzon Press, 1988, 53-73.

34 Indeed, these very concepts have never had the "stable" meaning which they were deemed to have. Their use was very elastic. For example, we see that from the 8th to the 12th century the distinction between autoritas and potestas was used to justify both a papal theocracy and a royal theocracy. In this respect, the contribution of Gelasius was decisive. In these matters see R. L. Benson, 'The gelasian doctrine. Uses and transformations' in G. Makdisi (et al.), *La notion d'autorité au Moyen-Age. Islam, Byzance, Occident*, Paris, Presses universitaires de France, 1982, 13-44. With regard to the specific question of obedience, see C, Capelle, *Le voeu d'obéissance des origines au XIIe siècle*, Paris, 1959. For the rest, see P. Rousseau, *Ascetics, authority and the church in the age of Jerome and Cassian*, Oxford, 1978.

35 See, for example, J. B. Mahn, *L'ordre cistercien et son gouvernement des origines au milieu du XIIIe siècle (1098-1265)*, Paris, Coll. Bibliothèque des Ecoles françaises d'Athènes et de Rome, 1978.

36 See J. Strayer, *L'origine mediévale de l'état moderne*, Paris, Payot, 1970.

37 See, once again, B. Badie, 'Formes et transformations des communautés politiques', in J. Leca and M. Grawitz (eds), *Traité de science politique*, vol. I, Paris, Presses universitaires de France, 1985, 633-634.

38 We must make the necessary distinction between the various "lines of development" of christian monotheism (the "reformist" line, its "puritan" extensions, "lutheranism", the "latin" line...) and avoid taking too little account of its irreducible plurality.

Indeed, the interaction between the two "domains" was more complex that this – of necessity – cursory view might suggest. We know, for example, that in the feudal period the majority of bishops implemented deliberate policies to increase the number of parish centres, with the object of augmenting the income brought in by ceremonies of consecration and visitation.[39] We also know that it was through such initiatives that the church acquired a major part of its domanial properties, since the creation of new parish units depended, from the material point of view, not only on the gift of land from the lords but also on the allocation of a given number of serfs to provide labour.[40] Throughout this interaction, the church institution borrowed not only a certain number of the characteristics of decentralised feudal society. The feudal system turned the institution into a series of satellites through the patronage system. This system rapidly resulted in the personal appropriation of a substantial number of ecclesial units by private individuals, usually great lords.[41] The allocation to the church of domanial prebends and temporal fiefs not only resulted in the servants of the sacred finding themselves propelled into secular activities[42], it was, to some extent, the cause of the institution and its dignitaries gradually being reduced to vassalage, and their co-option into what can only be called the "feudal historic bloc".[43] This accommodation with the centres of power offered them the opportunity to become linked into the channels of accumulation[44], and to carve out positions for themselves within the networks for the redistribution of resources, influence and prestige.[45] This "satellization" became even more marked when the appointment of bishops became one of the royal prerogatives (the right of enjoying the revenues of vacant sees and abbacies). The kings' habit of appropriating the "effects" of a deceased bishop (in other words, helping themselves to the proper-

---

39 In this regard, see Imbart de la Tour, *Les paroisses rurales du IVe au XIe siècle*, Paris, 1900. It is also true that the majority of these parishes answered a corresponding real growth in population. But the two motives are in no way mutually exclusive.

40 See E. Lesne, *Histoire de la propriété ecclésiastique en France* (6. vols), Paris, 1910-1943. A shorter work is the excellent synthesis by D. Herlihy, 'Church property on the european continent, 701-1200', in: *Speculum*, 36(1961), 781-105.

41 See P. Thomas, *Le droit des laïcs sur les églises et le patronage laïc au Moyen Age*, Paris, 1906. Gradually this patronage was transformed into control over the appointment of priests and even the running of the churches.

42 See, for example, what E. N. Johnson has to say in *The secular activities of the german episcopate, 919-1024*, Chicago, 1932.

43 J. W. Thompson, *Feudal Germany*, Chicago, 1928, 44 shows clearly how the "liberal" policies of Otto made the bishops into the pillars of the throne and how this "co-option" fitted into the king's plans for gaining greater control over his secular vassals. As vassals, the bishops had the right to levy taxes, to develop land and to exercise military duties in the fiefs granted to them.

44 See, for example, the information recorded by D. J. Osheim in *An italian lordship: the bishopric of Lucca in the Late Middle Ages*, Berkeley, California University Press, 1977.

45 Naturally this co-option into the "feudal historic bloc" resulted in the erosion of the principle of election, replacing it, on the contrary, by a sort of ecclesiastical "baronry". S. E. Gleason gives good account of this in *An ecclesiastical barony of the Middle Ages. The bishopric of Bayeux, 1066-1204*, Cambridge, Cambridge University Press, 1936. With regard to the decline of the principle of election, see Imbart de la Tour, *Les élections épiscopales dans l'église de France du IXe au XIIe siècle*, Paris, 1891.

ties attached to the see) only served to emphasise the secular dimension of the function.[46]

This is, however, but one of the many historic examples of the organic relationship between the religious and the political in the medieval West. And it would be simplistic to note only the instrumental aspect of this interaction, feudalism making use of the religious "reserve" to establish its social project and to bring about political innovation, while the religious dignitaries became marginalized in their sinecures. We must realise that what is at work here is an historical "labour" of re-interpreting an institution in such a way that it becomes "plausible" in a given context. It is also a "labour" of the specific allocation of different types of resources, a "labour" in which the appropriation of power is directly involved. This activity is carried out within a common rule of meanings, a common "world". In the socio-historical profile of the feudal world, christian monotheism effectively served as a code which was constantly clarified and which was constantly re-invested with meaning. If this is indeed the case, then the real breach lies not in the "exit" of politics from the prison of religious matters and its constitution as an allegedly "autonomous" domain. Rather it lies in the manner in which politics becomes involved in the production of a meaning which, because it seeks to invest not only the world but all those who inhabit it, because it tries to take over all the areas of existence[47], is "problematic".[48] It lies, too, in the way in which that which is religious produces a power which, because it functions according to principles which are, to a large degree, similar, is also "problematic". In other words, it is the act of "coming together" and not of "severing" which is problematic, the power producing meaning and the meaning producing power.

But I must interpret the complexity of the historical models of Western christianity rather than seek to simplify them on the basis of the sole example described above. I shall therefore now move on to examine another profile of the

---

46 For other aspects of this "feudalization" of the ecclesial institution during this period, readers might find it useful to consult J. T. McNeill, 'The feudalization of the church' in J. T. McNeill (ed.), *Environmental factors in christian history*, Chicago, University of Chicago Press, 1939, 187-205. How this model influenced more specific areas such as the celibacy of bishops, see A. Houtin, *Histoire du célibat ecclésiastique*, Paris, 1929, or an earlier work, H. C. Lea, *History of sacerdotal celibacy*, 3rd ed., London, 1907.

47 We need only look at the way in which, in the course of the Middle Ages, this investment extended to all fields, be it the institutions or morals, art or popular literature, or science, to the extent that it became the monopoly of the clergy, or the way in which the so-called secular sciences were considered the "servants" of theology. On some of these aspects, see E. Gilson, *L'Esprit de la philosophie médiévale*, Paris, 1932.

48 I am not trying to claim that the issue of the way in which the symbolic network and the meaningful structures within society gained their autonomy should not be raised or that it is superfluous. What I should like to suggest is that within a given rule of domination, the historic constitution of new networks of meaning (the supports or the objects of practical investment) must, of necessity, take place in relation to "that which at all times offers itself as the indisputable and undisputed meaning" within that society. On these issues, see C. Castoriadis, *L'Institution imaginaire de la société*, Paris, Seuil, 1975, 203.

language about the uniqueness of God and the way in which it has been the origin of a grammar of the concrete relationships of power: the grammar which during those same Middle Ages made Christ take upon Himself the claim to a universal empire.[49] This profile is directly linked to the rise in power of the papal monarchy and to the developments resulting from its confrontation with the Empire.[50] We know that the 13th century marked the culminating point of this process, as a result of the energetic action of Popes Innocent III and Innocent IV. What I must try to consider here are the conceptual supports which served to express such a search for hegemony and which, in actual fact, reduced it to one dominant theme: the "lordship" of Christ.

I have suggested above that the movement to feudalize the church resulted in a situation in which ecclesiastical properties came to be considered fiefs and, as a result, were integrated into feudal common law. Such a confusion bore within it the potentialities of a sovereignty conflict between lay barons and ecclesiastical dignitaries.[51] Perhaps I have failed to suggest adequately the way in which, given the organic nature of the interests within the local historic blocs, the baronry had increased their margins of autonomy in comparison with central authority. The result of this was a noticeable erosion of imperial authority, an authority which, from the 10th century onwards, some emperors sought to restore.[52] As for the

---

49 Due to lack of space I shall have to omit a description of the socio-economic context in which these developments progressed, and which was characterised by, among other things, the decline of the countryside, made inevitable by the clearing of vast areas of forest (see G. Duby, *Rural economy and country life in the medieval West*, London, 1968), and the conflicts surrounding the acquisition of land which followed; demographic pressure and the its long term effects on the systems of handing on inheritances, matrimonial regulations, the whole sexual economy (the notions of continence and chastity), and the modalities of family relationships, the appearance of the "poor" as a new economic and social category recognized as such (see with regard to poverty, for example, J. M. Bienvenu, 'Pauvreté, misères et charité en Anjou', in: *Le Moyen-Age*, 72(1966), 389-424; then 73, 1967). With regard to the economic changes as such, see R. Latouche, *The birth of western economy*, 2nd ed. London, 1967; with regard to the importance of the urban factor, see H. Pirenne, *Medieval cities*, Princeton, Princeton University Press, 1925; with regard to the expansion of education and the link between school and society, see J. Le Goff, *Les intellectuels au Moyen-Age*, Paris, 1957.
50 For an exhaustive view of these historic developments to which I allude, see C. Morris, *The papal monarchy. The Western church from 1050 to 1250*, Oxford, Clarendon Press, 1989.
51 We cannot go into these numerous and violent conflicts. One well known example is that, in 900, between the bishop of Constance and a noble house which claimed the ducal crown of Souabe. In this specific case, the intertwining of secular property and ecclesiastical property was so great that it was possible for some villages to be dependent upon two or three different supreme authorities. In the case of Dinant, some of the inhabitants were subject to imperial law through the intermediary of the count, the representative of the emperor, whereas others were subject to ecclesiastical jurisdiction, see the study by H. Pirenne, *Les villes et les institutions urbaines*, 2 vols, 2nd ed., Paris-Brussels, 1933.
52 One of the most striking examples in this respect is that of Otto the Great. He attempted restoration by bringing the abbeys and the bishoprics under his control. He filled the higher échelons of the church with his friends, and increased church property by the donation of lands taken from the barons. With regard to the importance of the centralization movement, see M. Bremond and J. Gaudemet, *L'Empire chrétien et ses destinées en Occident du XIe au XIIIe siècle. Essai sur les forces d'universalisme et de particularisme dans l'Europe du Moyen Age*, Paris, Librairie générale de droit et de jurisprudence, 1944, 86-88.

church, it drew enormous benefits from this work of restoration, because, in the long run, it found itself endowed with privileges even more vast than those granted by the emperor to the lay barons themselves.[53] This was the case with the so-called royal privileges. In those territories granted it, the church could exercise the right to impose tolls and market taxes, or mint its own coinage.[54] Its responsibilities went far beyond those areas which traditionally were considered its own. The church's tribunals could, henceforth, deal with civil and criminal cases. The "transfer of sovereignty" was so extensive that ecclesiastical lands became lands enjoying "immunity", and which, as such, lay outside the control of the officers of the crown. I shall leave aside certain of the non-religious consequences of such transformations (the practice of simony, the selling of bishoprics and abbeys on the "open market" as a means of replenishing the coffers of the Empire, the "liberation" of ecclesiastical morality: the cases of bishops living in concubinage with domnae epsicopissae), nor shall I dwell on the reform movements resulting from such developments.[55] This whole process demonstrates that we are committing a certain injustice if we only seek to interpret the christian modality of monotheism as a regime of domination "in itself", without taking into account either the place, the period, or the role-players involved in this "labour" which is basically historical in nature. This remark, however, in no way diminishes the fact that from a strictly political point of view the roman christian path of monotheism can quite validly be seen as a means of affirming a specific principle: the principle of power.

This becomes clear when we examine the procedure by which the papacy was able to nurture its universalist claims which it sought to realise through a policy of centralisation and unification, and which, in the internal government of the church, was to benefit Rome first and foremost. These same universal claims constituted one of the corner stones of its relationships with the so-called tempo-

---

53 See the study by R. Genestal, *Le privilegium fori en France du décret de Gratien à la fin du XIVe siècle*, 2 vols, Paris, 1921-1924. With regard to England, see L. C. Gabel, *Benefit of clergy in England in the Later Middle Ages*, Northampton, 1929.

54 This perspective is examined by H. J. Legier in 'L'église et l'économie mediévale. La monnaie écclesiastique de Lyon', in: *Annales*, 12(1957), 561-572.

55 The monastic movement probably was part of this. At least, we cannot deny its contribution to the work of reformation. For a general view, see W. J. Shields (ed.), *Monks, hermits and the ascetic tradition*, Oxford, 1985; C. H. Lawrence, *Medieval monasticism*, London, 1984, and T. Asad, 'On ritual and discipline in medieval christian monasticism', in: *Economy and society*, 16(1987), n.2, 159-203. With regard to the impact of a specific monastic order on the reform movements, see H. E. J. Cowdrey, *The Cluniacs and the Gregorian Reform*, Oxford, 1970; and D. Loades (ed.), *The end of strife*, Edinburgh, 1984, 155-179. With regard to the way in which the "satellization" of the churches within a domanial economy had repercussions on the debate on poverty within that economy, some information is to be found in M. Mollat, *Etudes sur l'histoire de la pauvreté*, 2 vols, Paris, 1974, and the same author's more recent work, *Les pauvres du Moyen Age*, Paris, 1978. On the reform movement itself, see A. Fliche, *La réforme grégorienne*, 3 vols., Paris, 1924-37. G. Tellenbach makes major corrections to these theses in his book, *Church, state and christian society at the time of the investiture contest*, Oxford, 1940. On specific aspects such as the reform of the clergy and the celibacy issue, see A. L. Barstow, *Married priests and the reforming papacy*, New York, 1982.

ral power.[56] Historically, this growth of hegemony worked against, on the one hand, the forces of implosion within the institution itself (this was the case during the battles against simony, or against the interference of temporal authorities in ecclesiastical elections and ecclesiastical life in general) and, on the other, the claim of temporal princes to be outside religious control; and, finally, against the effects of the Eastern schism.[57] This movement towards pontifical centralisation increased the privileges enjoyed by the church. Such privileges were both honorary and liturgical. To give an example: the honorary rights included the wearing of imperial insignia (the mitre, the pointed headdress, without a slit, the purple chlamys, the scarlet tunic, purple sandals, a white horse for processions) and borrowings from the imperial ceremonies of the Later Byzantine Empire (the example of kissing princes, reserved, however, for the pope alone). The result of the liturgical prerogatives was to affirm the assumed holiness of the sovereign pontiff. But such prerogatives were not purely symbolic, because in terms of the internal government of the church the definition of pontifical powers came to include the right to ordain all members of the clergy, no matter their diocese of origin; the right to alter the boundaries of dioceses by creating new bishoprics; the division of bishoprics which were too wealthy or which were too large; the right to transfer bishops from one diocese to another, or to depose them.

All these developments must be understood in the light of the previous arrangements, and, in particular, royal infringements with regard to the appointment of bishops. For the church, the process briefly described above opened the way for a gradual exit from feudalization. As a consequence it put an end to the vassalization of the bishops. Their role was freed from the suzerainty, even although – as I have suggested – feudalization did not represent inconveniences alone. We need only think, for example, of the royal prerogatives, of the immunity privileges, of the lands, of the rents, and the other services. The other side of this liberality was, of course, the dependence of church fiefs on kings and great vassals. The latter, after all, retained their prerogative to exercise their rights of ownership when "vacancies" occurred. The whole undertaking described above sought to take the church out of the relationship of vassalization, to dissociate it from the feudal system and from the fast grip of the laity on all levels of the ecclesiastical hierarchy, and in so doing, to enhance the principle of power, of which the papacy wished to be the specific, universal manifestation.[58]

---

56 See the – controversial – book by W. Ullmann, *Medieval papalism*, London, 1949. A more nuanced view is presented by A. M. Stickler, 'Concerning the political theories of the medieval canonists', in: *Traditio*, 7(1949-1951), 450-463; and B. Tierney, 'Some recent works on the political theories of the medieval canonists', in: *Traditio*, 10(1954), 594-625.

57 This was the reason for the attempts to base the legitimacy and the primacy of the roman church on divine origins (it owes its foundation to God alone) and to prove that the Eastern churches are mere creations of man. According to these views, the universality of the pope is based on these divine origins. And it is this universality, as well as the infallibility deriving from it, that were gradually translated into legal formulae and theological doctrines.

58 As was to be expected, this did not happen without violence. This was the case in Milan in the course of the 11th century. Simonist priests and those who kept concubines took up arms in

The conviction began to grow that the "lordship" of Christ should be exercised in the world as a whole, in all its activities and in every corner. Since the whole world was His dominium, then the church and the princes had the responsibility of making Him known there. Within this universal economy, the church's specific role was that of intermediary. The pope was allotted a kind of "vicarious power". As for the princes, they had to exercise a "christian policy". Their power had, however, almost no autonomous base. In fact, since nothing escaped the "lordship" of Christ (not even political power), everything had a christological base. The government of princes could have no justification unless it formed part of a general economy of salvation which went beyond its own objective. And, strictly speaking, this government was but a means to this end. The prince himself derived his leading role from the fact that he was one of the arms of God, the instrument of the Celestial King in the government of the world. He had no existence of his own. Thus we are confronted by the "ministerial" concept of royal power.[59] But the decisive factor in our argument is most certainly the pontifical "religious policy" derived from these concepts.

And one of the best examples in this respect is the policy of the crusades and of the so-called Holy Land. It was strictly in line with the idea that Christ had not only "dominium" over the world and the right to command it but that He also enjoyed "imperium": active domination. As I explained, His claim to a universal empire is derived from His status as the head of humanity. In other words, His power to rule cannot be dissociated from His right of ownership. This right of ownership was, of course, exercised over the so-called christian lands. His sovereignty and His domination, however, extended "from sea to sea and to the ends of the earth" (to quote Pope Innocent III), as a result, the property of the "infidels" also belonged to Him by virtue of the universality of His reign. This was a direct opening to the right of conquest.[60] Moreover, the issue of the "Holy" Land was of especially interest because of the idea that Christ's possession (in the

---

their defence. For other cases, less violent but which nevertheless demonstrated the greed which accompanied the vassalization of ecclesiastical affairs to overlordship, let us consider the case of Guifred, Archbishop of Narbonne (1019-1079), for whom his father, the Count of Cerdagne, had bought the episcopal see from the viscount of the city and from the Count of Rouergue. In an effort to recoup this money, and in order to buy the bishopric of Urgel from his brother, Guifred sold the ornaments of his church to Spanish jews and began to dispense the sacrament to the faithful in return for payment. For greater detail see M. Bremond and J. Gaudement, *L'Empire chrétien*, 137. For detailed information about the "Investiture quarrel" itself, see the examples recorded by A. H. J. Cauchie, *La querelle des investitures dans les diocèses de Liège et de Cambrai*, Louvain, 1890.

59 In putting forward such ideas I have, to a large extent, taken as my source, D. Leclerq, *L'Idée de la royauté du Christ au Moyen Age*, Paris, Cerf, 1959, 20-63.

60 The impact of this upsurge of "christian militarism" is well-known. On this subject, see the classic study by C. Erdmann, *The origin of the idea of crusade*, Princeton, Princeton University Press, 1977. This should, however, be amended in the light of J. Gilchrist, 'The Erdmann thesis and the canon law', in P. W. Edbury (ed.), *Crusade and settlement. First conference of the Society for the Study of the Crusades and the Latin East*, Cardiff, 1985, 37-45. We can resituate this upsurge of christian militarism in the context of the collapse of the authority of princes, which meant that many bishops took over responsibility for the maintenance of public order.

feudal sense of the term) of Palestine is of a very special nature. It is, indeed, the concrete and historic place of His presence and of His earthly life. This land was "bought" on the Cross by blood. In one word, it is the centre of gravity from which He embraces the whole world. It is because of this particular place that, henceforth, no land can escape Him. Thus His right of ownership and of conquest are exercised under particularly distinguished titles. By providing soldiers and resources to "liberate" this land from the "infidels", christian princes fought "under the standard of the Cross".[61] The concepts of royalty and of "lordship" as applied to Christ thus resulted in an ecclesiology which was, at the same time, a political economy.[62] And it was by virtue of this political economy that the papacy invested Christ with the powers and the rights of the lords and sought to impose the obligations of vassalship upon the temporal princes. But what do such developments tell us about the historicity of christian monotheism?

It would be wrong to claim that the two lines of development discussed above (the feudalization of religious affairs by the baronry, and the papacy's vassalization of things "temporal") sum up, by themselves, the ways in which monotheism in christianity was brought about. We can, however, draw some conclusions. It is clear, for example, that the way in which the christian language about the uniqueness of God poses the political problem and itself produces power, draws on a number of traditions. Thus this language, in its structure and even in its principle, is polysemous. As are its social significances. But as an "original structural principle", i.e., as Castoriadis explains, as "the source of that which on every occasion professes to be the indisputable and undisputed meaning, the foundation of the interactions and distinctions of what does and what does not matter"[63], this language reproduces an imperial fiction, even when pronounced from a subordinate position. In this perspective, the period in which it was pronounced, the objects which it chose to institute practically or the institutional mediations to which it gave preference, are of little matter.

Finally, one of the characteristics which distinguishes biblical monotheistic language from the christian configurations of the same type is the fact that the one is based on a tribal fiction, while the other is based on the idea of a "domi-

---

61 For a general history of the crusades, see *Crusader institutions*, Oxford, Oxford University Press, 1980; J. W. Riley-Smith, *The crusades*, London, 1987. Readers might also usefully consult the study by R. W. Southern, *Western views of islam in the Middle Ages*, Cambridge, Cambridge University Press, 1962, and more recently that by B. Z. Kedar, *Crusade and mission. European approaches towards the moslems*, Princeton, Princeton University Press, 1984. With regard to the war ethic underlying these expeditions and their legitimation, see F. H. Russell, *The just war in the Middle Ages*, Cambridge, Cambridge University Press, 1975. With regard to the expeditions to rescue the Holy Sepulchre, see M. Benvenisti, *The crusaders in the holy land*, Jerusalem, 1970.
62 It is in this sense that we can interpret the facts reported in J. Rivière, "In partem sollicitudinis'. Evolution d'une formule pontificale', in: *Revue des sciences religieuses*, 5(1925), 210-231. On the concept of "plenitude of powers", see R. L. Benson, "Plenitudo postestatis'. Evolution of a formula', in: *Studia Gratiana*, 14(1967), 193-217.
63 C. Castoriadis, *L'institution imaginaire de la société*, Paris, Le Seuil, 1975, 203.

nium" which was universal both in time and in space. Biblical monotheism is based on a fiction of withdrawal and an imprisoning within oneself, despite Israel's certainty that it was "elected" by God. At the outset, the Davidic dynasty possessed no universal empire, nor did it ever claim one. It is, without a doubt, simplistic to reduce its language with regard to the uniqueness of God to a rite of consolation or a metaphor for its historic despair (which typifies its temporal failures, the loss of sovereignty, and the suffering which constantly resulted from it). Nevertheless, this historical vulnerability is placed within a narrative and rituals which set a limit to the power of forgetting. Indeed, God must "remember", especially in times of trouble. There can be no biblical language about the uniqueness of God without the act of remembering (God's actions in the present, his mediation in the past...).[64]

The historic figures of christian monotheism, on the other hand, in their diversity, display an appetite for conquest. We do not find among them that same logic of suspicion with regard to authority which to a large extent represents the inherent identity of biblical tradition.[65] Biblical tradition, indeed, draws on a sort of "critical reserve" founded on the central fact that there is No God but God. It therefore follows that authority is not God. Authority is, however, constantly suspected of seeking to usurp the divine attributes and, in so doing, of creating unfaithfulness to the covenant which itself is postulated as the central meaningful fact. It is the meaning of this alliance which, in the biblical language with regard to the uniqueness of God, is articulated at different periods of history. The rules, acts, rites, symbols – in short, its entry into a given history – take place in relation to this covenant. It is the alliance which is remembered; it is the alliance which God is asked not to forget. On the other hand, and no matter the forms in which it appears, what we are witnessing is a growth in the hegemony of a "sect" whose public status was transformed by Constantinian edict. The omnipresence of the mediaeval church in society began the minute christians stopped expecting the imminent end of the world and took upon themselves the task of offering that society a vision which claimed to set out the criteria likely to hasten the historic vision of the revelation. Hence the progressive exercise of normative and legal roles affecting practically all the areas of life (from marriage[66], to usury[67], by way of the civil state, legal procedures, the setting up of an education system, the sacralization of social authority, the condemnation of heresies, sexual practices

---

64 On these points, see Y. H. Yerushalmi, *Zakhor. Histoire juive et mémoire juive*, Paris, La Découverte, 1984.

65 Let us consider, in particular, the case of the prophets. To a large extent, prophesy was instituted against society. It is for this reason that it encourages the taking of distance vis-à-vis authority. With regard to these arguments, see M. Gauchet, *Le désenchantement du monde. Une histoire politique de la religion*, Paris, Gallimard, 1985, 149-160.

66 See J. Goody, *The development of the family and marriage in Europe*, Cambridge, Cambridge University Press, 1983; and P. Daudet, *L'établissement de la compétence de l'église en matière de divorce et de consanguinité*, Paris, 1941.

67 See L. K. Little, *Religious poverty and the profit economy in medieval Europe*, London, 1978; T. P. McLaughlin, 'The teaching of the canonists on usury', in: *Mediaeval Studies*, 1-2(1939-1940).

and pleasure[68]). To such an extent that between the 4th and the 6th centuries a process of institutionalization and bureaucratization resulted in the church assuming the appearance of a formidable "machine", or at least a dominant position in relation to the temporal powers, whose decline was quite obvious by the beginning of the 9th century. It was these developments which, towards the 11th century, led to the conflicts with regard to power and hegemony between the papacy and the empire.[69] The affirmation of christianity's political status is thus a constituent element of the whole christian modality of monotheism. This affirmation is founded on the idea that the revelation must be confirmed historically.[70] At the heart of this paradigm (the historic verification of the faith) lies a plan which, strictly speaking, is a total one; and which, by virtue of this, should involve all areas of existence. This plan perceives politics as a tool necessary for its accomplishment. In other words, and in concrete terms, it imposes upon authority the duty to create a christian society and to conduct christian policies. Thus, as opposed to the tribal withdrawal into the group and a world closed in upon itself which was characteristic of the biblical economy of the One, we find an imperial dynamic, the desire for expansion and universalization inherent to the christian economy of transcendence.

"Sin" as a political category

Thus the christian paths of monotheism cannot be dissociated from the institutionalised forms of domination (or of forms of domination in search of institutionalisation). That is why it is difficult to deal with them without raising the concomitant question of the emergence of the subject. In other words, under a monotheistic regime, as with other regimes, any language with regard to the forms of the divine, at the same time, means taking a position with regard to the human subject, i.e. about his capacity to define himself and "to govern himself". More specifically, the basic question raised by human language with regard to the divine (be it in the economy of the One or in the economy of the many) is that of knowing whether or not the human subject is master of his own liberty, or whether his capacity to "govern himself" depends upon areas which he himself cannot define. It is this question of the "possibility of government of self" that I should like to examine at present. In order to do so, I shall take as my point of reference Augustine as the turning point in the formation of the christian conscience and of Western

---

68 With regard to this last aspect in particular, see M. Foucault, *The history of sexuality*, vol. I, tr. R. Hurley, New York, Vintage Books, 1980; vol. II, New York, Pantheon Books, 1985; and vol. III, New York, Pantheon Books, 1986. Readers might profit from consulting P. Aries and A. Begin (eds), *Western sexuality. Practice and precept in past and present times*, tr. A. Forster, Oxford, Basil Blackwell, 1985; A. Rousselle, Porneia, *De la maîtrise du corps à la privatisation sensorielle (Ile-IVe siècles de l'ère chrétienne)*, Paris, Presses Universitaires de France, 1983.
69 See M. Pacault, *La théocratie. L'Eglise et le pouvoir au Moyen Age*, Paris, 1957.
70 I owe the essence of this argument to G. Alberigo (et al.), *La chrétienté en débat. Histoire, formes et problèmes actuels*, Paris, Cerf, 1984, 27-44.

anthropology in general.[71] We know, indeed, that a whole series of circumstances, which it would take too long to set out here but which had a more or less direct link with the collapse of the roman empire in the West, enabled his theologico-political positions to triumph, and his authority to win the field over the views of his adversaries (in particular, Pelagius, Julian of Eclanum, the monks of Lerins...)

Since it is almost impossible to deal with the problem of "the government of self" without going directly into the Augustinian theology of sin, I shall centre my discussion on this theme. Recourse to the category of "sin" is inevitable because at the period which we are examining here, the debate on power was not conducted in a language which we, today, should consider political. The story of Adam and Eve was accepted as the appropriate metaphor for discussing the issues of the ordering of human societies and the division of power within them. To return to the Augustinian theory of sin, it must be said that it is based on a deep-seated pessimism with regard to the flesh. Indeed, what he calls "original sin" (which thereafter became the epicentre of Western christian tradition, from later Antiquity to the Middle Ages and down to modern times) is closely identified with sexual sin.[72] With Augustine, the movement towards the gradual downfall of the body and of sexuality gained depth. Such a development, as far as the fundamentals were concerned, was in complete opposition to jewish tradition. It is thought that the radical break with jewish tradition took place during the later Antiquity period.[73] At the turn of the 3rd century, a change took place which made the body and sexuality into social markers, points of reference and indicators of power.[74] This change resulted in a complete recasting of all the previous views with regard to "free will" and the very possibility of an "autonomous government of self". But what is Augustine's thesis?

His thesis was that the place of sin, par excellence, is the flesh, and that all sexuality must be ill-fated.[75] The basic message of the biblical creation story is

---

71 For this examination I shall base my self almost exclusively on the work of E. Pagels, *Adam, Eve and the Serpent*, New York, Random House, 1988; and on another study by the same author, 'La politique du paradis'. L'Occident, le sexe et le péché', in: *New York Review of Books*, 12 May 1988. I also take account of L. Dumont, *Essais sur l'individualisme*, Paris, Seuil, 1983. With regard to works on Augustine himself, readers might find it useful to consult the biography by P. Brown, *La vie de saint Augustin*, tr. J. H. Marrou, Paris, Seuil, 1971; and the contributions by C. Lorin, *Pour saint Augustin*, Paris, Grasset, 1988; and M. Caraki, 'L'émergence du sujet singulier dans les Confessions d'Augustin', in: *Esprit*, February, 1981.
72 For greater detail see G. I. Bonner, 'Libido and concupiscentia in St Augustine', in: *Studia Patristica*, 6(1962), 303-314. For a more general view, see P. Brown, 'Sexuality and society in the fifth century A.D.. Augustine and Julian of Eclanum', in: *Tria Corda. Scritti in Onore de Arnaldo Momigliano*, Como, 1983, 49-70.
73 According to E. Pagels, jewish and christian writers of the first centuries of our era rarely dealt with questions of sexual behaviour, or at least only very discreetly. They produced few theses on marriage, divorce, or sex, and when they did so it was through a re-interpretation of the story of creation.
74 See P. Aries and G. Duby (eds), *Histoire de la vie privée*, vol. I, Paris, Seuil, 1985.
75 We should contrast this position with one of the visions which predominates in islam, in which the promise of a paradisiacal here-after tends to become confused with a promise of lascivious-

that sexual desire is sin: worse, it is "original sin". In Augustine's eyes, the biblical creation story does not bear a message of liberation as was previously believed; what "original sin" ushers in is the era of the servitude of man. At the outset, "original sin" meant nothing other than Adam's arrogant attempt to establish his own autonomous government.[76] It was this desire for "government of self" that brought about the fatal fall. As a result, this desire should be interpreted as the translation of human inability to profit from the experience of liberty. According to Augustine, the question of "government of self" is determined by a major factor which is man's enslavement to his sexual impulses. In other words, because the human "subject" is a slave to his sexual desires, and because he is moved by insatiable lust, he does not possess an autonomous capacity for free choice and free decision. If this is the case, to whom, then, belongs the right to govern, since the preceding statement indicates an explicit hostility with regard to the possibility of a "government of self"? Moreover, Augustine saw in such a desire the very root of "sin" to the extent that the ambition to be master of oneself reveals nothing short of a disdain for God. Such is the great and fatal temptation.

It thus follows that what constitutes the true glory of man is obedience and not autonomy. And de facto, man was created in such a fashion that it was to his advantage to be submissive, not to follow his own will but that of his maker. It is in this way that Adam's experiment in affirming his own autonomy and establishing his own government led him into insubordination towards his divine Master. Thus, under a monotheistic regime, the affirmation of an autonomous human subject was equivalent to rebellion against God and against His law. Hence the Augustinian concept of "free servitude". The concept of "free servitude" is derived from the fact that no human power can redeem man from the state of "original sin". Outside this space of "free servitude" there is nothing but death.

This is where the concept of "sin" becomes a political category, or, rather, it has a political efficacity which we must now examine. To demonstrate this, however, we must provide a brief elaboration. We must first appreciate that Augustinian theory did not develop within a neutral context. It must be resituated in a given historical context which transformed the christian movement from the status of a suspect sect to that of the official religion of the roman empire. In the course of

---

ness. A. Bouhdiba, *La sexualité en islam*, Paris, Presses Universitaires de France, 1975, records this description of the muslim paradise: "Their (the women's) bodies are so diaphanous, so transparent that one can see the bones through the skin and the marrow through the bones, just as a drinker can perceive the ruby colour of the wine through the crystal... The penis of the Elect never becomes flaccid. The erection is eternal. To each coitus corresponds a sensation so unknown here below that were one to experience it, one would fall senseless". See, in particular, the chapter entitled "L'orgasme infini".

76 As I have emphasized, I have based this argumentation on the study by E. Pagels, which I have from time to time paraphrased; it is from this study that I take the present quotation, attributed to Augustine.

this long period, there were many christians who, while living as citizens of the empire, nevertheless considered themselves foreigners. Their adherence to imperial power presented a problem. It was within the context of this problematic adherence that their doctrine with regard to the possibility of a "government of self" was forged. This doctrine was based on an interpretation of the biblical story of the creation which gave a central place to the theme of free will and liberty in all its forms (vis-à-vis social and sexual obligations, with regard to tyrannical power, with regard to fate...). This liberty and this free will were won over sin and against the demands of roman authority once these requirements came into conflict with the commitment to the person of Christ. This was the case, for example, when the christians refused to offer sacrifices to the roman gods or to worship the emperor himself.[77] The moral liberty to "govern oneself" (autexosia) could lead to martyrdom. But then martyrdom was interpreted as divine approbation of the conduct of those among the christians who, in the very act of their death, proclaimed their independence vis-à-vis the authorities, because, it was believed, the power to govern is given by God alone. It is given not to the king or to the emperor, but simply to humanity. This gift of sovereignty, as a result, brings with it complete moral liberty, which means that despite the forms, man is not, in principle, subject to any power. Conversion to christianity, in this respect, was considered the key to "government of oneself". The implacable nature of imperial tyranny (persecutions, martyrs, coercion...) could thus do nothing: the christian was ordained to liberty, be it in public life or even within the church in which he recognised himself.

This perspective changed, however, once the christian movement saw its public status transformed, and once imperial favour began to shine upon its members. The conversion of Constantine in 313 once again raised the question of the relationship between christians and a christian emperor; what was the legitimacy of his law? Thus it brought about a reinterpretation of the biblical creation story, to the detriment of the principle of autexousia. By offering to interpret the christians' new position – a position born from a gradual familiarization with the Empire, which henceforth accorded them a public status and poured privileges upon them – Augustine at the same time interpreted power. He responded to the new questions by defending the position which states that the members of the human race (including those who had been redeemed) were incapable of governing themselves. They required an external discipline, capable of curbing that obscure and irrational part of themselves which finds expression in the pleasures of the flesh. Since the essential task was the building up of defenses against the forces of "sin" unleashed by human nature, any form of human government, even tyrannical government, would prove indispensable, if its actions formed part of this struggle against "sin". Be that as it may, given the fallen nature of man, it followed that the law of one man over others, that of the master over the slave,

---

77 On these issues, see P. Allard, *Histoire des persécutions pendant les deux premiers siècles d'après les documents archéologiques*, Paris, Librairie Victor Lecoffre, 1892.

that of he who governs over his subject, became a necessity. From this point of view, the difference with the paradisiac order derived from the fact that henceforth, slavery, coercion or oppression were penal in nature. The evils of power and its arms (orders, threats, coercion, punishments, brutal force and other disciplinary measures) were a necessary evil not only for the pagans but also for christians. The force and the coercion needed to govern people outside the church were also necessary to govern christians within.[78]

In the beginning, the Augustinian theory of "original sin" was accepted only by marginal groups of christians. It achieved universal acceptance only gradually. It was the Council of Orange (529) which finally endorsed it. In the meantime, it had received support from imperial authority. It is clear that it responded not merely to theological concerns. Its political effectiveness was two-fold. On the one hand it was a question of forging an alliance between the church and the imperial power and of justifying this alliance in the eyes of christians while taking into account the subjection of christians to the emperor. Thus it was claimed that it was necessary, not for reasons of opportunism, but because it flowed from the economy of salvation itself. On the other hand, and within the church, it endorsed the constitution of a specific form of the exercise of episcopal authority. This totally Augustinian form did not exclude the use of force, since it was convinced that force was sometimes necessary for human salvation.[79]

From the strictly historical point of view, the three situations which I have just examined clearly demonstrate that in the various economies of language with regard to the uniqueness of God in Western christianity there exist several human attitudes towards the divine and towards power. This is not surprising, to the extent that any monotheistic regime, simply because it is a regime of domination, is propelled by an organic tension between the power of God which crushes man while at the same time liberating him. Moreover, in the way in which this tension finds concrete expression in the history of a specific society, the very possibility of

---

78 He implemented this authoritarian concept of power in his own practices within the church. Thus when his authority was challenged by the Donatists, he used force (laws refusing civil rights to non-catholic christians, the imposition of fines, their dismissal from public posts, coercion, exile...). An advocate of the right of the state to suppress non-catholics, he acquired a taste for the manipulation of the advantages which he gained from his alliance with the repressive power of the state under the pretext of liberating "people from themselves". For greater detail, see P. R. L. Brown, 'Saint Augustine's attitude to religious coercion', in: *Journal of Roman Studies*, 54(1964), 107-116.

79 See the way in which this was expressed in terms of the battles against heresies, schisms and the "inquisition". With regard to the concept of heresy, see W. Lourdaux and D. Verhelst, *The concept of heresy in the Middle Ages*, Louvain, 1976; for a general view, readers might profitably turn to the article by C. Brooke, 'Heresy and religious sentiment, 1000-1250', in: *Bulletin of the Institute of Historical Research*, 41(1968), 115-131. A more recent work is that of R. I. Moore, *Heresy and authority in medieval Europe*, London, 1980. Above all, see D. Baker (ed.), *Schism, heresy and religious protest*, Cambridge, Cambridge University Press, 1972. With regard to the inquisition itself, see the case study reported by J. Given, 'The inquisitors of Languedoc and the medieval technology of power', in: *American Historical Journal*, 94(1989), n.2, 336-359, and more generally, B. Hamilton, *The medieval inquisition*, London, 1981.

a "inherent subject" of man and the fate of the pressures in which the specific power regimes maintain him almost always play a role. It is to this extent that we can say that the languages with regard to the uniqueness of God derive their prodigious political effectiveness from the fact that they are both, and by definition, the forming (or the institutionalisation) of specific regimes of domination, and at the same time the specific models of their de-construction. We cannot determine the circumstances leading to these operations. What does emerge from this short investigation is the fact that in the diversity of its paths in the West, the inherent quality of christian monotheism resides in the simultaneousness of this two-fold maximization: formation-institutionalisation on the one hand, and de-construction on the other.

The contexts of plausibility

This long detour through non-African history is worth while if we wish to give serious consideration to all the consequences of that movement which impelled the christianities of the West to conquer those lands which they claimed were "pagan". The christian forms of monotheism forced their way into Africa, with all the weight of their long history behind them. Many studies have sought to respond to the question of how Africans agreed to trade in their religious learning for that which was offered – and sometimes imposed upon – them. In other words, on what conditions did Africans adhere to an historical regime of domination which, in its principles as in the larger part of its symbolism, could only conceive adherence in terms of the abdication of the "converted" subject? I shall not go into the debate yet again, for it is sufficiently well known. I should, on the contrary, apply to the indigenous religious regimes, prior to christian penetration, the same treatment I have just applied to the various paths of the language with regard to the uniqueness of God in its historical relation to powers and to domination. In the present state of the sources available to research such an undertaking would be extremely difficult. The majority of the works available lack historical depth. At best, they are the works of ethnologists more concerned with reconstituting the invariables of "traditional" African societies than in giving account of the way in which the various African forms of the divine were, at the same time, forms of ordering power and domination, open to risk and therefore to change.[80] The major

---

80 With regard to earlier periods, however, we possess many and complex studies. See, in particular, K. Fields, *Revival and rebellion in colonial Central Africa*, Princeton, Princeton University Press, 1985; D. Lans, *Guns and rain. Guerrillas & spirit mediums in Zimbabwe*, Berkeley, University of California Press, 1985; J. Comaroff, *Body of power. Spirit of resistance*, Chicago, University of Chicago Press, 1985; J. Fabian, *Jamaa. A charismatic movement in Katanga*, Evanston, Northwestern University Press, 1971; J. D. Y. Peel, *Aladura. A religious movement among the Yoruba*, Oxford, Oxford University Press, 1968; G. Bond, W. Johnson and S. Walker (eds), *African Christianity. Patterns of religious continuity*, London, Academic Press, 1979; W. M. J. Van Binsbergen, *Religious change in Zambia. Exploratory studies*, London, Routledge and Kegan Paul, 1981; See also J. Fernandez, *Bwiti. An ethnography of the religious imagination in Africa*, Princeton, Princeton University Press, 1982; W. M. J. Van Binsbergen and M. Schoffeleers (eds), *Theoretical explorations in African religion*, London, Routledge and Kegan Paul, 1985; W. MacGaffey, *Religion and society in Central Africa*, Chicago, Chicago University Press, 1986; J. M. Janzen, *Lemba, 1650-*

fact is, however, that christianity, just as the market system and the state, was unable to "reproduce" itself in Black Africa in the same way as it did in the West. More specifically, the concept of the uniqueness of God became crystallised, but Africans very soon managed to explode the matrix it brought with it, as well as the institutions and the apparatus which supported it. There have been many studies devoted to this "uncoupling". Most are based on somewhat dubious arguments: namely that, on the one hand, African religious regimes, prior to the advent of islam and christianity, were derived from polytheism, and, on the other, that there was a radical difference between polytheism and monotheism.

Now if, despite its a-historical and a-political approach, the ethnology of African religions has taught us anything, it is precisely this: while Africans may not accept the monotheistic paradigm as the dominant paradigm (i.e. as the ultimate determining factor in the social order), they do not necessarily argue systematically against it. Historically, and with very few exceptions, African societies were never "polytheist" in the Greek sense of the term.[81] Nor were they "pagan" societies.[82] The complexity of their language with regard to the divine is linked to the fact that the conscious acceptance of a transcendental order dominated by a primary power (the one God, distinct from the world) has its origin in a form of interaction in which the visible order is in permanent dialogue with the invisible order. More specifically, there can be no unique figure of God unless it is in a dialectic with distance and autonomy; a dialectic by means of which the said figure – to be recognised as such – must make itself both close and distant. In order to bring about its inherent being, and as a basic precondition of the emergence of the subject here and now, this unique figure must "retire" once it has been consciously recognised as the unique image of that which is divine.[83] This withdrawal frees a space for mediation. This role of mediation is carried out by "bearers of power" (in actual fact therapists) who are not necessarily gods as such but who exercise forms of sovereignty over specific areas of individual

---

1930. A drum of affliction in Africa and the New World, New York, Garland, 1982. For reports of studies seeking to take explicit account of the history of the religious regimes themselves, see the two works edited by T. O., Ranger and J. Weller, *Themes in the Christian history of Central Africa*, Berkeley, University of California Press, 1975; and T. O. Ranger and I. Kimambo, *The historical study of African religion*, London, Heinemann, 1972.

81 With regard to the plurality of divine beings and the diversity of their use within Greek cities, characterised by their independence the one from the other, see the works collected by F. de Polignac, *La naissance de la cité grecque*, Paris, 1984, and V. Ehrenberg, *L'Etat grec*, Paris 1976.

82 Unless we understand "paganism" (like "fetishism" or "animism") as a process of "inventing" the "other", something which is essential for any strategy of domination which seeks to find its place in the long history of mentalities. On this point, see V. Y. Mudimbe, *The invention of Africa*, Bloomington, Indiana University Press, 1985; L. Hurbon, *Le barbare imaginaire*, Paris, Cerf, 1988.

83 This is well expressed by all the myths with regard to the "withdrawal" of God, no matter the reasons invoked in order to make it understandable. See, for example, R. Jaouen, 'La mythe de la retraite de Bumbulvun', in: *Afrique et Parole*, n. 33-34. With regard to the depth of the unique figures of the divinity themselves, see the example given by the ancient sage Ogotemmêli to M. Griaule, *Dieu d'Eau*, Paris, Fayard, 1966.

existence or over the polity as a whole.[84] This is why African religious paths are inevitably linked to a therapeutic economy, i.e. a specific settling of differences (power, inequality, domination, cause of death, renunciation of property) and the methods of its negotiation. This therapeutic economy, or in other words, this creation of difference, manifests itself as the historic area in which what we call the birth of the "individual" takes place. Here there can be no "individual", except within the interstice left free by a legitimately recognised method of confronting the difference and of negotiating it. It is also in this interstice that the problem of the "government of self" arises. It is impossible for me, here, to take up again the comparative analysis of the various paths of this therapeutic economy, or even to dwell on the other profiles within the African scene as I tried to do with regard to monotheism. Should such a comparative analysis be made, it must, first and foremost, be an historical analysis.[85] It must take into account such important variables as the material bases of power in these societies, the paths towards their centralisation and their implosion, the management of ecological domains, demographic rhythms and technological memories.[86]

As to the supposed difference between monotheism and polytheism, it is based on the belief that polytheism constituted a pragmatic and intra-societal modality which gave priority to the here and now over the hereafter, and preference to day-to-day events as opposed to the extraordinary. Polytheism was assumed to be an anthropocentric religion in which no god was all-powerful and omniscient. There was no claim to universality. Moreover, it was a religion into which one was born, to which one belonged by virtue of one's lineage and descendance. It knew no heresies and it was tolerant. Unlike monotheism, which always followed its own model, there was more or less no model of polytheism, because its forms were so diverse.[87] While, strictly speaking, African religions are not derived from "polytheism" – even when they have been described as paganisms – such characteristics have nevertheless been ascribed to them. The fundamental idea is that there is a radical incompatibility between the two paradigms. The outcome is a confrontation between two distinct and irreconcilable anthropologies.[88] This is understandable, if we choose to apply a "phenomenological" approach. On the other hand, we arrive at quite another result if we study them as historical constructs.

---

84 In this respect, I share the feelings to be found in the study by G. Waite, 'Public health in precolonial East-Central Africa', in: *Social Science Medicine*, 24(1987), n.3, 197-208. See also, J. M. Janzen, 'Ideologies and institutions in the precolonial history of Equatorial African therapeutic systems', in: *Social Science Medicine*, 13B, 317, 1979.

85 It is in this way that one can interpret the study by J. M. Janzen, *Lemba. 1650-1930. A drum of affliction in Africa and the New World*, New York, Garland, 1982.

86 See the indications provided by S. N. Eisenstadt, M. Abithol and N. Chazan (eds), *The early state in African perspective. Culture, power and division of labour*, Leiden, E. J. Brill, 1988.

87 With regard to the traces of such an attitude in the works of Max Weber, see J. Freund, 'Le polythéisme chez Max Weber', in: *Archives des science sociales des religions*, 61(1986), n.1, 51-61. Note, too, that for Max Weber, polytheism was also the paradigm which accounted for the conflict of ideas and values which tear men apart when they lose the feeling for things religious in the traditional form of the faith.

88 This is, for example, the thesis of M. Augé, *Génie du paganisme*, Paris, Gallimard, 1982.

Let us take, for example, the case of christianity before it became bureaucratised and transformed into a powerful machine, in other words its institutionalisation into a specific regime of domination. In the beginning there was a group of people who sought to understand what one among them, a certain Jesus of Nazareth, crucified on the cross by the roman authorities, signified and signifies hic et nunc. They formulated an "account" of His life and death, in so far as this life and death represented an "event", i.e., it left behind some traces. At the same time, this "account" sought to be an account of the meaning which they attributed to what they said had happened and of which they tried to record the "memory". Once this "tradition" was invented (or parallel with its invention), there arose the problem of its "transmission" from "generation" to generation. But this tradition becomes pluralised because it is constantly re-invented within areas and units which initially belonged to a common "epistem", but later to several competing epistems. Thus each time it was a question of deciding, of discriminating and of marginalizing. This was the responsibility of an authority which, as it was exercised, became autonomous and produced its own logic, created its own universe of meaning which it sought to impose on others by using all the means available.

Thus, historically, the language with regard to "God, One in Jesus" emerges as a narrative proposition. It develops an interpretive tradition which professes to be meaningful. But what does it interpret? It interprets what it calls "the Kingdom", in other words, strictly speaking, a complete concept of man and his limitations, of time and of its duration, of authority and of its ends, of order and of death. This language with regard to the "God, One in Jesus" is therefore, in its very principle, a language with regard to human existence placed within an identifiable historical development. The problem is to find out what gave this language its power of truth, its margin of plausibility. Historically it was, first of all, the way in which this narrative proposition managed to adopt the network of meaning of greco-roman paganism, in particular the major issues to which the mystery cults sought to respond.[89]

One of these major problems was, in fact, that of the "government of the world".[90] To the extent that it was assumed that the "government of the world" was exercised by authorities, the problem was one of knowing how to organise a

---

89 Due to lack of space, I shall merely limit myself to two examples. For the remainder, and in particular the way in which the christian community managed to institute its methods of dividing history and time and the importance of the eschatological dimension, see E. R. Dodds, *Pagan and christian in an age of anxiety*, Cambridge, Cambridge University Press, 1965; A. Momigliano (ed.), *The conflict between paganism and christianity in the fourth century*, Oxford, Oxford University Press, 1963; S. Benko, *Pagan Rome and the early christians*, Bloomington, Indiana University Press, 1984; R. Lane Fox, *Pagans and christians*, New York, Alfred A. Knopf, 1987; M. Sordi, *The christians and the roman empire*, tr. A. Bedini, London, University of Oklahoma Press, 1986.

90 Here "government of the world" must be understood in the widest sense: the course of nature, the growth of time, the movement of vegetation, the multiplication of the herds, human prosperity, the yield of the earth and of the flocks, success in warfare....

system of mediation through which man could be involved in this task, guiding it towards the elimination of evil; in other words, to his own benefit. Associating man in the "government of the world" involved the invention of an economy of ritual whose basic aim was to win over the forces and powers, or at least to guarantee their regulation.[91] The public nature of these rituals clearly demonstrates that they were acts of common interest and, as such, formed an integral part of the regime of social life. What about the "individual subject" in this economy dominated by the gods? First of all, it should be said that the latter were distinct from men, over whom they had authority, yet their models of action were more or less copies of human models. Generally speaking, we find ourselves confronted with a method of producing gods marked by a sense of tribute in which the good offices of the divinities had to be repaid in order to guarantee their on-going goodwill. The other major problem is that of the "civilization" of the areas of death.[92] Indeed, the cults claim to guarantee their initiates the special privilege of individual access to a practical knowledge of the world of death. More specifically, this privilege is immortality. At the heart of this approach lies the idea that earthly existence does not mean an end to life, and that another existence, beyond the life here below, is possible.[93] In the beginning, christianity presented itself as a language about the death and the resurrection of one man.[94] We could multiply such examples. They demonstrate that what gives a margin of credibility to the language with regard to the uniqueness of God is its ability to offer a new "truth" which, somewhere or other, takes on the language of a "tradition" of pre-existing narratives and memory. On the other hand, there where authority and the position of power were intermingled (as was the case among the "pagan peoples" of Africa), the imperial logic lost no time in gaining the upper hand.

---

91 This was the case with the ancient festivals of Athens and, specifically, the roman festival of Fordicidia, in the course of which cows were sacrificed, cut open and the ashes of the calves were preserved. With regard to these issues, see A. Loisy, *Les mystères païens et le mystère chrétien*, Paris, Emile Noury, 1914.

92 In terms of its domestication.

93 The guarantee of survival is derived from some examples taken from the lives of the gods themselves. These gods had ushered in and instituted a never-ending cycle of life which the initiates could make their own. For example, Dionysus was devoured by the Titans but was then reborn immortal. Korah descended into the country of death before returning to Demeter. Attis had tasted death and immortality because he had been resurrected.

94 I do not have time to deal in detail with Egyptian influences. The christian concept of the resurrection of the dead was, in fact, not new. It was a concept which was highly developed in the cults of Isis and Osiris in Ancient Egypt. In the beginning, when christianity first began to expand, the hellenization of this cult was very far advanced. To a large extent this worship had been "denationalized" and made available to non-Egyptians. On these aspects, see Apuleius, *Metamorphoses*, XI; Moret, *Rois et dieux d'Egypte et mystères égyptiens*, 1911; and the work by the same author, *Le rituel du culte divin journalier en Egypte*, Paris, 1902. See also L. Petrie, *Religion of Ancient Egypt*, London, 1908. We should note what was involved in this worship of Osiris; it was a case of retelling the action by which a god had been resurrected, i.e. returned to the integrity of his person. The difference lies in the fact that, unlike Jesus, Osiris had no personal existence. Thus, at the outset, his rite was a mime of royal funerals which gradually became democratized. By the time christianity adopted and consolidated it, it had long been transformed into the common ritual of all the dead.

Whatever the case, what is valid for our argument is the fact that that which monotheism, polytheism and paganism all have in common is not, principally, the manner in which they adorn history; rather it is the fact that, first and foremost, they all represent standpoints with regard to mankind, on the production of death and ways of disciplining it, and on the development and the limitations of power. From a functionalist point of view, it could be said that they are meaningful propositions whose aim is to "standardise" societies, to integrate them into the duration of time, on the basis of a means of agreeing upon the acceptable level of disorder, a means of producing death which does not lead to the disintegration of societies, a sense of disagreement and the need to negotiate it both practically and symbolically. What divides them are the processes and the formalities which they use in order to institute themselves as meanings, and the way in which, by instituting themselves as meanings, they institute a world, they produce power and, at the same time, they control it. They share in common the fact that, as central meanings within a society, they claim to cover all aspects of that society in such a way that henceforth nothing may be thought, said, represented, or have meaning outside of them. In other words, they have in common the fact that they constitute both the difference and, at the same time, the method of their own negotiation. They have in common the fact that they are schemes of meaning which institute themselves in different ways, indeterminately and according to societies and cultures and their specific histories.

Thus I have just "de-dramatised" the problem of the "conversion" of Africans to christianity. Now I must try to explain why, despite all the advantages which they might obtain by attending christian churches, Africans "snub" them. Or, more widely, in relation to what points of reference can we harmonise this understanding of popular piety in contemporary Africa? There can be no response to this question without an explanation of the concept of the "post-colonial event".[95] This is a category which is both objective and subjective. It is the area of plausibility of African practices, be they political, cultural, economic or symbolic. It is that which marks an era, which marks African time within the time of the world. The "post-colonial event" includes what has happened "recently" or what is in the process of happening. It is something which "speaks"[96], which is sufficiently remarkable to escape immediate consignment to oblivion, and to be shaped into knowledge.[97] And thus it is remembered, while the means of remembering are many. Moreover, it is not merely something which is "memorable", it is also

---

95 I used this concept for the first time in *Afriques indociles*, 12, with an intentionally flexible meaning. I explained it as "all those things which have happened to the indigenous person and which he is able to recount and retell because he has been a witness to them, a role player and sometimes the victim".
96 In the sense in which I. Szombati-Fabian and J. Fabian, in 'Art, history and society. Popular painting in Shaba, Zaire', in: *Studies in the Anthropology of Visual Communication*, 3(1976), n.1, 1-21, say that popular painting is a language, a speech, "a narrative", "a visual story".
97 For example: "the price of quinine cuts the throat". Or, again: "while the state arrests you, it doesn't kill you, it only wants the little it can get from you", in: F. Streiffeler (et al.), *Zaire. Village, ville et campagne*, Paris, L'Harmattan, 1986, 44 and 85.

something which, at the same time, structures and organises the memory.[98] Because these things form a whole which is "memorable", stories can be composed about it. Thus it is something which cannot be dissociated from the narrative. There are many means of producing this narrative. What is true is the fact that the narrative itself and the story contained within it deal with objects which one comes across almost daily, with events which are repeated often and which can, as a result, be set alongside each other and compared to each other against a background of time which is sufficiently lengthy and which goes beyond the post-colonial period as such.[99] As a result, the post-colonial event is that whole group of happenings which offer themselves as a reading of the fictions of the "societies after colonization", the weight of this fiction in the creation of the realities of these societies, and the different meanings which these societies attribute to them contradictorily. It is what individuals within these societies remember, because they encounter them on a daily basis, in their lives; and because these networks of the imaginary play a role in the way in which they form themselves into historic "operators". It is also that about which people can speak and to which they can witness, which they can shape in story-telling, in tales, and which they can pass on to those who have not experienced them directly.

It is in this context that we must situate the enormous traffic in rituals and religious language which is characteristic of the post-colonial period. The intensity of this traffic is the result of two major elements: on the one hand, the fact that, strictly speaking, there is no insurmountable difference between monotheism and what is sometimes referred to as polytheism and sometimes as paganism. This is why, from the point of view of the users, the passage from one order to the other no longer bears the dramatic character which the first analyses of African

---

98 For example: "Those with power in the chieftaincies of Zaire kill the people. At one time, the District Officer (...) would assemble the people: 'You, the leading men of the chieftainries,' he would say, 'I'll be coming to visit you on such and such a day, invite the people'. When he would arrive, he would stand there and ask: 'Who has a problem?' People would speak in turn. If everyone agreed with what was said, he would take note. Today, authority (...) knows about aeroplanes, and Isiro, Buta and Bunia (centres of the trade in gold and ivory tusks). The authorities do not know the people; they come for the elephant tusks, for goats and for ducks, not to listen to the voice of the people", in: F. Streiffeler (et al.), *Zaire. Village, ville et campagne*, 84.

99 For example, a letter: "To the Prefect, Dear Sir, We should like to tell you, without any anger, that we do not understand the beatings which we receive. Here in our country what is it that's making progress? Is it our work or is it the lash?", quoted in J. M. Ela, *L'Afrique des villages*, Paris, Karthala, 1982, 207. See, elsewhere, with regard to popular urban painting, B. Jewsiewicki, 'Collective memory and its images. Popular urban painting in Zaire: A Source of "Present Past"', in: *History and Anthropology*, vol. 2, part 2, 1986, 389-396 (see also, in an appendix to the text, the paintings themselves). For the text, knowledge or sung narrative, listen, for example, to the music of Fela Anikulapo Kuti: "I go many places... Waka waka... I go government places... I see all the bad bad bad things,... Dem steal all the money... Dem kill many students.... Dem burn many houses... Dem burn my house too.. Dem kill my Mama... So I carry the coffin... We go Dodan Barracks... We reach dem gate... We put the coffin down... But dem no won take am...", in: *Coffin for Head of State*, Kalakuta Records, Side A (n.p., n.d.).

conversions led us to believe.[100] It is not a question of denying the violence (including violence to the fiction) borne by the missionary movement in the majority of the regions proclaimed "pagan".[101] It is a question of reaffirming the hypothesis which states that each of the orders under discussion is, in itself, a regime of truth which seeks to institutionalise itself and, in so doing, is transformed into a regime of domination, but one which, at the same time, conceals within itself the potentialities of its opposition and of its own de-construction, based on the very domination which it seeks to institutionalise. The political efficacity of the monotheist proposition, like that of the pagan proposition, is thus, in principle, contingent. Under the semblance of ever-lastingness – in its forms at least – both languages are basically "capable of review". It is this which makes them different from the simple mythical accounts (in the strict sense of the term) to which they are in other ways related, at least in certain of their categories.

The other major fact which explains (while not necessarily being the cause of) the explosion in popular piety in the post-colonial situation, is the fact that while the religious creates power, the opposite is also true. In the post-colonial period, authority sees itself as a rule of truth. The state is not merely an apparatus, the institutions and their architecture. The economic processes and the markets are also networks of meaning woven around the areas of daily life. There can only be a state, a market and a society in post-colonial Africa to the extent that there are these acts and rites of investment of meaning, i.e. the ability of African role-players to see beyond the immediate appearances and beyond their canonical meanings. In the post-colonial situation, the power or the merchandise is constantly enclosed in symbolism which eventually comes to constitute "realities" which are just as central as that which is considered material "reality". The same is true of the narratives, whose objective is to interweave a language with regard to the uniqueness of God or to disperse it among diverse figures. The margin of plausibility of such a language, within a given social formation, is, first and foremost, historical in nature and not phenomenological. More specifically, it resides in the ease with which their "phenomenality" can successfully dovetail into their "historicity" and vice versa. Now, to a large extent this depends on the adroitness of the "entrepreneurs" who elect to target them and the depth of the social validation which a proposition is capable of receiving at a given moment in the history of a society.

---

100 At the time, for example, it was believed that the only alternative for an African who had become "christian" was to lose his "African-ness". This is the cornerstone of the African theologies of so-called "inculturation", which are preoccupied by the questions of identity and of difference. For a typical case, see O. Bimwenyi-Kweshi, *Discours théologique négro-africain. Le problème des fondements*, Paris, Présence africaine, 1981.
101 In other areas, see the information recorded by P. Duvois, in *La lutte contre les religions autochtones dans le Pérou colonial. 'L'extirpation de l'idolâtrie' entre 1532 et 1660*, Lima, Institut français d'études andines, 1971; and S. Gruzinski, *La colonisation de l'imaginaire. Sociétés indigènes et occidentalisation dans le Mexique espagnol (XVIe-XVIIIe siècles)*, Paris, Gallimard, 1988.

It happens that if we must, at all costs, define the post-colonial situation, there is no more appropriate concept than that of a "rule of constraints"[102] (a characteristic which it shares with the colony and which means that there is a close relationship between the "spirit of colonialism" and the "spirit of post-colonialism").[103] These constraints are not only state-based and administrative. They must be understood in a context in which the claim of reasons of state to be entitled to exercise absolute "dominium" over the indigenous peoples becomes transformed into a magic sovereignty. Since this magic space has imploded under the weight of the welding, escapes take place. They are expressed in a proliferation of the social, professional, family or religious networks. Within these networks various forms of submission hold sway. Within them, too, we find a large degree of that creativity and "improvisation" which are the most obvious characteristics of the post-colonial situation. This capacity for "improvisation" resides in the common people's ability to create and to transform their practices, by using interiorized cultural determinants, but determinants which are constantly re-invented "in situ".[104] It is in this sense that we can say that the culture of the post-colonial era is a culture of "trade" and of "bargaining". What counts are strategies of accommodation.[105] Now the logic of accommodation supposes, in principle, a certain distance. Thus it is also a culture of distance. This distance is created in all the major areas of daily life, be it family relationships or otherwise, relationships between the sexes, of illness, of money, of poverty, of food, of clothing, of housing, of leisure, of death itself. This is why the issue of "dissidence" and of "heresy" is both dramatic (in the political sphere for example) and at the same time banal (because dissidence forms part of the daily lives of the role players).

Thus it is a regime of constraint, but constraints which are aggravated by a context of "welding", which leads to the draining of the reserves, and creates difficulties with regard to re-stocking.[106] Such a situation not only has its conse-

---

102 An apparently banal example: "This evening, they ring for the people to go to work. Now, if I had set my traps, I would say that first of all I had to go and look at them. When I came back I would find a summons, so I would go and present myself. There the chief of the community would tell me that because I hadn't taken part in the collective labour I would get two months' imprisonment and a fine of 50 or 25 zaires", in: F. Streiffelled, *o.c.*, 83.

103 It is in this sense that we can say that "the spirit of colonialism did not die with independence"; or that the latter has not made the issue of the "subject" "obsolete". For a brief exposé of the questions, see A. Mbembe, *Afriques indociles*, (in particular the section entitled "pour une lecture politique du paganisme" - "a political reading of paganism"), 205-212.

104 See Abdou Touré, *Les petits métiers à Abidjan*, Paris, Karthala, 1985.

105 This is particularly obvious in the cities, be it in the area of housing, of city dwellings, the supply of food to urban centres, trade as such, or clothing. For some examples, see S. Bredeloup, *Négociants au long cours. Rôle moteur du commerce dans une région de Côte-d'Ivoire en déclin*, Paris, L'Harmattan, 1989; J. D. Gandoulou, *Dandies à Bacongo. Le culte de l'élégance dans la société congolaise contemporaine*, Paris, l'Harmattan, 1989.

106 This is the whole problem raised by the politics of so-called "structural adjustment". Ever more is being written about this. For some case studies see, G. Durufle, *L'ajustement structurel an Afrique (Sénégal, Côte d'Ivoire, Madagascar)*, Paris, Karthala, 1988. With regard to the procedures themselves and the way in which they can be phrased or articulated to fit idioms with a "universalist" meaning (as with "democracy"), see R. Joseph, *Democracy and prebendal politics in Nigeria*, Cambridge, Cambridge University Press, 1988.

quences when it comes to the distribution of largesse and sinecures. It also alters the nature of the struggles between those who aspire to "intermediate" positions within their collective units, and who, in a personal capacity, become involved in multiform transactions at the level of the state itself, seen as the ideal warehouse in which to stock scarce resources.[107] Even more it complicates the disagreements around the issue of "food", and thus forces us to redraw completely the metaphor of the "stomach" (witchcraft, devouring, the constitution of inequalities, in short, the economy of death).[108]

In such a context it is understandable that the depth of the reality calls for the use of categories which are able to give account of the subjectivity of the role-players and not only of the formalities or the institutional arrangements. For example, the situation of advanced "poverty" raises afresh the old question of "covetousness", but this time under entirely new aspects. Yet behind this metaphor of "covetousness" lies the very construction of the social order. In one sense, all social orders are based on a mode of production of death, admitted as such, because, in the long run, it provides the guarantee of the reproduction of a given society. Specifically, the dramatization of the theme of "covetousness" means that there is no longer a consensus on the issue. A disagreement has been born which has bearing on the very epistemology of the social order. The dramatization of the issue of "covetousness" takes place within a context in which post-colonisation is increasingly seen as a death-dealing path. "To skim off", "to buy up", "to disappropriate": all such acts bring us back to the problem of the "devouring" – the dominant paradigm, if there is one – of African constructs of the "individual" and of the "government" of societies. And it is the historical paradigm par excellence. The "non-subject" of the post-colonial era does not only seek to integrate into a line of descendants. It is still a central issue, to the extent that part of what is at stake in the practices of religious rapacity is specifically linked to the methods of redefining social cohesion and civic life. Contemporary religious poaching takes place against the background of changes in feelings of belonging. It would be no exaggeration to say that it serves as a factor in the production of specific senses of solidarity and of new "fictional communities". It is none the less true that the same "non-subject" is haunted by the fear of "being devoured" and of finding himself in a situation in which he believes that unless he can protect himself adequately, he will be "eaten" by the other person, unless he "eats" the other person himself. Under such circumstances it is no longer enough to believe that the explosion of the market of the sacred will serve as a "substitute for the class struggle". Certainly, post-colonial African "paganism's" potential for opposition is not a foregone conclusion. The process of its "routinization" and

---

107 See J. F. Bayart, *L'Etat en Afrique. La politique du ventre*, Paris, Fayard, 1989.
108 With regard to witchcraft, see the works of P. Geschiere, 'Sorcery and the state. Popular modes of action among the Maka of Southeast Cameroon', in: *Critique of Anthropology*, 8(1989), n.1, 35-63. Or M. Rowlands, J. P. Warnier, 'Sorcery, power and the modern State in Cameroon', in: *Man* (N.S.), 23(1988), 118-132.

its "institutionalisation" is actually far advanced. Moreover, the post-colonial state rewards this process liberally, at least with regard to those forms of "paganism" which pay allegiance to it, and whose principle themes follow in the wake of the language and the symbolic practice of the state itself: where necessary, authoritarian practices, whose post-colonial pagan forms reproduce, at the outset, the epistem. Thus there can be no question of under-estimating the "softening" effect of a patronage which sometimes can be highly "corrupting". At the extreme, we could say that post-colonial "paganisms" "ignore the state" more than they "contest it".[109] Unable to eliminate the state, they seek to trick it.

This method of posing the question leads us to conclude that they have had no impact on the – on-going – dismantling of the post-colonial field of authority. Now, it is difficult to deny the fact that, with regard to the state, popular forms of religious action constitute, organically, matrices of disorder. It is for this reason that the state tries, if not to "militarise" them, at least to "regulate" them, just as it tries to "formalise" (in order to control) spontaneous housing or the so-called "informal" economic sectors, to choke smuggling or to limit the so-called "parallel" markets, to penalise "rumour mongering", to legislate with regard to "witchcraft" and the "invisible", to sanction illness and madness, to censure the dead who, within a given society, crystallise within themselves the unfulfilled potentials of the past. Has it managed to do so? Apparently not, even if we cannot deny the efficiency with which it has "decapitated" the majority of these undertakings: by taking over their "intellectuals" (prophets, marabous, the practitioners of black magic, healers...), by placing them in the "historic bloc" which it then cements, and by so doing, blocks the growth of a "counter-elite" which might eventually disrupt the dominant scenario. Thus, simultaneously, we can consider them as rites which work to preserve order.

But this is not enough if we wish to consider contemporary "paganisms" as the product of history, and that, as a result, they have several faces. They must, therefore, be defined, in terms of the "post-colonial event", as a "total social fact". If this is the case, the question then is whether, by coopting them as rites which, through the influence of the imaginary and the symbolic, work for order, the post-colonial state has succeeded in eliminating the very awareness of disorder among the masses. Has it succeeded in integrating itself into the mental universe of the subjugated peoples as a sign of order, authority and abundance? Apparently not, because the very body of the narratives invented by these peoples in the framework of post-colonial religious migrations are constantly built around conflicts such as sickness, famine, disorder and "evil" as conflicts which destroy individuals and ravage them internally. Hence the problem of knowing how to "localise" them and to identify them, because, generally speaking, they always appear "in disguise". They are always situated beyond what one sees here and

---

109   J. F. Bayart, *op. cit.*, in particular the whole section dealing with "the passive revolutions in the Sub-Sahara".

now. Hence also the problem of knowing how to "govern" them, those elements of that which defines a human order. It is in this sense that it can be said that in a post-colonial pagan regime, "evil" is a political category. The problem, however, remains that of the effective policy appropriate to such a category. It resides in what we ought to call the process of imputation.

In a pagan regime, evil is, in principle, hidden. Hence the importance given to the occult and to knowledge of it. Hence also the strategic importance accorded to the agents and the bearers of this specific power which is the power of revelation: the revelation of the active force or the agent of evil. The concept of the process of imputation is useful because, from the heuristic point of view, it is more beneficial than that of "mediation". It is therefore a question of naming the "place" of the "evil" and of identifying the nature of the conflict, while at the same time "imputing" it to specific figures of reality, be they beings or things. Religious poaching in the post-colonial era is part of a general migration, in a critical period, when indigenous agents question and consult the many instances offering themselves to them, which claim to reveal both the place of the "evil" as well as its nature and those responsible for it.
To this extent, post-colonial forms of paganism in Africa form part of the continuity of the antique practices of divination and oracular processes. They function on the basis of the fresh circulation of ancient memories of the religious and a tapping of the symbolic shreds and detritus arising from a monotheistic space/time. In doing so, their area of definition lies at the meeting point between diverse historical heritages. Their relationships with these diverse heritages is not a purely genealogical one, but is of an historical order. They represent a historical moment in the sedimentation of religious idioms, a sedimentation which began long before the penetration of the narratives of the Book, even if, since then, the latter have become unavoidable constituents thereof.

What makes post-colonial forms of African paganisms so effective is that they impute the "evil", in other words, the "discord", not to the state but to the native dweller himself. It is true that they do not deny the reality of the "aggression" and the affliction which follows. But in their eyes it is secondary to the "transgression", which is central. Through this process, the eruption of "evil" into the lives of the indigenous peoples is blamed on the peoples themselves. Thus the state is discharged of responsibility. It does not appear as the central figure in the general economy of discord in the post-colonial era. Still less does it have a place in the imagination as the creator of this discord. Under such circumstances, no significant place is given to its representation as an up-side-down order.

As a result it is the indigenous people who are up-side-down. Thus it is they who must "readjust themselves". But this readjustment is a strictly "private" operation. Thus limits are imposed on the imagination of the evil and on the methods of transcribing it in concrete political areas. It is to this extent that we can affirm that in this post-colonial era the pagan order functions as a means of domestication and de-virilization of the subversive powers of the imagination that it helps to "abort".

In the Hobbesian context which typifies the post-colonial period, the reproduction of religion is, first and foremost, the production of "subsistence". The post-colonial religious economy is an economy of "collage". This is one of the reasons why we can consider that the present religious "poaching" fails adequately to brutalise a state logic which defines the latter as the absolute subject, functioning according to the principle of non-contradiction. Who can, however, seriously maintain that this "poaching" has nothing to do with the on-going implosion of the dogma? All the efforts on the part of religious grammar in the post-colonial era consist of legitimising the principle of a language on the "non-liberty" and the "birth of the individual", a language which independence has certainly not made obsolete. More specifically, however, for the time being, this "non-liberty" signifies nothing more than what it is, i.e. the subjection of the native peoples to the "authoritarian principle" and the exercise of "brute" force.

Popular religiosity
A liberative resource and terrain of struggle

Takatso A. Mofokeng, South Africa

Popular religiosity, like all religion that has emerged in the social history of societies, is a social product of society.[1] It is, however, at the present stage of the historical development of societies, no longer possible to determine which came first, society or religion. What is apparent, however, at this stage of history is that religion, in one form or another, is so deeply entrenched in most social formations that it seems to have preceded the earliest human social formations and is able to outlive even the oldest of them. By so saying, we are not denying the impact of religion in the further moulding and reforming of social formations. It undoubtedly does exercise a considerable influence, depending on the society in question. It is more influential in some societies than in others.

Our own operative position on this matter is that religion is undeniably a product of society. But since society as we know is not a homogeneous entity it would be grossly insufficient to describe it only as such. We are, as a matter of fact, obliged to go further and add that, if we view social formations in terms of people's relations to the means and processes of material production, distribution and consumption, we have to accept that society consists of different classes, and that every class would therefore have its own religion. If, as is the case in many societies like South Africa for example, the prevailing religion is an imposition, then that dominant religion in society will invariably exhibit all the characteristics of a religion of the dominant class(es) in that particular society. And if it is true that, as Marx says, the history of society is that of the class struggle, then contemporary religion will not only be a social product of society, it will be the social product that invariably emerges in the class struggle that rages in society and will have his place and role in the cutting edge of the societal processes. It emerges in the course of the struggle of a particular group or class to exist and produce the means of subsistence as well as to make sense of its existence.

Popular religion in South Africa

Popular religion in South Africa can also be understood in terms of the above mentioned theory. As a matter of fact, many writers (from B. Sundkler to I.J. Mosala) on the African independent churches as the traditional South African

---

1 See P.L. Berger, 1973, 12ff.

institutional home of popular religion, agree that the overwhelming membership of these churches is from lower working classes of the black population, be they urban industrial workers or rural agricultural workers. This religion appeals more to these classes than it does to other classes of black people. In itself popular religion provides resources that enable the groups or classes referred to above to survive the stressful social, economic, political and psychological contradictions of an emerging industrial society that is permeated by racism. It also gives meaning and strength to the struggle of these weakest and most vulnerable sectors of the black population to exist, survive and progress.

In South Africa, popular religion arose historically in the earliest violent colonial meeting between Africans and European colonizers who used colonial christianity to reduce the costs of conquering and subjugating the African population. It arose in that social context as a means of unarmed cultural resistance to incursion, dispossession, subjugation and social disruption at a particular period in the social history of that country. Its relevance and effectiveness should therefore be measured not only in terms of the challenges facing black South Africans today as well as the goals they are presently pursuing, but rather also in terms of the challenges which faced the indigenous population and the goals which they had set for themselves at the time when a particular form of that religion emerged and rose to prominence. As I.J. Mosala correctly puts it, "Man's understanding and positing of divine reality must of necessity, correspond in some important ways with the level of development of historical society".[2] Many analysts of this religion make the mistake, to our mind, of assessing it in terms of challenges and goals that are foreign to the historical period in question. Such challenges and goals are thus wrongly universalized and eternalized. They then insist that the African independent churches, as the traditional home of this religion, should be the contextual home of modern black theology, and their religion the primary source of this theology. They are consequently surprised that all prominent black theologians disagree with them on this score and instead assert a different context and different sources. Some analysts of religion, on the other hand, consequently reject it as being totally irrelevant for all time, while others tend to glorify it and assert its relevance to all of black South Africa and for all time.

As a social product of a people who exist at a particular epoch or period in history, every popular religion bears the indelible mark of that historical period. That historical epoch, in turn, gives a distinct mark to the comprehensive struggle of its adherents as they define their struggle during that particular historical period. It also bears the mark of its geographical and socio-cultural and political location. This location distinguishes it from other popular religions in other places and countries. It is well known that in the social history of South Africa this religion has manifested itself in different forms at different historical periods. Of

---

2 I.J. Mosala and B. Tlhagale, 1986, 86.

the many forms of its manifestation, the African independent churches' religion is the best known to researchers of African religion. There are other less known and less recognized forms of this religion which are more modern and more effective in the present historical period and which exist in tension with the religion of the African independent churches. Like the African independent churches, they too emerged as modern forms of unarmed cultural resistance to the intolerable brutalities of a racist and capitalist social order and are openly committed to overthrowing the present inhuman order and bringing into being one which is nonracial and nonexploitative. Unlike the former churches and their religion, they are most visibly confrontational and their theology is more abrasive and, consequently more effective and popular among very large sections of the politically conscious and active black christians. These religious formations are consequently starting to chip away at the outer edges of AICs as young people start to experience a religion that is reconcilable with their socio-political commitment and practice.

This religion has emerged as a timely and necessary solution to the dilemma which was facing the African independent churches and which led to their inability to penetrate the black youth, especially the student sections, namely how to respond to the growing and justified critique of their lack of revolutionary relevance in a situation that cries out for it. It also succeeds in providing a haven as well as spiritual resources to those revolutionary workers who are presently in the forefront of the struggle against apartheid capitalism and its state, but who would not contemplate abandoning the christian religion or making the choice between it and marxism. (By the way, we have always been puzzled by a strange phenomenon of the lack of unity among the African independent churches as well as their rapid proliferation as churches of the lowest classes in society and their susceptibility to frequent splits on the one hand and the coherence, unity and revolutionary fervour among their membership in their industrial organizations (trade unions) and activities on the other hand. We have been asking why the workers who constitute the overwhelming membership of these churches and adherents of their religion are unable to stick together in church while displaying a remarkable unity when engaging in industrial confrontation).

The 1970s and 80s ushered in a new revolutionary popular religion that operates within the context of the struggle for liberation as it is waged on the factory floor, in the classroom, in city streets and dusty black townships. It is communicated through new hymns and choruses with liberative content that places God in the frontline of struggle where the crudest brutalities of the police and the army are experienced. The singing of freedom songs to the rhythm of modified African dance movements which come from the depths of the black ghettos of our land is an integral part of the new liturgy. Like the well known AICs the theologically untrained industrial workers and peasants form part of the large force of its religious leadership. Unlike the AIC-religion, they are already showing an ability to unite and keep the struggling black working people of South Africa together and provide them with necessary religious dynamic and language, symbols and values as well as defend and legitimize their dreams and aspirations against a powerful and vicious state propaganda apparatus. What may soon give cause for concern though, is the durability of the prominent leadership role played by some powerful leaders of historical churches on some formal occasions where this religion is practised. While their integrity and commitment to the socio-political goals supported by this religion may be beyond question, it remains to be seen how long they will successfully withstand the tension of operating in two mutually exclusive religious contexts. It is also a question of which side they will choose if and when they are forced by their institutions to do so.

It is important to note that the historical churches are not the alternative home for this religion. They are not a substitute for the churches we have been discussing. They too, as impositions with much doctrinal irrelevancies, liturgical rigidity and inflexibility, as well as very little space for innovation, are not a suitable context for this revolutionary popular religion. This is the only conclusion one can come to when one notices, with amazement, how even the powerful leadership of these churches abandons them and their official theology for the periphery of the established church where this popular religion is located, when it is time for a revolutionary religious practice. There is general dissatisfaction with the above state of affairs in the established churches and resistance to the tendencies of these churches to co-opt, mould and redirect whatever falls into their clutches instead of accepting the critique represented by this religion and transforming themselves, their theology, symbols and liturgy. The frequently given official support to the liberation struggle on the part of some of these churches is not enough to remove this resistance and suspicion. Nor does the ecumenical flavour and colouring of this religion permit such an institutional change of context.

It is the religiously neutral but politically defined space outside of the official church, be it independent or historical, that constitutes the context for the popular religion of liberation. Here the fringes of the church, on small soccer fields and in huge stadia, in the open air, in the commuter trains that ferry the huge army of black industrial workers to work, in the small homes and shacks of workers, in the streets where committed people lock arms together in the face of the vicious police and armies of the racist state there is more than adequate freedom to practise a religion that brings together and merges elements of traditional African religious practices like dancing and a high emotional spirituality, liberative elements of African culture, such as a strong sense of solidarity and sharing and a theology with a distinct political, economic and social agenda. This religion is rationally informed, and this we wish to emphasize by a social analysis of society that is critical as well as appreciative to the positive role of religion in society.[3]

---

3 See S.S. Maimela and D. Hopkins, 1989, 105ff.

This is where the demarcation line between the new revolutionary religion in South Africa and AIC-religion in other parts of Africa as well as South Africa lies. When we criticize African religion and theology, as we have done before, it is on the basis of this above mentioned role of religion and culture, To us, religion does not exist for itself. It serves a clearly and consciously defined purpose of making people human and the world a peaceful home. Culture is not the central concern of religion nor the goal to be pursued and realized. It is a source from which we tap what is needed for the enhancement of the struggle for liberation, power and justice.

POPULAR RELIGION, MOBILIZATION AND STRUGGLE

In a class and racist society, popular religion as a religion of the oppressed who always constitute the overwhelming majority of the population, has to operate on the side of the oppressed, with their interests at heart and it must perform several functions.

Operating in sectors of the population with a low level of literacy and lack of formal analytical skills, the protagonists of popular religion must utilize the tools of such religion together with formal sociological ones, and publicly as well as audibly, in the old prophetic and sangoma (spirit medium) tradition, analyze the societal processes and dynamics in order to enlighten the oppressed through the medium of a religious language they understand. It is necessary for them to understand clearly what God says about their situation and conditions of enslavement; they must get a clear picture of God's involvement in social struggles and their place, role and participation in the light of God's involvement in such struggles. This analytical work constitutes part of the sermon of the preacher. All the preachers in our form of popular religion perform this function as a matter of necessity. Popular religion functions polemically in a religious field where the religion of the powerful and the rich claims hegemony. Its claims of exclusive ideological rule over the hearts and minds of the oppressed and dispossessed have to be challenged and denied openly and in public. In such circumstances, to enter this terrain and contest the exclusive claims of custody of religious truth and all images and symbols which serve as vehicles of that truth is part of the struggle for religious freedom which is fought simultaneously with that for concrete freedom.

This religious polemic against the religion of the powerful and the rich also serves as a necessary process of delegitimation of the right of the powers that be to rule with God's blessing. It strips their power of all religious protection, thereby removing all fear and respect for it. Mass religion also must be projective and not moribund. It has to be deliberately infused from a organically related theological think-tank with new images and symbols that portray in clear and tangible terms, the socio-political ideal which the struggling masses are envisaging as it gradually becomes a reality. These images have to become part of the conceptual load carried in the memory and the many religious forms of expression of the religious masses. When popular religion, as a religion of the huge masses of oppressed

56

people who are hungry for freedom, does this it will invariably become a very successful instrument of social critique, mobilization and legitimation, a source of cohesion and empowerment in the struggle for liberation of oppressed groups and classes.

Popular religiosity as a terrain of struggle

There is, historically, overwhelming evidence that historical christianity, conservative and progressive, as a christianity that shares a common history of imposition on the colonized and dominated people, also shares a common intolerance of every indigenous effort at religious creativity. Both wings of colonial christianity have a hegemonic intolerance of other religions in their conquered spheres of influence. They consequently regard popular religion as a cultural creation of conquered and vanquished people, as a great treat and a challenge to their long established regimes of truth and territorial spheres of influence and will oppose it as fiercely in the name of orthodoxy and religious uniformity, as the state does, in the name of social uniformity, law and order.

As we have just pointed out, these two powerful social institutions provide different motivations for their common intolerance of popular religion. That the motivations or reasons for intolerance are different, makes no difference as far as their actions on the religion of the masses are concerned. They both dislike and combat it, using different means because they are both powerful institutions with a long history of periodical cooperation in certain ventures, in societies with colonial history. In South Africa, christian churches and other religious forces and institutions ideologically aligned with the state, and which share the same material interests among themselves and with the state, namely: maintenance of white supremacy in politics and economic sphere, have acted against popular religion of the masses because it posed a threat. They have also launched an offensive against it because it creates and provides images of struggle that help to criticize and sharpen concrete instruments of struggle. This is, among other factors, what prompted the emergence of the Kairos document with its analysis of the church and theological situation and a very fierce attack on the theology of the church and the state.

We should realize that popular religion, as a means of psychological and spiritual survival under conditions adverse to the survival of the weak and poor in society, will obviously be viewed with great suspicion. As a for of cultural resistance to an order of society that does not promote the welfare of the underdog, it will automatically attract the attention of the state that is always coopted by the powerful ideological and economic forces in capitalist societies. The state is able to see very clearly that it does not perform an ideological role reconcilable with the one assigned to institutionalized religion nor can it operate with the same kind of rules and regulations that allow for easy monitoring. As a religion with a low level of rationalization and organization, if any at all, unlike the institutionalized churches, it is also difficult to bring under state control and manipulation because it programmes and course of action are not very predictable.

The South African state has decided to make a direct entry into the sphere of religion, thereby violating its own rule of the separation of religion and politics. It has decided to turn the relatively peaceful side with serves as a base for the production of images and symbols of struggle into a battleground for images of struggle. The purpose for this entry is nothing but to contest and, if possible, win the ideological space in which the popular religion of the oppressed informs and controls, as it were, the hearts and minds of the lowliest people in South African racist and capitalist society. This programme is carried out with a two pronged course of action – an overt as well as a covert programme of action. It has overtly launched a widely and highly publicized campaign of criticism of mass religion and its high profile leadership in as well calculated effort to delegitimize it. There is no doubt, to my mind, that the ultimate aim is to cut off this mass religion from the mass political action to which it is related in order to deprive the latter of the necessary images and religious symbols of struggle.

The next more overt form of state combat against progressive mass religion in which some conservative churches had a hand is that of trying to win over some elements of formally organized AICs and to use them against the other black church people and religious organizations. We have recently seen the appointment of bishops in the AICs who are well disposed to the government, and their very swift rise to more powerful positions within these religious organizations. They have access to state-run and controlled television and radio which other black mass religious organizations do not have. They use religious language for the benefit of the racist state and against the best interests of our oppressed people. They also use the state communications media to delegitimize the struggle for liberation and cut off the connection between black christianity and its social base in the black community and replace it with a piety with no social commitment to the struggle of the oppressed and which, to our mind and our circumstances, is nothing but a reactionary piety. The former state president cultivated cordial relations with some AIC leadership and actively participated in some of their huge religious festivals which were televised. In that way an attempt was made to bring popular religion within the ideological network of the state as well as to link it with the government's reformist programmes which are unpopular among the black masses because they do not come close to the historical project of the oppressed masses. One programme of state intervention which, to my mind, is more dangerous because it is so subtle and seemingly innocent, is that of state financing of the formation and facilitating of black gospel musical groups with the aim of co-opting black religious music and the symbols it projects for use against black people's historical project of liberation. This religious struggle for images and the subtle invasion of the subconsciousness of religious people has been internationalized through the organized forceful intervention of American tele-evangelists and massive importation and utilization of their video programmes on state television.

This religious offensive did not, however, remain uncountered. No sooner had this religious offensive been launched that the protagonists of this mass religion deliberately launched a counter offensive. This resulted in a growing body of new choruses, hymns, plays and poems with the express purpose of exposing and flushing out the components of the state-promoted mass religion. *The Road to Damascus* as the successor of the well known *Kairos Document* originated within this context of struggle to defend and regain lost ideological advantage. It serves as a systematic articulation of a religious struggle that took place and is still continuing at the level of mass religious practice.

Preliminary conclusions

The above exposition on popular religion leads us to several conclusions, some of which are the following.

1 Popular religion is a very significant phenomenon which cannot be wished away nor ignored by those who are committed to the course of justice for the oppressed and the poor.
2 The oppressed will not be left alone to develop their own religion and forms of worship without interference.
3 Popular religion, as a growing force in the on-going ideological contest, will never be free from attempts to co-opt it for use as an ideological weapon by the powerful in society.
4 That Steve Biko was right when he said that the most potent weapon in the hand of the oppressor is the mind of the oppressed. It is therefore imperative for the mass organizations of the oppressed to develop ways of actively defending and protecting popular religion against co-option and manipulation by the enemies of the oppressed. They should regard popular religion as a liberative resource that can be harnessed to facilitate the process of liberation, as well as a terrain of struggle for control of ideological resources of the oppressed.

South African popular religion and contextual theology

It is important for theologians who are organically involved in the mass liberation struggle as social activists as well as formal theologians to ask themselves what the significance of the above mentioned mass religion is for theologians that emerge in the cause of struggle and vice versa. In what way does mass religion serve as a resource for theology? How does it affect theological conceptualization of social struggles? Those are some of the questions which must concern theologians of the oppressed during the entire realization of the social project to which the form of popular religion under discussion relates. Other questions dialectically related to the former are the following. How are the subversive theological concepts, images and symbols produced by such organic theologians infiltrated and smuggled into the subconsciousness of the worshipping masses of our people? These are crucial methodological, tactical and strategic questions which must be confronted as a matter of urgency, in a honest desire to consolidate the social and ideological gains which our worshipping and toiling people have paid for dearly.

We have already referred to popular religion as one of the sources which inform black theology in South Africa. It has a privileged mediational position between black theology and the social project of the oppressed. As a religious practice that has a closer affinity with concrete practice it undoubtedly has a more sensitive antenna that is capable of capturing the subtle nuances of grassroot articulations of the broad struggle for social power. It is, consequently, better placed to filter through to the theological drawing board, the fundamental framework, social images and dynamics that articulate the mass social project, albeit in religious forms. It is also better placed to translate en filter through critical, new and more dynamic theological resources that can correct and qualitatively enhance the process of realization as well as the content of the social project itself.

If we accept the mediational location and role of mass religion, what remains to be done is to identify some, if not all, the social symbols of the social project, and carefully search for their religious and theological translations in the two directions of our theoretical exercise (social praxis to theological praxis and theological praxis to social praxis). In our country the following slogans used by the African Congress, the Pan-Africanist Congress and the Asian People's Organization respectively, encapsulate individually and collectively, the broad goals and the process we have been discussing: "Amandla ngawethu" (power is ours), "Anzania-One nation". Referring as they do to the political sphere (power), the social sphere (solidarity) and the material basis of a free society (land), they form the social matrix of a mediational popular religion that informs and transforms South African black theology.

Bibliography

Becken, H.J., *Relevant theology for Africa*, Mapumulo, S.A., Missiological Institute, 1973.
Berger, P.L., *The social reality of religion*, Harmondsworth, England, Penguin Books, 1973.
Goba, B., *An agenda for black theology. Hermeneutics for social change*, Johannesburg, Skotaville Publishers, 1988.
Kruger, J.S., *Studying religion. A methodological introduction to the science of religion*, Pretoria, Unisa, 1982.
Maimela, S. and Hopkins, D. (eds), *We are one voice*, Johannesburg, Skotaville Publishers, 1989.
Mosala, I.J. and Tlhagale, B., *The unquestionable right to be free*, Johannesburg, Skotaville Publishers, 1986.
Segundo, J.L., *The liberation of theology*, Maryknoll, New York, Orbis Books, 1975.
Villa-Vicencio, C. (ed.), *Theology and violence. The South African debate*, Johannesburg, Skotaville Publishers, 1987.

The religious role of African women

Yvette Aklé, Benin

In Africa, as elsewhere, the malaise remains. A great many consultations and seminars have studied the question of the role of women within society. Women themselves have struggled to redefine their social and religious roles. Yet they have still not managed to find their place in secular life and in the sacred domain. Thus we must once again analyze the roles which the woman plays – and which she is called to play – in African societies.

Any critical analysis of the position of women, if it is to be valid, must take into account the diversity of the communities and the complexity of the societies to which they belong, as well as the changes taking place within these communities and societies. The very nature of the relationship between the sexes is dependent upon the cultures, the religious traditions and the political structures which are typical of each society.

If we are to grasp the nature of these relationships in the African context we must first of all study the religious traditions. How, indeed, can we redefine the role of women unless we analyze the myths and the rites, the practices of witchcraft and magic, the composition of the whole range of gods, cults of possession, etc.? All these beliefs and practices influence the concept of the relationship between the sexes. If we are to understand the full meaning, then we must, in addition, provide a platform where those women – who while they may chatter much, have been reduced to silence and are condemned to hold their tongues – can be heard. In consequence, the question which we touch on here is too vast to be dealt with in all its complexity. Nevertheless, we should like to offer some guidelines for analysis and reflection. Before examining the religious role of African women, we must review the situation.

African women in scientific literature

Historians and anthropologists, ethnologists and African specialists have studied religion on the former slave coasts. Despite a vast number of publications, their contribution to our knowledge of the religious role of women in the societies of Ghana and Togo, of Benin and of Nigeria is limited and – to be frank – inadequate.

Writing the history of the position of women in Africa raises very specific problems. In Western societies history is codified and documented. The problem of the historian seeking to uncover the position of women in Western societies lies in the fact that he (she) must re-interpret history as written by learned men who were searching for their own identity. In Africa, and in other societies which possess no writings, documented history with regard to societies is of recent date. Moreover it has been written from the perspective of their discovery, their colonization and their evangelization. The memory of historical facts is preserved in oral tradition. The problem facing the historian seeking to study the active participation of women in African society is that of re-interpreting the oral traditions which tend to lock women into the stereotyped roles of mother, wife or witch.

It is true that some traditions have preserved the memory of illustrious examples of women who, by their wise and timely advice, or by military action traditionally limited to men have left their mark on the political history of some peoples. This is true, in particular, of the Akan mothers, or those who waged war, who led campaigns of conquest, and who took over command of armies. They readily mention, in this regard, Queen Aminata, who gained glory in the mid-15th century by her victories throughout Katsina, or the valiant women's armies of Monomotapa, and the amazons of the kings of Dahomey.[1] Then again, like B. Quentin, we can emphasize the dignity of the queens-mother in the empire of Benin. Quentin writes: "In the Oba's entourage, his family – with the exception of his mother – plays a secondary role. The latter has equal right to be enthroned with her son and she then takes the title of Iyoba (Queen Mother)". With regard to the relationship between the mother and the son, Olivier Daper, a Dutch merchant, writes that the prince honours his mother greatly and does nothing of any matter without asking her opinion. What conclusions can we draw from these testimonies to the major role played by African women in history and in politics? What do they tell us of their role as social actresses and participants in religious rites?

The question is all the more relevant, given the fact that the ethnographical studies are more or less exclusively based on male evidence and thus, as Denise Paulme remarks, provide a picture of a society which is purely male.[2] Under such circumstances, the woman's identity and her social position can only be seen at second hand. She is, to a certain extent, diminished. Claude Lévi-Strauss expressed it well when he wrote: "Women have never been subjects side-by-side with men, but rather the objects of commerce, like the coinage of which, in many societies, they bear the name".[3] The assessment of the British anthropologist, Herbert Spencer, was no better. Like the other theoreticians of the Victorian era he agreed that in primitive societies women were but a piece of property to be bought or sold, that they had a right neither to sympathy nor to respect.[4]

---

1 See *La civilisation de la femme africaine. A meeting organised by the Société Africaine de Culture, Abidjan, 3-8 July 1972*, Paris, Présence Africaine, 1975, 388.
2 D. Paulme, *Femmes d'Afrique Noire*, Paris-The Hague, Mouton, 1960, 204.
3 Cl. Lévi-Strauss, *Les Structures élémentaires de la parenté*, Paris-The Hague, Mouton, 1967, 294.
4 See H. Spencer, *Descriptive sociology*, London, Williams and Norgate, 1930.

We should note that the comparative method used by the precursors of anthropology only served to emphasize the hypotheses with regard to the pitiable state of women, to the extent that these anthropologists based their judgement on their own attitudes towards women, their opinion with regard to the position of women, and their prejudices with regard to the superiority of the civilized woman vis-à-vis her "savage" sister.

Fortunately, however, the situation has improved. Evans-Pritchard records that, on the whole, anthropological discoveries today agree that the status of the "primitive" woman was misunderstood and under-estimated. In this respect, he quotes the thesis of R. Lowie who, already in 1921, claimed that the Crow Indian woman of North America "is not a chattel", and that "her position is far from being an adverse one" because she is the subject of few religious bans and her social position is stable, or even to a certain extent privileged.[5]

It was women anthropologists who were the first to become aware of this discriminatory approach to the question of the sexes in anthropological analysis. Phyllis Kaberry, of London University, corrected current opinion by demonstrating that the aborigine women of Australia were involved in all the social activities and very often played an effective role, and that aborigine men and women, within a union which was more or less stable in the fullest sense of the term, were partners with reciprocal duties and privileges. In a study of the economic position of women amongst the Bamenda in the British Cameroon, the same author emphasizes the fact that women there were held in the highest esteem, and she describes the liberty and the responsibility which they enjoyed in some West African societies.[6] While certain African observers and some African specialists accuse the feminist world of frivolity, Michèle Dacher raises questions about the basic conditions for serious anthropology. How can we build up an anthropology with regard to women, she asks, when the anthropologists and their sources are almost always men. How can we succeed if it is true that when women are questioned they simply reproduce the image of themselves imposed from the outside and are apparently incapable of communicating their own experience?[7] As long as women remain a silent group with no right to be heard, the difference between the specific reality of the woman's position and the image of it built up outside will remain hidden, and the issue of the relationship between the sexes will be spurious. But why should it be so?

It is not enough that our anthropologist should be a woman in order to be capable of establishing open communication with African women and thus of identifying the religious element in their vision. The growing feminist consciousness within

---

5 See R. Lowie, *Primitive society*, quoted by Evans-Pritchard in *La femme dans la société primitive*, Paris, Presse Universitaire, 1971, 36.
6 See Ph. Kaberry, *Women of the grassfields. A study of the economic position of women in Bamanda, British Cameroons*, Paris, Musée de l'Homme, 1952.
7 M. Dacher, *Des femmes sur l'Afrique des femmes*, Cahier d'Etudes Africaines, n.65.

French society has, nevertheless, meant that it has been women ethnologists who have produced the studies to which we can look for support. Here we should mention the works of Nicole Echard[8] with regard to the Hausa in Niger and the phenomena of possession, and that of Marie-Claude Dupré[9] on the Mukisi rite among the Téké of the People's Republic of the Congo. We can only regret that women ethnologists have, as yet, made no study of religion in Benin. Such regret is well-founded, for none of the general works by the pioneers such as Herkovits, Le Hérissé, Maupoil and many others – some of which contain a wealth of descriptive detail – give any room to the lives of women, except perhaps to note that they exist and to interpret their lives in a rather generalised manner.[10]

Research has concentrated on the voodoo religion and interprets the latter on the basis of concepts accepted by the science of religions, for example, fetishism, animism, traditional religion, popular religion, and religious practice. I shall summarize the structure of this religion as follows.
Under a creator God, Mawu, are spirits known as voodoo, each of whom bears a name, has its own history, is male or female, and fulfills a specific role. Ako-voodoo for the extended family; Henno-voodoo for the close family; To-voodoo for the village; Kome-voodoo for the neighbourhood, etc. Whereas Mawu, the supreme and original divinity is only worshipped on rare occasions, worship – involving rites, offerings and sacrifices – is regularly offered to the voodoo. The worship offered at the time of the festival of sowing and harvest links the dead ancestors with the living. The latter are the first to be served during ceremonial rituals. At the gate, crumbs of food are laid out for ancestors unknown to the lineage. The seats used by the ancestors are kept as relics in a hut and are the objects of constant worship, veneration and offerings.

Did christianity take root?

The presence of several christian churches – catholic and protestant – on the former slave coasts would lead us to believe that the years of evangelization had met with success. Yet we must ask whether christianity has become rooted in the region.

---

8 See N. Echard, 'La pratique religieuse des femmes dans une société d'hommes. Les Haoussa du Niger', *Revue française de sociologie*, October-December 1978, 551-561, and 'Petites lectures sur les phénomènes de possession', *Archives de Science Sociale des Religions*, 1975, n. 40, 145-156.
9 See 'Comment être femme. Un aspect du rituel Mukisi chez les Téké de la République Populaire du Congo', *Archives des Sciences de la Religion*, 1978, n.46, 57.
10 In addition to the works mentioned, readers may also care to consult the works of P. Verger, J. Speith, P. Bouche, E. Foa, Ch. Merlo and P. Mercier, as well as the publications of researchers from Benin and Togo such as Hazoumé, Alapini, Aguessy, Adanté, Agossou, G. Johnson, and Nuatépé. With regard to Togo, Claude Rivière has brought together a number of articles in a work entitled *Anthropologie religieuse des Ewés de Togo*, Lomé, Nouvelle Editions Africaine, 1981. This represents a synthesis of the issue following an in-depth study carried out by A. de Surgy into the phenomena of divinization among the Ewés of Togo: *La divination par Afa chez les Ewés du littoral*. Doctoral thesis, University of Paris, 1974.

From the time it arrived there, christianity believed it must combat everything which was opposed to its truth. Religious ceremonies, with their dances and their chants, traditional medicine, and even the techniques used by local craftsmen were seen as manifestations of the devil. Everything had to be destroyed.

Despite the long years of evangelization and efforts to encourage the introduction and the practice of the christian life, traditional cultures preserved their vitality. This was true in all regions of Africa. Today we are better able to appreciate the fact that christianity damaged the structures of indigenous societies. While it wished to be a factor of progress, missionary action was in fact an instrument of destruction. By forcing converts to break with traditional religion, the missionaries cut them off from their families, their tribes and their economic system.[11] By abolishing the traditional system which provided him with a sense of security, mission left the convert in an emotional, cultural, material, and – finally – spiritual vacuum. Having reached this stage, the convert then began to search for his roots.[12]

While this return to one's roots brought about specific reactions in the various cultural areas of Africa, A. Andrianary's comment with regard to Madagascar is also valid beyond the frontiers of that country. "We believe," writes the author, "that sooner or later the Malagasy will be forced to make a radical choice between his hereditary beliefs and the absolutism of christianity. Such a choice can be made easier by basic christian education and the desacralization of those things which, for the Malagasy, are more or less sacred even today: the taboos, secular customs, the corners of the ancestors".[13]

This all goes to show that the convert is not deeply touched by European christianity or other beliefs which are foreign to his culture. It often happens that a christian comes into conflict with his church because his family or clan responsibilities sometimes lead him to share in community meals prepared with animals which have been sacrificed to the gods and to the ancestors, and to fulfill ancestral religious acts such as the "épé ékpé" of the Ge-Mina of southern Togo. This festival tells us much about a very specific approach and therefore merits our attention.

The Epé ékpé

This is a festival, the prerogative of one tribe, whose ceremonies are of significance for the social and religious life of the other clans in the community.

The épé ékpé ceremonies are founded in the worship of the ancestors and the gods of the seasons found all over West Africa, where the majority of the people are involved in agriculture. These cults divide the year into several periods according to a natural calendar determined by the position of the sun and the

---

11 See P. Guillaume, *Le monde colonial au XIXe-XXe siècle*, Nancy, Armand Colin, 1974.
12 The same is true of islam in its encounter with the surrounding world. See P. Guillaume, *op. cit.*
13 See A. Andrianary, in: *Foi et Education*, 1972, n.99, 26.

appearance of several natural phenomena, some of which foretell the coming of the rainy season, and others the appropriate season for sowing the fields; yet others announce the coming of the period of great heat and of the harvest. Each natural phenomenon which plays a role in agriculture is thus classified and symbolized. Thus we see that the African has achieved, as Calame Griaule tells us, a very extensive knowledge of the natural world and that his knowledge of astronomy is sometimes astonishing.[14]

The épé ékpé festival (which means "the year renews itself") is celebrated among the Ge-Mina of Lower Togo at the beginning of the year, which is some time in September. The aim of the religious ceremonies is to propitiate the gods and to make them shower favour on the work in the fields which will be begun or delayed depending on whether the oracles predict that the year will be a good one or not. All the people attend and take part in the ceremonies, the beginning of which is marked by the ékpé soso, or the "taking of the stone".

The "taking of the stone" involves looking for a stone hidden in the bush on which one can read, depending on the colour given it by the priests, what kind of year has been decreed by the will of the ancestors. Each soothsayer consults the oracles and, under the direction of a fetishist chief, they arrive at a synthesis of all that has emerged from the consultations and this they inscribe on a tablet (ékpé) in white clay. This ékpé is then placed in the sacred forest, to await its ceremonial discovery; hence the expression ékpé soso.

The ceremony continues with a community meal prepared from all that has been collected. The basis of the meal is yèkè-yèkè, or steam-cooked flour, rather similar to Moroccan couscous. Once it has been moistened with a little sauce, this yèkè-yèkè is first of all spread around the Yo homè – the hut of the ancestors – then it is spread over the tombs, on the paths and all round the house. Finally it is eaten by everyone in a meal which symbolizes fraternal reconciliation. On that particular day family members or neighbours who are involved in a dispute must make up their quarrel and, if possible, eat and drink together. Part of the meal is even distributed among those who were unable to contribute to the offering. Hence the name Yakja-yéwokè, which means "that which is freely given".[15]

Prior to independence, some missionaries and administrative authorities tried to abolish this festival because, to christian and Western thinking, is seemed a form of idolatry and a barbaric custom. I have seen christians excommunicated, or young catechumens suspended for have taken part in and danced at épé ékpé ceremonies.

But the years have gone by and the épé ékpé has always preserved its basic traditional aspects. The authorities – christian and administrative – finally acknow-

---

14 See C. Griaule, 'Culture et humanisme chez les Dogon', in: *Aspects de la Culture Noire*, Cahiers n.24, 1958, 10.
15 See G. Condaminas, *Le jour de l'an Mina*, Lomé, Orstom, 1952.

ledged that they were in the wrong and adopted a conciliar attitude with regard to ritual ceremonies the aim of which was merely to call down the blessing of the gods on the work in the fields which was about to begin. In Togo, this festival is the occasion of official celebrations. The Ministry of Cultural Affairs has undertaken research in order to collect the elements essential for the ceremony of ékpé soso. On this occasion, the christian leadership offers masses and prayers.

Christianity and African culture

For a number of years now, African theologians have begun to appreciate and to re-examine the relationship between christianity and animist culture. Far from seeking to revive the integral character of a culture, certain elements of which are incompatible with modern life both at the economic and at the cultural and religious levels, they have adopted the major principles, to the extent that these are able to make an original contribution to the creation of a christianity appropriate for Africa.[16] In South-West Benin, "l'Action Apostolique Commune" (Common Apostolic Action) has found in the practice of the blood pact expressions (words, hymns, gestures, dances...) which can be used in a catechesis adapted to meet the needs of the deep mentality of the village peoples. Instead of seeing merely those aspects of the pact which might represent a danger for the person involved and those around him/her, it concentrates on the beneficial aspects of such ceremonies, which highlight the idea of communion, of confidence, of sharing and of solidarity. In short, liberation from all those inevitabilities which weigh down upon the peoples of the soil and which they must ward off by means of the blood of victims offered to voodoo gods; a liberation which has a certain analogy with the blood shed by Christ.[17]

These facts mark a development in religion in West Africa. Yet there are certain ambiguities with regard to these developments. Indeed, to what extent do women take part in this universe? What access do women have to religious practices? What is the form and the importance of their participation – if any – in the formulation of the symbolic and ritual universe which orders a relatively major part of the ideological construct? Such questions remain.

Women have never been reluctant to introduce innovations in the religious field. To support this thesis, allow me to return to the area of voodoo and to offer the example of the account of the installation of the voodoo Mawu-Lisa in Abomey (Dahomey) recorded in the work by Maupoil. "The cult of Mawu-Lisa," writes Maupoil, "was brought to Abomey by Hwadjelé, the mother of King Tégbessou, in order to put an end to a quarrel with regard to the succession. Tégbessou had seized power, despite his brothers, and Hwadjelé, 'as strong as a man', used all

---

16 See *La théologie Africaine s'interroge. Colloque d'Accra*, Paris, L'Harmattan, 1979.
17 See *Le Pacte de sang. Réflexion sur les grandes lignes d'une catéchèse*, Bohican (Benin), 1976, Paris, CEVAA Archives.

her powers to ensure his stability. She went back to Adjahomé, her native country, and there acquired Mawu-Lisa voodoos and brought them back to Abomey. From Abjahomé she brought back two wooden statuettes representing Mawu in the form of a woman carrying a crescent moon, and Lisa, in the form of a chameleon, bearing the sun in its mouth. She became the high priestess and handed on the secret language of these voodoo, and the rite".[18]

We should also point out that women soothsayers exercised exclusive authority in some cults and were able to rival their male counterparts. In a thesis on the role of women in the church in Togo, Seyi Paabissih mentions a large number of women soothsayers within Togolese society.[19] The names of a great many other women leaders – prophetesses, founders, inspirers of tens of thousands of followers and the victims of harsh repression – are recorded, as are the names of those who have encouraged the setting up of the syncretic sects and messianic movements which are on the increase in Africa today.[20] The evidence is there. Women play a role in the formulation of the symbolic and ritual universe of Africa. Yet this evidence notwithstanding, men continue to ignore the religious function of women.

The position of women in the church

Let us limit ourselves to the christian church, in order to demonstrate that despite the conferences, seminars and consultations devoted to women, African women are still ignored within the christian community.

The report of the Consultation of African Women organized by the AACC (All Africa Conference of Churches), held in Lomé from 16-22 October 1989, is quite clear. Dr Musimbi Kanyoro, secretary of the Lutheran World Federation's division on "Women in church and society", has no hesitation in writing:

> "Those African women who have grown up in the church have been taught that they must accept everything in silence. Even when their culture allowed them to speak out, the church, following the teachings of Timothy 2:12-15, imposed silence upon them. The church has taught nothing but total and even blind obedience. This was the only chance for a woman to enter paradise.
> I am often asked: what is the role of women in the church in Africa? Most of the time I do not know what to say. To a certain extent christianity has

---

18 See B. Maupoil, *La géomancie à l'ancienne côte des esclaves*, Paris, Institut d'Ethnologie, 1981, 69-70.
19 See Seyi Paabissih, *Le rôle de la femme dans l'église. Exemple de Togo*, Master's thesis, Faculty of Theology, Porto Novo (Benin). This is backed up by Gert Chesi's documentary book, *Vaudou*, Paris, Fournier-Diffusion, 1980, which contains photographs of Mamissi Kokoé and Mamissa Dosa, Ewé or Mina priestesses of the cult of Mamiwata, celebrating certain rites.
20 See M. P. Hebga, *Emancipation d'églises sous tutelle. Essai sur l'ère post-coloniale*, Paris, Présence Africaine, 1976, 31.

opened new perspectives for women in Africa, by offering them an opportunity to escape from their cultural and family contexts and to enter a much wider christian community. Christianity has also offered Africans in general greater opportunities for education. But it is here that we encounter the differences. The christian faith has given power to men. It has brought them education and the liberty to decide as they wish. Christianity has taught men that they are the head of the family and that the women and the children owe obedience to them. It has not placed the same emphasis on the gospel of the love of the father for his children, and the love of the husband for his wife. Even today, the work of women in the church is limited to making things for sale, to welcoming people and to providing food, etc. Such activities have their value. But could our churches not envisage new ways of using the potential strengths represented by women?"[21]

By recognizing women as individuals with the talent given them by God, the church could become a community of all the believers, men, women and young people. Its witness would then be the witness of all the people of God. To become this people of God, consisting of laity and of clergy, of men and women, of adults and young people, the churches will have to make room for a larger number of women in parish councils and in decision-making bodies. It is up to the women to convince them. Opening the Lomé conference, Leah, the wife of Anglican Archbishop Desmond Tutu, said: "Is it not time for us (women) to say: 'Arise, Shine' and to give direction rather than always to be looking for a leader to follow."[22]

I should like to end with an account of a meeting which for the Africa specialist, Jean Claude Barbier, was to represent the beginning of a complete change of attitude towards women. "One day when I was questioning a venerable old man with regard to the initiation rites among the Betis of Cameroon," he tells us, "a woman of around eighty years of age came and sat beside me, and without beating about the bush she said: 'My son, why do you forget the woman? When you are foetus, I carry you in my belly; when you are a baby, I carry you on my breast; when you are a child I carry you on my back; when you are an adult I carry you on my knees (an allusion to sexual intercourse); and when I stop carrying you, it is because you are dead!, So why do you forget the woman?'."[23] We can draw our own conclusions! Why are African women still the forgotten and the neglected ones?

---

21 See *Report of the Consultation of African Women*, organised by the AACC (All Africa Conference of Churches) and held in Lomé from 16-22 October 1990, mimeo.
22 See *ibid.*
23 See J. C. Barbier, *Femmes de Caméroun*, Paris, Karthala, 1985, 10.

Liberative ritual and African religion

Mercy Amba Oduyoye, Nigeria

If it is a challenge to try to distill the liberative potential of religion it is even more difficult to draw a line between religion and popular religion. On the African continent religion is popular, it belongs to the realm and is within the reach of all the populace. The festivals that mark the high points of Africa's autochthonous religions have their "popular" aspects marked by processions, feasts, ritual cleansing and prohibitions that affect everyone. Christianity in all its forms, but especially as found in the African instituted churches and Roman catholicism fills churches to overflowing and binds people in beliefs and practices that constitute the source of their courage to live. Religion, as such, is popular in Africa, therefore in this survey what is highlighted are the popular beliefs and practices of Africa's three major religions, some of which are found in all.

As to whether these beliefs and practices are liberative or not thus depends on one's view of what human life is about and how the optimum conditions for this life are to be arrived at. Religion is experienced as a two-edged sword. It can be a means of creating an illusion of well-being or a conditioning for the acceptance of fate. But religion can also fuel discontent and promote protest against and struggle to rectify what is experienced as sub-human, anti-human and dishumanizing. In Africa we have experienced christianity both as a religion for alienation and domestication, as well as one for promoting human dignity and the struggle of a life-affirming community. The same can be said of African traditional religion and of islam in Africa. Whether religion is liberative, domesticating or alienating also depends to some extent on one's personal situation in life. Since there is so much hierarchical and patriarchal structuring where religion is concerned, people who are on the periphery or at the receiving end of the ministrations of organized religion can evaluate the role and influence of religion in their lives as oppressive if and when they begin to question their place in those structures. This is the case with women, who in most structures and especially the religious structures find themselves on the receiving end of the do's and dont's of their communities, and whose lives and participation are subject to many limitations. We shall illustrate this power of religion in the lives of African women and then attempt to draw some conclusions with regard to the subject under discussion.

African religion

Africa is very hospitable, she has played host to both christianity and islam, expecting them to be just as tolerant. They have not. They could not be, since they claim to posses unique and superior revelations. Both continue to compete for the conversion of the adherents of the traditional religion of Africa. In this contribution, I should like to concentrate on the traditional religion of Africa, which in this offering will be referred to as African religion. There are Africans who are christians and others who are muslims, but so are many peoples from many other nationalities across the continents and islands of this globe, so those two religions have sufficient advocates. Secondly, I shall focus on African religion, because whether christian or muslims most Africans operate by the norms of African religion in the primary instance since it is an integral part of African culture. Thirdly, African religion exhibits an affinity with the religions of the peoples of the Pacific and those of native Americans. In that respect we may be able to treat my contribution as affording an intercultural perspective on our study. I find it necessary to do this because there is a tendency amongst scholars of African religion to expound upon it as a unique occurrence.

Fourthly, I have elected to focus on African religion because of the tendency Africanists have to claim that African culture is fairer to women than the Western culture which was super-imposed by colonial governments and by christianity. The fact that the continuous metamorphosis of this culture in Africa keeps it moving more and more in the direction of the anti-women provisions in Western societies is often ignored. In the present discussions of women in Africa assertions are being made by both men and women that African religion, (sometimes culture) affords full opportunity for the liberative participation of women. An initial reading of the actual involvement of women in festivals and other religious events indicates that this assessment is biased in favour of what is deemed to be the welfare of the whole community of women and men as we experience it in Africa today, and is anchored on the approved roles of men and women as circum-scribed by an unchanging set of norms enshrined in an equally unchanging culture.

The classic and oft-quoted illustration is the participation of women in religious ritual. Here no question is raised concerning the exclusion of women of child-bearing age on the assumption that menstruation is inauspicious, if not positively dangerous, to all things holy. The status of blood as sacred/pollutant needs a thorough investigation by scholars of religion. In the African instituted churches women are more visible in the structure of authority, but even here the blood taboo still excludes women (some of them being church founders) from the churches' sacramental roles and sacred spaces. A de-mythologizing of blood may be a way out; without that, there can be no liberation of women's energies for liberative roles in religion. African religion, our present focus, has been chal-lenged by the impinging religions in several aspects, but where they relate to women these religions very often reinforce what from a feminist perspective, may be designed as negative factors and obstacles to the full expression of women's humanity. To assess the role of African religion in women's lives two fundamental questions have to be asked and answered in connection with religion. What responsibilities do women have in the structures of African religion? In what way does religion serve as a liberative force in women's lives?

Women in African religion

Much has been said to suggest that the participation of women in African religion is adequate, and that equality, as a concept, cannot be applied since role differentiations in Africa are clear and not meant to be valued hierarchically. It is true that in African religion we have women in charge of shrines and cultic centres, just as we have men in these roles. Two questions have yet to be raised: one, how influential are the women-led cults? And two, what percentages of cultic functionaries are women and what are their specific duties by comparison with men's roles and duties at the shrines. At any rate it is a demonstrable fact that there are more women in the secondary roles of mediums and cultic-dancers than as high-priests of shrines and healers. Even more obvious is the fact that more women than men are clients of the divinities of these cults.

In family ritual, men officiate and menopausal women only do so *in extremis* or in supportive roles. Hence, while a small boy can officiate at the ceremony of "splitting kola" among the Igbo of Nigeria, a mature woman cannot. There are stories of people who, upon the appointment of a woman as a commissioner, asked: "Are we going to present drinks to a woman and have her split kola?" Her competence for the assignment ceases to be an issue and her place as a ceremonial head takes centre stage.

It is important that now, at least, this kind of cultural orientation has been given voice. When silence reigned, the exclusion of women from centres of power and authority seemed quite irrational; now, at least, one surmises that there was a subconscious rejection that comes from layers of religio-cultural provisions. This realization at least enables one to ask the question "why not", to go ahead to investigate and to stimulate rethinking, and to promote a rational approach towards women as community leaders.

There are very many central cults from which women are excluded except as clients. They are forbidden to handle the instruments of divination. An important example is the exclusion of women to be found in Yoruba Ifa divination, Ifa being the most important means of knowing the will of the divinities of the Yoruba religion. The will of the divinities is therefore communicated to individuals and to the community through and by men only. This reminds one of the reaction of the followers of Jesus of Nazareth when the women returned from the tomb to deliver the message the risen Christ had charged them with. The response was "these are idle tales told by women". The Yoruba religion ensures compliance with the will of the divinities by having men be the interpreters of the divinities.

Parallel cults exist in African religion with practices of mutual exclusion. Why not? There are areas of life that are gender specific. But whereas the women's cults do not turn public, to become oppresive to men, the exclusively male cults do. When freshly circumcised boys parades in the cities and towns of Kenya women must stay away. When Oro and ancestral masks come out to parade in the streets of Yoruba cities and towns women must stay away. The huge processions of men in the streets in the city of Ibadan that terrorize women and some specific ones used as a camouflage to frighten them from the market so their wares might be looted by men, have recently been banned at the insistence of women. The excesses of others are also being regulated by traditional rulers who see their anti-women regulations as incompatible with life in contemporary cosmopolitan communities. One ought to be able to argue that what is private to men should remain so and not interfere with the public of which women are equally members if women's private cults can apply to women only and not cause men to remain indoors and out of sight. We either accept a strict double standard in the management of community life or we become more inclusive and reciprocal in our demands. Fear and exclusion are incompatible with the liberation and dignity of the human spirit.

Ritual

African religion gives a major role to rites of passage. One's path through life is monitored and marked and celebrated from "before-birth" to death and thereafter. So are the events of the community aside from the personal rites of passage. Throughout one's life several rituals may be occasioned by specific circumstances. To start a new farm, a new business, a journey, a building, every new venture demands a foundational ritual. There are supplication rites for rain, good health, and children. There are purification rituals to expunge negative influences that have accrued and the contaminations that one is liable to acquire in the daily course of interaction with other people, animals or whatever is taboo. There are protective rituals to ward off future negative influences by making one immune to particular sources of danger. There are rites for harvest as for other accomplishments, while festivals provide occasions for the celebration of significant events in a community's history. Observing the rituals of these festivals can also give us an insight into how religion informs and shapes life and, to some extent, how life and environment shape religion. All these are ways of attaining a feeling of security and self-realization. We shall now examine how women are affected in this ritualistic approach to life.

Birth

Birth is marked as the passage from the Other Dimension of Time and Space (ODTS) to this one. Among the Akan, all the ritual applicable to this stage apply equally to babyboys and babygirls. Family names are derived from the generation before one's own parents and may be the masculine or feminine version of a name, depending on the sex of the child. Girls may bear the feminine version of grandfather's name and boys the masculine version of grandmother's name. So far so good. The spiritual, and therefore religious, link is preserved with the forebears as well as with posterity. For both women and men this could be either oppresive or liberative, depending on one's approach to the importance of community.

We now need to note the role of the men and women assembled for the ritual. The father pronounces the name of the child for all to hear; the choice of which ancestor is being reincarnated in the baby is his prerogative. The mother, and all women, are excluded from this choice. The actual actions of carrying the baby, putting water or wine in its mouth may be done by the oldest member of the father's family and a woman could do that. Where paternity is not acknowledged the whole ceremony may be performed by the mother's family, but the role of men and women would remain the same. It is interesting to note that among the father-centered Yoruba women take part in giving names at these ceremonies. The balance of patriarchy and matriarchy is rectified at the ceremony and both sides feel included in the new person being inaugurated.

Puberty

The passage from childhood to adulthood is marked by rites that sometimes include circumcision for both males and females, and for some peoples not at all, or for males only. The central significance, however, applies to all ethnic groups. With those rites performed one becomes a member not only of one's family but of the whole community and may be assigned community responsibility, notably that of replenishing the race. Among the Asante pregnancy is an abomination if the puberty rites have not been performed and the couple is liable to banishment. It is a religious ritual acknowledging, accepting and celebrating human sexuality and its expressions. Marriage is not a necessary criteria for childbearing, although the gradual patriarchalization of society shows through the spiritual role accorded to fatherhood. The ritual of puberty confers adult responsabilities upon adults and demonstrates to what extent they are gender-specific. The acknowledgement of one's adulthood by the whole community is what empowers and liberates the person at this stage.

Ritual itself is performed for women by women and for men by men. This is the beginning of Africa culture' bicameral organization of society. The ritual for girls include fertility rites whilst for boys virility rites are replaced by evidence of bravery. It is significant that one of the euphemisms for first menstruation is "She has killed an elephant" and for birth "She has returned safely from the battle-front". Coming face to face with one's blood is itself an act of bravery; for women this is part of what it means to be a human being, while a man does not have to kill a lion to be biologically male. Other societies require this, or some comparable *achievement*, before a man would be admitted to the rank of husband. It could of course be oppressive, as all socialization is, if one is not inclined to conformity or, as in this case, to acts set to demonstrate bravery and masculinity or feminity.

74

Marriage

With marriage one's majority is fully recognized and one is publicly admitted as having accepted the responsibility of child-bearing and rearing. The ritual is that of bonding, primarily of two families and physically that of two individuals to be recognized as coital partners. The performance, however, underlines the transfer of the woman from the spiritual power of the father to that of the husband. The Yoruba perform a ritual of the crossing-over with actual washing of the bride's feet at the threshold of the man's house. There is an element of purification as ablutionary rituals imply. It is like washing one's hands upon return from a burial. Her old self is buried with the marriage ceremony that took place in her parents' home and she begins a new life "in the husband's house". This transition then becomes more significant for the woman than for the man. The threshold ceremony becomes a territorial marking by the family of the man. She is "hedged in" by him and his people; the reverse does not apply, for the ritual is not reciprocal.

The Akan, whose main interest in marrying off "their daughter" is in her duty to be the channel for returning ancestors, will at the marriage stage repeat the feeding of the fertility symbol of eggs to the new bride. Prayers in this ceremony are for fecundity peace and prosperity, blessing and protection. The support and solidarity pledged by both families to the new unit become a liberative atmosphere in which to contribute one's share to community needs. Participation becomes a responsibility that liberates the creative powers with which all human beings are endowed. Marriage liberates and empowers individuals for full participation in the African community.

Giving birth

When all the prayers and rituals work and a woman delivers a baby the marriage is then truly stabilized. The birth chamber, and in some cases the house were a birthing is taking place, are taboo for men. African women strictly forbid men from sharing in the secrets of child-birth. If the birth is normal no special ritual is required except for thanksgiving rites and the soul-washing ones to congratulate the soul of the woman for a job well-done. She is showered with gifts by the husband and other relatives. If the birth is complicated the labouring woman is encouraged to confess her sins; generally she is accused of adultery and she has to name the illicit partner and have sacrifices made on her behalf to ensure safe delivery. Needless to say, several fatalities have resulted from what is essentially a religious belief.

Mourning

The death of a spouse marks another stage in the life of the individual, and separation rites are then performed to terminate the coital rights of the partner. What is done for men in this case is minimal and not much has been recorded on it. The popular evidence is that in the case of men, they are encouraged to obtain a sexual partner as soon as possible because the spirit of the deceased wife will then be so disgusted she will never visit him again. Whatever the truth of this saying, the fact remains that in the case of a woman it is assumed that the husband's soul will not rest until the widow has gone through mourning rites and has been purified before she can be rendered safe for re-marriage. For most African women this is an extremely intense period of their lives. The separation ritual is marked by purification rites that may involve carrying hot coals to a stream or to the sea to have a pre-dawn ritual bath. For some it involves the shaving of the widow's hair, while others will require burning all the clothes she was wearing at the time of the death and those she wore during the mourning period. In addition, a "decent" length of time must elapse before she can re-marry. Even then she may not have any choice there where provisions are made for her to be "inherited" by the husband's successor. If she refuses she goes away with no material benefit from the marriage, except through her children, there where inheritance is patrilineal. Mother-centered groups expect nothing from the marriage alliance beyond the gift of children.

Before these purification rites, none of the concourse of people who stream in to mourn with the bereaved family can shake hands with the widow; the inauspiciousness of losing one's husband is contagious. The unprintable things that widows bound by African religion go through are many. Whatever the details there are three main factors:
- To survive a husband attaches negative influences to a woman which may contaminate others and so she has to be purified.
- The spirit of the husband stays with her until rites are performed to separate them. This is necessary, so that she is made safe to be passed on to another man, the assumption being that a woman is better off married. The state of widowhood is a modern one in African society as symbolic marriages are arranged to keep even very old women attached to men.
- A man's soul can only rest peacefully when the spouse has meticulously observed all the widowhood rites. So, in addition to all the people being sent off in proper style, a man must have in addition, a thoroughly dejected wife, at times thoroughly humiliated by in-laws, before he can rest in peace. Male sexuality shows up as belligerent, if not vindictive and malevolent.

These rites are most demeaning and have been opposed by several groups. Over the years, they have undergone many modifications but the fundamental religious issue of inauspiciousness remains. As do the socio-economic and legal consequences of a system that does not recognize the official status of "widow". Female sexuality does not have an autonomous value outside marriage and motherhood. It is these widowhood rites that rob marriage rituals of any liberating potential they may have for women. It is as if the death of a husband is being blamed on a wife. The non-acceptance of death is for me, a sign that African religion lacks a liberative theology of afterlife. This lack is countered by the belief in re-incarnation which, in turn, demands that women must have children, and makes children into a religious duty in this religion just as it is in christian tradition.

Death

The final passage, death, comes to women as to men, and apart from the absence of elaborate mourning by husbands, women's funerals are every bit as meticulously performed as men's. As departed spirits both men and women are equally powerful, and as improper funeral for either might spell a lot of trouble for the living. The ancestors to be re-incarnated are both men and women so all have to be sent off in the prescribed manner so that they might return. Women's souls, however, do not demand the demeaning of husbands in order to rest in peace! The rituals surrounding death are imbued with pleas for life and the coherence of the living community. Death is a liberation into a larger realm of life as the dead are believed to continue to participate in our realm, as well as in the other dimension of time and space.

A matter of belief

At every stage, a principal of religion is involved and since religion plays such a key-role in enforcing societal norms and ethics, each stage has a social significance that reflects what store society places on women. Socio-political participation is truly imbued with these religious beliefs even when they are not explicitly stated. In this journey through life one finds more rituals for women than for men. Several injunctions are issued to men who are embarking on important tasks to avoid women thus reinforcing the belief that women shed negative influences. We also find the failure of men at their tasks being attributed to the unfaithfulness of a wife. Thus men's incompetencies are blamed on the ritual impurity occasioned by contact with women or caused by a woman's lack of sexual fidelity or even her practice of witchcraft. Put simply, African religion attributes a much greater spiritual strength to women than to men, but seeks to curb its use except where it is to the benefit of men or, as is often said, for the good of the whole society or pointedly for women's own good.
The potential for liberation in the possession of spiritual strength is impeded, causing these religious practices to take on more oppresive and domesticating aspects.

Bio-logic

The rituals for women, whether positive or negative, are related to procreation. The logic being that to ensure the survival of the human race depends on its female components. The conclusion drawn, however, is not that the female principle should therefore regulate the human community, but rather everything should be done to ensure that, the female principle is closely managed by the male principle. In African religion this has meant that procreation is placed at the centre of the woman's universe and multitudes of taboos and ritual for protection and purification are developed to direct her life. Thanksgiving, congratulatory and celebratory rituals are meticulously observed to compensate for the burden of the former, and it is these that empower and encourage a woman's life among several groups in Ghana: puberty rites for girls are designed to fill them with a sense of worth and pride in being a woman. Birthing rituals of renewal and revitalization of the woman are performed to prepare the female for the next pregnancy. Thus women's lives are regulated around their biology. These are self-affirming, as long as a woman fulfills the life cut out for her by her being female. There are no liberative rituals affirming the personhood of a woman if she does not join the biological task of reproducing the human race.

Participation

These are two issues to which we need to pay attention as we look at women and ritual. The first is the gender of the person performing or enforcing the ritual. The second is the reason for the ritual. This will enable us to begin to see whether they need to continue as they are, be modified or that, having no liberative potential, they can be dispensed with altogether. Since these are deeply psychological as well as political issues, it is those whose rituals they are, who will have ultimate responsibility for a reassessment of the situation. The approaches of christian and islamic missions, and those of Western colonial government and their successors, have all been ineffective, precisely because none has been ready to admit the resilience of religious ritual and the hold it has on a people's understanding of life. The security and inner satisfaction people derive from complying with these provisions cannot be ignored.

Among the Akan naming is the prerogative of men because only men are deemed to have the capacity to be spiritual protectors. Food and drink for the spirit world is prepared by people who are free from any flow of blood; blood being deemed sacred has the dual character of being both holy and inauspicious (when found where it should not be). To be sacred is to be separate. This is the root of the limitations put on women's participation in ritual.
Women feature prominently in ritual dances and singing as in *mmomomme* a war support ritual which is a specifically female activity. When rituals are performed to show our unity with the ancestors, women join in the feasting and the dressing up but not in the sacrificing and not in the wearing of masks, for behind the mask are real men, never women, even when the ancestor being represented is a woman. Men have arrogated to themselves the prerogative of representing the spirits that shaped the history and destiny of the community, when we know fully well that some of these history-makers are women. The exclusion of women from rituals performed to recall the ancestors should be of considerable interest to researchers, for these are community activities that have very important political implications and consequences. They may be what lies behind the unwillingness

to see women take responsibility when this includes authority over men, but they also hold within them an untapped liberative potential.

Purification rituals for women are more frequent, for in addition to rituals that both men and women undergo to combat economic and other failures the procreative role heaps more rituals on women. They are very often prescribed by men who are the interpreters of oracles and are performed on women by women. For the liberation of the whole community, however, women of course take part in the cathartic "mocking rituals" intended to release pent up feelings against powerful personalities in the community. Not being in power, women throw themselves most heavily into these rituals to get back some of their "stolen" dignity. In these respects, traditional society has several "shaming" and reconciling rituals that women use to restore equilibrium in societal relations.

Projecting

Religion and ritual operate in the human community as space for power, influence, domination and oppression. It is often an arena of intense passion, especially of fear and, hence, an arena within which those in a weak position can, with very little effort, be made to give up their autonomy. If it turns out that, in this interaction, women more often than men find themselves in weaker roles, then the influences of religion and ritual in the lives of women deserve more attention if women are to be enabled to get on the path for autonomy and full participation according to their innate abilities and acquired skills. One can say with some confidence that, as in all religions, there are liberative elements inherent in African's primary religion. One needs to affirm in addition that, as in all religions, its constituent beliefs and practices can be manipulated for the oppression of those whose spirituality and life-style are answered in the tenets of the religion.

Popular religion in Africa
The cry of hope

Sidbe Semporé, Burkina Faso

To speak about popular religiosity in Africa today is to touch upon a massive reality which is present everywhere and in which all sections of African society participate. We can, therefore, state immediately that in no way are we speaking here of a class phenomenon. Notwithstanding the predictions of numerous sociologists, the religious character of the African peoples is far from having evaporated in its contact with technology and modernity. On the contrary, it seems to be regaining its strength and finding a new vitality. Everywhere churches, fraternities and religious movements are flourishing, and the whole of Africa is experiencing a fever of all kinds of religious manifestations, devotions and practices. This phenomenon is not peculiar to Africa, but here it takes on certain specific forms. As such, it questions the theological reflection and the pastoral practice of the African churches.

What is it all about?

Popular religiosity is, so to speak, the very lifeblood of the peoples springing from an immemorial source and flowing through the veins of a humanity that is anxious to express its aspirations and to gauge the potentialities and limits of its condition. For people lost in the immensity of the universe and struggling with all kinds of oppression it is a matter of exorcising fear and anxiety and of reaching a settlement with the powers from above and from below in order to assure a modus vivendi based on balances of power and agreement that have constantly to be renegotiated.

In Africa, where a holistic understanding of existence has always prevailed, the history and the tradition of the peoples are characterized by the original conviction that humankind is linked with metahuman beings by working and living together with them. These powers, which are called gods, spirits or forces, are not considered as simple projections of human fantasy, but as inevitable interferers in daily life. Popular religion, the religion of the people, appears in its historical dimension as a struggle for vital interests, a Jacob's fight in laughter and tears. Hence, on the part of the people, those endless practices and incessant acts of recourse which are meant to place them back within the cosmic network, to insert them again into the harmony and balance of forces, to reconcile them with the society and with themselves. Their religion thus mobilizes the living forces of the people for the conquest of the life-beyond, the preservation of life and the realization of their destiny. In Africa this existential struggle takes place along three principal lines: the relation with God and the veneration of the suprahuman forces; the recourse to consultation as an attempt to master and to control the unknown; the permanent care for the integrity of the human person and of the environment.

God and the powers

The central dimension of popular religiosity appears in the piety towards the divinity and related powers. The cult in its many forms and expressions translates, here and now, the innate belief in a solidarity which links the destiny of humankind to the active presence of invisible powers capable of influencing life's course. The cult is a symbolic act in which people recognize an existence which establishes and controls their existence. Sacrifices, prayers, offerings and other cultic acts proclaim, in a most serious manner, the dramatic character of the struggle of people who assume their condition in an act of allegiance and submission to the powers with whom they conclude truces and alliances. Before this invisible presence of the "numen", people are fatally covered up with contradictory sentiments: they venerate and revere, they adore and abhor, they hope and fear.

In Africa, we find this ambivalence of sentiments with regard to transcendence in the ancestral religions as well as in islam and in christianity. On the one hand, god and the transcendent powers (spirits, manes, jinns and other angels) have united themselves with humankind and its destiny which they control and influence; on the other hand, they do not appear as partners, but as masters. The traditional image of the African god: powerful, far away and kindhearted, coexists with the despotic image of Allah and the cold and severe face of the christian God. The popular imagination remains struck and even traumatized by the neojansenist pictures which, even today, are still being brought by catholics, protestants and numerous pentecostal preachers who, take delight in emphasizing the image of a severe, intransigent and impatient God. The African god, whom popular wisdom, by tricks, has removed from the human theatre, creates less fear than the christian God with this judgement and hell. Popular belief sees in Him the One who determines people's fate here below and their reward in the hereafter, and it multiplies the cultic acts (masses, novenas, penances, devotions, etc.) to try to bend the divine decrees in its favour.

The popular mentality of all believers without exception always manifests itself in a deep preoccupation with the interference of the world of the spirits in, and its impact on, the world of the humans. Thus the cult of the spirits, and in particular the cult of the ancestors, is added to the christian tradition of angels, devils and saints. In African tradition, the dead are truly dead. Hence the importance, among catholics, of the cult of the dead and the saints. The piety towards the dead, which is traditional among the majority of the African peoples, finds a new vigour among christians. To their Requiem masses and the many prayers which they offer for the dead, they add sumptuous and expensive funeral and anniversary ceremonies. The church, and sometimes also the state, fight against these practices, but in vain, as long as the hold of tradition and the pressure of the environment prove irresistible. The obligation to help each other and to take care of the living disappears behind the duty of piety towards the dead. This constitutes a defiance of common sense and of faith. A reason for this stubbornness among the people is certainly the fear that the dead who do not receive enough for their last journey will change into ghosts ready to torment the living. And there is also the fear that they themselves will be deprived of a worthy funeral and be condemned to wander as phantoms on the earth. The same fear manifests itself with regard to those who meet a violent end (suicides, accident victims, lightning, etc.) and whose remains, according to a tradition scrupulously observed also by christians in many places, cannot pass their domicile without serious damage to the survivors. The reaction of the apostles when confronted by the wandering 'phantom' of their Master is echoed vividly in African belief. The world of the hereafter constitutes an enigma full of anguish. The christian image of heaven, which essentially consists of a beatific encounter with God, moves African believers little, and the mystique which dichotomizes the human route by over-emphasizing the heavenly pole at the expense of the earthly dimension of existence cannot have a lasting hold on them. After what it is hoped will be a long and happy life, they prefer the company of the saints and the ancestors whom they consider as their powerful intercessors and efficacious protectors here below.

Deciphering human existence

If God and the metahuman powers emerge as a fascinating reality in the African religious universe, human existence and its thick veil of mystery constitute, for the African believer, a crucial question which permanently mobilizes their wisdom and their resources. What is the ultimate meaning of existence? Does the past determine present life? Which pertinent, meaningful and motivating secrets does the future hold? Briefly, what is the impact of the hidden realities on the course of human existence?

In an environment where the precariousness of the conditions of life multiplies the obstacles and aggravates the handicaps, people are ceaselessly confronted with issues which are virtually fatal for their existence and their projects. Mistakes or failures are signs of damnation or curse. Hence the feverish will to foresee and to prevent one's fate by incursions into the wreck of time gone by, into the flow of running events, and into the obscure field of the future. People therefore attach great importance to visions and dreams which symbolically coagulate realities that are significant and enlightening for human destiny. In such a perspective the dream does not appear as an epiphenomenon, nor even as a pure psycho-analytical phenomenon. On the contrary, it is integrated into the dynamic of existence both as an apocalypse, a revelation, a beacon, and as a prophecy anticipating the world to come.

In African religions, as well as in islam and christianity, the need to consult pushes the crowds of poor and rich, of illiterates and literates, of weak and powerful, to seen out diviners, marabous and seers. The enthusiasm of African christians for apparitions, phenomena of clairvoyance, esoteric associations, collections of revelations, prophesies or secret messages of mystics or people of extraordinary lucidity, novenas or illumination, etc. can be explained by the vital desire to decipher existence, to decode the chain of events, to exorcise the existential anguish and reduce the element of risk and of the unknown which hides life. They consult people, cosmic elements, Sacred Scriptures, the dead and the saints; they consult God whom they ask for readable and tangible signs of His will and His presence here and now. The leap into the unknown, the walk in the *clair-obscure*, the passage through the night are not images that motivate the faith of the masses who are on the lookout and watching. The certainties and the lights of science are not enough to extinguish in the people the irresistible need for lights that have come from elsewhere.

'In the shadow of your wings ...'

The third important element in the life of an African believer is the constant and assiduous search for effective means of protection against the forces destructive of humankind and its environment. The influence of traditional beliefs and practices on the behaviour and the activities of muslims and christians in the struggle for the preservation of life is evident everywhere. It was, and still is, a matter not only of guaranteeing the integrity of individuals, but also of protecting nature (waters, flora and fauna) through sacred laws. The family taboos, be they alimentary or sexual, as well as the social bans meant to guarantee the integrity of life and the equilibrium of society and nature are observed by christians without any drama of conscience. The amulets, talismans and other medals made by diviners or marabouts, or imported from Europe or Asia, are, by popular sentiment, invested with quasi-sacramental powers of protection and defence against evils, bad luck, sickness, spells.

On the one hand, they are searching for everything that, in their thinking, conserves or increases life, protects health, cures sickness: christian sacraments, objects of piety and images of saints who are reputed as mighty and "miraculous" (e.g. Michael, Jude, Benedict, Anthony, the Miraculous Virgin, Rita, the Sacred Heart, the Infant Jesus, Padre Pio, Martha Robin, etc.). Certain "marvelous" prayers have proved their worth: the Key of Psalms, the Fifteen prayers, the 40 orations, the prayers of Father Julio, the prayer of St Charlemagne, the chains of prayer which must be multiplied – at times up to 81 copies – and be distributed in the churches and, not forgetting, the messages of Medjugorje and of Father Gobbi. Undoubtedly, we are dealing here with practices and formulas with a poor and artificial doctrinal content, but with a powerful and explosive emotional charge. They touch the conservation instinct and mobilize the dynamism – one should say: the dynamite – of the human irrational. Just as the official teaching of the churches promotes sacramental practice in order to increase spiritual forces, in the same way popular devotion has recourse to a tissue of signs and parasacramental symbols, tropicalized and resensitized in the African manner, in order, itself, to take charge of its need for security. Under the unbridled accumulation of a curious hotchpotch of objects and formulas, the old reflex of a shattered humanity manifests itself, seeking refuge not in the achievements of rationality but in the ridiculous symbols of hidden powers.

On the other hand, it is not enough to requisition heaven and earth in order to guarantee and increase the goods of life (health, fertility, riches, security). We must also – human wisdom obliges us – track down and neutralize the real enemies of humankind. The generalized belief in the existence of sorcerers and fortune-tellers is so strong and so natural to African societies that popular piety, by wearing certain objects, using certain formulas of cursing and anathema, as well as by having recourse to seers, searches for the means to detect evil powers, to immunize people against the invisible poison of the "drinker of blood", and eventually to annihilate the "eaters of souls". Here again the Old Testament find acceptance. The revelations and confessions of active or repentant sorcerers strengthen a belief whose roots lie deep in the night of the times and regularly perturb the psychology of individuals and masses, the cohesion of families and the peace of societies.

Such a mentality poses the problem of evil and violence in the midst of African societies where nothing is attributed to change and where a new-born baby can be accused of sorcery for the same reason as a ninety year old woman who lies paralyzed in her hut. Since death before one's term (i.e. in full youth or in the prime of life) is always suspect in the eyes of the community, people in many regions of Africa interrogate the dead who always indicate a culprit. This procedure opens the way to bloody settlements of accounts, criminal injustices or hereditary hatred of which, alas, christians are both the agents and the victims. Sharing in such a mentality, they search for means of protection in the arsenal of christian religion, brandishing the cross against fetishes, holy water against lustral waters, psalms against incantations. The frequency of "demonic possessions" and exorcisms in characteristic groups and in the Afro-christian churches reveals the mentality of sorcery which underlies the psychology of many for whom the evil personifies and incarnates itself and emigrates at will. Prior to the question of evangelical love, the problem facing us here is that of the African understanding of culpability and innocence, of sin and forgiveness.

Questions for theology and for the missions

This summary description of the three concrete aspects of popular African religiosity raises serious questions for theological reflection and pastoral practice in Africa.

84

First of all, I think that the existence of popular religion in its christian and non-christian forms is a fact that imposes itself on us and that we must always discover with interest and sympathy. The answer of the people to the message proclaimed and to the cult celebrated, always takes a colouring and a turn which stretch and overflow the frame of official orthodoxy. The dialectical tension: cleric-lay, learned-ignorant, literate-illiterate always produces, in the church, a duality of feelings and of practice of the one and the same and unique faith. Jesus behaved differently with regard to the masses, that tired and harassed flock, that mob which did not know the law, than he did with regard to the religious leaders, the officers of the Temple and the scribes. The theologian and the religious leader run the risk of despising and ridiculing the faith of those who live their religion in the depths of life, with few means and little to fall back on. Certainly, we must not canonize the religious practices of the peoples. It is an attempt, sometimes desperate and unfruitful, to grasp the parable of the mystery of Christ, the Saviour, and before the diffuse clarity of the Gospel, its roots in perversion and sin. Do we, however, have to pass by on the other side of the road?

Popular religion in Africa has its strength and its limits. As far as it is the lived reality of the great majority of christians, it is in itself a force of witness and of life according to the gospel: a gospel, sometimes truncated and betrayed, but a gospel all the same, a message of hope and a reality of salvation. The people who believe make the incarnation of Christ visible in the African realities today, and this constitutes a title of nobility. Certainly, this force which is derived from Christ's sacramental presence in the midst of the people can be recuperated and diverted by the powerful towards less evangelical ends: they build shrines and basilicas with looted money in order to lock up the people in factories of devotions. They multiply in abundance the celebrations and objects of worship in order to wrest from the poor the penny of their credulity. They adapt and inculturate pastoral practice in order to control and rule the faithful better. The risk for theology is great and the temptation for the missions is to turn to ideology and tactics. All the more because the weaknesses of popular religion are evident: the illiteracy of the majority prevents them from having direct access to the Scriptures. This makes the believers easy prey for manipulators of the Word. The weight of certain antiquated and antihuman African traditions (eg. the fate reserved for woman, the deadly belief in sorcerers, the tyranny of funeral customs, etc.) places a heavy mortgage on their evangelical freedom and practice. The unconditional search for happiness now, at this moment, will in time remove the scandal of the Cross. Finally, the mystique of mankind, co-creator of the world and ruler with God of the universe, is far too absent from, and strange to, the faith of the believers. This shows that popular religion, just like learned and official religion, is called to permanent conversion. In our catechumenal churches the religion of the "people of little faith" is fully in its place.

African popular religion throws the question about God back to theology and to the missions: Who is God? Is the reply to this question above all of a notional or an existential order? "No one has ever seen God." No one, therefore, can speak about Him in an adequate manner and theo-logy, our talking about God, cannot claim any normative character whatsoever. The stammerings of popular piety about God, just like the learned theological treatises, are childish prattle that cannot lay any claim to orthodoxy. "Only his Son has revealed him." Orthodoxy is not established on the level of notional or symbolic knowledge of God. The revelations belong to the existential order: it is through His person, His witness, His living word and His example that Jesus reveals God to us. God allows us to know Him only in the *kenosis*, in the descent into the hell of the human condition, in the incarnation. He reveals Himself only through humanity. There is no liberation of humanity without the Exodus of God; there is no salvation for humanity without the *kenosis* of God; there is no knowledge of God without the experience of humanity. Popular religion is one of the places, among others, where God reveals Himself to humanity in a process of mutual exodus. It recalls that God is first and foremost a revelation, a being in Exodus, not a brute given of reason of faith. On the other hand, the life of the relationship between the Africans and their God is characterized by extreme discretion, in strong contrast to the interventionism of the christian God, the use of liturgies and the multiplication of temples. Does this discretion not come close to the Johannine sobriety of the worship "in spirit and in truth"? Is it certain that the cult of a God who comes out of His silence to proclaim his commandments one by one, to demand submission and to dictate human behaviour, means progress for the African religious sensitivity? The popular cult of saints and spirits, notwithstanding its alienating aspects, replaces the service which God refuses to impose on humankind. And the true worship of God? Would it not be to serve in the temple which is humankind?

African popular religion also throws the question of eschatology back to theology and to the missions. African people are haunted by the brevity of time and the precariousness of existence. The evolution of African society, the progressive impact of science and technology, the secularization of structures and ways of life have not yet damaged their hope in the quest for happiness here and now. For the African people, religion in a very specific way, constitutes an eminent means of that happiness. The enigma of suffering and the mystery of evil today call for a redefinition of christian eschatology. The spontaneous identification of African christians with the Suffering Servant and with the Crucified Christ of Golgotha, the emphasis placed on the passion to the detriment of the Resurrection make a new approach to the Paschal mystery necessary. The darkness of Good Friday is today in Africa called: drought, Aids, political tyrannies, apartheid, pauperization, unemployment, illiteracy ... The daily struggle for survival and the fervent devotional practices express that inarticulate cry: why did God allow his Son to be crucified? Why is Africa prey to so many evils?

We can then understand what Fr. S. O'Leary, a missionary in South Africa, means when he writes that people identify strongly with Jesus on the cross, with the abandoned Christ. It is interesting to notice, he adds, that when thousands of people joined us for the celebration of Good-Friday, only a few hundreds did participate in the joy of Eastern. The life of our people is the life of the cross. The burden of this cross blur the view of a luminous future.

Gabriel M. Setiloane, a South African writer, expresses the same reality in a moving poem:

"And yet for us it is when He is on the cross,
This Jesus of Nazareth, with holed hands and open side,
like a beast at a sacrifice:
When He is stripped naked like us,
Browned and sweating water and blood in the heat of the sun,
Yet silent,
That we cannot resist Him."[1]

Suffering and misery are not the exclusive lot of the Africans. But why is Africa, in the person of Simon of Cyrene, in an impromptu manner requisitioned to carry Christ's cross? It is at the foot of that cross, under the gaze of the Crucified One, that the believer becomes aware of the injustice of its lot, of the scandal of violence and of the absurdity of death. Is it there that he, secretly, draws the strength to hold on, to hope and, at times, to act. "Today...": the cross announces, every day, the last day, the eschaton, the end of the time of humankind.

Conclusion

Popular religion in Africa is a living and complex reality which implies the Message and its irreducible specificity, the context and its factors of liberation and oppression, and the African people and their desire for salvation. It is a cry which expresses the multiform suffering of a people in search of happiness and liberation; it is a cry calling the messengers of and those responsible for the Word to help; it is the cry of a newly born child in contact with a hard and cruel world, struggling and kicking in the arms of its liberator whom it searches gropingly: the cry of hope.

---

1 G.M. Setiloane, 'I am an African', in: G.H. Anderson, Th.F. Stransky, (eds), *Mission trends n.3. Third World Theologies*, New York – Grand Rapids, Paulist Press – Eerdman's Publishing Co., 1976, 130.

PART II

LATIN AMERICA

Social transformation and the religious vision of the world among the underclasses of Nicaragua

Amando J. Robles, Nicaragua

The presentation which I shall offer here is a very concise synthesis of some of the major lines and findings of on-going research into "religion and rationality as a vision of the world in social structures of dependent capitalism".[1] Its empirical point of reference is the vision of the world among the under classes of Nicaragua.

Our approach to popular religiosity is a sociological one and it is deliberately limited.[2] To begin with, in our research we shall deal only with popular religiosity as that whole group of representations which constitute a vision or an image of the world, leaving aside all the other dimensions and aspects. It is therefore with a rather heavy bias that we dare to speak of popular religiosity. On the other hand, as with any research, the object of our study is limited by the scientific manner in which we shall seek to deal with it. As a result the "vision of the world", in the sense in which we choose to see it here, is not only the consequence of a general need for a definition of the object of the study and the operationalization of the concepts, it is also an indication of our sociological position. It is a position which is critical with regard to other positions[3], but which, for that very reason, is also prepared to submit itself to that same critical exercise on the part of others.

---

1 This research forms part of the background work for a doctoral thesis in sociology at the Catholic University of Louvain, Louvain-la-Neuve, under the direction of Prof. François Houtart.
2 For information with regard to the new religious awareness among the popular classes in Central America readers should see, among others, the following works: A. Opazo, 'El movimiento religioso popular en Centroamérica: 1970-1983', in: D. Camacho, R. Monjivar (eds), *Movimientos populares en Centroamérica*, San José, C.R. Educa, 1985; *Costa Rica. La iglesia catolica y el orden social*, San José, D.E.I.; G. Blando and J. Valverde, *Honduras. Iglesia y cambio social*, San José, D.E.I., 1987; R. M. Pochet and A. Martinez, *Nicaragua. Iglesia: manipulación o profecía?*, San José, D.E.I., 1987; F. Houtart and G. Lemercinier, 'Conscience religieuse et conscience politique en Amérique Centrale', in: *Social Compass*, 30(1983), n.2-3, 153-154; J. H. Pico, 'Religión y revolución en Nicaragua. Análisis de diez años de experiencia', in: *Cuadernos de Sociología*, 9-10(1989), 69-90.
3 We think, obviously, of the positions taken by the "desarrollista" (developmental) school of sociology, but equally of the positions of culturalist sociology as represented by Pedro Morande, *Cultura y modernización en América Latina. Ensayo sociológico acerca de la crisis del desarrollismo y de su superación*, Cuadernos del Instituto de Sociología, Santiago de Chile, Pontificia Universidad Católica de Chile, 1983, and the positions of those referred to as "catholic intellectuals", and even certain positions of Latin American sociology of religion.

The central religious vision of the world and popular religiosity

It is important that we begin by defining the relationship between the central religious vision of the world and popular religiosity. Indeed, since we are dealing with two different religious realities, but realities which, under certain social conditions, are closely related, the transformations taking place the level of the central religious vision of the world can be considered as one indication of the transformations which have taken place in popular religiosity.

The general impression that the two realities are superimposed the one upon the other and that they are mutually inter-related is only true with regard to the traditional or pre-capitalist social structures and the social forms resulting therefrom, which are sub-capitalist.[4] Thus, in our Latin American societies, during the period of colonization, not only popular religion but even institutional and official religion was identified with the central religious vision of the world, seen in christian terms.

The elements inherent to a pre-capitalist or traditional society, when compared with the so-called "primitive societies" are:
a the existence of socio-economic classes,
b the existence of a power which can be shaped into a central state, and
c a central vision of the world which can be developed into a religious system whose principal role is to provide legitimization.[5]

In the case of the Hispanic social structure and the newly colonized societies whose structure was based on conquest, the central vision of the world is a religious and a christian one. As we see, the religious vision of the world was a social function of the only existing religion – since it was central, it was considered unique, universal and exclusive – and as a result part both of the institutional and official religion and the popular religion.

By the central religious vision of the world we mean the way of looking at and considering the reality (the attitude and the knowledge), built up on the basis of a meta-social point of reference common to people living within the traditional or pre-capitalist type of social structure, or in the resulting, and thus sub-capitalist, social structures.

As far as Nicaraguan society was concerned, it took a very long time before the popular classes sensed that their central religious vision of the world was being

---

4 By "sub-capitalist" we mean the non-capitalist forms which capitalism, as a method of production, adopts or recreates, or which it reactivates according to its logic, and which are not merely the heritage or something left over from the past but which are, to a large extent, a contemporary creation.
5 See J. Habermas, *Teoría de la acción comunicativa*, vol. 2., Madrid, Taurus, 1987, 235 and 271-280; *La technique et la science comme "idéologie"*, Paris, Gallimard, 1973, 25-26; *Raison et légitimité. Problèmes de légitimité dans le capitalisme avancé*, Paris, Payot, 1978, 34-37; *La construcción del materialismo histórico*, Madrid, Taurus, 1981, 19-20.

eroded. For a number of reasons, agrarian capitalism was late in arriving on the Nicaraguan scene, and as it developed it found itself grafted onto the backwardness of the existing structure of production, thus preserving the former relationships among people and between people and their environment.[6] It was only in the course of the 1950s that Nicaragua experienced more radical and major social changes under a capitalism which sought to modernize the country and which gradually subjected the labour force of the pre-capitalist sector to the power of capitalism. First of all, it was subjection to capital in the form of free international capitalism, particularly in the 1960s, with such violent social repercussions that they constituted an element in the fundamental social conditions for a people's revolution, which brought about the capitalism of the mixed economy, to the benefit of the major groups and under the control of the state.

Here we must make a remark which we believe is true of the other Latin American societies: in the course of such a social transition, the central religious vision of the world loses its structure, it loses its central character, it becomes "decentralized", and this occurs in those social sectors identified by this vision of the world. At the same time, however, certain other elements and functions of popular religiosity do not disappear, for example, the role of the production of meaning and of symbolism, of motivation and of direction of action, of ethical legitimation. These are roles which, indeed, perhaps become even more important than in the past. All this, however, demonstrates the real difference which exists between the religious vision of the world and popular religion, as well as the need to deal with it as a limited, dynamic and changing social reality, which goes beyond any kind of idyllic position, if we are truly to appreciate the nature of the subject before us.

The plurality of world visions

THE PLURALITY OF RELIGIOUS LANGUAGE

In an earlier study of the cultural models of religion among the under classes in Nicaragua[7], we already pointed out a number of important factors. Firstly, we were able to prove that there is no single language, but rather several, religious languages; that there are different way of thinking of things religious, which erupt into the socio-symbolic space while centring on different axes. Such forms extend from what one could describe as the traditional-community-based model which still retains a number of mythical elements with regard to extreme situations in any order of reality, to the praxis-utopian model typical of the members of the BECs (base ecclesial communities), and even to a secularized model which sees

---

6 J. Wheelock, *Imperialismo y dictatura*, Managua, Edit. Nueva Nicaragua, 1985, 15-35 and 57-95.
7 J. A. Robles, *Production de sens religieux et transition sociale dans les classes paysannes subalternes au Nicaragua*, Master's thesis, Catholic University of Louvain, Louvain-la-Neuve, 1985. Spanish translation: 'Producción de sentido religioso y transición social en las clases subalternas campesinas de Nicaragua', in: *Senderos*, Aug.-Dec. 1986, 1-59.

itself as autonomous vis-à-vis matters religious. Popular religiosity is not mono-lithic, it is pluralistic; there is no such thing as popular religiosity; there are several religiosities or popular religions. This also means that some elements typical of the religiosity of the past become eroded and, indeed, in certain cases disappear, while other elements emerge.

Secondly, by analyzing the sequences which make up the religious elements of the language, we note that there is practically no religious reading of the social and practical relationships. While there is a religious reading of the relationship between man and nature, it is rare, at least in explicit terms. In other words, the area of social and political relationships and the area of nature gradually create their own autonomy vis-à-vis the area of religion. On the other hand, a general religious understanding of life and an ethic of inspiration and of religious motiva-tion, with both a social and an individual projection, are present.

In general, we see that the popular sectors can no longer, sociologically speaking, reproduce the religious language of the past, while, on the other hand, we cannot consider them the bearers of an already-instituted language. There where the language changes most, it is a language in transition. And the basic logic which guides this language is a good expression of the last two elements which we have just mentioned: the religious meaning of life, history, the world, and social commitment. It is a religion of commitment for justice.

THE PLURALITY OF THE VISIONS OF THE WORLD

So far we have only dealt with variations of religious language among the under-classes in Nicaragua. But do these types of various language not appear in the symbolic or cultural fields? What relationship, along these lines, might there be between the two manifestations? Thus we raise the issue of the analysis of world visions within the under and rural classes in Nicaragua. This is the subject of the work underway at present.

The purest models of the visions of the world are three in number, along typico-ideal lines. A traditional vision of the world applied to nature, as opposed to a rational and analytical vision of the world applied to the social domain, and a traditional ethico-social vision which, likewise, is opposed to a vision of the world in mythical terms and a vision of the world purely in analytical and rational terms.

The mere act of noting this fact says much about the plurality and the hetero-geneity of the visions of the world among the popular classes in Nicaragua. Only in the first model does religion, as a central vision of the world, persist. The second model can co-exist, empirically or otherwise, with a religious sense of life and with a religious social ethic. It would appear to be autonomous, and is based on an analytical rationality applied to reality as a whole, but more specifically to society. The third model, the ethico-social vision, falls between the two. In principle, the phenomena of nature are seen as a reality which is self-explanatory, which is made autonomous by God, but as far as everything related to the cosmos is concerned, one still feels the need for religious clarification, and the perception of society is conceived in terms of the ethico-moral categories of rich and poor. It presents all the aspects of a profile of a vision of the world in transition.

In this heterogeneity we perceive opposition and order. There is clear opposition between the traditional vision of the world and the analytical vision. In this respect, Houtart and Lemercinier say that we are witnessing a "national debate".[8] The opposition is strong and marked. It does, however, present a specific characteristic which might well be due to the Nicaraguan revolutionary context. First and foremost, it is not merely an opposition between tradition and modernity as two specific forms of knowledge, between religious and non-religious language; rather it is an opposition between two ways of approaching matters social. It is an opposition in the manner of considering and analyzing social matters, between the traditional religious vision and the modern vision. This opposition comes into play in the acceptance or the rejection of a vision of society as the product of natural laws, exempt from all control by the social sector.

Order is reflected in the sequence which emerges from a traditional vision with its mythical elements applied to nature, to an analytical vision applied above all to the social sector, by way of a position intermediate and equidistant both with regard to the passive attitude of a traditional vision and the purely analytical attitude. Nevertheless, the character and the dynamic of this sequence is never mechanical or linear; rather it is a true social and dialectic dynamic, filled with challenges and contradictions.

Finally we note something else: the strong presence of the ethical factor. By this we mean the recurrent interpretation of the reality in terms of the "ought to be" of good and evil. Ethics permeate all the models, but it is in the ethico-social vision that it would appear to play a more modulating and "nuclearizing" role. Here ethics would appear to represent a point between extreme visions. Hence we arrive at a analytico-social concept on the basis of an ethical valorization of the social.

VISIONS OF THE WORLD, SOCIAL ACTORS AND FACTORS

To those factors already mentioned we must add others: the heterogeneity of the registered visions of the world is not arbitrary when looked at from the point of view of the social role-players as the bearers of those visions. In a decisive way, the traditionalist-natural vision and the analytical vision are associated with very different categories of social role-players. In the first case, those whose living conditions are precarious and who have no educational future. These are groups whose socialization takes place within a family and local culture which is practical and oral. In the second case, they are role players who enjoy success on the professional and technical levels and who have a high level of education.

---

8 *La cultura en Managua. Una cultura en transición*, Louvain-la-Neuve, CETRI (Centre Tricontinental), 1988, 18-23. They also speak of an "antagonism between two socio-religious visions (which) constitute the culture of Managua" (Ibid., 20).

Such affirmations are endorsed by the studies carried out by Houtart and Lemercinier with regard to representations of health and culture, largely among the same sectors.[9] With regard to popular representations of health, these authors speak of "a disintegration of popular culture and, as a result, the irreversible loss of their monolithic character". As for urban culture in Managua, while that traditional culture which finds expression through a traditional cultural model is, numerically speaking, the most important, an analysis of the heterogeneity and the tension between the cultural models leads the authors to conclude that popular religiosity no longer plays a homogenizing role in Managuan culture.[10] In rural areas, as in the cities, the whole area of culture is much taken up with the cultural debate with regard to ways and means of representing and analyzing the natural and social reality.

With regard to culture in Managua, we see that there is a correspondence between the cultural profiles and models and the socio-professional groups, with the sole exception of the workers who do not appear to be the bearers of a specific cultural model. This would appear to be due to the social heterogeneity of the group. Among those factors which play a role, we should highlight education. It has a strong influence on the decline of traditional thinking and on the emergence of analytical thinking. According to the evidence, it is among those who have completed secondary studies that we see the greatest break with a traditional type of thinking. The same phenomenon can be seen in the countryside: we witness the major social impact of education and cultural diversification, parallel to social diversification. As for religion, it does not appear to be a determining variable in the cultural profiles; indeed, on the contrary, to a greater extent it is religion which is influenced by other factors.

To summarize, in the countryside, as in the cities, with certain specificities in each case, we see the same phenomenon of cultural transition. Transition, however, does not mean a linear and mechanical passage from one to the other – states of doubt, uncertainties, questioning and anomies deny this. What it does means is that it has become impossible for popular thought and religiosity to continue to reproduce themselves as they did in the past, just as it has become impossible for

---

9 F. Houtart and G. Lemercinier, *Creencias y prácticas que conciernen a la salud, en los grupos populares rurales y urbanos nicaraguenses*, Louvain-la-Neuve, Centre de Recherches Socio-Religieuses, C.U.L., 1985; *La cultura en Managua. Una cultura en transición*, Managua – Louvain-la-Neuve, Centre d'Analyse Sociale de la Culture, UCA and Centre Tricontinental (CETRI), 1988, and a whole series of monographs on the influence of religion and education on culture, among young people, women and agricultural workers: *Campesinos y cultura. Análisis de los perfiles culturales de una población campesina nicaraguense*, Managua – Louvain-la-Neuve, Centro de Analisis Socio-cultural, UCA and Centre d'Analyse Sociale de la Culture, CETRI,1988. The research into culture in Managua involved, among other things, measuring the permanence of religiosity as a factor of homogeneity. See *La cultura en Managua, o.c.,* 12.
10 Of a sample group of 872 people questioned in Managua, 55% considered themselves close to traditional thinking; a closer analysis of the facts showed, however, that the majority of the sample group – 78.4% – no longer reproduced the traditional model in all its aspects. See *La cultura en Managua, o.c.,* 60.

this religiosity to act as an area of social consensus, because it is becoming increasingly diversified and distinctive.

Popular religiosities and social functions

The facts recorded here prevent us from speaking of religiosity or of popular religiosity, of its potentials or the social functions which it might fulfil, as though it were a whole; we prefer to speak of the various existing forms of popular religiosity and their respective social functions. Were we to speak of popular religion in the singular, and of its social potential, then we should require to realize that we most probably are trying to speak of a given type and a given potential, and that most probably it is a question of religiosity as something which is capable of making the transition towards a rational and analytical vision of the world, or of the religiosity which is in the process of coming into being.

This type of religiosity undergoes certain specific social conditionings and as a result, what really matters is the possibility of a social transformation of the relationships among people and between people and their milieu. This possibility implicates neither the fact nor the concrete direction which it might take. It is here that we see the importance of the convergence of role players and of the inductive practices. If, however, the conditions for real social transformation are not present, they cannot be replaced by any type of voluntarism.
The transformation of popular religiosity in Nicaragua would not appear to be the result solely of the revolutionary situation of the last ten years, it represents a whole series of social conditions which, together with others, might explain the more specific orientations, the immediate needs and the content, but which have their roots in prior social transformations. The same may be said of Central America as a whole. There the transformation of popular religiosity has been closely linked, as a part and consequence of the characteristics of the historico-social process which the sub-continent has experienced since the end of the last century and which has resulted in the emergence of under classes as a new historical subject.[11] The revolution cannot be separated from this process; on the contrary, it is the result, and its impact is obvious in the very extent to which it widens, accelerates and deepens the social transformations.

The constant factor in this transition is the gradual disappearance of a religious reading of nature, whereas a religious awareness of life, of the history of the world and an ethico-religious attitude with regard to the social reality continue to exist. The aspiration of our Western way of thinking – and in saying this we limit ourselves to a statement of fact, without seeking to make a value judgement – is

---

11 See the special issue of *Envío*, January-February 1986, 'El Nuevo sujeto historico. Centroamérica 1979-85'; E. Torres Rivas, *Crisis del poder en Centroamérica*, Educa, 1981, 88-89 and 103-107; A. Opazo, 'El movimiento religioso popular en Centroamérica: 1970-1983', in: D. Camacho, R. Menjivar (eds), *Movimientos populares en Centroamérica*, San José, C.R., Educa, 1985.

to be able to assist the popular sectors to disengage themselves as quickly as possible from this former function and, in exchange, to support them (the popular sectors) and to deepen the strength of their motives and their mobilization in the struggle for liberation.

This is the struggle being fought today by the peoples in whom this potential resides; people of whom, until now, we have only known a very small sample.

We know even less, indeed very little at all, of the relationship which exists between these functions which we also try to distinguish. On the one hand, this distinction would appear to be at the root of the emergence of the ethical attitude of compromise and of the new analytical rationality. By freeing itself from a mythico-religious reading of nature, there is an initial liberation with regard to others and with regard to things social, and thus emerges the need for an ethic as life and the exercise of analytical rationality in all areas, including that of social life. It is here specifically, in this ethico-rational heart, upheld by a religious understanding of history, of one's own life and of the life of human beings, that the source of the liberating potential of religion is to be found. But is it not here that its own weakness and its future, perhaps, indeed, its disintegration also develop? The more religious awareness becomes subjectivized, the more it divides, the more it becomes a reflection of itself, the more it becomes individualized and privatized. The result is that the more popular forms of religion become pluralist, the more religious consensus becomes impossible, and the less religion can fulfil a homogenizing role in society. And, as with other issues, is it not true that here, too, we shall only begin to become aware of what is happening when its very existence is threatened?

To the extent that the religious becomes ethical and becomes rational, and where social consensus is less and less to be found in religion, even among the popular sectors, of what historical and social subject are we thinking when we speak of the liberating potential of religion? Of the religious peoples of the Third World in general? Of the popular sectors among these peoples? Of certain specific sectors or groupings? Can we conceive a global strategy which might have some meaning? So many questions and so many challenges, which does not mean that we intend to play into the hands of that paralyzing paradox which makes us abandon any form of analysis. Rather they should encourage us to carry out more careful and rigorous analyses. The liberating potential of popular religiosities would appear to be weaker and more limited that we tended to imagine, less decisive, than perhaps we thought, more cyclical and transitory. But this does not mean that their contribution is any less important. In any case, it is more important than if it were to be absolutized.

An ethico-rational religiosity is one which can go hand-in-hand with a very strong individual and social identity, with scientifico-social analyses as mediation, and with an awareness of class and of the people. While this is, perhaps, only incarnated among certain sectors and groups, this support can prove very important within civic society.

To end, we should like, briefly, to specify another role which popular religiosity often fills and can continue to fill from time to time, and this can have even greater bearing. Here we refer to the symbolic role which it can have for whole cultures and peoples, or for certain sectors of these peoples, with all the influence which such a symbol contains[12], in the service of an historic and social identity, and in mobilizing the people. This is, for example, the role of certain national and popular festivals. In Nicaragua, this is true of the celebrations of "La Purisima" and of the festival of Santo Domingo in Managua. In such cases, the religious-symbolic aspect extends beyond the various cultural religiosities and mentalities to become a point of reference common to all. This ability to serve as a source of linkage and identification can develop in situations of aggression and cultural domination. We need only think of those islamic movements which are incorrectly referred to as "integrist".

Conclusion

In our presentation we have sought to emphasize the social transformation which takes place to a greater extent in popular religion than in the political and social domains. Thus this presentation places the social element of popular religion within the social reality of which it is part, allowing us to appreciate its possibilities within a given situation, as well as its limitations and the transformations which influence it. In other words, in such a framework, we can take a more critical view.

Thus we have seen that popular religiosity is becoming transformed, and, in the process, it is losing its more mythical and traditional functions – such as that of a religious reading of nature – and its centralizing role, as well as its role as a source of social homogeneity and of consensus. This would appear to be the price which it must pay in order to acquire its new ethical functions of motivation and orientation, of identity and of commitment which can turn it into a liberating force. In this process of transformation, as in its repercussions, this popular religiosity has a partial and limited – but none the less major – contribution to make.

---

12 In the opinion of Hernandez Pico, it is the strength of the symbol which is most important in the religion of the people of Nicaragua. See J. H. Pico, 'Religión y revolución en Nicaragua. Análisis de diez años de experiencia', in: *Cuadernos de Sociología*, 9-10 January-June 1989, 70 and 73.

Popular religion and liberation in Latin America
Between common sense and good sense

Julio de Santa Ana, Uruguay/Brazil

The historical process of Latin American nations over the last twenty years has shown the relevance of religion and its influence upon other realms of reality, especially over political events. The second general conference of the roman catholic bishops (Medellín, 1968) was a striking moment, providing proof that the evolution of the religious field in Latin America needs to be carefully followed by those who wish to understand what is happening in that part of the world. The Rockefeller Report[1], published in 1969, already gave reason to this need, underlining the important role played by the roman catholic church in Latin America and the Caribbean. Since then, many events have confirmed this trend: in Central America's conflicts, religion has almost always been present. In struggles for the defence and promotion of human rights, religious forces have played a major role. The same thing happened in Haiti, when Duvalier was obliged to resign as head of state and then to leave the country and go into exile. Last, but not least, all the observers who have followed the course of the last presidential elections in Brazil have perceived that religious symbols, religious personalities, as well as religious institutions, had a relevant function supporting one or other of the most important candidates.

For the first time in twenty-nine years the Brazilian population had the opportunity to vote directly for its president. The previous election took place in 1960. In 1964, the Armed Forces staged a coup d'etat, and declared a state of national security, as a result of which the military took control of the political life of the nation. This situation continued until 1985, when a government of transition prepared the way for a new era characterized by liberal democracy. The presidential elections of 1989 offered an opportunity for a wide national debate, which often became heated and even passionate, especially during the last weeks of the campaign. Through it, the role of religious forces became clear. Some candidates accused the "progressive church"[2] of taking the side of the Workers' Party (PT),

---

1 The *Report on the State of the Americas,* was the result of a mission by John D. Rockefeller III, when, Vice-President of the USA, he was requested by President Richard Nixon to visit Latin America in order to find ways of improving relations between the USA and Latin American countries. "The Rockefeller Report", as it is known (Washington, 1969), underlines the great historical importance of the roman catholic church in the life of Latin America.
2 This concept indicates the practices and thought of sectors of the christian churches in Latin America and the Caribbean who, besides looking for the renewal of the christian church and its theology, align themselves with the social and political sectors aiming at transformation of the

and at the same time they appealed to other religious leaders to participate in the campaign on their side. Religious services, on several occasions, were disturbed because the faithful openly manifested their disagreement with the views expressed by the clergy in the homilies during the worship. The "progressive church" and the "conservative church"[3] were mentioned continually throughout the campaign. The churches (as well as other religious institutions) were divided. Traditional religious confrontations became irrelevant during this process: the problem was between "progressive" and "conservative" roman catholics, evangelicals, pentecostals, and so on.

Two things must be noted at this point. On the one hand, the language used by the candidates (especially by the two who came through to the second and final stage of the elections: Fernando Collor de Mello, a rightist populist, and Luiz Ignacio Lula da Silva, who represented the leftist forces) appealed to the consciousness of the public, openly using the concepts popularized by liberation theology: "the preferential option for the poor", "the role of the people in history", etc. In other words, in a country where the vast majority of the population lives below the poverty line, the religious language which gives pride of place to the poor became important for the candidates. This means that religious symbols and images are very much present in the awareness of the Brazilian masses. Therefore even a linguistic code forged by ideological forces which took the side of the dispossessed classes, was co-opted by those who defended conservative interests. Language was no more than the means which helped to distinguish the progressive from the conservative. On the other hand, such a distinction could be made if individuals were taken into account. Those personalities whose practices are well-known represented clear positions to the public. They were like images. Their options helped the people to recognize the orientation of the forces in confrontation. Among those who supported one or other of the candidates, a privileged role was given to religious leaders and even institutions. For example, Collor de Mello received the support of the Igreja Universal do Reino de Deus (the fastest-growing pentecostal church in Brazil), while Luiz Ignacio Lula da Silva received the backing of a great number of pastors of the Assemblies of God (the biggest pentecostal church in the country). In the same way, some "progressive" roman catholic bishops endorsed the leftist candidate, while other leaders of the same church gave public support to the candidate of the right.

---

present state of affairs in Latin America. From the ecclesial point of view, the base ecclesial communities are its clearest expression. From the intellectual perspective, the Latin American theology of liberation is a manifestation of its theoretical orientation.

3 Opposed to the "progressive church", we find the "conservative church". It claims to seek to stop the process of renewal involved in the new forms of being church and the theology of liberation. Politically is characterized by its support for rightist populist political parties, as well as other more conservative forces in Latin American societies. It also manifests a clear trend towards a reversal of the results of the roman catholic episcopal conferences in Latin America: Medellín (1968) and Puebla (1979).

However, for the observers who followed carefully the evolution of the results of public opinion polls before the elections, it became clear, first, that the success of the candidate of the Workers' Party in reaching the second round of the elections, could not be explained without the support of the "progressive church" and the organized action of the base ecclesial communities. Second, that most of those who voted for Collor de Mello were people who were more or less illiterate[4], and whose monthly earnings fluctuated between a half and two minimum salaries.[5] In other words, the support of the religious movements for the candidates indicates a gulf: on the one hand we find those who participate in religious communities whose activities are in some way or another an expression of permanent popular education (for example: the base ecclesial communities). On the other, those whose religious practice is characterized, basically, by the supremacy of images and symbols over conceptual and logical arguments.

Of course, such a sharp distinction as we make here cannot be made at the level of material life. Things are not so clear. However, there is a consensus among observers that the bulk of the population who voted for one or other of the candidates could be characterized from the religious point of view along the lines we have just mentioned. Using Gramsci's categories, it is possible to say that the gulf is between those who practise a religion of common sense and others who witness to an awareness seeking a praxis based on good sense.

A religion of adjustment

The relevant role of religion in the class struggles in Italy was underlined by Antonio Gramsci in the last twenty years of his life.[6] He carefully analyzed the functions of religious institutions (especially the roman catholic church), as well as those of the intellectuals at the service of those institutions. But, for him, more important was the role of popular religion, which he said was an expression of what he called "common sense". He saw it as an expression opposed to philosophy. Or, to be more precise, "it is the philosophy of the non-philosophers". To put it in other terms: "It is the conception of the world absorbed un-critically by different social and cultural sectors among which the moral individuality of the common human being is developed".[7]

This is already a paradox for the Italian thinker. As a matter of fact, for him, "all human beings are philosophers"[8], potentially at least. However, we must recognize that there are many who reject the exercise of this human possibility.

---

4 Though official statistics indicate that the illiteracy rate in Brazil is as high as 14 %, they also recognize that *practically*, if the daily exercise of reading and writing is taken into account, the proportion of illiterates rises to 55 %. See IBGE, *Estatisticas do Brasil*.
5 At the moment of writing, the minimum salary in Brazil corresponds to US $ 45,00.
6 See de Hugues Portelli, *Gramsci et la question religieuse*, Paris, Editions Anthropos, 1974.
7 A. Gramsci, *Il materialismo storico et la filosofia de B. Croce*, Roma, Editione Riuniti, 1971, 139.
8 *Ibid.*, 3.

Philosophy means thinking as coherently as possible, applying rigour and being accurate. Philosophy is a manifestation of critical thought which guides those who practise it towards critical action vis-à-vis the prevailing order in society. In other words, philosophy cannot be separated from transforming praxis. Philosophy cannot be isolated from the historical conditions in which it is shaped. Then we must recognize, that many people cannot become philosophers as they might.

Although all human beings can be philosophers, many reject the exercise of critical thought, and – what is even more important to Gramsci – of critical action. Most people give no sign of aiming at a praxis of transformation in history. Thus, they show that they are not fulfilling their possibilities at the level of intellectual activity. When human beings reject the opportunity to be philosophers, they at the same time deny themselves the opportunity to be guided by reflection. Philosophy is a guide for action. In this sense, it has a orienting function in order to help the individual to affirm his/her self identity and autonomy.

This does not mean that those who reject their philosophical vocation do not think. Of course they do! But their reflections are not guided by the critical exercise of their own minds. Most people think by looking for and adjusting to the prevailing state of affairs in society. That is, they reflect in themselves the need to fit into an order of the world over which they have no control, which they do not manage, but which is ruled by others who act according to interests contrary to those of the people.

They share a vision of the reality which has been shaped by those who hold power over the world and over people in society. They share with those in power the sense that it is better to preserve the status quo. Following this line of thought, it is possible that for the subordinated sectors of society, common sense is founded on an ideological base which is foreign to the consciousness of the people. It is neither neutral nor naive. It assumes a philosophy produced by intellectuals who are subordinated to the dominant class. This common sense mechanically absorbs that vision of the world. It also adapts such a philosophy to the immediate needs of the subordinated classes, organizing such alien thinking into norms of life and moral principles. It sanctions the order of the world as it is, managed by the people in power. Through this process, common sense considers that it is the awareness which safeguards the wisdom necessary for the preservation of what are seen as "eternal truths" (which, nevertheless is nothing more than the views of the dominant classes). In this sense, common sense is the deformed reflex of that view of the world among those people of the subordinated classes who have resigned the exercise of critical thought and critical action.

Apparently common sense can be considered a spontaneous impression which is shared by the people and the dominant groups. This gives common sense its realistic dimension. In this sense, because it is uncritical, common sense is like a belief. When common sense dominates the religious experience of the subordinated classes, the awareness of the need for change which can exist among these sectors is never expressed openly. Such expectation is manifested as a dream. That is, in symbolic terms. People expect change. But they do not commit themselves to transformation. They hope that change will happen as a miracle, coming from above, brought about by someone who will act as "saviour of the nation". It is an expression of that kind of awareness which, based on the feeling of powerlessness of the people, hopes that things will be changed by the intervention of supernatural forces. At some moment or another, as indicated in the book of Revelation, the final battle will take place between the powers of evil and the agent of God (see Rev. 16.16ff). The power of God will be victorious, inaugurating a new era in human history (Rev. 20.1-5). This millenarianism is a manifestation of the religion of common sense.

It is necessary to recognize that, when people accept this kind of ideology, then it is as though they are paralyzed with regard to social and political action. Their religion aims at adjustment to the order of this world. It is an understandable reaction for survival. In situations of historical crisis and rapid social change, many people experience a fear of being lost. This is the case of those who experienced horizontal mobility involuntarily. The consequence for many is anomy. In a new situation, their survival very often depends on the ability of the people to adjust themselves to the new situation. In such cases, the power of symbols which express the need for change is countered by the material interest in avoiding change. This is a common sense shared between many sectors of the popular masses and the dominant groups of society. Therefore, it is no surprise that Pinochet has been supported by the wealthy classes of Chile and by the popular sectors who participate in the pentecostal worship in that country. In the same way, a mayor sector of the masses of the Northeast of Brazil felt that they were represented by Fr. Damião[9], when he gave his full support to Fernando Collor de Mello during the electoral campaign.

These sectors of the masses wait for liberation. However, they do not dare to commit themselves to it. In this way, they believe that someone will bring freedom and wealth to them. But they do not have faith that they can change the situation in order to create conditions which would help towards satisfying their interests and needs. They believe in an order managed and controlled from above. They do not engage themselves in the struggles for transformation.

A religion of commitment

Moreover, as we have said previously, this religion of "common sense" is not characteristic of those who participate in the Base Ecclesial Communities (BECs)

---

9 A Franciscan Friar, proposed by Fr. Cicero as his successor in Juazeiro, a small city in Cariri, state of Ceara, where Fr. Cicero promoted a social, economic and religious renewal. Fr. Damião is considered a charismatic personality by the people of the Northeast of Brazil. Political support given by Fr. Damião is like the "canonization" of the candidate in the eyes of the people.

and other new forms of being church, including some forms of pentecostalism in Latin America. At this point it is necessary to recognize, once again, that at the level of material life and historical practices, things are not so clear. Sometimes support for the candidate or the parties who represent the interests of the people is not based on the evolution of the consciousness of the religious masses alone. This can also be the consequence of other factors (for example: rivalry between two different denominations of the same confessional branch, as was the case when we consider the electoral options of the Igreja Universal de Reino de Deus and the Assemblies of God during the second round of the Brazilian elections; among these, economic, etc. developments are very important.

It is important to realize that the religious practices of the BECs, and to a certain extent also a growing number of the pentecostal communities (especially, for example, the Assemblies of God in Brazil; the Evangelical Pentecostal Mission in Chile, etc.) give a major place to precesses of building consciousness in the development of religious awareness. In these cases, conscientization implies that permanent adult education and continuous formation are seen as activities given high priority among the members of the communities. There is, in this case, a decision aiming at a religious practice based on something other than symbols and images. Critical thinking becomes a must! It is very clear among the BECs; it is perhaps more diffuse in the case of other religious communities, but among them there is an undeniable attempt to build up a critical awareness among their members. In this case, we can say that the people are assuming their human vocation as thinkers seeking their own autonomy.

Gramsci contrasted common sense with the good sense. He understood the latter as a position of the human consciousness which seeks to go beyond primary and elementary human passions. The goal of this new awareness is a conception of human needs as something which gives conscious orientation to individual action.[10] Good sense is built up on that part of the human being which exercises a healthy resistance to all efforts of domination coming from the outside. It is only with good sense that the ambiguities and contradictions of common sense could be broken and transcended.

According to what has been said above, good sense means orienting human action according to real human needs. When the latter remain unsatisfied because prevailing structures in society, managed by groups belonging to the powers-that-be hinder the fulfillment of peoples aspirations, then good sense leads towards action aiming at confrontation with these powers and such structures. The consensus which existed under the hegemony of the ruling groups is broken. Critical thought leads people to critical action. Then, liberation is not only a wish, a dream (expressed symbolically), but it becomes the guiding motivation for praxis.

---

10 A. Gramsci, *o.c.*, 8.

If chiliasm (millenarianism) is a characteristic of the awareness dominated by common sense, the action oriented by good sense, aiming at real transformation of social, economic and political structures (based on a moral, spiritual change in the human being), can be called messianic. That is, it is orientated by eschatological expectations. But it does not remain merely at the level of hope. Above all, it is praxis. Messianism is not only grounded in religious beliefs, it is also motivated by faith (anthropological or theological).[11] The goal of messianic action is to gain more freedom. Therefore, it is manifested by a praxis of liberation.

When the people who participate in the base ecclesial communities and other similar new forms of being church in Latin America support the most progressive political sectors, they are joining hands and participating with those forces which introduce the dimension of freedom in history practically. They are trying to go beyond the reign of need.

History is no longer seen as different from the salvation process. In the case of a religion oriented by common sense, the hopes and expectations of the oppressed can only be fulfilled in an otherworldly fashion. This means that the history of salvation does not coincide with human history. In this case, the brokenness of the human being is unavoidable. But this cannot be applied to the case of a religion oriented by good sense. Hopes and expectations do not belong only to the level of wishes and dreams. Hope is real when it becomes the substance of action. Then, history cannot be fragmented: human liberation is part of the historical struggle. That is, human liberation involves economic, social, political and cultural liberation. "Integral liberation" cannot be fulfilled without the other processes of freedom we have mentioned. Because they are historical liberations, a holistic liberation has therefore to take place, above all as an historical process.[12] Among those who act on the ground of a religion looking for commitment, this demonstrates the great relevance of praxis, and, also, of orthopraxis over orthodoxy.

Conclusions

ON PEOPLE'S RELIGION

The potentiality of a given, lived faith to contribute to a process of liberation depends, above all, on the social subjects who express their expectations and wishes through that faith. It is generally known how the same religion was lived as an expression of liberation when those who shared that faith were living under oppression. However, when the same social group came into power or became closely related to the powers, that same religion was used as a tool of oppression. Therefore the potentiality of a people's religion for liberation depends, on the one hand, on people's awareness. If people look for the transformation (justice and

---

11 See J. L. Segundo, *El hombre de hoy ante Jesús de Nazaret*, vol.I, *Fe e ideología*, Madrid, Ediciones Christanidad, 1982, 45-110.
12 See L. Boff and Cl. Boff, *Da libertação. O teológico das libertações socio-históricas*, Petrópolis, Vozes, 1980.

liberation), then they are moved by a 'messianic' consciousness, looking for something better for their lives. This is good sense. But when a people gives priority to survival and adjustment, trying to avoid being crushed, then common sense prevails: the believers in a religion oriented in this way are allied to those in power. Their praxis does not try to fulfil their hope. It is a matter of fact: their only expectation in not be swallowed by death (pentecostalists).

On the other hand, the transformation of the "awareness" of the people (expressed by religious symbols, which were reformulated through that process of change of consciousness) cannot be dissociated from the orientation of the leadership and of intellectuals, who are responsible for the articulation of the new vision of the world. In this way the believers are called to move from common sense to good sense; from a praxis of adjustment towards another praxis which aims at liberation. This is something which we see among the majority of those who participate in base ecclesial communities.

ON LIBERATION

On the basis of what has just been said, we can demonstrate the crucial role of leadership and the intellectuals in the process of liberation. Nobody can ensure that leaders and pastoral agents will always fulfil such a role positively. Therefore it is necessary to emphasize a process of formation which combines action and reflection in order to keep alive the messianic awareness in terms which correspond to the people's expectations. That is, leaders and intellectuals are called to support the people, to confirm their faith and to call them to action and not merely to "adjust" themselves to the existing structures.

For this purpose, the basic requirements are:
• A permanent attitude of listening to the people, remembering that, because they live in a situation of oppression, people do not speak frankly (if they would do so, they would have been already free). Therefore, it is necessary to listen and to discover the voice of the oppressed, the arguments of good sense among the words of common sense.
• To develop a critical mind. That is, to exercise permanent suspicion. Human beings are great producers of idols, and common sense is an awareness shaped by idolatry. Only a critical mind can help developing a critical praxis (anti-ideological).
• To practise hope. This means, on the one hand, not being satisfied with the prevailing state of affairs and, on the other hand, looking for a new tomorrow. For this purpose, utopian reason is necessary. Reality cannot be brought down to facts that can be quantified or measured. Instrumental reason merely gives account of a limited part of reality. Utopian reason is what inspires prophecy and poetry. Messianic religions are basically nurtured by the utopian reason.

ON THEOLOGIES IN CONTEXT

I think that we must recognize that theology has always been produced in context. The problem is knowing in what context. Most of the time, biblical theologies were formulated in a context which gave priority to the interests, expectations and hopes of groups in power (especially after the defining of the canonical writings). We can, however, affirm that the most living biblical theology was produced in contexts of people's praxis for liberation (the exodus from Egypt, the ideological combat against the israelite monarchy, the struggle against the Babylonian oppressors by those in exile, the combat of the Maccabees, the Jesus movement, etc.). It was always in this context of praxis for liberation that theology was faithful to the messianic movement. Or, to put it in different terms, it became an expression of good sense.

Popular religions and BECs in Brazil
What kind of liberation do they offer women?

Suggestions for a theoretical approach

Maria José F. Rosado Nunes, Brazil

I believe that we can discuss the validity of a proposal to deal with the base ecclesial communities (BECs) under the heading "popular religions". Indeed, the very concept of "popular religion" raises problems. Under what circumstances can we describe a religion, or a group of religious practices as "popular"? If we draw the dividing line between official religion and the religion of the people, how can we then consider the religion of the BECs – attached as they are to the ecclesiastical hierarchy from whom they derive their legitimacy – as popular? Or can we attribute the title "popular" to a religion by examining the beliefs and practices of the believers? What, then can we say about the BECs? Perhaps the "popular" aspect of the BECs is to be found precisely where we least expect to find it, in those combinations of all sorts of beliefs and practices – catholic and non-catholic devised by the believers in order to compose their own religious universe, a universe which takes its distance from orthodoxy, and even from orthopraxis. Yet it is precisely these very diverse combinations of beliefs and religious practices which are not taken into consideration in the majority of sociological analyses and theological reflections on the BECs.

This is a difficult and dangerous area into which I shall not venture. Yet without entering into this debate, we can agree on a proposition which is sufficiently wide and general to allow the BECs to be present in a Congress on "popular religions": The BECs constitute a form – or one of the forms – of a type of popular catholicism whose roots are to be found in the very history of the sowing of the catholic religion in Brazil. This is not so much an affirmation as a working hypothesis.

BECs – Do they liberate women? Existing sociological analyses do not enable us to deal with this question of what kind of liberation they offer women, because women are not treated as a social category, and even less are they integrated into the man/woman social relationship. My thesis is that the question can only be raised if we consider that, no matter the area of activities under consideration – including the area of religion – it is social relationships which constitute women and men in sexualized social categories. It is the analysis of the division of religious labour in relation to the division of social labour in sexual terms which enables us to understand the concrete forms of religious exclusion of women and the extent to which they are dominated in the religious domain. We must look critically at this analytical proposal which will allow us:

1 to call into question the so-called "natural" relationships between women and religions, by questioning the underlying concept of feminine "nature";
2 to try to understand how the position of women in social relationships determines their place within religion, taking religion as a social fact;
3 to understand the social relationships between the sexes as they function in the BECs;
4 to call into question the homogeneous treatment of women as a social group on the basis of their membership of a given class and a given race.

Is there such a thing as "feminine nature"?

The proposition that we take the social sex of the social role-players as a category for analysis implies the rejection of any reference to a certain "feminine nature" which returns women to "the specific": this "specific" which only exists for women. Men represent the norm, that which is universal. The rules of grammar in romance languages are clear evidence of this. The moment a man is present we have to say "ils". The category "man" is so dominant that it invades all the fields of knowledge and the field of theology as well. There is no "paternal vocation" which corresponds to the "maternal vocation" so dear to catholic language. There is no "paternity" considered "natural" for men, despite the fact that we know that maternity pre-supposes the natural involvement of a man. Women are real or potential mothers and that is what they must remain.

This "feminine nature" which is at the root of all religious reasoning with regard to women is also at the root of the unasked questions about the feminine majority in the BECs. The large body of women in the communities is only rarely, and marginally, referred to in the theological and sociological studies of the BECs. No one ever asks why women are in the majority. It seems to be accepted. It seems "natural" that women should show more interest in religion than men. The area of religious practice is considered "inherent to women". The latter are expected to be the privileged consumers of the religious goods produced by men. A woman is expected to be "pious", to be attached to a religion. This is supposed to be part of her "nature" which is more sensitive to religious values; it is part of her inclination to "devotion", to sensitivity, to submission. Between the mystery surrounding the religious space and this "mysterious feminine nature" – half angel, half animal; so desirable, yet so contemptible; ever Eve and Mary, always confronted with this insoluble contradiction of being virgin and mother at one and the same time – a sort of co-naturalness grows up. (Is it not precisely this relegation of women to the mysterious, to this area which has not been entirely mastered, which is more or less wild, which explains the role of women in black religions? That role which is often held up as proof of the "success" of women in the religious domain?)

Their place in the religious domain and social relationships

Such considerations lead us to another level of analysis. The critical rejection of a cross reference to the women/religions relationship to nature, to a pre-supposed "feminine religiosity" to be found somewhere in the bio-psychic structure of women, leads us to the proposition that the place occupied by women in the religious domain is determined by the place which they, as women, occupy in social relationships. The exclusion of women from areas of religious power is merely the measurable effect of the social relationships which exist between women and men as social groups. "The problem appears to me to be the problem of the links which exist between the division of religious labour and the division of social labour, in sexual terms. It is a problem which we can study by examining the relationships which exist between the domestic imprisonment of women and the extent of the handicaps affecting them in the religious area. As Leger said: "Women in the catholic church are lay people who are more lay than the others." It is not merely a simple mirror image, in the religious field, of the position of economic exploitation and of domination suffered by women. These relationships are much more complex, and the BECs provide proof of this.

How social relationships between the sexes function in the BECs in Brazil

I take as my starting point an observation: to be a faithful catholic woman, is not the same as to be a faithful catholic man.
Yet the way the sociology of religions, from the classics to the modern specialists, deals with the role players in the religious domain fails to take into consideration the sex of these role players, or at least does so only in a very marginal or accidental fashion. This observation is equally true of a large majority of the texts on the BECs, if not all of them. Be they sociological or theological texts, those who people the communities are divided into the classical categories known to the sociology of religions: clergy and laity or hierarchy and laity, with no reference whatsoever to the fact that the clergy as a whole is male and the laity is composed of – or divided into – men and women, and that to be a woman lay person or a male lay person is not the same thing. Nor is any reference made to the race of these religious actors and actresses. It is as though the fact of being a woman or a man – of belonging to the social group of women or the social group of men – contributed nothing to sociological analysis or to reflection on the faith. Given the social origins of the lay people in the BECs, such people are perceived as belonging to the "popular classes"; they are often referred to as "the people", both of which are homogenizing categories.

Remaining at this level we have perhaps managed to "reveal" women, we have made them visible beside men, but we have not yet uncovered the relationship which opposes men and women as social groups. Analysis of the apparent homogeneity of the "people", of the "popular classes", of the laity reveals a contradictory situation caused by the conflictual and hierarchical social relationships between two groups which are socially (and not biologically) opposed to each other: women and men. If we examine the socio-religious practices of women and men in the BECs, and on condition that the category of social sex or gender is accepted as a category for analysis, we see this opposition emerging. Indeed, women and men do not become members of a base community in the same fashion. We need only recall that women represent the majority of members of the community – a fact that is often obscured – not only as simple participants but also among the socio-religious and pastoral "leadership" and as pastoral workers. Yet once one begins to move up the structures, there is a noticeable decline in the number of women, and an increase in the number of men. This is no accident. It is because there is a decline in the number of women that the number of men increases. This means that if one is a woman there is no chance of ever reaching a position of influence or of decision-making within the ecclesiastical structures.

The national meetings of the BECs provide a very clear illustration of women's position of inferiority. Even when women are in the majority within the team preparing these meetings – in other words doing the hardest and most thankless work, the work which has least social visibility – it is men who run things.[1] We should note that in all the national meetings so far, the total number of men has been greater than the total number of women. This has brought reactions amongst the women in recent meetings. The reasons the men use to justify such a situation is their refusal to allow women to participate and the fact that "they (the women) have their children"! Yet this doesn't prevent them from working daily in the BECs or being militant at the grassroots of the social movements.

With regard to the pastoral workers, we need only take the case of women religious to understand the extent to which social relationships between the sexes mould the communities, or more widely how these relationships are created and recreated within the space of the catholic church. Starting with the changes introduced into the lives of the religious orders after Vatican II and Medellín, people began to speak of an "exodus" of women religious towards the urban and rural periphery where the poor live. But the conciliar reforms did not affect women and men in the same way, among the women religious and among priests and male religious. Indeed, there are very few communities of men religious in the popular quarters. (Which does not, however, prevent the use of the term "integration of male religious ("religieux")" in the popular milieu".) Those men directly involved in the catholic church as an institution work in formation and training and in guiding the BECs as bishops, priests or experts (theologians, sociologists, politologists...). Despite the fact that the "option for the poor" was also a principle of internal reconstruction among the male orders, its translation

---

1 Data from the VIth meeting, 1986: preparatory team, 3 women and 1 man – of course, the power relationship changes if the man is a priest; Executive Committee – 8 women and 7 men; Experts: 28 men and 2 women.

in terms of pastoral action has been very different from the form it took among the congregations of women religious. The women religious are, first and foremost, "among the poor" to "share their lives"; as women, they become involved in the daily life of their neighbourhood. The women religious do their own housework (they clean, they wash, they shop), things they did not do when they were employed as teachers or nurses. They are paid less than priests, even if they have direct responsibility for the pastoral work among the BECs. In addition, given the catholic nature of the BECs, the latter are under ecclesiastical authority which means that the pastoral activities of the women religious are controlled directly by the clergy. Thus there is a clear demarcation line between the way in which the process of renewal of the church has taken place among women and among men within the institution. The effects of this social "exodus" are not identical for both sexes.

The need to sexualize the sociological treatment of the BECs is therefore the result of the fact that the social and religious practices of women and men in these communities are far from identical. This differentiation must be brought out in the analysis.

In a study of political mobilization among women members of BECs in São Paulo, the author develops a hypothesis which claims that women reformulate, and reinterpret the theses of the theology of liberation and the practices of the BECs on the basis of the requirements of the sexual division of social labour (Drogus). They are concerned by the theses of the BECs to the extent that these correspond to a certain "feminine language" of action on behalf of others. These women are prepared "to do something" to improve the position of their own families and their neighbourhood. It is precisely their role as women in the sexual division of labour – their reproductive role – which leads them to call for better conditions in which to fulfil their "duties" as wives and mothers. "Committing oneself to the struggle," taking part in the actions for better conditions launched by the BECs is legitimated by the idea of "serving others": the people, the community. It is not for themselves that they struggle, but for their children and for the people. If there is no sense of guilt in the militancy of the women in the BECs – a militancy which has an impact on their domestic roles to the extent that they have less time for their children and for their homes – it is not because the sexual division of labour has been called into question; quite the opposite; it has been strengthened.

It is precisely this reinterpretation by women on the basis of the questions raised by their prime role in the sphere of social reproduction which, according to Drogus and Caldeira, explains the fact that a large majority of women do not become involved in the class-based parties, nor do they vote for them. We might well ask if this is not the result of a different "class awareness" forged by, and in, their experience of being, at one and the same time, exploited in economic terms and dominated in social terms. Women in the BECs and more generally the women of the popular classes know from their own experience, from their lives, that even a class-based party will not offer them, as women, very much. The

113

language and the practices of the trade union and of the class-based parties have their origin in an abstract concept of "class", which amounts to saying, in actual fact, a class which is completely male, and which has little to do with the real class situation of women.

Finally, it is part of the very logic of the exploitation and social domination of women – through which their position of inferiority is constantly created and re-created in all areas of social life, including the field of religion – it is within this logic that we find women being constantly returned to the home, to their traditional status of mothers and spouses, to housework, or more generally to reproduction.

The co-extensiveness of social relationships

The last point of reference with regard to our way of dealing with the women/religions relationship seeks to account for a false postulate to which the preceding theories might lead us. It is the postulate which states that the variable "women" has a universal explanatory value. This proposition denies that membership of a class and of a race have an impact on the differentiation of the concrete social positions of women. While the variable "women" "enables us to demonstrate the major social regularities (wage discrimination to take only one example), it is incapable of accounting for the diversity in women's positions" (Kergoat). This is a diversity brought about at least by class and by race. In other words, the fact of being a woman means something different for a black woman from the popular classes and for a white woman from the upper or middle classes. Third World women are constantly reminding us of this.

With regard to the religious domination of women, it is not only different from the domination suffered by men (laity), it also is different depending on whether one is a woman from the dominant classes or the dominated ones, whether one is a white woman or a black or Indian one.

Conclusion

Such a presentation of the problem of the relationship between women and religions offers a proposition and a challenge.

We must escape from those analyses which isolate women, which treat women as a particular phenomenon, and we must learn to think of women and treat women, like men, as social categories, as social groups in inter-relation. The sexes as social categories are at work in all areas of social practice, in all their dimensions, including the imaginary and symbolical ones. The social relationships between the sexes thus represent one of the principal organizing forces of any social formation.

With regard to theological work – if it is to be truly liberating – women cannot be confined to one "issue" or be conceded the last chapter. It is all of theological reflection which must be informed by the new paradigms.

Bibliography

Battagliola, F., e.a., 'A propos des rapports sociaux de sexe. Parcours épistemologiques', in: *Recherches féministes et recherches sur les femmes*, CNRS, ATP, September 1986.

Benhabib, S. and Cornell, D., *Feminism as critique. Essays on the politics of gender in late-capitalist societies*, Cambridge, Polity Press.

Caldeira, T. Pires do Rio, *A política dos outros. O cotidiano dos moradores da periferia e o que pensam do poder e dos poderosos*, São Paulo, Brasiliense, 1984.

Drogus, C. A. *We are women making history. Political mobilization in São Paulo's CEBs. Discussion Paper n.81, November 1988'*, Center for Latin American Studies, The University of Wisconsin, Milwaukee.

Guillaumin, C., 'Race et nature. Système des marques. Idée de groupe naturel et rapports sociaux', in: *Plural*, 1977, n.11, 39-55.

Hervieu-Léger, D., 'Oppression des femmes et religion. Introduction au colloque de l'Association française de Sociologie religieuse', in: *Travaux et Documents VIII*, Paris, Centre d'Etudes sociologiques, CNRS, 1980.

Kergoad, D., *Les ouvriers*, Paris, Le Sycomore, 1982.

'Les rapport sociaux de sexe. Problématiques, méthodologies, champs d'analyses', in: *Cahiers de l'APRE*, 1/3(April-May 1988), n.7.

Uncertainty reduction in the candomblé religion of Brazil

Allard D. Willemier Westra, the Netherlands

As is publicly known, a religion is not only a system of belief but also an organizational whole. This implies, of course, that a religious organization is subject to general organizational laws. In this article I shall discuss some of the laws recently revealed by organizational sociology and relate them to religion.

I shall take a relatively small religion as an example, an Afro-Brazilian possession cult called candomblé. It is a religion in which elements of the West-African Yoruba religion still prevail. It was taken to Brazil by slaves. Although it underwent modifications to meet the restrictive requirements[1] of the slaveowners and their allies in the roman-catholic church, the African core of its belief system was generally well preserved until the present day (see Bastide 1978).

Nowadays this religion has many millions of followers, which is an indication of its vitality.[2] Therefore it is quite understandable why most studies of candomblé seem to concentrate on its remarkable survival, the result of it being a general upgrading of black culture and religion in Brazil.

Reviewing literature on candomblé and related religions[3] I believe that the image improvement of this black religion[4] has not yet been completely finished. It is true that nobody seems to deny that candomblé believers are well qualified in the symbolic and ritual field. As soon as it comes to an adequate approach to worldly matters, however, the same qualifications no longer seem to be attributed to them. Judging from literature, the endeavour to take their fate into their own hands seems to be almost exclusively symbolic. As a consequence, people belonging to this black religion usually are described as being pushed around by others – mostly powerful whites – or by all kinds of anonymous circumstances.[5] There-

---

1 A striking example is to be found on the candomblé altar. Most of the statues standing there look exactly like those in a roman catholic church. In reality, however, they represent African gods (*orixás*).

2 Some sources indicate that no less than 60 % of the town population and about 30 % of the total Brazilian population regularly participates in candomblé or other Afro-Brazilian religions. (For a brief overview of these sources see A.D. Willemier Westra, 1987, 217).

3 They are generally subsumed under the term Afro-Brazilian religions, the most important of them being umbanda. Xangô, Batuque, Casa das Minas, and Seravá are other examples of these religions.

4 More whites are gradually participating in it, however.

5 Oliven (1984) and Menezes (1982) give the impression that candomblé is manipulated by the national elites, whereas DaMatta (1985) shows this religion to be moulded by national symbolic laws which are said to be basic to the "social grammar of Brazil" (for an English overview see A.D. Willemier Westra, 1990).

fore they are simply not capable of exercising power over others, at least outside their own religious circle.

To my surprise I found this to be compatible with my own field data. They gave me reason to believe that the focal activity of candomblé, *cura* (that is social assistance and healing), is partly based on the manipulation of others both inside and outside this religion (Willemier Westra 1988). To some degree this passive impression is due to the image-building activities of candomblé itself.[6] It publicly shows off as a religion dealing with spiritual beings, symbols and rituals alone. Behind this religious smoke screen however, all kinds of this-worldly activities take place, aimed at the exercise of power to the benefit of its priests and their followers.

When I started my fieldwork in a town in the interior of the state of Bahia[7], this highly power-conscious and businesslike attitude came rather as a surprise to me. I discovered that, on closer observation, the ritualistic side of candomblé was only one side of it. The spirits, symbols and rituals sometimes seemed to be not much more than a beautiful shop window. Behind it, highly commercial and power-oriented activities were taking place, almost hidden to the eyes of outsiders like myself. A sophisticated and extended social network existed, by which favours, social claims, money and materials were collected and distributed, being nothing less than the material infra-structure of candomblé social assistance and healing, *cura*.

On earlier occasions I already described this infra-structure.[8] In some of these publications I have tried to delineate the business-like aspect of candomblé, by giving details of its management and its marketing procedures.[9] This time I should like to make a few remarks on its organizational characteristics.

Even people only slightly acquainted with candomblé know that its priests or priestesses occupy a strong position of power in their own group. A complicated system of social ranking exists, as well as many specialized and well circumscribed functions. Still, at the beginning of a candomblé religious celebration, there seems to be no organization at all. Things just appear to be happening by themselves. Just before such a *festa* starts, everybody hangs around, with no observable objective whatsoever. People enter and leave the temple – *terreiro* – whenever they feel like it, and nobody gives any sign that the rituals are finally starting. Apparently this is the case when a lonesome drummer starts to play, because a few minutes later two or three woman and an old toothless man join in. After ten

---

6 Every ritual performance underlines its preoccupation with spiritual matters. In addition, material assistance is sometimes sought and found by powerful people, mostly whites, who feel indebted to such rites.
7 Most of the field work took place in 1978 and 1979 in Alagoinhas, a provincial town with (at the time) 100.000 inhabitants. Since then regular contacts have been maintained to keep the data up to date with recent local developments.
8 See A.D. Willemier Westra, 1987 and 1988.
9 See A.D. Willemier Westra, 'Het marktgedrag...', *a.c.*.

minutes a fully fledged ritual dance is – literally – in full swing. At the beginning of my fieldwork candomblé appeared to be pure improvisation; an organization-less organization.

Of course this impression was entirely wrong. After a while it became clear to me that such an apparent absence of leadership, in this case, was only an indication of its quality. In the following sections I shall try to demonstrate the organizational sophistications of candomblé.

Five organizational parts

In the so called "contingency theory" origanizational sociologists[10] embrace a rather Darwinistic-sounding theory. Organizations – be it profit or non-profit, secular or religious – are said to be a response to an environmental challenge. Only the fittest among them can survive.[11] If the societal context changes organizations will have to adapt to them. If they fail to do so, they will be eliminated unconditionally by more successful organizational species. The key word in this dynamic view of organizations is uncertainty reduction. The idea is that any successful organization is designed to eliminate internal[12] as well as external uncertainties. As daily circumstances are ever-changing, this activity has to be carried on forever.

The concept of "flow" is another crucial element in the contingency theory. The word "flow" indicates the interplay between the organizational parts, like flows of decisions, information, symbols, materials, favours, claims, power etc. All together these different flows constitute an interdependent whole, which – in principle at least – can be controlled by the secular or religious leader.[13] Viewed in this way the management of flows is the *sine qua non* of every organization.

I have the impression that religions are all too often regarded as structures; structures of belief as well as organizational structures. Some of them are sometimes even regarded as almost eternal social structures. Therefore it might be useful to look into their most dynamic internal and external aspects, without discarding, of course, the more conventional approaches. It may throw light on the way religions reduce their environmental and internal uncertainties by controlling their own – highly interactive – system of flows. Taking candomblé as an example, the first point I shall try to elucidate concerns the organizational parts between which the flows are moving. The second point has to do with the substance of the flows.

---

10 This article is mainly based on Mintzberg, 1979, still considered the leader in this specific subject (see C.J. Lammers, 1987, 447).

11 See C.J. Lammers, 1987, 414.

12 Though Mintzberg (1979) makes use of the ideas of Kieser and Kubicek (1977), who stress the importance internal as well as external contingencies, Mintzberg focusses on the internal part of the organization.

13 Management literature indicates that the controllability of organizations should not be over-estimated (see C.J. Lammers, 1987, 18 and 32-33).

In candomblé the top of the organization, its strategic apex[14] consists of a priest or a priestess (*babalorixá* or *iyalorixá*). Ideally speaking he or she has a general overview of the internal and external relations and interactions. Usually the candomblé leader is assisted by one or more underpriests or under-priestesses. Occasionally also well-trusted high-ranking members of high seniority will be consulted.

Immediately below them in the hierarchy is the second main part of the organization, its middle line.[15] It consists of respected and prestigious mediums, who are well known for their experience in spiritual, as well as worldly, matters.

Thirdly, in our top-down picture of candomblé organization each group has an "operation core".[16] This workforce consists of low-ranking mediums and ordinary members who are not yet mediums, or who have no aspirations whatsoever to become one. They assist their superiors in ritual and curative activities. Without them the bulk of the work in the *terreiro* could not be carried out.

A fourth organizational part, consisting of specialists, occupies a somewhat independent position alongside the hierarchical lines. The specialists are responsible for the achievement and maintenance of a high standard of quality of the candomblé ritual and curative product.[17] Formally this product is purely symbolic and ritual. It is considered vital to the well-being of everybody taking part in candomblé that these rituals are performed perfectly. The *axogun* (a Yoruba word) is responsible for the sacrifice of animals, the *iyabassê* for the preparation of special meals "to feed the spiritual beings" (*orixás*, *caboclos* and others[18]). The *iyalaxê* is responsible for the maintenance of the altar (*peji*), the *ekede* for the proper training of new mediums and the *alabê* for the playing of the right rhythms on the drums at the right time, so that the spirits can descend as they should.

The fifth organizational part, which may be called "the support staff"[19] is harder to circumscribe, as it consists of an ever-changing group of unofficial assistants like assistant cooks, seamstresses making the beautiful dance costumes, assistant trainers of mediums, assistant drummers etc. They usually belong to the circle of regular participants in the group rituals. Without their commitment and dedication candomblé simply could not function.

---

14 H. Mintzberg, 1979, 24-26. People charged with overall responsibility for the organization.
15 See H. Mintzberg, 1979, 26-29. Ideally speaking, the middle line manager collects feed-back from the support staff, technical staff and the operating core. He coordinates their work and keeps the strategic apex of the organization informed.
16 See H. Mintzberg, 1979, 24. They secure the inputs for the production and transform them into outputs and by doing so form the heart of every organization.
17 H. Mintzberg (1979, 29-31) calls it a technostructure. It is somewhat removed from the operating work flow.
18 *Orixás* are the strongest among them, originating from West Africa. *Caboclos* are said to be of Amerindian origin (see O.G. Cacciatore, 1977, 74 and 206).
19 See H. Mintzberg, 1979, 31-34.

Regulated flows

The work of all five organizational parts (and more specifically of all the people belonging to them) must be coordinated; brought into line with group objectives and ideals. As I indicated briefly before, this is done by controlling the flows between these parts. Some of the flows between them are intended – "designed" – by the leaders. I shall call them "regulated flows".[20] After having described some of them I shall turn to the unintended, informal, flows of the candomblé organization. Although they were not deliberately designed to come to grips with group affairs, they are indispensable for its management. There are various types of regulated flows.

The first one consists of decisions taken by the priestess or priests in charge. For example, a decision as to whether, or when a public ritual (*festa*) must be held should be communicated to the specialists involved, either directly, or via the middle line of the organization. As most of the tasks of the specialists are highly standardized[21], every one of them usually knows exactly which ritual procedure is prescribed in a given situation. In other words, in most cases obtaining explicit orders from the priestess or priest is not necessary at all. This is one of the reasons why candomblé seemingly functions without any visible organization.

A second regulated flow, called "work flow"[22] is connected to the route the candomblé product takes through the organization. Material goods, like articles of food used in the preparation of meals, are transformed into the form needed for the curative product (*cura*). This product is in high demand by group members, but most of all by patients from outside who are paying for it. Significantly enough the financial survival of candomblé is ensured by a *symbolic* added value rather than by a *material* added value, as is the case in secular profit organizations.

Symbols and rituals are moulded and sometimes changed in the process, to fit the demands of the market, consisting of paying customers, clients and patients. Symbols and rituals are constantly being produced, reproduced and altered on their behalf, thereby unavoidably gradually changing the candomblé system of belief. Of course the central position of possession is a great help in sustaining this flexible attitude. The words and actions of mediums are never completely under the control of the leaders governed by tradition. The effect of this is that the mediums – responding to the questions and problems of their clients – are bound to deal with the hot issues of society, thereby keeping their religion optimally in tune with the demands of the market. This is the way uncertainty

---

20 The term is borrowed from H. Mintzberg, 1979, 37-46.
21 In management terms this is called pigeon-holing. For most problems of candomblé clients, more or less standarized procedures, known to the priestess or priests and some experienced group members, exist.
22 These flows involve the movement of materials and information in a variety of combinations (see H. Mintzberg, 1979, 38-42).

reduction works, both for the candomblé organization itself and for the many people turning to it for help.[23]

Thirdly, a constant flow of information is needed for the decision-making process of the leaders. Their subordinates report the daily events and incidents inside and outside the religious group. Without such a constant and trustworthy flow, management would be built on quicksand. People are very eager to assist the leaders in the collection of data, as they hope to obtain favours in return. If necessary the priests or priestesses do not simply wait passively for the information to flow in, like a spider in a web. Sometimes, however, they find it imperative to initiate the data-collecting activities of their followers, and an active attitude in their effort to do whatever is possible to reduce the environmental uncertainties of the group.

A fourth type of regulated flow concerns communication between the middle line of the organization (consisting of senior mediums), specialists and the support staff (assistants). In the first place these three organizational parts have to coordinate the work among themselves. Secondly, coordination is needed between these parts and, thirdly, all of the three parts have to coordinate their work with low-ranking group members. These members help wherever they can, but because of their modest skills and experience, they are only able to do so on an *ad hoc* basis. The effect of this triple coordinative interdependence is that all kinds of complicated activities, like public celebrations, processions and ritual meals, take place without any observable structure of command. Things run smoothly, as if they were done instinctively, which is of course only an outward appearance.

Informal flows

I shall now briefly sketch out a few flows which are complementary to the regulated flows. The regulated flows discussed so far belong to the official organizational outfit of candomblé, although as we have just seen, they are not always easily observable. Still, they do not belong to the secretive side of the possession religion; to its backstage. All the regulated flows belong to that part of candomblé which – in principle at least – is open to everybody. In this sense the flows we are now going to describe are completely different. We shall now look at a number of informal, sometimes deliberately hidden, flows, therefore – in my terms – belonging to the backstage. I shall call them informal flows.[24]

The first one is informal communication. Everybody participating in candomblé, like everybody else, likes to chat informally with anybody around. In this way a variety of information is gathered which might eventually or immediately be

---

23 In a sense candomblé can be considered an optimum in uncertainly reduction. It not only maximizes this basic organizational principle for its own group but to an even greater extent for his members and clients.

24 The word "informal" indicates spontaneous and flexible ties and communication among members, guided by mutual feelings and personal interests (see H. Mintzberg, 1979, 46).

useful for the effective management of the group. It is typical for this type of information to reach the leaders outside the official hierarchical lines. High-ranking members also benefit greatly from this flow of unofficial information. From various sources in organizational sociology[25] it appears that no organization can ever function without this informal coordinative instrument.

A second flow, tightly linked to the first, is informal power. All group members try to reduce their uncertainties inside the group as much as they can by the exercise of power related to their own position. As we have seen, they try to be of use whenever they can, hoping to get some kind of favour in return. On other occasions, however, they may be overtly non-cooperative[26] in order to exercise a little pressure. Another way of gaining influence is to maintain tight relations with other lower ranking group members on a reciprocal basis. In that way mini-nuclei of power can arise, sometimes endangering the official positions of power.[27]

Another equally related flow, is related to the formation of cliques not completely under the control of the official management. Groups of mediums who are initiated together – the so called *barcos* – develop strong ties of solidarity which, among other things, express themselves by the provision of mutual support if a member of the *barco* is confronting difficulties; financial assistance, help in finding a job, etc. In doing so they not only reduce their personal uncertainties, but also provide for a minimum amount of invulnerability in their interactions with powerful group members. This solidarity lasts long after the initiation has been completed.

So far we have discussed, almost exclusively, *internal* regulated and informal flows, all leading to a reduction of group and personal uncertainties. However, the same principle of uncertainty reduction can also be observed in the *external* flows of candomblé. Flows of favours granted and claims laid upon the outsiders and the resulting flow of materials and money etc. are extremely important for the successful management of the group. Although material flows are also important for the internal affairs of the group, they are absolutely vital to the effectiveness of *cura* (healing and social assistance); that is to the quality of the candomblé product.

Internal and external flows

As we saw, the curative system of candomblé is characterized by an effective management of a complex system of internal and external flows. These regulated and informal flows are generated and controlled by the candomblé leaders. Flows of formal decisions find their way down the line (trusted and experienced as-

---

25 See H. Mintzberg, 1979, 46-50.
26 My impression is that it is primarily, *de facto* powerful members who do not enjoy the corresponding *de jure* recognition who have recourse to this method.
27 From time to time this leads to the break-up of the group. From the point of view of candomblé as a whole this means a constant multiplication of retail outlets for the curative product.

sistants), technical staff (ritual specialists), support staff (other assistants like seamstresses and drummers) and operating core (ordinary group members responsible for the bulk of the work).

These flows of decisions have to be based on trustworthy internal flows of information about people belonging to the various parts of the organization. External flows of information, for example with regard to the neighbourhood and all kinds of town affairs, must also be added to the internal system. In addition, the five organizational parts have to coordinate their work by communicating among themselves. Public religious celebrations, private ritual and social services (*cura*) have to be organized.

We already know that *cura* is to candomblé what soap is to a soap factory. *Cura* is produced by this religion to meet the demands of the market. Goods flow into the organization, flow from one organizational part to another and finally flow out of the organization again. Although, in this process, these goods are gradually transformed into the form needed for the *cura*, their real added value is obtained through the rituals which accompany it. Herbs used to cure a chronic headache are collected in the fields, dried, stored, packed and sold by people belonging to various organizational parts and, in this way, flow through the organization. In a factory specializing in herbal teas, the product value would increase with each of these steps. In a curative organization like candomblé this is also the case but these steps are considered rather insignificant, since it is the added spiritual force (*axê*) which is believed to be responsible for the cure and not the chemical substance of the herbs. Likewise daily problems are thought to be solved by driving out evil spirits rather than by implementing forms of material aid. In this way the complex organizational infra-structure of candomblé aid, its back stage, is almost covered up by its rituals, symbols and beliefs, its front stage.

These two examples are illustrative of the way in which candomblé *cura* is organized. Flows of rituals and goods with a symbolic added value firmly attached to them are exchanged for flows of "raw materials" (goods needed for the ritual services), favours and money. After having been processed, and having been charged symbolically as a result of this interplay of various flows and rituals, the curative product is sold to outsiders, some of whom are rich and powerful. The money and influence resulting from the contacts of candomblé members and these people are partly redistributed in the form of *cura*. In this way *cura* is sometimes even effective according to Western criteria. Clients who find themselves in precarious economic and social conditions may benefit especially from candomblé aid.

Uncertainty reduction and liberation

As we saw, candomblé produces *cura* (material, social, medical and psychological assistance with symbolic added value) and receives money, raw materials and favours in return. In other words: outgoing symbolic flows result in incoming material flows. Goods qualified as symbolic both by the producers and the consumers are exchanged for material income and power.

The essence of this is that an organizational system which reduces uncertainties to survive, as a system, in its own socio-economic context, is also actively engaged in reducing uncertainties for its own group members as well as for paying outsiders. People facing serious personal problems feel that the special assistance of candomblé really helps. Therefore they are prepared to pay for it, just as they would do for any product that supplies their wants.

The customers of this curative product are primarily interested in finding short term solutions to pressing *ad hoc* problems and not so much in solving their long term problems in whatever form. This type of attitude does not encourage adherence to or the development of an idea like liberation which, at least in a Western sense, has a much broader connotation.[28]

Still, most true believers in candomblé feel that their religion has liberated them from psychological chaos and despair and has given them a better life-perspective. Most of them also gain in social prestige and some of them even improve their economic position. In addition, most group members enjoy a certain amount of protection by their group, for example against the misuse of power by the authorities and upper class outsiders. At the same time, however, their religion makes them subject to their leaders and to the discipline of the group, without which the management of the complex system of flows could not function.

So, looking at the liberating potential of candomblé, I find it to be virtually non existent. *Cura* is strictly confined to individuals and, furthermore, is partly counterbalanced by new repressive forces closely bound up with the organizational structure of candomblé. These findings with regard to the conservative nature of candomblé are completely in line with the ideas on curative religions in general as advocated by Schoffeleers (1988). He states that religious healing is always linked to a conservative world view and leads to an anti-reformist political attitude.

---

28 It is my opinion that much of the discussion on liberation is blurred by a rather programmatic and ethnocentric significance given to it by some theologians, and a pragmatic understanding of the term based on field work by anthropologists and sociologists. This difference in approach is not always made sufficiently clear and therefore leads to confusion.

Bibliography

Bastide, R., *The African religions of Brazil. Towards a sociology of the interpenetration of civilizations*, Baltimore/London, The John Hopkin University Press, 1978.

Cacciatore, O.G., *Dicionário de cultos Afro-Brasileiros*, Rio de Janeiro, Forense Universitária/ SECC, 1977.

DaMatta, R., *A casa e a rua. Espaço, cidadania, mulher e morte no Brazil*, São Paulo, Brasiliense, 1985.

Kieser, A. and Kubicek, H., *Organization*, Berlin/New York, De Gruyter, 1977.

Lammers, C.J., *Organisaties vergelijkenderwijs*, Utrecht, Spectrum, 1987.

Menezes, E.D.B. de, 'Elitelore versus foclore, ou de como a cultura hegemonica tende a devorar a cultura subalterna', in: *Cadernos*, 1982, n.17, 9-14.

Mintzberg, H., *The structuring of organizations*, Prentice Hall, Englewood Cliffs, 1979.

Oliven, R.G., 'The production and consumption of culture in Brazil', in: *Latin American Perspectives*, 11(1985), n.1, 103-115.

Schoffeleers, J.M., *Gebedsgenezing en politiek. De medicalisering van het christendom in Zuid-Afrika*, Afscheidscollege, Vrije Universiteit, Amsterdam, 1988 (to be published in *Africa* soon).

Willemier Westra, A.D., *Axê, de kracht om te leven. Het gebruik van symbolen in de candomblé-religie in Alagoinhas (Bahia, Brazilië)*, (Axê, the powers of life. The use of symbols in the social assistance of the candomblé religion in Alagoinhas (Bahia, Brazil), Amsterdam, CEDLA, 1987.

Willemier Westra, A.D., 'Symbolic paradoxes. The internal dynamics of popular candomblé religion in Alagoinhas, Bahia', in: G. Banck, K. Konings (eds), *Social change in contemporary Brazil*, Amsterdam, CEDLA, 1988.

Willemier Westra, A.D., 'Het marktgedrag van de Braziliaanse heilconsument. De publieke opinie ten aanzien van het pinkstergeloof en Afro-Amerikaanse religiositeit in de provinciestad Alagoinhas (Bahia)', (On the market orientated attitude of the Brazilian religious consumer), Paper, Conference on pentecostalism, Free University, Amsterdam, April 10, 1988, soon to be published in Spanish.

Willemier Westra, A.D., 'Street and home. The symbolic framework of Afro-Brazilian religion in Alagoinhas (Bahia, Brazil)', in: *European Review of Latin American and Caribbean Studies*, June 1990, n.48 (forthcoming).

Popular religion and pentecostalism

Francisco Cartaxo Rolim, Brazil

First of all I should like to point out that my reflections on the subject will be limited to the Brazilian context. Nevertheless, here and there I shall make brief allusions to certain South-American aspects of the question.

Without claiming to enter into the complex question of the character of popular religion, I should like to limit myself to certain features which link it to pentecostal religion, nor shall I repeat what I have already written elsewhere.

Let me first set out those points with which my reflections will deal: a) the exterior aspects; b) those directly religious aspects, or the religious vision of the world; c) social conditioning. With regard to the first point, I think immediately of its spontaneity. We need only recall how this comes through in the hymns with their simple melodies. All those present, and not a group apart, sing together. This is an external sign of the fact that the humble and poor people like to sing. Emile Léonard, in his study of Brazilian protestantism, already noted the great feeling which the peoples of the interior have for religious songs. A song, and the simpler and lighter the better, gives joy to the poor people who sing it, and it is certainly for this reason that they are greatly moved by it. To this we must add the public prayers, which, for them, are the outward expression of feeling and emotion itself. Psychologists and psycho-analysts have found food for reflection here, and we can only thank them for the help which their analyses have provided. As for preaching, what can we say about that? Even today we find simple lay people, people who are not pentecostalists, who preach in public places and in small villages, free from the restraints of the church. Doubtless we should not forget that these practices, like devotion to the saints which they preach, are to a certain extent linked to the ecclesiastical institution. Indeed, they have taken certain formulae – such as the novena, the Our Father, and the Hail Mary – directly from the institution. But the use which they make of them has gradually brought them into an area of autonomy and of spontaneity. This spontaneity and liberty are related to the lack of social control, something highlighted by Lalive D'Epinay in his studies of pentecostal religion.[1]

---

1 On this subject, see Ch. Lalive D'Epinay, *O refúgio das massas (Brazilian translation)*, Rio de Janeiro, Editora Paz e Terra, 1970; *Religion, dynamique sociale et dépendance*, Paris-The Hague, Mouton, Paris, 1975. See also F. Cartaxo Rolim, *Pentecostais no Brasil*, Petrópolis, Vozes, 1985.

Finally, at this point, the social position of the poorer classes and their very limited level of education is of great significance. It represents concrete forms of organization among the poorer classes by the people themselves: groups become organized in order to achieve various social goals, community centres are founded to improve sanitation in the areas in which the poor live, or to demand a public transport system; around such centres the poor, through dialogue, build up a holistic vision of their interests and learn to take part in collective action. This gives birth and encouragement to an awareness of a new historic subject: that of the poor classes. The poor begin to realize that social inequalities are not natural, they are the products of society. This means that such inequalities are gradually identified as the outcome of the action of certain groups which enjoy economic and decision-making power. The formation of groups, which are organized to a greater or lesser extent, participation, the identification, to some extent, of the social roots of poverty are all the signs of the mobilization of the poorer sectors within our society. A new vision of the world is born and explodes; it is a vision which is different from that of the past, and which is directed towards social transformation.

In my opinion, the problem which then arises for pentecostalism is the following. Given this new perception of both the political and religious world, what is the vision of the world produced and presented by the pentecostalist churches? Let us not forget that the vast majority of their adherents have come from, and still come from, among the poor and the uneducated. Yet this socio-cultural situation does not represent an obstacle to a process of growth towards socio-political awareness among these same social classes. How do the pentecostalist churches stand vis-à-vis this growing awareness?

Such questions lie at that point where the visions of the world cross, a central point which, according to Max Weber, directs human action along paths opened up by interests.
At the same time as they call for a theoretical framework which will direct us in our reading of empirical facts, such reflections also force us to take a reasonable distance with regard to certain methodological formulations.

Thus the Durkheimian-style positivist optic – by only seeing the external aspects of pentecostalism and by proclaiming a radical separation between factual judgments and value judgments – is incapable of presenting us with a vision of the world. The functionalist approach, to the extent that it gives priority to the roles which pentecostalism is called upon to play in our society, be they therapeutico-subjectivist in nature or an attempt to reconstruct primary relationships which have been broken in the process of internal immigration, demonstrate what the pentecostalist religion does, and not what it is. Even if we consider the opportunities to aspire to responsibility which these churches offer to the poor, who are denied such chances in society, this still does not reveal the internal aspect of pentecostalism. The organicist concept which lies at the root of such a perspective hinders the birth of a vision of the world.

127

The idea of a return of the sacred is linked to the concept of secularization arising from a renewed interest in the theories of Weber. However, observes Ferrarotti, "it is interesting to note that the term 'secularized' is found only once in Weber, when he deals with the consequences of the centralization of worship in Jerusalem".[2] For Weber, the process of rationalization assumes a global character and involves the disenchantment of the world. This, however, does not mean that the modern world has become desacralized.

To speak of the return of the sacred supposes an eclipse of the sacred in the face of the glittering light of techno-scientific knowledge. Yet we need only look at the Brazilian socio-religious framework to appreciate the unceasing and enormous growth of pentecostalist churches and the ready multiplication of Afro-Brazilian centres. All this leads us to conclude that the sacred has not been eclipsed. In our country, we see that what lies behind the return of the sacred – an idea which, moreover, is chiefly spread by clergy who traditionally are dogmatic and apologetic – is a plan to highlight the almost exclusive emphasis of the spiritual in religion, detached from its links with things social and political. It even reaches the stage where "politicized" sermons are condemned on the pretext that they "put off" a certain number of the faithful. The latter then go and knock at the door of other religions and end up becoming pentecostals. This is a pure illusion, and an affirmation without any empirical base.

We should like, as far as possible, to look at pentecostalism in a dialectic relationship between its vision of the world and our capitalist society. At the outset, the dialectic encounter was between religion and the sacred, taking social conditionings into account. The sacred space and the religious space did not entirely coincide. This leads us to believe that the basic beliefs of pentecostalism – the belief in divine power and in the millennium – can occupy different positions in the representations of the sacred. In theory, they appear to be linked, but they can also appear individually in actual experience. Hence our hypothesis: under the influence of certain religious practices and of certain historical and social conditionings, millenarian belief can play a secondary role, while the belief in the power of the Spirit can assume a principal and dominant one. As a result, if we can demonstrate such a situation at least approximately, the vision of the world, in such a case, would appear entirely different from a vision in which the millenarian belief predominates, or where the two beliefs are of equal importance. Thus the question is one of knowing what the religious practices and the social conditions are. Here we find ourselves in the area of experiential belief, rather than theoretical doctrine.

Religion and the sacred

This title might appear a little disconcerting to those who cultivate the, now classic, Durkheimian formula of the radical opposition between the sacred and

---

2 F. Ferrarotti, *Le paradoxe du sacré*, Brussels, Edit. Les Eperonniers, 1987, 46.

the secular. We shall not deal with this opposition (sacred/secular), for it has already been the subject of pertinent critique[3], but with another aspect mentioned by Durkheim, namely that religion pre-supposes the sacred. He defines it in relation to the sacred. The two do not necessarily occupy identical fields, as Ferrarotti points out in his work to which we have already referred. Moreover, with regard to organized religion, he adds: "We could probably maintain with some appositeness that as the need, the hunger for the sacred grows, organized religion declines. The paradox is that 'organized religion' is basically desacralizing, and that the pure experience of the sacred, even in its relation to the divine is hindered rather than assisted by the religious hierocracy".

We shall consider religion not in its all-encompassing meaning but rather as the field of religious practices and the organization of religious groups. As for the sacred, we shall examine this as it is characterized by beliefs. Following this line of thought, we shall not consider practices as a mere concrete form of religious practice. They are, of course. But they are more than that. And this additional element is visible in actual experience.

To put this in more concrete terms: there are dialectic relationships between the practices and the religious organization on the one hand, and beliefs on the other. We believe that practices can influence religious representations, while the latter, under the influence of practices can, in turn, reinforce the practices themselves.

Before entering the empirical field, I should like to point out that pentecostalism, which came to Brazil from the United States in 1910 and 1911, already bore a religious experience which was dissociated from socio-political commitment. The first pentecostal missionaries to arrive in Brazil belonged to white pentecostalist groups whose experience of the faith in the Spirit was limited to the purely religious field. Initially they met together around those blacks who were the first to receive the gift of speaking in tongues, in 1906, in the celebrated event of the Azzura Street Mission, which historians regard as the starting point of the modern pentecostalist movement. These whites only parted company with the blacks some four years later.[4] This means that what we received was a pentecostalism already imbued with a certain predisposition towards a predominant belief in the miraculous gifts of the Spirit, i.e., in divine power. But, theoretically at least, this belief was also linked to belief in the millennium. This aspect of its historical origin is important for Brazilian pentecostalism.

Firstly, at a time when Brazilian urban workers, influenced by European immigrants, began to organize and to acquire their first experiences of political participation, the fact that the early pentecostal churches – the vast majority of whose members were urban workers – rejected social issues had a very negative

---

3 F.-A. Isambert, *Le sens du sacré*, Paris, Les éditions de minuit, 1982.
4 See, in this regard, V. Synan, *The holiness-pentecostal movement in the United States*, Grand Rapids, Michigan, 1971; W. Hollenweger, *El pentecostalismo, historia y doctrinas*, Buenos Aires, Editorial La Aurora, 1976; F. Cartaxo Rolim, *Pentecostais no Brasil*, Petrópolis, Vozes, 1985.

impact. The second Workers' Congress, held in Rio de Janeiro, warned workers to take their distance from religious associations and religious sects. Most probably, the expression "religious sects" referred to the Baptists and the pentecostalists who were concentrated in the Braz suburb of São Paulo.

This exclusive religious experience very probably marked out the historic path of the pentecostal churches. Indeed, during its first period of expansion, pentecostalism absorbed the supernatural-protection aspect of devotional catholicism. From protection by the saints, people moved over to protection by divine power. Thus we can imagine that the belief in the power of the Spirit, by its elective action, brought with it the dynamism of popular religion. It provided a larger area for the spontaneity of the religion of the simple people.

If, now, we examine the facts, we find a series of religious practices which give pride of place to divine power, the power of the Spirit. First, the practices of speaking and praying in tongues. One of the oldest churches in our country, and the largest numerically – the Assembly of God – systematically directs its members towards requesting the gift of tongues. Public, and above all private, worship represents a religious space where it is hoped that the divine power will manifest itself. Acclamations to the all-powerful God, to the miraculous Jesus are signs of the proclamation of divine power.

What, however, provides the spectator with the best evidence of the entry of divine power onto the stage is without doubt the practices of healing. The invocation of divine power, with the ritual imposition of hands, has a two-fold meaning: to heal the malady and restore health and, in addition, to fight the devil, who is seen as the source of physical and mental illness. With regard to this struggle against the devil, the pentecostal churches – above all the two most recent ones "Universal do Reino" et "Deus e Amor" – have launched a fierce and furious battle against candomblé and umbanda, which they consider the foremost areas of manifestations of the devil. The Universal do Reino, on occasion, uses television to demonstrate to viewers that the umbandist trance is really satanic possession.

What concerns us here is the fact that healing practices and the practices of praying in tongues have an impact on the fundamental beliefs of Brazilian pentecostalism. With regard to actual experience, the first sign of this lies in the fact that divine power becomes the central and predominant belief, while belief in the millennium becomes increasingly peripheral. In the older churches, such as the Assembly of God, belief in the millennium is mentioned from time to time in Sunday School publications, and is illustrated by statistics simply to prove that Christ's second coming is at hand. But, concretely, as far as actual experience is concerned, what matters, what registers in the minds of the adherents is belief in divine power. In the newer churches – Universal do Reino and Deus e amor – which grew out of the Assembly of God and Brazil for Christ, and which are principally interested in healing practices, belief in the millennium has almost disappeared. Their members ignore it altogether; their pastors do not mention it.

Weber's idea of elective affinity can lead us to this provisional suggestion: on the existential level, belief in divine power, in the power of the Spirit, dissociated from belief in the millennium, tends to introduce other beliefs, for example, that of God the Creator, Jesus the Saviour, who changes the life of those who give themselves to Him. The faith in the eschatological millennium is something distant and, to me, appears secondary. We could say that it has not been destroyed but that it is dormant.

This dissociation of religious representations can have repercussions at the ethical level. It represents a serious obstacle to entry into the historical process. This does not mean that belief in the millennium, as such, leads to involvement in the transformation of the social structure. According to observers of the pentecostal churches in Nicaragua, belief in the millennium encouraged these churches to see war, the death of thousands of people, and the famine in that country as signs of the imminent coming of Christ. Nevertheless, de facto, concrete situations force pentecostalists to adopt certain types of social practices, as has been the case in Brazil, in the Maranhão or within the "Ligas Camponesas". When the issue of social justice is raised among those pentecostalists who take part in these movements, we can, with some justification, imagine that some flashes of millenianism inspired their participation. We could imagine that this represented the beginning of a modest link between this belief and the historical process. Alas, these experiments were destroyed by the military coup d'Etat.

Finally we must remember that the economic-social position of Brazil under the military governments, with systematic repression of the social protest movements, left the pentecostal churches in peace. This created conditions which favoured purely religious practices, among them the rite of healing. Such practices did not disturb the military regime in the least.

A conservative vision

According to Max Weber, the vision of the world has considerable importance for human action in society. "It is the interests (material and moral)," says Weber, "and not the ideas which directly control human action. Nevertheless, the visions of the world created by the ideas very often direct human actions onto paths determined by the dynamism of the interests".[5]

In his commentary on this passage, J. Habermas situates the relationship between ideas and interests in terms which, on the one hand, are conceptual and, on the other, empirical: "Material necessities should be interpreted with the assistance of ideas".[6] This means that material necessities have their place within the contexts of meanings. They are not meaningful in themselves. In the vast area of religion, the relationship between interests and religious paths is filtered by the

---

5 M. Weber, 'Morale économique des grandes religions', in: *Archives de Sociologie des Religions*, 1960, n.9.
6 J. Habermas, *Théorie de l'agir communicationnel*, vol. I, Paris, Fayard, 201.

vision of the world. Without the latter, we cannot understand the different directions taken by religious groups.

In the generic sense, interests reveal the desires and the aspirations to be satisfied. In pentecostalism we find them in many forms: psychotherapeutical, moral, the liberation from habits which are considered sinful (in pentecostal language) – smoking, drinking, gambling, public entertainment; the need to come together again and to re-establish primary relationships which have been broken by the social atomization of the large cities. But there are also material desires – healing those who are physically and mentally ill.

Thus different interests follow different paths. The light of the vision of the world falls on the chosen path, directing and stimulating the steps, or holding them back... And here we can perceive the similarities and the differences between popular religions – including devotional catholicism and Brazilian pentecostalism.

In the Brazilian context, pentecostalism generally has a vision of the world derived from the sacred, and dissociated in its religious representations. The predomination of belief in divine power tends to shut the door to any effective participation in the structural transformation of society. This does not, however, prevent the members of these churches, as individuals, from becoming involved in social movements. Let us look at certain facts in this respect.

The "Ligas Camponesas" episode, prior to the 1964 military coup d'Etat, witnessed the active participation of a certain number of pentecostalists. There were some who, Bible in hand, spoke out in the political meetings against the social injustice suffered by the rural labourers of the North-East. Among them were leaders who organized rural groups, thus making concrete use in society of that technique of "nucleation" which formed the basis for the growth of their churches.

Another episode was that of the Maranhão. The pastor of the Assembly of God, Manuel da Conceição, gave a detailed account of the peasants' struggle against the invasion of the new rich. In the beginning, it was a question of defending subsistence farming. But the outcome of the struggle was the creation of rural unions which raised awareness and active involvement among pentecostals and catholics alike.

Alas, military repression destroyed these two experiments, experiments in which social practices played a significant role. These short-lived happenings nevertheless showed that the people not only saw the social inequalities, they also identified their social roots.

Yet we must note that the institutional apparatus of the churches, with their decision-making bodies, prevented these isolated, but nonetheless valid, experiments from changing the rigid system of religious control. It is very revealing that once these experiments had been eliminated by means of military repression, some – though not all – of those who returned to their churches were welcomed as reconverted.

On the other hand, the last presidential elections demonstrated a clear leaning to the right on the part of the pentecostalist churches, which did not prevent some of their adherents from voting for the Workers' Party candidate. Here, however, we are looking at the institutional aspect. It would appear that while part of the pentecostalist churches did not come out officially against the Workers' Party, some pastors did advise people to take their distance from socialism because it was contrary to the gospel. Other churches, however – Evangelho Quadrangular (Four-Square Gospel), Universal do Reino, Deus e Amor – campaigned on behalf of the candidate of the right.[7]

If we now look at popular religion, and here I think principally of devotional catholicism, let us take as our starting point Ferrarotti's formulation: "organized religion is basically desacralizing". In this sense, the practice of devotion to the saints, to the extent that it lies outside ecclesiastical control and thus retains a certain autonomy, preserves a dynamism which is capable of opening up to a non-conservative vision of the world. This does not mean that it is always the case. Here, too, the sacred retains its ambiguity. Everything depends on the positions of the social sectors within the social structure, committed to a greater or lesser extent to their individual or collective interests. We can be sure that the aspiration of the poorer social strata is liberation from their sufferings. And such liberation, even if it is dependent upon the protection of the saints, offers two major aspects: first of all this appeal represents a rejection of the actual experience of the poor, who long for a better and more human life; hence the rejection of that which is painful, that which is harsh, that which is bitter in life; and there is the aspiration, be it implicit or explicit, towards a more human world.

To the extent that these poor strata become organized in order to confront their concrete problems, such practices tend to awaken a perception of the social roots of poverty. Devotion does not disappear; it is present in these practices. Thus new factors emerge. Base ecclesial communities, where devotion to the saints continues, with novenas, processions, and popular prayers, reveal some extremely interesting elements: the request for health, for happiness, for the family, persists, but to a much lesser extent than before. On the other hand, the saints are requested to give strength and courage in order to struggle against injustices; they are requested to increase faith; people ask for a change in ways of thinking and help in the work of the community.[8]
Yet devotion seeks to retain its identity: "A procession should not be confused with a political march," a group of the faithful told those who carried political placards. But there are other ways. Under the military regime, we saw rural

7 "Discussing the forthcoming presidential elections on 15 November, we have given them due consideration and are notifying and requesting pastors that they should not vote for, and that they should encourage the faithful not to vote for the candidates of the left – Lula, Freire, Brizola and Covas. We do so, since we consider that the whole ideology of the left is completely opposed to the gospel", O Globo, 14 November 1989; see Jornal do Brasil, 3 December 1989.
8 See F. C. Rolim, Religião e classes populares, Petrópolis, Vozes, 1980.

labourers from the North-East carrying the statue of St Joseph in order to call people together. It was a form of procession-gathering, but this gathering turned into a collective meeting where the labourers could discuss the problem of the invasion of their plantations.

While we have mentioned these aspects with regard to the base ecclesial communities, it does not mean that the latter created them; merely that the BECs created the conditions necessary for the blossoming forth of a latent religious dynamic.

While the opening up of popular catholicism may be more readily received by the poorer sectors of society, it is not exclusive to them. The problem remains one of knowing, empirically, whether industrial workers and rural labourers or the wage-earners in the service and commercial sectors are more sensitive to devotional dynamism. As far as the middle classes are concerned, they tend towards conservatism.

Social conditioning

The forms of conditioning which we deal with here are neither economic, cultural nor political conditionings perceived in mutual interaction. It is a question of class relationships. In addition to these social groups we should, no doubt, also consider their common interests. We should. however, remember that those social groups whose common interests are not truly economic do not, as a result, constitute social classes in the true sense of the term. They must, in addition, embody ideological and political relationships. In concrete terms, this means that common interests should either be directed towards the transformation of the social structure or towards the maintenance of the status quo.[9] This orientation, however, implies certain practices, and follows its own route, guided by its vision of the world.

The pentecostal churches do not constitute social classes. The vast majority of their adherents, however, belong to the under classes: according to a study which we carried out on the periphery of Greater Rio de Janeiro, and on the basis of evidence from other regions, we find that there are very few industrial workers, but that there are many salary-earners from among the commercial and service sector.[10] We can describe these classes as dominated in that they find themselves either within the fundamental capital/labour relationship or they find themselves dominated by commercial capital.[11]

Here, no doubt, we are touching on structural issues. But the socio-religious practices, and even the organization of the churches, provide enlightenment with regard to the ideological and political aspects. Here we should look at two points at least: firstly, the absence of any positive and permanent social commitment

---

9 In this respect, see L. Goldmann, *Le dieu caché*, Paris, Gallimard, 1959, 26ff.
10 F. Cartaxo Rolim, *Pentecostais no Brasil, o.c.,* 176.
11 N. Poulantzas, *Les classes sociales dans le capitalisme aujourd'hui*, Paris, Ed. du Seuil, 1974.

which could create, amongst the adherents, an awareness of those who are the subjects of social transformation. Poor and subjugated, the pentecostals do not become organized in an effort to liberate other poor people through a constant struggle against capitalist domination and exploitation. Secondly, to this rather negative aspect there corresponds an intense interest in matters related to worship and a passive conformity to the existing social situation.

Last year's presidential elections clearly demonstrated the ready reception accorded the anti-communist language of the candidate of the right in pentecostal milieux – although not only there. Other pentecostal churches echoed the Foursquare Gospel Church, although they limited themselves to advising people not to vote for the candidates of the left. The anti-communist language of the right, despite the fact that it was out-of-date and old-fashioned, was generally well-received among pentecostal groups as a whole, thus revealing the conservative air which these churches breathe. Despite these facts, however, we cannot generalize. It would appear that the political and religious behaviour today also reveals close similarities with the attitude of the pentecostal churches sixty years ago, when the workers first became mobilized. It is true that in the 1920 it was a question of trade unions, whereas in 1989, the people of Brazil were to elect their president after 29 years without any democratic elections. In the first case, the adherents were forbidden to join trade unions. As far as the presidential elections were concerned, the religious language was very much that of the right. The churches as a whole took the side of the dominant groups.

The consequence of the facts which we have just outlined is that the pentecostalist religion is not a religion which is politically neutral. The churches as a whole took an openly political position (official publications, preaching in the churches, political campaigns, advice to individuals). This means that these churches have declared themselves in favour of the continued existence of the dominant groups, for the continuation of social inequalities, and the poverty of wide social strata, in order to prevent the pentecostalists from becoming involved in the struggle for the liberation of the poor.

Since they are not politically neutral, the conservative vision of the pentecostalists cannot escape class conflicts. It is influenced by the ideology of the dominant class. This means that it is permeated by a secular ideology in which and through which that which dominates continues to dominate. As a result, social inequalities are not seen as the product of groups who become ever more rich. According to the pentecostals, this inequality is part of the natural order. In turn, the pentecostal religious ideology as disseminated by the church leadership, tends to sacralize the social order. In this case, ideological domination, in the shape of biblical formulae, in our capitalist society represents the social and political condition – and not merely the economic one – of the strongest.

In such a perspective, the electronic reproduction of beliefs plays a major role in the reproduction of the system of domination in the present stage of dependent monopolist capitalism. The electronic churches, such as the Assembly of God, the Universal do Reino, Deus e Amor, by using the media to spread belief in divine power, manage to create thousands of small centres in the most diverse areas, and these centres guarantee the active presence of the conservative vision.

Conclusion

Faced with the proliferation of christian sects and the arrival and the acceptance of eastern religions in our country, those who speak of the return of the sacred merely look at the cultural aspect, isolated from the system which is characteristic of our society. Among them, there are some clergy, still impregnated by meaningless apologetics, who criticise a catholicism which they consider politicized because it is involved in the social struggle and movements, and wish to see a religion which is purely directed towards the spiritual, or, at least, a religion which is above social matters. They forget, however, that religion bears a vision of the world, and this vision alters depending on the position and the interests of its subjects in the social structure. Such people fail to appreciate that the pentecostal response, and the response of other over-spiritualized groups (or para-religious groups) misses the point with regard to the basic problem of theodicy: man is called to give meaning to the created world and, hence, to his society.
The partiality of the response given by such groups scarcely translates human dissatisfaction when faced with the contradictions of modernization. While doubtless the subjective world may be satisfied with this "junk food", yet it remains in the heaven of illusions, with no strength to walk on terra firma.

The Brazilian social context, and indeed the South American situation, requires christianity to take up a clear and concrete position, not beside or above the vast mass of the poor, but in the midst of them. The poor wish to escape from their poverty and their misery. They question their faith, they question the validity of a religious vision of the world which is passive and dormant, and which has been handed down to them.
We can no longer be content to talk of heaven and abstract spiritual matters. We must get to the base of social movements, to the legitimate social and political aspirations of the poor; we must listen to what they can teach us, so that we can bring them the gospel message.
The positivism which inspired the radical opposition between the sacred and the secular, as a principle universal to all religions, is still to be found today in the language which preaches the separation of the spiritual and the social, of religion and of politics.

The absence of politicization implies more than a mere rejection of the world. Indeed, and this is true of pentecostalism in Brazil, it means legitimizing – as natural – the vast social differences and their repercussions on the growing mass of the poor, and the gradual accumulation of wealth in the hands of the rich.
Pentecostalism claims that it is not up to people to solve social injustice and socio-economic inequalities between those who dominate and those who are

136

dominated. God always comes to the aid of the poor. But the poor continue to be poor.

It is true that we can see, in pentecostalism, a protest against the formalism of worship. But behind the spontaneity of its collective prayers we must discern the activities of the decision-making organs in directing belief. Above all the belief in the power of the Spirit.

Given several of its aspects, pentecostalism can been called a popular religion. But to the extent that it refuses to commit itself to the liberation of its poorer members and of other poor people, it is not. By drawing on the analyses of some South American sociologists and anthropologists of religion, I can say that, basically, it is anti-popular, to the extent that it distances itself from the deep-seated aspirations to liberation emanating from the poorer sectors of our society.

The assessment of pentecostalism which I have just given here is, as you will have gathered, closely related to our concern for our real situation. Other contexts will require different types of interpretation. Our problems in Brazil, and in Latin America, are not the problems of the developed countries.

PART III

ASIA

Popular religion, church and socio-cultural change in India

Anthony B. Fernandes, India

From the outset, some preliminary remarks are very appropriate. The presentation of this paper does not intend to cover the subject of popular religion, church and socio-cultural change in India as a whole but from a very contextualized situation that I willingly underwent in the second half of the sixties in a lower middle class orthodox hindu environment in the inner city area of Pune in Maharashtra, India. What is being presented, in short, is part of a journey in which I ventured into hinduism as part of my genuine search for my own religious and cultural roots on the one hand, and my concern to reconcile my christian faith with the faith I was witnessing around me of those who professed hinduism. It was a journey I dared to undertake with a sense of urgency without realizing what it had in store for me. It has been a powerful experience which has not left me till this day, though I must say, it was not all smooth sailing. It is against this personal and communitarian background – fortunately I could fall back on a core group of fellow passengers and journey with them together at times during those eventful five years – that I am setting out on this reflection on popular religion, church and socio-cultural change in India.

Contextual experience

To begin with, some characteristics of the context must be presented in order to situate the kind of questions to which one was trying to find some answers, and the reflections that have been drawn from this particular contextual experience.

The area chosen lay very much at the heart of the inner city of Pune. It was indeed a pulsating heart, because it was one of the strong orthodox hindu centres, not only in terms of living out its hinduism but one that was a source of power in the civic life of the city. It was a place where there were several writers, poets and dramatists; a place where there were journalists and editors of some of the major newspapers of the city; it was the place where there were some very vocal political and social activists and leaders of political parties. And yet the place was overcrowded, shabby and dilapidated. In fact, quite a major part of it needed complete repairs.

Economically, the majority were poor, while some 10 to 15 per cent belonged to the middle class. And it was staunchly hindu – quite a few of them belonging to the Brahmin caste representing all types of stances – from the extreme chauvinist and nationalist, to the most progressive liberal and the most interesting combination of the hindu marxist.

From the above, it is pretty apparent that the area oozed a very clear identity. There was no doubting this one fact – of one's origins and of one's religious and cultural traditions. It meant that if you were going to become part and parcel of this community you were steeped in hinduism because the whole of life here was just that from the very start.

It was a very gripping context that was lively and enervating no doubt. But it was also very trying because of the new awakening and the continuous struggle to re-shape society now that we Indians were masters of our own destinies from the sordid poverty and, worse still, trying to reconcile the immense diversities. Not in spite of, but because of, the new awakening, the grind of poverty could be extremely harsh at times when the space for the making of effective choices was rather limited. The specific context of poverty turns out to be important in this journey as many of the reflections are quite clearly influenced by this all pervasive factor.

Situating the questions

The questions were shaped by the growing inner unrest and, at times, inner protest against the slow but definitive process of alienation that we were growing into because of our practice and formation in the christian faith. Basically, it was trying to redress the imbalance caused by the negation of our own historical, cultural and religious traditions. It dawned on us one fine day that the uprooting was rather complete and unless we took some effective steps to rediscover ourselves in terms of our own religious, cultural and historical traditions, we would end up as well-cultivated general zombies.

Therefore the questions that just swelled before us were the following. What is it that keeps the hindu people on the move? What is that motivates them and inspires them? What and where is one to find the binding element that is intangible but irrevocable? What is the hindu religious and cultural consciousness and how is this manifested? What is the hindu perception of the individual, community and society?

More than the questions, there was the urge to experience hinduism from within by plunging into it, realizing full well that my own faith and religious practice was christian. There was only one way to do this and that was to go and live among them and do as the hindus do – dare to undertake the discourse in all openness and in a spirit of learning on the themes of death, sin, redemption, sacrifice, salvation and liberation. It meant gradually learning to begin the day with the morning prayerful bath, discovering and keeping pace with one's chosen marga which is further manifested in the choice of foods, fasts and celebrating life at the individual, communitarian and societal levels.

It meant joining them in going to the temples, moved by the desire to offer something or make known a wish at appropriate times, days and seasons. It

142

meant harboring the inner wish to witness the sacred by visiting the sacred Godavari river, the holy city of Nasik and its holy temples. It meant joining the pilgrimage to Alandi, the place were Jnaneshwar, a saintly young man experienced his liberation and joining thousands of *vakaris* – devotees of Vithoba – to Pandurpur and singing and chanting the thousand names of God following the example of the holy persons before us, like Namdev (1270-1350), Eknath (1548-1599) and Tukaram (1608-1648). It meant experiencing the binding element of brotherhood and sisterhood and witnessing the shine of Vithoba's blessing on the faces of the pilgrims.

It also meant whiling away time in *bhajans* and *kirtans* where, rhythmically, the thousand names of God were sung in community and his wonders commemorated. And it meant taking part in great socio-religious feasts like Ganesh chaturthi, holi deepawali and makar sankrant, the feast of reconciliation.

One of the most moving discoveries was the special psalm-like incantation sung to the household deity. The form of the incantation is often hundreds of years old because it carries with it the history of the family and the community – the sorrows and struggles and also the periods of prosperity and happiness. This was another binding element where you discovered who you were and where you came from, and how the community has fared till now. It was a living prayer sung during the feast days in honour of the deity, witnessed as one of the myriad manifestations of God.

This is the place were one witnesses the answers to what moves the hindus, who is calling them to prayer, who is keeping them on the move, what is binding them together. The incantation always begins and ends with: *"Jai, Jai Deva"* which means "Praise, praise be unto you, o God". It is moving to see how it gets to your bones when the whole family joined by the children, almost shouting, sing the praises not to some unknown god but to the known deity of the family, one that belongs to them and one whom they have witnessed in that particular manifestation and one to whom they, in turn, belong. What a sense of identity and rootedness!

The incantation then goes on to describe the manifestations – both the external and the internal – of the deity in terms of beauty, kindness, and caring love. This is then followed very often by the commemorating of certain events of sorrow, struggle, prosperity and happiness. Then the family joins together in making petitions for happiness; petitions crying to remove hurdles in their way of happiness, and petitions for prosperity. And the incantation ends up once again, as we said earlier, with praise which clearly carries within it the undertone of thankfulness and the joy of being present in their midst, in fact of always being present in their midst.

One other binding element that I should like to highlight that is very touching, and one where one witnesses the constant awareness of the divine, is the silent fasts undertaken mostly by woman. This is sensed within the family as being present by the sacred which is concretely manifested in the choice of foods –

certain foods are not touched that day or during the period of the fast. The daily *puja* acquires a special significance as mother mediates with God (in hinduism God is mostly mother) for the whole family. Next to the psalm-like incantation of the household deity, the fast is the most tangible expression of the awareness of the sacred and the divine in the daily life activities.

Reflections

Religion as lived out by the hindus in this particular area of Pune, by means of the private incantations to the household deity, prayers, offerings and fasts; in the solemn moments of life by means of the rites of initiation (upanayana), marriage and death; celebrating life in the major social feasts, pilgrimages, *bhajans* and *kirtans*, portrayed a remarkable sense of identity and destiny. The feeling that the hindu "comes from", rather, he or she is linked with the divine is one of the most striking experiences one who undertakes such a journey comes across. This linkage with the divine is simply taken for granted and is kept alive until today through the exemplification of the sacred in symbols, myths and legends.

Every feast, be it at the individual, community or social level is couched in symbols, myth and legend. Even the fasts and the incantation to the household deity are explained by means of myths and legends. There is no question whatsoever that the hindu believes that he or she is directly linked with the divine and the sacred. It is interesting to note that linkage in sensed not just in individual terms but in terms of the family. The family again is unquestionably taking for granted to be the extended family – the *jati* or the community. In fact, the household deity is the deity of the *jati* or the community.

Another striking experience is the fact that the hindus see this linkage with the divine as the discovery of existence itself. It is practised in terms of the discovery of one's own humanity and the discovery of the self. This is where the link with the divine is experienced in terms of enlarging one's consciousness. And it is in the enlarging of the consciousness that the entire gamut of relationships is placed in its proper perspective – relations to nature, to the universe, to other human beings as other existences, that are an integral part of the same divine existence. The other relations are seen as relationships of equal acceptance, rather than of similar possibilities and opportunities. This latter is the key to the understanding of the role that popular religion plays or can play in socio-cultural change.

Its role in socio-cultural change

Popular religion as a vehicle for socio-cultural change in this popular contextualized situation prized the acquisition of knowledge as one of the highest values. Acquisition of knowledge is seen as a religious value as part and parcel of the enlarging of consciousness, which is where one experiences the divine.

But the acquisition of knowledge is not to be understood as a simple linear function but one that has to comply with the complex of historical factors. In concrete terms, the hindu tries to explain the process of acquiring knowledge as first going through the process of shifting the various heritages in terms of one's own values and in terms of the bindings expressed through structures (family, joint family), customs, traditions and religious practices.

The shifting of heritages also explained as coming to terms with progress, locally and globally, was again viewed from the hindu liberational or salvivic values. In practice, the hindu people I was part of as a member of the community through mutual acceptance, saw the shaping of society as the creation of a sphere of similar opportunities from which each could draw on for his or her liberation. In other words, you had to liberate yourself and nobody would or could do it for you. You have actively to contribute to this corpus, to this sphere of similar opportunities in order to benefit from it.

Popular religion, as I witnessed it, has tremendous power to come to terms with the adjustments called for by the changes taking place, particularly if these changes come from outside. The socio-cultural change it can initiate by itself would seem to me to be of an even more important order than coming to grips with the changes from outside. In this sense, popular religion would seem to me to have the potential to criticize, protest and advocate change. It is also at this level that popular religion is able to overcome and get rid of the dead wood which has become merely ritualistic and farcical.

For example, the people I lived with were able to see the misuse made of religion by many a political party and political leadership; that this misuse might bring some gains in the short term, but that eventually they turn out to be detrimental to deal with the two most central problems of Indian society: the eradication of poverty and the bringing together of diversities. It is a sharp-edged sword which certainly is capable of creating disharmony through the wrong use of its outward expressions. But then, the problem is not to be placed at the door of popular religion as lived out by sincere and genuine hinhu people but at the door of those who misuse it, whoever they be.

Popular religion and Asian contextual theologizing

Felix Wilfred, India

One of the significant cultural phenomena we are witnessing today all over the world is the conversion to the small, the micro, the periphery as a result of disillusionments with the macro, the large, the grand – be it political and economic systems or ideologies, theories and institutions – regarding their capability to answer the pressing problems and issues of humankind. The attention which popular religion has gained in the past few years – partly in the context of liberation theology – in contradistinction to official, institutionized religion is an expression, at the religious level, of this general phenomenon. The grand theological systems and theoretical constructs today stand challenged by the religious experience of the people, which calls for a different theological approach, an approach that would mirror more closely the day to day realities of life, interpret them meaningfully and help to transform them.

Against this general background, I wish to offer a few reflections on the experience of popular religion among our neighbours of other faiths. This experience can be a rich source for Asian theologizing; it also represents a challenge to traditional theology, its orientation and approach. This paper does not pretend to be comprehensive; it reflects on a few selected issues and areas related to popular religious experience.

Understanding popular religion from an Asian perspective

In the first place it is necessary to view the reality of popular religion itself in proper perspective. This will avoid the danger of transposing ideas about popular religion derived from the christian experience and context on to another religious tradition that has its own specific characteristics and features, particulary history, socio cultural configurations and structures. It is very important that Asian popular religiosity be understood on its own ground and not with reference to definitions and descriptions formulated elsewhere. What popular religion is, is largely determined by the particular social context. Without entering into the current discussion about the understanding of popular religion in Europe, Africa and Latin America, let me make three observations from the perspective of the Asian religious traditions.

POPULAR RELIGION AND OFFICIAL RELIGION

In christian theological circles today, popular religion is often understood in contrast to official religion. This contrast does not correspond to the experience of most Asian religions. For these religious traditions do not form an officially well-organized system of beliefs, rituals, structures from which the popular religion and its practices could be differentiated.[1] In confucian and taoist China, religious cults and practices gravitated around the two pillars of its social organization – state and family. The ethical and rational approach to life, characteristic of Chinese civilization did not call for any separate official system of religion. Religiousness expressed itself either as public worship connected with the imperial court or cults connected to the family, without needing any religious system.[2] The reflection of this long tradition can be observed today in communist China's attitude to organized religions.

In the hindu tradition of India, what is called *dharma* – religion – is something which belongs to the total way of life of a people, and therefore the introduction of a contrast between institutionized, official religion and popular religion would be out of place. In hinduism there is a diversity of ways of religious experience – the way of knowledge *(jnana marga)*, the way of love and devotion *(bhakti marga)* and the way of action *(karma marga)* to be followed according to what best suits one's temperament and natural propensities. They do not exclude each other. Though the advaitic hindu tradition would consider *jnana marga* as superior to the way of *bhakti* which is meant for the ordinary people, another important strand in the tradition, even among the Brahmins, the *Saiva Sidddhanta*, maintains the inadequacy of knowledge (since it can only free us from bondage) and considers devotion as indispensable for salvation. This is different from the view that sees official and popular religion as antithetical realities.

LITTLE TRADITION AND GREAT TRADITION

Another contrast that is generally made is between the "little tradition" and the "great tradition", identifying the former with popular religion. This polarity, too, does not fit in with the Asian religious experience. Lawrence Babb and McKim Marriot studying, respectively, the village religions of Chattisgarh in Central India and Kishan Garhi in North India come to identical conclusions.[3] The relationship between the great and the little tradition, or textual and non-textual tradition, or Sanskrit and non-Sanskrit tradition – to mention the category used widely in the study of Indian religions since M. N. Srinivas[4] – is not one of opposition nor of

---

1 See F. Wilfred, 'Faith without "Faith"? Popular religion. A challenge to elitist theology and liturgy', in: Paul Puthanangady (ed.), *Popular devotion*, Bangalore 1986, 594-613, specially 595.
2 See J. M. Kitagwa; 'Some reflections on Chinese religion', in: *Ching Feng*, 29(1986), n.2-3, 145-157; see also C.F. Yang, *Religion in Chinese society*, Berkeley - Los Angeles - London, University of California Press, 1961.
3 L. A. Babb, *The divine hierarchy. Popular hinduism in Central India*, New York-London, Columbia University Press, 1975; Mckim Marriot, 'Little Communities in indigenous civilization', in: *Village India*, Chicago-London, 1972, 171-221. See also M. Amaladoss, 'Popular religion. Some questions', in: *Vidyajyoty Journal of Theological Reflection*, 53(1989), 357-370; id., 'Popular religion in India', in: *Pro Mundi Vita Studies*, 1988, n.6, 12-17.
4 M. N. Srinivas, *Religion and society among the Coorgs of South India*, London, Asia Publishing House, 1952.

mutual exclusion.[5] Popular religion as lived in villages is a confluence of both the great tradition and specifically local elements in continuous communication with each other. There is, then, in popular religion a parochialization of the great tradition providing significance and explanation to popular practices from a wider horizon, and a universalization of the local elements in as much as what is called the great tradition is often a transmutation of something that has often been drawn from the local people's cults and practices. Thus even in the present form of hindu Sanskritic or Aryan tradition, a lot of pre-Aryan elements of popular Dravidian folk religion can be discerned.

The communication between the great tradition and the little tradition which is manifest in hindu popular religious festivals, practices, rituals etc. is rendered possible because the symbols in which both this traditions share are multivalent and pluridimensional. What may be used at the popular or empirical level is capable of being interpreted at various other levels of meaning. A popular worship like that of *Kali*, a tender mother as well as a blood-thirsty, gruesome woman could be interpreted at various levels, cosmic, ontological, personal, exterior, interior etc.

In Asia the great tradition and the little tradition are not dichotomized, but are held together in a holistic perspective. This does not leave room for any interpretation of the relationship of popular religion or the little tradition and elitist religion or the great religion in terms of a conflict between the religious experience of two different classes. The relationship between the little tradition and the great tradition in Asia is too complex and nuanced as to permit any such interpretation.

POPULAR TRADITION AND FUNDAMENTALIST RELIGION

Today's developments in Asia call for a contrast not so much between official and popular, or elite and popular, religion, but rather between a popular religion which is open, flexible and universal in its spirit and a fundamentalist religion which is sectarian, closed and dogmatic. The emergence and intensification of the fundamentalist religious trends and attitudes is opposed to the spirit of openness which has characterized the Asian popular religious traditions.

Among other things, fundamentalism is due to the economic interests pursued by certain sections and groups in society. It is remarkable that, today, fundamentalism is fostered by middle and upper-middle class people – not by the elites – and they carry along with them the masses to achieve their purposes; they twist and shape the religions of the people to suit their interests. A case in point is the present conflict concerning the Ram Janma-bhoomi – Babri Masjid – a dispute between hindus and muslims in North India concerning a popular place of worship in Ayodhya. This conflict, associated with a popular cult, is so sharp and volatile that the political stability of India hangs in balance. This is also a case of the exploitation of the emotional power invested in popular religion to achieve economic goals and political power.

---

5 This can be said also of the relationship between the elite *priyayi* tradition and *abangan* tradition of the poor classes in Indonesia.

Theological method and language

Popular religions, particularly in Asia, involve the whole person of the devotee, with feelings, aspirations, trust and hope, as he or she stands before the mystery of life. This religiousness of the people is rich in symbolism, in stories and myths; through them, people interpret their experience, analyze and understand society and affirm themselves as a community. If culture and religion are always intimately interlinked, this is all the more true of popular religious festivals, rituals etc. which cover the whole spectrum of the cultural universe, its moods, values etc., and reveal the collective unconsciousness of the people. Soaked as it is in the life and cultural stream of the people, popular religion offers a rich source for contextual and inculturated theologizing in Asia.

Anubhava or experience lies at the heart of Asian theologizing, In South Asian traditions, God, or rather the Divine, is not simply an object which theologians try to understand primarily by the means of *logos*, but the subject which is experienced through *mythos*, and, consequently, symbol becomes a primary reality in theologizing. The Divine mystery is something that is ultimately connected with the mystery of the subject – the self of the one who seeks it. Theology is not, unlike the dominant Western christian tradition, a "progression from the obscurity of faith to the intelligibility of logos"[6], but a movement towards an ever deeper experience of the Divine in the depth of one's self. A theology with anubhava as its score becomes profoundly transforming. Anubhava presupposes a different epistemology. It does not operate on the basis of a distinction between subject and object. In this epistemological framework, experience is considered not as something pertaining to the subject or as in danger of subjectivism. Anubhava is something that happens through identification with the reality and not through differentiation. If anubhava is so central to all theologizing in Asia, in distinction to mainline Western tradition, this Asian characteristic of theology receives a particulary powerful stimulus from popular religions with their intense experience of love and devotion. Intoxicated with the Divine, the *bhakta*, the devotee, breaks into trance; dancing and singing the Divine name the bhakta moves towards the shrine of his or her Lord or *devi*, goddess.

If the Indian and South Asian tradition focus on the subject, the self and its experience of the Divine as the source from where theology wells up, we have in the subjecthood of the *minjung* and their experience of suffering and oppression the locus of an emerging Korean theology. As an outstanding representative of minjung theology, Kim Yong Bok notes, "we have in mind the total subjective experience of the minjung, their aspirations and sufferings, their struggles and defeats which form their social biography. Therefore, our reflection involves not only objective socio-economic analysis, but also an empathy for their experience,

---

6 J. B. Chethimattam, 'The spirit and orientation of an Indian theology', in: *Jeevadhara*, 1971, n.1, 452.

language and culture".[7] The experience and language of the minjung – and therefore of their theology – are precisely the experience and language of popular religion – the traditional religious practices, rituals, the mask dance and shamanism, which all have been despised and sidelined. Stories, parables and narratives are the privileged theological idioms of minjung.

Asian theologizing is bolstered up by the symbolic universe represented in popular religion and culture. The elitist form of christian theology – which has been the only recognized way of theologizing – is built on a system of universals that transcend all particularities, and the quality of this theology is identified with its high degree of abstraction and the elucidation of the interrelationship between concepts, their meanings, their interpretations etc. The language of Asian theologizing, fostered by peoples' culture and religion, is a language of symbols where the particular is not allowed to vanish in a timeless universal, but is palpably present. Symbols and myths are not things simply to be decoded to obtain a meaning for them, but are powerful expressions of the very life of the society from which they emerge. The symbol or myth in all its particularity and space/time-bound concreteness appeals to the universal in the human, and that explains why epics like the Ramayana and Mahabharata, or The Monkey, a supernatural fantasy written by Liao-Chai-Chi, based on popular stories, could move millions of Asians to religious and social commitment, in spite of, or rather because of, their concreteness; whereas cogently argued and conceptually well-formulated christian theology met with only cold indifference, if not total rejection.

The language of symbols and myths indicated by popular religion and culture is a language that can become theology in the hands of every committed believer. An idea of how much Asian theology is moving today in the direction of popular culture and religion – their stories, songs, symbols and myths – can be had by reading Asian authors like C.S. Song and Kosuke Koyama. The language of myth, stories, and parables draws the devotees into a dialogue with reality; it is based on experience and is capable of creating critical consciousness. It is the theological method and language of Jesus himself.

Dialogue and community

Popular religiosity assumes great importance in the context of two crucial and interconnected issues in present-day Asian life, and, consequently, in its theology: dialogue and the creation of community. In an Asia that is torn by the self-assertion of threatened ethnic, linguistic and communal identities, there is no gainsaying the importance of unity, harmony and concord in justice and fellow-

---

7 Kim Yong-Bok, 'Messiah and minjung. Discerning messianic politics over against political messianism', in: D. W. Fern (ed.), *Third World Theologies. A Reader*, Maryknoll, New York, Orbis Books, 1985, 374; see also C.S. Song, 'Building a theological culture of people', in: *CTC Bulletin*, 5(1984), n.3 and 6(1985), n.1.

ship. Religions are not infrequently the cause of conflicts, riots and violence. But religions are also a great cohesive force. Meetings, dialogue and communication among various faiths would seem to be indispensable for peace, and unity among the various groups of people in a particular society. But the dialogue pursued today has been a meeting of religions at the *macro* level – meetings of religions as systems and institutions and discussions on their respective doctrinal tenets. This macro dialogue at the level of religious elites does not really respond to the challenges of creating a community in the face of conflicts and divisions. What is required is a dialogue of life, a sharing in day-to-day life by the people of various faiths living together in a society.[8] This is possible only when dialogue becomes a meeting at the level of popular religion – the rituals, festivals, worship, etc.

Christian theology has much to draw from the resources of popular religion and the role it has played in the history of the Asian nations. Popular religion cuts across religious barriers and draws together believers of different faiths in a common quest for the sacred. The history of Indonesia illustrates – as is well shown by the prominent Indonesian historian Prof. Sartono – how popular religious syncretism and mystique have been a welding force among hinduism, buddhism and islam.[9] A religion which comes into a society from without and is not born out of the cultural matrix of a people can be a divisive force, as buddhism was in the early stage of its presence in China, Thailand, Korea, Japan etc. However, buddhism, without failing to make its own contribution to these societies, was able to become a force of unity and be truly inculturated when it made place within its fold for the spirits and deities of the people – the *nat* of the Burmese, the *phi* of the Thais, the *neak-ta* of Cambodians and the *kami* of the Japanese. In this process buddhism itself became a religion of the people.

All this raises a very important question for Asian theology: could there be a deep relationship between us christians and neighbours of other faiths if we do not also share and participate in some way in what they hold as most sacred? The faith of the people in the sacred is not an abstraction, but is concretely lived out as loving devotion to the various deities. As for hinduism, this kind of popular religion is, in a way, the concretization of the very essence; hinduism sees in the multifarious names and forms of the gods, the ultimate one, the one without the second.

The crucial question in whether these deities on whom popular religion centres itself are to be rejected as simple polytheism and, consequently, idolatry or can the various forms and names, the various goddesses and gods – Lakshmi, Parvati,

---

8 'Living and working together with sisters and brothers of other faiths. An ecumenical consultation, Singapore, July 5-10, 1987', *Joint CCA-FABC Report*, Hong Kong 1989.
9 Sartono/Kartodirdjo, *In search of social order and cosmic harmony. Consciousness in Indonesian context*. A Paper presented at the Tenth Bishops' Institute for Inter-Religious Affairs (BIRA IV/10) of the Federation of Asian Bishops' Conferences, June 24-30, 1988, Sukabumi, Indonesia (shortly to be published from Hong Kong).

Saraswati, Ganesh, Ayappan, Hanuman etc. – be positively related to christian belief in One God. Popular religion in Asia throws up a challenge to re-examine the traditional understanding of monotheism (taking into account the socio-political role it has played), and the "polytheism" of popular religion (taking into account the spiritual transformation it has effected on the devotees and the sense of communion and solidarity it has created).

In finding a solution to this question which is, in my view, very important for Asian theology, we should be aware of the fact that the Old Testament had to face the question of the various gods of the neighbouring peoples of Israel, while early christianity had to confront the greco-roman popular god and religious practices. This has influenced and shaped the concrete form of christianity, its beliefs, symbols, worship forms etc. Every socio-historical situation is different and the approach of the past cannot be simply repeated in the new Asian context. How can we, *today*, creatively relate to the various religious expressions – gods, goddesses, rituals etc. – of the popular religion of the neighbours of other faiths? This is a central question of interreligious dialogue, and, therefore, of Asian theologizing. No theological reflection in Asia is possible without facing the religion of the people, with their gods and goddesses, and making sense of our christian faith in relation to the non-christian popular religious world.

Asian theology should explore the possibility of christians sharing in the popular religious symbols of other faiths – festivals, rituals etc. – thus realizing one community and fellowship with followers of other faiths, without losing one's genuine christian identity. The interpretation of these symbols could be very different, since symbols are ambiguous and polyvalent. They make it possible for christians to form one community with the people of other faiths through participation in their popular religious symbols while remaining true christians by their interpretation of these same symbols at a different level. This is a question which requires deeper reflection and consideration.

Popular religiosity and an Asian theology of liberation

It is undeniable that social structures condition the nature of religion and its practice, even though one may dispute the extent of this conditioning. This is also true of popular religion. In South Asia, for example, there are popular religious manifestations and ritual practices which reflect the social structure of caste discrimination and even reinforce and sacralize it. Through the principle of hierarchization and purity-pollution, the social structure and inequality even become constitutive of peoples' understanding and approach to the sacred.[10] All this should make us aware of the limitations of popular religion for the project of liberation and prevent us from romanticizing it in the Asian context.

---

10 See A.A.M. Ayrookuzhiel, *The sacred in popular hinduism*, Madras, CLS, 1983; see also G. Dietrich, *Religion and peoples' organization in East Thanjavur*, Madras, CLS, 1976.

These limitations notwithstanding, peoples' religiosity presents an immense resource for the process of liberation and for a theology of liberation in Asia.[11] This is so because, in the first place, popular religions associated with myths, with *ithihasas* and *puranas* (hindu texts of religious myths) in the crystallization of the experience of the people, their aspirations and dreams. It is understandable, then, that many religious movements for social change have popular religion as their base. Even in China where, traditionally, religion has served the interests of the state, we have numerous examples of protests and rebellions inspired and sustained by popular religious movements. We may recall, here, the Taoist Yellow Turban Rebellion, the White Lotus uprising, the Taiping Revolt etc. In times of social, economic and political crisis, popular religion kindled in the people a new force to fight against oppressive regimes and their misgovernment. As C.K. Yang notes, "economic hardship and disaster constituted a frequent type of crisis that bred religious movements and rebellions. Famine due to crop failure was a current crisis, typical of any agricultural society, leading to many forms of mass action. We may say that no major politico-religious upheaval in China was without some form of extensive agricultural crisis as a backdrop".[12] It is no wonder that the Chinese state and its rulers tried to suppress popular religious expressions and movements, realizing their potential to overthrow the existing socio-political order.

The culture and religion of the people connected with shamanism and its expressions constitute a great force of liberation in Korea. The Korean theology of liberation – minjung theology – is very much associated with *'han'* which is a deep awareness of the contradictions in a situation and of unjust treatment meted out to the people or a person by the powerful".[13] The shamanist ritual *kut* is a ritual where in the spirits of all those who suffered unjustly are rendered present so as to impel the participants to protest against all kinds of oppression and injustice.[14] Korean minjung theology is not only a result of drawing from the popular religious resources, but also a fruit of the re-interpretation of Korean religious history from the perspective of the oppressed and marginalized. A similar re-interpretation can be found among the *dalits* – the outcasts and oppressed people of Indian society, in whose popular religiosity the traditional religious symbols and figures are reinterpreted in support of their struggles. Thus, Aryan-dominated and Brahmin-centred classical epics of *Ramayana* and *Mahabharata* are today re-constructed and re-interpreted from the perspectives of the oppressed Dravidian and outcast peoples.[15]

---

11 See 'Religion and liberation. Statement of the EATWOT Consultation, New Delhi, December 1-5, 1987', in: *Dialogue*, 15(1988), n.1-3, 11-27.
12 C. K. Yang, *o.c.*, 225.
13 Kosuke Koyama, *Mount Fiji and Mount Sinai. A pilgrimage in theology*, London, SCM Press, 1984, 185 (with reference to Kim Young-Bok); see also Younghak Hyung, 'Minjung theology and the religion of han', in: *East Asian Journal of Theology*, 3(1985), 354-359.
14 See 'Religion and Liberation. Statement of the EATWOT Consultation', *l.c.*, 17.
15 A.A.M. Ayrookuzhiel, 'The religious resources of the Dalits in the context of their struggle', in: *Essays in celebration of the CISRS Silver Jubilee*, Madras, CLS, 1983, 111-127.

No one would deny the important role played by the popular religious symbols in the Indian struggle for independence from the colonial powers. We could recall the *Ganapati* festival which proved to be a great school of education of the masses about their experience of oppression and a rallying point for protest against colonial domination.[16] This is in line with the Medieval *Bhakti* movement in India, with the difference that here was it a movement not against foreign domination but against the oppression of the lower groups of the people by the upper castes and classes of the same society.[17]

In a caste-ridden society with gross social discrimination, the Bhakti movement was a protest on the part of the outcasts and lower classes against caste, and a movement for an egalitarian society, though the co-option and domestication of this movement by the upper castes and classes reduced much of its social poten-tial and élan. The *Narada Bhaktisutra* of 10 century A.D. stated how God himself is with the lowly:

"Isvarasya dainyapriyatrat abhimanibvesitvat Ca"
(Because God loves the lowly and hates the proud)

Bhakti sings and praises the special love and dilection of Lord Krishna for the most low and socially insignificant *gopis* – milk maids (see Lk 4:18). The Bhakti movement was a religious movement of the people, also because it did not use the classical religious language of Sanskrit, but local languages – Tamil, Bengali, Gujarati etc. – for its religious and devotional expressions. Furthermore, many of the saints of the Bhakti movement, men like Namdev and Turkaram, belonged to the lower castes.

As history and present-day experience show, in many Asian societies, the project of liberation requires a religious, and indeed a popular religious point of refer-ence. This indicates the crucial importance of popular religion for contextual theologizing in Asia. One of the central tasks of Asian theology is to draw upon the popular religious resources, to interpret and re-interpret them, and channel them for liberative practice in Asian societies.

Popular religion and the place of the goddess

One of the most important questions facing humanity today is the issue of the forgotten, neglected and suppressed half – the woman. The wholeness of the human cannot exist without the conscious recovery of the female in all areas and dimensions of human life. There is a reluctance, if not a refusal, to make this recovery because it will challenge the present model of the world and its develop-

16 S.M. Michael, 'The politicization of the Ganapati Festival', in: *Social Compass*, 33(1986), 185-197.
17 See S. Kappen, *Jesus and cultural revolution. An Asian perspective*. Bombay, A Build Publication, 1983, 43ff; W. Fernandez, 'Bhakti and a liberation theology for India', in: Paul Puthanangady (ed.), *Towards an Indian liberation theology*, Bangalore, 1986, 83-108.

ment. The place of woman, the feminine in human and social life is duly recognized when it is rooted in the very conception and approach to the Divine. While the judeo-christian tradition is almost silent with regard to the feminine in its understanding of God, non-christian popular religions, specially hinduism abound in goddesses.[18] This is paradoxical. Hindu tradition has been one of the traditions most oppressive of women, yet it is the same tradition which perhaps offers the most religious potential for the liberation of women.

It is noteworthy that goddesses are most popular with the lowest strata of society. The village deities worshipped are in great part goddesses. In buddhist popular religion, too, we have the popular goddess figure of *Kuan-Yin* who is associated with so many miraculous stories of favours bestowed upon devotees. It is interesting to note that, whereas male deities were connected with other-worldly salvation, almost invariably the devotion to goddesses were centred on this-worldly material benefits. And this explains why goddess worship has been very popular among the marginalized groups.[19]

In popular worship and myths, the goddess is very much connected with liberation. She is the *sakti* – energy, and she struggles with the evil powers, vanquishes them and becomes victorious. In the Tamil story of *Chilapathikaram*, the deified Kannaki is the heroine who confronts the unjust king who executed her innocent husband and destroys the whole city of Madurai by the fire of her holy anger. The goddess Kanaki, also worshipped as Pattini in Sri Lanka – as Gnananath Obeyesekere shows – is a Jain-buddhist goddess later co-opted into hinduism under other names.[20] Long before this story found literary expression, it had been enacted for centuries as a popular drama. What is particularly noteworthy is that the energy and valour held as high values among the Tamils have, in this story, been personified in a woman. Similarly, we have the myth of *Mahisa-Mardana*, connected with popular *Durga* festival.[21] It is the myth of the *devi* – goddess who, mounting a lion, in a fierce battle conquers the demon in the form of bufallo who causes evil both in the world of gods and men. From the Japanese world we may cite here the popular goddess *Amaterasu*, symbol of energy and valour, whose worship was latter monopolized by the imperial power.

The goddesses of popular religion often represent a *coincidencia oppositorum*: on the one hand, the goddess is the giver of life, bestower of gifts, the nurturing

---

18 See R.M. Gross, 'Hindu female deities, as a resource for the contemporary rediscovery of the Goddess', in: Carl Olson (ed.), *The Book of Goddess. Past and present. An introduction to her religion*, New York, Cross Road, 1985, 217-229.
19 See S.M. Bhardwaj, *Hindu places of pilgrimage in India*, Berkeley, 1975. "The scheduled castes pilgrim distinctly favour the Modern Goddess shrines, especially where animal sacrifices can be performed" (227).
20 G. Obeysesekere, *The cult of the goddess Pattini*, Chicago-London, 1984, 509-618.
21 Subash Anand, 'Mahisa-Mardana. A myth of holistic liberation', in: *Towards an Indian theology of liberation, o.c.,* 66-87.

mother. On the other hand, she is the black, terrifying, gruesome and blood-thirsty warrior and destroyer.[22] Both these apparently contradictory aspects are symbolized in one of the most popular goddesses of hinduism – *Kali*. Ultimately strength and beauty are not opposites, nor does the nurturing and mothering aspect contradict that of an energetic and fighting woman. On the contrary, the destruction of evil and injustice which calls for energy and fortitude is part and parcel of the protective and caring aspect.

The popular worship, festivals and myths centred around goddesses are a strong stimulus for Asian contextual theologizing. I see the significance of this aspect of popular religion in three areas: 1) The oppression of women is something pervasive all over Asia – in China, India, Japan, Korea etc. – both in the past and in the present. Contextual theological reflection oriented towards the liberation of women can derive much from the goddesses of Asian popular religions. 2) It is a fact that the language of human dignity and human rights (not its content) do not vibrate with the mood, ethos and psychological make-up of the Asian peoples who find in the liberation stories connected with the goddesses a powerful inspiration for historical commitment, justice and liberation. Therefore, in an Asian theology of liberation, the goddess figure will occupy a significant place. 3) Finally, the popular worship of the goddess poses a great challenge to the traditional understanding of God in our theology. If the human reality has two fundamental and inalienable poles – the male and the female, the *yin* and *yang* – could our conception of the Divine be reduced to one pole, the male figure of God, without basically distorting the concept of God who created Adam in his own likeness and image – male and female he created them?

Conclusion

Seen from the Asian perspective, popular religion and its recourses are not a matter of the past; it is not a question of recovering the roots and drawing from the past. It is a matter of *awareness* – awareness of a dimension of religiosity which is alive and present. If I do everything with my left hand and for a long time have not used my right hand, and then suddenly become aware of the unused hand, I am not recovering anything past; so is it with popular religiosity. It is a *present* experience and reality to which we and our theology should awake in Asia. The Asian popular religions should be understood on their own ground and in relation to the society in which they flourish. They represent a great potential for contextual theologizing. Popular religion is a religion of experience – *anubhava*, the beginning and foundation of all Asian theologizing. The theological language which popular religions dictate to us is not that of *logos* but that of *mythos* – language of symbols where the subject-object polarity is transcended. Popular religion opens up the avenue for an existential and experiential theology

---

22 R.M. Gross, 'Hindu female deities', *a.c.*

156

of religion and dialogue, and enables the creation of community across conventional religious and social frontiers. Certain limitations notwithstanding, popular religious expressions and movements have been a force for the liberation of the marginalized in Asian societies and, as such, they offer very pertinent elements for a contextual Asian theology of liberation. The significant place which Asian popular religions give to the goddess is a source for the liberation of women in Asian societies, as well as a stimulus for a reconceptualization the traditional image of God.

Finally, from the Asian experience and perspective, it looks more and more important that the followers of various faiths participate mutually in each other's popular religious manifestations, leading to the creation of true fellowship and community on the basis of what each one lives and hold most sacred. Such a sharing should be possible without being unfaithful to one's faith, given the polyvalent and multi-dimensional nature of religious symbols open to various levels of interpretation – interior, exterior, cosmic, ontological, individual and communitarian.

The strength of popular faith in the Chinese catholic church today

Jeroom Heyndrickx, Belgium

When discussing the situation of the catholic church in China I have, in my own evaluation, always stressed two points, namely: that there is only one catholic church, even if this church is internally very divided, and that the recent developments now, for the first time in history, show us the emergence of a truly Chinese indigenous catholic local church.

If the evolution of recent years continues, the danger of a formal division inside the catholic Chinese church becomes more and more threatening. There is, on the one side, the officially established Catholic Patriotic Association and the bishops appointed and consecrated by it without the agreement of the Holy See. They indeed are the ones officially recognized by the Chinese government; they are the official hierarchy in China. They are in the process of officially and openly recognizing the catholic church in China: by trying (with much difficulty) to get back the church properties, by opening churches, convents and seminaries. Many catholics attend the services led by them. Among those catholics one finds a large majority (I estimate at least 90% of these CCPA members) of very faithful people who try to make the best of their situation for the church. They try to keep the church alive in their socialist country. They insist that "what is of Caesar must be given to Caesar; what is of God must be given to God". Their faithfulness also includes faithfulness to the universal church through the Holy See. Only a very small group among them remains unclear about this point. Some individual leaders even seem to be opposed to unity with Rome. It is because of the open and public statements of these few, critical CCPA leaders that a great group of catholics turned against the whole CCPA and organized themselves into the "underground catholic group". They insist that there are two churches.

The so-called "underground bishops, priests and catholics" are the ones who refuse any collaboration with the CCPA bishops or with the official Bureau of Religious Affairs. They have all suffered much for their faith in the past and lost their trust in the government and in those who collaborate with the government. Any collaboration with the officially established CCPA group is branded by them as "working with the devil". They admit of no middle road. Their refusal to cooperate or even to dialogue with the CCPA members – until now at least – causes the total "impasse" in which the church finds itself today. And to the extent that underground bishops and priests have significantly increased in numbers over the past five years, they feel that they are strong and can succeed in drawing away from the official CCPA group a number of catholics who joined the "underground". This internal conflict has now grown to such a proportion that the situation is critical. Chances of a split are now very real. The underground group often clearly opposes any form of socialism which, in turn, gives the government a reason to consider them as "enemies of the country" and arrest their leaders.

The point I wish to bring out in this short lecture is that, in my view, the strength of the Chinese church lies in the faith of the catholic flock. Their faith is traditional, and in many ways mixed with folk devotion, pilgrimages, etc. It is striking how much attention is paid to miracles, apparitions, etc. These and other practices of folk religion which have penetrated church life, are like ways in which the faithful seek strength and affirmation to confirm that the road they walk is the right one; defence mechanisms against the unclear guidance and teaching of some of their own church leaders. Whatever pressure is brought to bear upon them from the "official side" – be it from church officials or government officials – the faith of the Chinese catholics as a group is solid. True, they are now divided because some of the leaders have misled them by a catechetical teaching which was often mixed with politics. Catholics have read those signals and interpreted them in different ways. Hence the "division" into the official, open group and the "underground group". The main hope and the saving factor that can help the church out of this impasse lies in the genuine faith of the flock. Catholic church history in China also proves this.

The history of the Chinese catholic church shows that the faithful have, on several occasions, had to deal with very confusing situations, with pressure from officials, persecutions, etc. But the flock, as such, was able to resist and overcome it all. Little research has been done on christianity as folk religion in China (except some studies by Dr. Robert Entenman – which I use here below – and Dr. Dan Bays). Their research reveals to us a true christian faith expressed in a Chinese christian folk religion that was perhaps more "inculturated" than we have been ready to believe.

Catholics in Sichuan in the eighteenth century[1]

In 1798, a eminent scholar and official warned that the people of Sichuan and Hupei were being led astray by heterodox religions – the White Lotus, the Eight Trigrams, and the Lord of Heaven sects. The religion of the Lord of Heaven was the Chinese name for christianity in its roman catholic form. Between 1724 and 1860 christianity was illegal and was perceived as subversive in China. In many ways it resembled the indigenous heterodox folk religions such as the White Lotus sect. Members of each formed tight-knit communities with a sense of common identity and fate, ever wary of the threat of persecution.

---

1 See R. Entenmann's paper 'Clandestine catholics and the state in eighteenth-century Sichuan', presented in Taiwan in 1968 at a symposium on church and state in China.

Catholicism and the White Lotus sects were successful proselytizing religions, enjoying rapid expansion in Sichuan in the second half of the eighteenth century. The growth of the catholic church was particulary remarkable, since the number of catholics in China as a whole declined during the eighteenth century. In Sichuan the church grew tenfold from 1750 to 1800, despite its insecure and underground existence. This growth took place, in part, because the authorities increasingly distinguished catholics from followers of other "heterodox" and illegal popular religions. By the end of the century the church enjoyed a degree of tacit toleration.

Settlers, as well as natives, tried to make their lives more secure by relying on groups and institutions that offered mutual support, protection and organization. Often family ties were at the core of these. Religious organizations also provided people with mutual aid, companionship, a sense of community, and spiritual solace. Here the catholic church, as well as the White Lotus sects, played an important role. They provided an alternative society, and their explanations of the world proved more appealing than that provided by Confucian orthodoxy.

Most catholics lived in small tight-knit communities, known as *chrétientés*. Most consisted of sixty to eighty people. Catholic communities were concentrated in several areas: the Chengtu Plain, the Chungking area, around Anyueh in Central Sichuan, around Chiating and Hsuchou in the south, and around Kuangyang in the north. There were surprisingly few catholics in the major cities, probably because the authorities would not tolerate a visible catholic presence in these administrative centres. Chengtu, the largest city, had no more than fifty catholics in 1760.

Most of the *chrétientés* were small hamlets. Because they were scattered over a large area, priests had to travel almost continuously to serve them. Even after the number of priests increased later in the century, it was impossible for them to visit each community often. The priest would interview the catechumens, baptize those ready for baptism, visit the sick, and celebrate mass – often at night to avoid detection.

In the absence of priests, the day-to-day leadership in these communities devolved upon lay leaders. A *chrétienté* would elect a *hui-chang* ("head of the congregation"), who would be vested with authority by the priest. He would be put in charge of religious instruction and assumed the leadership of the community during the absence of the priestm – in other words, almost all the time in most cases. He conducted church services, prepared the sick for death, and made reports to the priest when he came.

There was also an organization of women who had taken vows of celibacy. Their duty was to instruct the young, train catechumens for baptism, and baptize dying infants.

Lay catholics played a mayor role in proselytization. Catholic families who moved into a new area sometimes spread the faith to their neighbours. Lay catholics not only sought converts but often baptized them as well.

Catholic lay evangelism may have drawn upon the example of White Lotus teachers, especially in faith healing, a strong tradition in the White Lotus sects. Catholics also used healing as a means of spreading their religion, often gaining access to sick infants because of their knowledge of medicine. The infants were baptized and, if they survived, the family often converted. Priests sometimes practised medicine as well.

By the end of the eighteenth century catholicism in Sichuan was in many ways a Chinese popular religion. Christian communities relied on Chinese leadership, both lay and clergy; by 1800 most of the priests in the province were Chinese. (This was not true elsewhere in China).

Christianity and folk religion in China[2]

One aspect with regard to the nature of rural christianity that needs to be mentioned is the tendency towards syncretism in a few village groups. One is reminded of the ambiguous relationship of christianity to the White Lotus in the last century. It is quite possible for some christians to move in the direction of traditional pattern of rural dissent or to incorporate aspects of Chinese folk religion into their religious practices.

There is little doubt that faith healing and exorcism are two areas where Chinese christianity, especially in the countryside, is directly related to traditional concern within Chinese folk religion. Government officials are likely to view faith healing and exorcism as verging on "superstitious" practices, but in fact in the context of a society in which possession by spirits is widely accepted as a valid understanding of mental and even physical sickness, a christian approach can be truly liberating, removing the fear that can dominate the daily routine of people's life. Chinese traditional medicine is itself holistic, and, freed of the element of fear and exploitation, is able to make an invaluable contribution to world medicine.

Faith healing and exorcism formed an important aspect of christian life in the past. The usual practice was for local congregations to pray for people, sometimes with them present, and for the sick person and a relative to live in the church for several months.

It may well be that for many rural people their first experience of the church will be as a result of a desire for healing or exorcism. Faith healing has played an important part in the growth in the number of christians. Folk religion exercises a profound influence and demon possession is felt to be a reality. In this situation christianity offers freedom of mind and body to people seeking to escape from the financial and spiritual burdens imposed by many of the practices of Chinese popular religion.

---

2 See B. Whyte, *Unfinished encounter. China and christianity*, London, Fount paperbacks, 1988, 410-414.

Christianity can also be seen as a progressive force in traditional rural communities in a situation of rapid social and economic change. Faith healing and exorcism in themselves tell us little about the quality of christian life. Christian communities that are dominated by a concern with healing may succeed in converting many people, but their faith will be distorted so that ultimately there is a real danger of them being absorbed back into the traditional rural culture from which they emerged. A true ministry of healing and reconciliation within rural society can indeed be a powerful force for good, and in its own way may open up another channel through which christianity can deepen its encounter with the riches and wisdom of Chinese tradition.

Catholic life in China today[3]

The controversy with Rome has affected the internal development of church life, but it would be quite wrong to draw the conclusion that the issue has dominated the lives of ordinary believers. Reports from many different parts of China relate that catholic life is flourishing in spite of a shortage of priests, a lack of buildings and religious materials. An urgent task has been the restructuring of the 147 previous diocesan units, many of which were established in relation to former missionary patterns of work, and, in any case, frequently no longer conform to administrative boundaries.

Sichuan was reported as having 300.000 catholics in 1985 compared to fewer than 200.000 in 1949. Sichuan's growth and reordering is but one example of the process of renewal that has been under way since 1980.

Inner Mongolia, formerly with five dioceses, now has one under Bishop Wang Xueming. In 1983 this diocese had ninety-six priests, thirty churches and 160.000 catholics. The revival of catholic life is well reflected in this huge and sparsely populated Autonomous Region. In Quahar Right Wing Front Banner in Meigui Cathedral during Bishop Wang's visit in May 1983, five thousand people attended; in nearby Liancheng three thousand attended. Altogether 3.477 people from the area were confirmed. At the re-opening of the church in Siziwang over five thousand people were present. On a visit to Tuquan Country, in the far east of the Region, Father Tian Weiyung married twelve couples, give extreme unction to 208 people, received 113 converts into the church, confirmed 1,284 and give first communion to 1,167. Altogether he said ninety-six masses attended by a total of 46,984 people.

Similar reports came from Chifeng City in Zhaomeng, an area incorporated into Liaonung during the Cultural Revolution but restored to Inner Mongolia after 1978.

It would be tedious to go on listing figures and details of similar reports, but enough has been said to demonstrate the vitality of local church life. The vast

---

3 See B. White, *o.c.*, 446-453.

majority of catholics still live in rural communities, and because of the foreign missionaries' policy of settling converts in catholic villages, there are many villages where the overwhelming majority of the population are catholic believers. We have noted the phenomenon of the strong catholic tradition amongst the fishing people of the Yangzi Delta who flocked to Sheshan. The non-urban nature of much catholic life is reflected in the fact that the Cathedral in Suzhou diocese is far from the centre of the city. Of the 40.000 catholics in the diocese, half are fishing people. Jiangsu has at least 170.000 catholics, and four dioceses, each with an active bishop. The life of small, compact catholic villages is deeply traditional, but, as with protestant home meetings, there have been problems in some places because of isolation and an absence of priests. On the other hand, the catholic community in parts of China has had a long tradition of survival against the odds, and consequently of lay leadership.

A vivid picture of life in a Shandong village was given by a visiting priests who returned to his family village for a five-month stay in 1981. While the report dates from the early period of catholic reorganization there is no reason to think that attitudes and customs will have changed very much since then. The village of Weijia is about 150 km. east of Jinan, the provincial capital. It has a population of 4.000, of whom 3.750 are catholics. According to the visitor, relations with local officials are relaxed and the village is known throughout the province as a model, with productivity twenty per cent higher than the average. The reasons are similar to those we have found amongst protestant christians – hard work, honesty, community spirit and commitment to the Four Modernizations. The one area of potential conflict with the autorities was attitudes towards family planning. Reports from other catholic villages have suggested strong opposition to the policy.

The catholic community in China is a community still in transition. The Chinese catholic community is now a truly indigenous church, but indigenization does not go far enough. The question facing the catholic church in China is how to relate to contemporary society in an active and not a passive manner.

Concluding remarks

In China there have always been two worlds living next to each other. The world of the intellectuals, officials, mandarins; all those who took part in the official government examinations. They adopted the Confucian tradition, remained closed, and rejected any foreign or new thinking. Then there was the world of the vast majority of the people who proved that they were open to buddhism and – over the ages – other new ideas which they adopted as valuable and enriching: islam, nestorianism, christianity. They suffered persecutions, prejudice and hardships from the continuously changing dynasties and regimes. But no regime was ever able to eradicate them. Quite the opposite. Religions came out of it more strongly than before.

Eighty percent of the Chinese catholics are farmers and fishermen. They are the catholics of Sichuan, Shanghai, Inner Mongolia of whom we spoke above. They are the ones who today fill the churches on Sundays and weekdays. They go on pilgrimage by the thousand; they say their prayers faithfully. Their faith has taken root in their daily life and in their own culture, so it seems, even if the external formula through which they express this faith has not really taken on a Chinese form. Mass, in the majority of Chinese churches, is still being said according to the old rite: hymns as well as readings in Latin, the priest saying Mass facing the altar.

Chinese catholics became christians from a true awareness of their need for salvation. They accepted the christian faith from their hearts, including suffering and the cross. They have, over the years, demonstrated a faithfulness to their conversion. Suffering and persecution in recent years did not change their conviction. They came out of it stronger than before.

Inside the much divided catholic Chinese church community today we find the same faithful among the CCPA flock as well as among the "underground flock". Even though they are internally divided in the interpretation about "collaboration with the government or not", their faith remains the same: traditional, faithful, strong. The few "church officials" who try, or have tried, to lead this flock away from the traditional faith by trying to stir up among them an attitude of rejection of a faith brought to China from abroad are bound to fail. The faith of the masses is stronger. Practices of folk religion, as lived inside christian communities, are often, for them, a way of keeping their strength of faith, a defense mechanism against aggression and pressure brought upon them from above.

In the 16th and 17th centuries Jesuit missionaries made their historic effort towards inculturation by adopting Confucian values and by addressing themselves to the intellectuals and leading classes. It did not succeed, not only because of internal struggles among the missionaries, but also because Chinese scholars, from their Confucian tradition, felt they had no need at all of salvation through the cross. The wisdom of Confucius had brought them salvation already. No need for christian faith for them. They remained impenetrable to this foreign faith. Spreading christian faith among the gentry in China, through the centuries, has therefore not been very successful.

At the same time, other missionaries were living close to the fishermen and farmers. These missionaries refused to follow the direction taken by the Jesuits. What were their motivations? Why did the French missionary Maigrot – who made a thorough study of local folk religion at the time and wrote books about it (which even today remain largely unstudied) – refuse to approve of the direction taken by the Jesuits? Besides the many studies on the Jesuit missionaries, more study needs to be developed on the other missionaries who lived close to the Chinese people in order to understand their view.

Shamanism and minjung theology in South Korea

Edmond Tang, Hong Kong

Popular religions or popular religiosity is becoming more and more a central challenge to the emerging contextual theologies of the world, particularly in the so-called Third World. Theologians there, in their option for the poor, discovered in the poor the tenacity to survive in extremely unfavorable conditions and the ability to create a culture which protected them through generations of external or internal domination. This power to survive, once articulated by a new understanding of history appropriate to their experience, e.g. a theology of liberation, becomes a formidable historical force in determining the shape of society as well as the church. This has been the experience in Latin America and is becoming that of Africa and Asia. As it was aptly put by Gustavo Gutiérrez, Third World theologians are beginning to "drink from our own wells".

This experience is by no means limited to the Third World alone. North American theologians are also discovering the Hispanic, black and feminist subcultures in their societies – although the word "popular" must be used with different connotations here – while ecological theologians turn to the Amer-Indians for a foundation of a new understanding of the world.

In almost all cases, the new awareness did not take place by accident. The contextual theologian starts by a critique of the power-relations in society and in the church, takes an option for the poor and oppressed and starts to search for the gospel message from the underside of history. Invariably he or she begins to discover the rich religious undercurrent among the underdogs of society. The transition is not an intellectual one; from an attitude of suspicion and contempt to that of admiration and identification, the contextual theologian goes through a process that can only be described as a "conversion".

As we survey the emerging theologies of Asia, we can find an abundance of examples. In the Philippines, theologians have attempted to construct a christology in terms of the Black Messiah of the popular Easter rites. Indian theologians have devoted an important amount of research to the popular devotions and processions which have attracted not only christians but hindus to their devotional practices. But it is in the "minjung theology" of South Korea and the "homeland theology" of Taiwan that we find the clearest examples of this shift in theological research.

It could be very interesting to make a comparative study of the latter theologies, since both share similar societal structures, histories of colonization as well as a Presbyterian background. Unfortunately, the present stage of research does not permit such a study beyond general observations. In the following we shall limit ourselves only to the minjung theology which has made a very clear option to build its foundation on the shamanist undercurrent of Korean history.

Theology as socio-biography

As minjung theologians readily admit themselves, no one remembers when the term "minjung theology" was actually used.

"Minjung" is a Korean word which combines two Chines characters "min" and "jung" – "people" and "masses". It is neither "people" as it is used in communist terminology, nor the crowd as the word "masses" suggest. "Minjung" are not only the poor proletariat, but also the oppressed women, the marginalized intellectuals; it can also be the whole people under domination, in short, the poor of history.

Minjung theology is the theological articulation of the political experience and suffering of the poor and oppressed in Korean history. It has been described by its practitioners as a socio-theological biography of the Korean people. This biography is often told in a narrative form, i.e. story-telling, a favorite medium of minjung theologians.

"I would like to tell you the story of the beautiful bell in the National Museum in Kyung ju, capital of the ancient Silla kingdom. At the time of Silla, the country was peaceful, but the devout buddhist king wanted to protect the nation from foreign invasion. The king was advised to build a huge temple bell to show the people's devotion to Buddha.

A specialist in the technology of bell-making, himself a devout buddhist, was given the responsibility. He used great care and all the right methods to cast the bell, but he failed again and again to obtain a bell that gave a beautiful sound when struck. Finally he took his problems to the council of religious leaders who were greatly concerned over this matter of national security.

After long discussion, the council concluded that the best way to give a beautiful tone to the bell was to sacrifice a pure young maiden. Soldiers were sent out to fetch a 'pure young maiden' who would be sacrificed for this worthy cause. They came upon a poor mother in a farm village with her small daughter. They took the child from its mother while the child cried out piteously, 'Emile, Emile!' meaning 'Mother! Oh Mother!'

When the next huge pot of molten lead and iron was prepared for casting the bell, the little girl was thrown into it. At last the bell-maker was successful. The bell, called the Emile Bell, when struck with the gong made a sound so beautiful that no other bell could equal it.

When people heard the beautiful sound of the bell, some gave praise and thanks to the technology and art that was able to cast a bell with such a beautiful sound. But when the mother whose child had been sacrificed to obtain that beautiful sound heard the bell, her heart broke afresh, and her neighbours, who also knew of the sacrifice and of the mother's pain, could not hear the bell's beautiful tone without pain. Only those who understand the sacrifice can feel the pain. Others simply enjoy the sound."[1]

The story was told by Lee Oo-Chung, a former professor of theology at a prestigious university, and at one time president of the association of women theologians. She was forced to resign by the martial law government, after which she went to work with the poor female factory workers and experienced the living emotions of "han", a word meaning the grudge, the profound bitterness of the oppressed. "Han" in the story she told comes from the recess of the heart and goes back down the ages. When martial law was relaxed Lee was offered reinstatement but she rejected the offer, preferring to work in a poor working class parish. It is clear that the ancient story retold is a strong indictment of the government's unjust development policy. The "minjung" is being sacrificed for economic and political goals. It suffices to put it against a more analytic analysis to see the analogy:

"Modern technology in its Korean form, is being experienced as another form of national messianism. There seems to be a conviction that technology and science, organized into the capitalist system, can solved all the human problems of the Korean people; and the political regime integrates and controls all the economic, military and cultural institutions. While doing this, the regime places itself and its authority above law and criticism, and claims the loyalty of the people by emphasizing filial piety, which was formerly a cardinal virtue of Japanese ultranationalism."[2]

The preference for the narrative form of the story lies in its origin in popular Korean literature. Stories like these are told in folk festivals and mask dances, involving the whole local population. Modern "minjung" poets such as Kim Chi Ha, a catholic, also uses traditional song forms in expressing the anguish and bitterness of the people. But for the minjung theologians, the story has a deeper meaning. For them the story is a different way of comprehending reality. The habitual world of false order and propriety is turned upside down by the minjung stories. Secondly, the stories are told with songs and dances, performed by the body in a rapid rhythm. It is felt and experienced before being reflected upon. The story acts and re-enacts. Thirdly, the story is a parable. In the view of a minjung theologian, David Kwang-Sun Suh, "minjung" is the hermeneutical key to the "parable of Jesus" while Jesus is the key to the "parable of the minjung". Minjung theology is then the interaction of two power metaphors, identified and yet distinct, which must produce the dynamic movement towards the Kingdom.[3]

1 Lee Oo-Chung, 'One woman's confession of faith', in: *International Review of Mission* (Geneva), April 1985.
2 Kim Yong-Bock, 'Messiah and minjung. Discerning messianic politics over against political messianism', in: Kim Yong-Bock (ed.), *Minjung theology*, Singapore, Christian Conference of Asia, 1981, 192.
3 D. Kwansg-Sun Suh, 'Theology of story telling. A theology by minjung', in: *Ministerial Formation* (Geneva), September 1985, n.31, 17-18.

In short, minjung theology is the expression of the social biography of the Korean people. The content of this biography may vary according to the character of the ruling regime and power, but it is the biography as seen by the minjung as subjects of their own history.[4] And in adopting the story as their favorite literary medium, minjung theologians tell their own similar histories thereby identifying their own biographies with that of the minjung.

Minjung theology as critique of culture

There is no better way to illustrate the coming together of the two histories, that of minjung and that of the minjung theologian than to follow the spiritual journey of one of its exponents, David Kwang-Sun Suh. Suh was a professor of theology and the dean of the College of Liberal Arts and Sciences at the prestigious Ewha Women's University at the time when he was arrested in 1980. "I was in the middle of a faculty meeting when a man from the Joint Investigation Head-quarters called and asked me to meet him at a nearby tea-house. I was supposed to be frightened by the call."[5]

At the interrogation centre, the first thing Suh was asked to do was write his autobiography, a common interrogation technique. He was asked to write about his family, his parents, his school, his education, the books he read and the friends he frequented, not overlooking anything. He understood this confession he was to write as "the story of Korean minjung people – my socio-political and theological biography".[6] Later on in the same centre he was to meet other christian professors and friends going through the same fate.

Suh was a scholar who trained first in Anglo-Saxon philosophy, and later special-ized in Paul Tillich in his doctoral studies in America. In 1969 he returned to S. Korea to teach at Ewha Women's University. The student world of the late 1960s in Korea was a volatile one. There were violent protests against Park Chung Hee's measures to change the Constitution so that he could run for a third term and extend his dictatorial reign. The student movement that Suh discovered was a well developed political force. This has been the historical tradition in Korean society. Already in the old kingdom, students were known for criticizing royal policies despite the danger of persecution. In more recent history, students were in the forefront of all national independence or democratic movements. They revolted against the Japanese in the 1920s, brought down the government of Syngman Rhee in 1960, and now they rose up again when the Park government trampled on democracy.

The students were socially involved as well, working in the villages and slum areas, and they applied their knowledge to study the sufferings of the people in

---

4 Kim Yong-Bock, 'Theology and the social biography of the minjung', in: *CTC Bulletin* (Singa-pore), 5(1984), n.3 ; 6(1984), n.1, 66-78.
5 D. Kwang-Sun Suh, *Theology, ideology and culture*, Hong Kong, World Student Christian Federation, 1983, 9.
6 *Ibid.*, 11.

the process of industrialization and modernization. The students went into the factories, into the countryside living with the workers and peasants in an effort to identify themselves with the underdogs of Korean society.

An important discovery by the students and one which affected Suh greatly was the strength of the culture of the people, especially the shamanist rituals and mask dances at village festivals. Shamanism has always been an undercurrent of Korean culture, shaped by the long history of oppression and foreign domination. They ridicule the rulers and mock at their own powerlessness. Through trance-like states and incantations, the "crowd" was brought through an oscillation of frenzy states and passive sadness, reflecting the people's inner depression and violence. Students learned the spirit of these rituals and performed them in the public places with new political themes. Thus the rituals and mask dances have provided a new sense of identity to the students as well as a new tool of political struggle.
Through all this, Korean christians like Suh became more and more conscious of their historical roots and their theological outlook changed. As Suh explained: "All the theological questions of the 1960s – the indigenization of christianity, the problem of text and context, and the issue of demythologization and the interpretation of the biblical language – all turned around to discover the language of the liberating gospel in the dance and plays. Korean christians found their own stories to tell alongside the stories of the Bible, the stories of a liberating Jesus and the christian gospel".[7]

For Suh, minjung theology is more than a political theology. It addresses itself not only to politics but to the whole history, religion and culture of the Korean people. In this sense it is a cultural theology, not in the style of Paul Tillich whom Suh had studied. Tillich's cultural theology was a response to a Western and aristocratic form of culture and Tillich's method of correlation presupposes a christian stance over against a given culture. "Korean cultural theology is a christian response within the culture, right in the middle of and at the centre of the culture of minjung".[8]

Minjung and shamanism

Why does shamanism exerts such a fascination for the minjung theologians? To answer the question it is necessary to take a brief look at the place of shamanism in Korean history and society.
It has said that Korea has a three-tier culture: a confucian head, a buddhist heart and a shaman stomach. Buddhism was introduced into Korea in the Koryo dynasty (918-1392) but was supplanted by Confucianism during the Yi dynasty (1392-1910). If buddhism remains the major organized religion in Korea, it is

---

7 *Ibid.*, 24.
8 *Ibid.*

Confucian values which have given shape to the social and political system for the last seven centuries.

The ruling elite has always despised the folk beliefs of Korean shamanism and tried to suppress its practice, as was the case under the Yi dynasty, the colonial powers of Japan and the modern Korean governments. In 1394 shamans were expelled from the Korean capital and forbidden entrance. In 1413 the government ordered all shamanist books to be burned. But shamanism, which is so well rooted in the social and religious life of the people could not be easily eradicated. Even the royal court continued to consult shamans and were publicly criticized by the Confucian officials.[9] Yet scholars of religion continue to observe that shamanistic practices remain very widespread among the population.[10] In times of sickness, ill-fortune or death, the shaman is always present. Although not recognized officially as a religion, shamanism remains the most prevalent religiosity in Korea. A 1972 survey estimated that there is one shamanist priest or priestess for every 314 inhabitants. In contrast there is only one protestant minister per thousand people and the ratio for buddhist monks is even less.

The culture of the minjung and especially Korean shamanism was discovered by the minjung theologians in captivity. In the late 1960s and early 70s many of them were imprisoned or expelled from their academic positions. In their forced exile they poured their energies into the study of Korean history and society, and given their own situation of oppression they paid particular attention to the undercurrents of Korean history. They searched not only for the causes of the ills of present-day society, but also for an original Korea before the arrival of buddhism, confucianism, Japanese colonization and liberal capitalism. They were looking for the soul of Korea.

A typical shamanist ritual, the *kut*, consists basically of the muga or ritual chant, dances and implorations to the gods performed by the *mudang*, the shaman priestess, to heal a sickness, to guide the deceased to a benevolent rest, to ask for good fortune or for protection of the village. During a *kut* there is chanting, dancing, drumming to a frenzied rhythm to induce the gods and spirits of the ancestors to provide blessings for the living.

For the minjung theologian, the "*mudang* religion" is the religion of the minjung's "*han*". When the people come to the *mudang* they are exorcised, their bitterness released, their grief consoled. It is the religion of the oppressed because they have no other place to turn to. Their sufferings cannot find justification in the dominant religions and philosophies or in the market economy of today.

Psychological studies of the *mudang* religion of Korea have shown clearly that the mudang kut is a dramatic process of counselling. Projection, catharsis, transference, consolation, admonition, release or salvation – all these steps and pro-

---

9 Li Ogg, "Les religions de la Corée", in: Henri-Charles Peuch (ed.), *Histoire des religions*, Tome III, Paris, Gallimard, 1976.
10 C. Osgood, *The Koreans and their culture*, 10th edition, Tokyo, 1965.

cesses are present. Projection and the power of suggestion call forth excuses or reasons for a woman's illness and misfortune. Her misfortune is projected out of herself. It is not her fault; it is because the dead ancestors' spirits are bothering her worldly affairs. Since her misfortune is the result of the doings of the spirits of her dead ancestors, she can talk about it. That is, she can talk about her han-ridden, unfortunate life. This desensitizes her guilt feelings through the above action by means of the *mudang's* trance, talking with the dead parents and explaining away her worries. And she will have a catharsis. She can cry out loud. And through her tears, laughter, rage and expressed frustration, she will relieve pent up emotions and *han*, the unexpressed and unresolved resentment. She reveals all her *han* to the *mudang*. It is a common thing to see – during the *mudang* dance – a daughter-in-law beating her mother-in-law, or the lady sponsoring the *kut* beating the *mudang*.[11]

Such experiences suggest an escape from the world of suffering into the world of gods and spirits, and shamanism can be criticized for being a religion which continue to submit the oppressed to their fate. Yet it is precisely this religion which has enabled them to endure their hardships and survive their fate.

The fascination of minjung theologians for shamanism is to be found in the latter's tenacity throughout Korean history. Denied civil rights, without education or any form of power, shamans have been related to the lowest classes of the Korean society. Yet they were able to maintain their traditions and practices up to present day Korea. In many ways the story of Korean shamanism parallels the story of the Korean people's domination in history. In their days of exile and imprisonment, the minjung theologians have gone through the same experiences of catharsis and discovered the shamanism in themselves.

Called to be a priest of "han"

"In this historical situation, what does it mean to be called to the *missio dei* to witness to the gospel faithfully? Sometimes I am misunderstood as calling *only* for the prophetic role of the church. I am not. I am also requesting that you do not give up the priestly role of the church.... Truly, it is the job of the priests to take care of the wounds of the minjung and enable them to restore their self-respect and courage, and to respond to their historical aspirations. This is to resolve their han. This is to comfort the han-ridden hearts of the people. I am suggesting that you become the priests of han."[12]

The christian, including the christian theologian, is called to be a *mudang*, the shaman woman who understands, consoles and heals. This is possible only

---

11 D. Kwang-Sun Suh, *o.c.*, 44.
12 Suh Nam-dong, 'In search of minjung theology', 1983, in Korean, translated and quoted by David Kwang-Sun Suh in: 'Called to witness to the gospel today. The priesthood of han', in: *CTC Bulletin* (Singapore), 5(1984), n.3; 6(1985), n.1, 66-78.

because the shaman woman belongs to the same class of the oppressed and share their helplessness. The *mudang* was once "sick with the spirit" which others treat as a mental illness. But she has overcome and transcended her "sickness" and is therefore able to understand, assume and resolve the sufferings and bitterness of her clients. "The *mudang* is full of *jung* (heart-warm feeling). Han can be resolved only through the *jung* of others. And when *han* is resolved, the feeling of *jung* is created between persons. And when *han* is resolved, the feeling of *jung* is created between persons. A person's *han* being resolved, he or she can live in this terrifying world with the warm feeling of *jung* in the family and among the people of his society."[13]

The first task of the christian theologian is to articulate the cries and groans of the people in their sufferings. To realize this task Korean christians bring with them a long tradition of social involvement and anti-colonialist struggle. The extent of christian involvement can be seen from the number of christians arrested in the independence movement of 1919. Among the 19,000 persons arrested, more than 3,000 were christians. During the martial law period under Park Chung-Hee the churches were in the forefront of the pro-democracy movement and the list of church leaders, both catholic and protestant, arrested makes an impressive list.

In the midst of political turmoil and violent oppression shamanism and social involvement came together. Historical pessimism and millenarian hope shared the same breeding ground. Today the "priests of *han*" are re-interpreting the history of Korea in interaction with a re-reading of the christian gospel. Whether it will move beyond the present stage to create an alternative but realizable vision of society remains to be seen. Certain hints are already being given by minjung theologians such as Kim Yong-bock who emphasizes the communitarian character of this theology.

In reflecting on the role of story-telling in building communities, he said:

"(The story) mediates between past experiences and the present in order to create a new future. It transmits the experience of one community to another, enabling both to share and to be reciprocally transformed into new communities. The story is a synchronic discourse, a synthetic scenario of the community – a drama sequence. One story is interwoven with another. The story is community-creating communication."[14]

Some observations

Minjung theology is a specific form of theological reflection which grew out of Korean politics in the 1970s, more specifically out of the milieu of student activism. It is both a theology of protest and a theology of popular religiosity as

---

13 D. Kwang-Sun Suh, *o.c.*, 46.
14 Kim Yong-Bock, 'Minjung social biography and theology', in: *Ching Feng* (Hong Kong), December 1985, 222.

expressed in Korean cultural forms. There is no consensus about how widespread this form of theological reflection is in Korea itself outside the intellectual and student circles, but there is no doubt about its distinctive character and its growing influence among other Asian and African theologians.

Several remarks and questions, however, could be made, not as criticisms but as points for a continuing dialogue:

The first concerns the interpretation of shamanism itself. Some basic differences exist between the view of Korean anthropologists and the minjung theologians. Although both agree on the widespread influence of shamanist practices, minjung theologians tend to overestimate the strength of shamanism as a social and historical force. Scholars such as Yim Suk-Jay have observed that with the collapse of the confucian system and the introduction of modern economic forces the social role of shamanism has been greatly reduced. Many shamanist priests are abandoning their practices to take up new jobs. To find an authentic shaman women one has to look in the age range above fifty years. Their number is diminishing, which was the difficulty Kim encountered in his research.[15]
Kim also differs from the minjung theologians in their description of the trance-state of most *mudangs*. While some trance-states are authentic, most are simulations. Kim also observes that the *mudang* as a medium of the spirits is limited to the Seoul and P'yong-yang area and not in the other parts of Korea.[16]

One cannot but ask the second question: if the minjung theologians have been inspired by the history of shamanism in Korea, to the extent that they have assumed the role of a christian *mudang*, what has been the interaction between these theologians and the original shamanist communities? Where have been concrete interaction between the "parable of the minjung" and the "parable of Jesus"? Are their efforts only limited to a simulation and transfer to an urban student milieu?
This last question may not be a fair one. Minjung theologians have always assumed the sufferings of the Korean people as a whole, and their witness as "priests of *han*" is a noble one. The question of effectiveness and nobility of purpose should be distinguished.

A third and important question is the compatibility of shamanism as a religion with a linear model of development in history. The strength of folk religions is their "timelessness" in which humans can interact with gods and spirits, and the transient sufferings can be identified with a timeless one to be absorbed and resolved. There is no doubt that the "parable of Jesus" will unlock the centuries of suffering and anger of the minjung and become a formidable historical force for change. In the process shamanism will also be fundamentally changed once

---

15 Kim Suk-Jay, 'Introduction au mouïsme', in: *Social Compass*, 25(1978), n.2, 189.
16 *Ibid*, 185.

the sense of history is introduced and concrete projects can be actualized. Will Korean shamanism still retain its fundamental characteristics and not dissolve in the linear, revolutionary change? Will a theology based on "resistance" and "resilience" in traditional societies be able to accommodate and transform a technological culture which is becoming more and more prevalent?

A final question concerns the shamanistic character of Korean christianity itself. To what extent is the rapid growth of Korean churches related to the shamanistic base in the Korean national character, see the enthusiastic response to the charismatic groups. This phenomenon has yet to be studied especially in the light of the rapid expansion of the new religions in Korea, such as the Unification Church and the Full Gospel Central Church which are very much dependent on a charismatic leadership. These new religions, no doubt a response to the fast mutations of society, are characterized by their conservative social and political ideologies. In this sense the minjung territory is not neutral, and a minjung theology is working not only against oppressive governments and structures, but against the fetishes of the minjung culture itself. More research and reflection in this area seems necessary.

PART IV

EASTERN EUROPE

Theology and liberation in the context of Czechoslovakia today

Libor Ovečka and Mireille Ryšková, Czechoslovakia

Czechoslovakia has traditionally been a strongly religious, mostly catholic, country. In 1948, nevertheless, all political power was seized by the Communist Party which exerted all its power to subdue fully all the elements of social life. It viewed the catholic church, as well as other social forces, mostly or even exclusively from the point of view of power and politics. It considered the church a political force threatening its monopoly of power, and the last and most dangerous enemy of the regime. It was therefore necessary for this "power" of the church, although predominantly a "power" of a spiritual nature, to be destroyed. Any means could be used to achieve this. These consisted of political and administrative measures, and also included the worst violence. Generally the measures were illegal.

Tens of thousands of believers were persecuted for professing their faith or for defending human rights. Some were tortured to death, thousands were imprisoned or held without trial in special labour units of the Army, or interned. They were, especially, believers active in the field of religion, members of religious orders, both male and female, priests, and practically all the bishops. Others were sacked from their jobs or expelled from schools, interrogated and shadowed by the police, their homes were searched, their telephones and flats bugged, their private correspondence was checked, they were intimidated and blackmailed. And all were exposed to massive atheistic propaganda which, for generations presented lies as truth, and was forced on everyone, including small children. More than any other group of the population, with the exception perhaps of purely political cases, the believers were denied, on ideological grounds, human and civil rights guaranteed them by law.

The whole life and activity of the church were seriously damaged, but the communist leadership of the state did not achieve its main goal – to create a split between the Vatican and the church in our country, to transform it into an independent national church, to exploit it for its own purposes and gradually to destroy it. This was prevented by the opposition and readiness to bear suffering of both the clergy and the lay people.

The marxist-leninist system

Severe as the external oppression of the whole society, including the church, was, it was far from the worst aspect of what the marxist-leninist system inflicted upon the society. Spiritual oppression and violence went much deeper. While pretending to build and guarantee happiness and wellbeing for all, communism strives for total materialization of human existence and seeks to eradicate the real self, the true being; it seeks the liquidation of the transcendental dimension of life and being, of everything that transcends the immediate here and now. Spirituality is prohibited, because it is essentially free, it cannot be controlled by administative or other means, and in this way it eludes totalitarian rule.

The affinity between people and transcendent, absolute values is intentionally and systematically suppressed in the name of the so-called scientific worldview. This worldview bears many features of some of the reductive streams of modern science which are destroying the "natural world" of human beings in the name of the ideal of verifiable objective truth. They reject everything that transcends the horizon of this kind of science; they kill God, and proclaim themselves the rulers, holding in their hands nature and the whole order of being. This kind of science, reduced and reducing, makes itself the only lawful possessor of all relevant truth, because it elevates itself above all subjective truths and is itself ultrasubjective and ultrapersonal, objective and universal. The power of this science, under the guidance of the Communist Party, will, of historical necessity, create a paradise on earth.

The omnipotent God is replaced by the omnipotent human power. But there is something in the communist regime which stands above even this materialistic god. And this something is the Party (the attribute "communist" is no longer needed, as the Party is absolute) and those who rule over the Party and through the Party, and its, or better their, ideology. In the interest of the so-called objectivity and historical necessity, which is in fact only a smoke screen for the arbitrary interests of the Party or personal power violating even science and natural cognition, the Party claims power over everything, including "objective reality" and the "objective truth", and the most secret corners of human conscience. It is the Party which decides what is true and what is not, what is good and evil, right and wrong, moral and immoral. The scientific fiction of pure objectivity, the abstract, purely rational concept of the world in which everything is calculable and technically accessible, which is controlled by historical necessity and in which it is possible to calculate scientifically, to programme and produce happiness for all, but in which there is no longer a place for the individual (not to mention God) – this fiction is overcome in communist ideology even before it can be sighted from afar in the limping communist economy. What is objective and where scientific truths lie is decided by the Party administration.

People, who are reduced to workers in the socialist system and who have the value of a productive unit, must be deprived of all the remnants of their own freedom and morality. These are taken over by the Party in the interest of achieving those goals, deemed objectively necessary.
The oppression and violence of a spiritual nature, justified by the ideology of the Party – which means the ideology of some powers within the Party – were

supposed to deprive people of more than their property, economic initiatives, culture, environment, human rights, outer freedom. They were supposed to deprive them of their inner freedom, their spirit, their souls, of their very lives. If this goal was to be reached, the destruction of the church and the eradication of christianity was unavoidable – as opponents with whom it was impossible to reach a compromise and agreement.

The life of the church

During the 40 years of oppression, religious life did not, of course, stop and die. All the time it was looking for, and finding, new forms which could escape state supervision and suppression, though they were considered illegal and were persecuted.

What was highly significant for the life of the church under the conditions of state oppression was a movement growing from below, from individual, committed christians and small communities, and strong interpersonal bonds – because every single individual and his/her faith, hope, love and courage, was most important. This wide commitment and movement from below were made possible by the fact that some groups of christians, especially the younger ones, consciously oriented their lives towards spiritual values, lived from vivid faith, and at the same time were active in the social sphere. They contributed to the growth of the activity of the whole church community, including the hierarchy (!), and in fact of the whole nation. Thanks to this, the church became a prominent spiritual force whose impact was growing all the time, transcending the boundaries of religious life in the narrow sense. For long the church was almost the only legal territory offering some space for free thinking in opposition to the power of the state; by its clear and uncompromising moral attitude it was a counterbalance to the state establishment.

Among the mass demonstrations which aroused the consciousness of our nation in recent years, religious gatherings were highly significant. Naturally they had their spiritual content, but at the same time they were an expression of protest against the regime, and a demand for freedom – not only religious freedom, but also general civil freedom. In recent years especially a major trend began to appear and to grow even in the official church documents in our country: the commitment of the church and the believers to the cause and to the interests of society as a whole. In this way the church gradually liberated itself from the ghetto of isolation and retreat, partly inherited from its own past and maintained for various reasons, including state oppression and its violent exclusion from the life of society.

The post marked expression of this attitude of the church was the address by Cardinal Tomášek to all the people of Czechoslovakia on 21st November 1989, an intervention in a dramatic situation when hundreds of thousands of people in

Prague and other cities of our country were demonstrating daily against the totalitarian regime. Cardinal Tomášek joined his voice to theirs and called for a democratic government in the interest of justice for all. And to the catholics he remarked: "In this decisive moment of our history none of you is allowed to stay outside. ... The right to faith cannot be separated from other democratic rights. Freedom is indivisible."

In this revolutionary proclamation the social commitment of the church and its opening to the world attained a new level. The freedom which we receive from Christ becomes manifest as a source of liberation for the whole of society, for both believers and unbelievers, in different spheres of our life. The Day of Freedom, which came with the events of 17th November 1989 and which had been prepared by the commitment of a larger number of people, including believers, can be also seen as the Day of the Lord, as a day which was a work of God's liberating love, a day when the power of God was revealed.

Theology of liberation

There can be no doubt about the influence of the joyful news of the gospel on the liberation of our nations; on the other hand, however, it has not become so prominent in our country as to be reflected in a theology of liberation. We must also admit that the committed attitude of the christians and of the church capable of influencing social reality has been a recent development. Nor is it a general attitude pervading the whole church in our country, especially not among all the clergy.
If we want to bring freedom to others, we must live this freedom, the freedom of Christ, ourselves, and we must understand our mission to the world. The problem is that this open attitude to the world outside the church encounters many obstacles in our country and it is not a clear and general attitude of the mass of believers, not of the priests and bishops.

Our situation has not, as yet, been sufficiently reflected upon theologically. Therefore no specific theology of liberation could have been worked out. It should be a theology capable of reflecting and inciting liberation, firstly on a spiritual and political level and leading, among other things, to a systematic confrontation with authority – that is, with that authority which is false and unauthentic. This situation is, to a large extent, still with us, despite the fact that political liberation has already been achieved. Therefore the people often need to hear of the liberation from all forms of slavery brought to us by Christ; they first need to be taught real spiritual freedom and the longing for it. And the liberation which must be proclaimed is a liberation of people who are poor and unfree in the spiritual, cultural, social, political sense, not so much in the material, economic sense.

It is also the church which need to go beyond its limited horizons, which needs to break out of the ghetto of self-interest into which it was forced by the external

180

power, as well as by its own inner immaturity. It needs to come to understand the greatness of the mission entrusted to it by God – to bring to Christ's freedom, justice, peace, love to all people. And to do so there where these people are, and in the way in which they need it and which is understandable and acceptable to them. A great task of the christian Good News, religion, theology, the theology of liberation, is therefore to liberate we christians from inner slavery, so that we can get rid of the distorted picture of God, the privatized God, and accept the God of Jesus Christ in order to be able to bring his liberation to others.

The urgency of this task is increased by the fact that social liberation in our country will probably open the door to some problems which we have not known in their acuteness so far, and which the church in other countries has to had to face already. If we want to be able to solve them, we must withstand the ancient temptation of all the strata of the church hierarchy to use religion for founding or strengthening one's power, though it be merely a spiritual power, over the others. Christians, in other words, must want to be servants, not lords; they must search for the truth and must not claim to possess it; they must seek, first of all moral, spiritual, trancendent values. Only then will we, as a church, have something to offer to the world.

Christians did much to contribute to the liberation of our society. But at present it is no longer sufficient if it is only christians, as individuals, who testify to Christ by their courageous attitudes, by their words, and by their work for the realization of true values in our lives in our live, both ecclesiastical and social. The proclamation of Christ's freedom must be a stream flowing from the life and activity of the church as such; it must not only be an activity of individual christians working in secular associations and movements. The church itself, as a community of the people of God, must contribute to the renovation and the formation of civic life in our country. It must carry christian values into society; it must defend truth and justice and oppose lies and injustice. It must do so at all times and in all circumstances, under every regime, in the interest of all people, not merely for its own freedom.

Liberation of theology

The many-sided liberation of society experienced by the whole of Eastern Europe now is firmly linked to a shift of political power. The fall of the communist regimes and the unmasking of their anti-popular, and even criminal, character, also contributes to the liberation of theology in another sense – the liberation from the temptation to cooperate with a marxist-leninist power and ideology, to look for a common path with it, and in this way to become, unknowingly, its instrument, misused for purposes of which theology itself may not know.

Our experience in European socialist countries shows that this kind of cooperation has always led to the misuse of religion for controlling and exploiting the mass of the population in a dictatorial regime. The reason is that the marxist-leninist ideology has always been an ideology in the full sense of the word, an instrument in the hands of the ruling power, for which the question of truth, of justification and legitimacy, of justice and of morality is irrelevant. On the contrary, truth, justice and morality are defined by what benefits the ruling power. Therefore when a marxist-leninist party takes over all the power within a state, it means the end of the legal state, the end of justice and morality, and the beginning of uncontrolled, arbitrary rule and misuse of power by a small group of rulers who use any means, including illegal acts, crimes of any kind and atrocities destroying human dignity and lives to achieve their goals. This at least is our experience with communist rule in Europe. Furthermore, it is also confirmed theoretically in the classic works of the revolution of the revolution of the proletariat, especially Lenin.

Czechoslovakia has now got rid of this communist power. Our country will certainly have to wrestle with many new problems, but they will be problems which will not prevent people from living spiritually. Though we may experience some social insecurity now and we may be forced to change our way of life in some ways which do not please us, we have new access to values that cannot be exchanged for anything.

Theology, which is now beginning to develop freely in our country again, enjoys the environment it needs to develop, as such, a theology of the church which will be the mediator of Christ's liberation to our nations, and in this sense to be a theology of liberation. If it is to be realized, then what we need, in many respects, is a liberation of theology. The conditions necessary for it are created by the fact that it is a theology developing in the situation of liberation.

The "second world" as context for theology

András Máté-Tóth, Hungary

The theologians of liberation developed their reflections and options in relation to the characteristics of the social environment of their particular regions, and, consequently, of the third world. Theologians from the "first world" reacted to this fundamental position of third world theologians with similar reflections on their own context on the social, historical and political level. This theologically reflected contextuality became one of the sources and conditions for the option for the "people of God".

The characteristics of the (real-existing) socialist world, i.e. the "second world", have not been theologically analyzed, a fact, which makes a new kind of option for the churches impossible, or at least difficult. Such an analysis could only be achieved through a collegiality which still has to be brought to life and through the collaboration of "second world theologians".
This article should be seen as a small contribution, like a small stone in a mosaic.

Basic sectors in the second world

1 Communism (socialism) means paradise on earth (!). The reconstruction (normally in a revolutionary way) of all relations of power and of all value-systems of this disastrous world (bourgeois) leads to paradise.
2 The leading group in this reconstruction is the Communist Party, controlling all areas of social and cultural life. The party initially gain the legitimacy to do this thanks to the liberating struggle and then through "democratic" elections.
3 The leading role of the party is visible in society through total control, in the economy through the planned economy, in the substantial questions of life through "clear, scientific answers" and a harsh struggle against religiosity and the church. This kind of use of power (leading to restored and just conditions of life) assumes that this ideal can be achieved through systematic struggle. These ideally accepted conditions will be modified according to the laws of reality.

Communism: a paradise on earth?

Due to the fact that socialism is also, according to the principles of dialectic materialism, the first stage towards communism deficiencies can be laid at the door of this preliminary stage. The conditions of the worldwide economy, weather conditions or similar external circumstances, were continuously used to explain the disillusioning reality.

The party too, used to express selfcriticism, but its own legitimacy and its right to exist were never touched. Any lack of efficiency was blamed not in the basic qualities of the system itself, but on insufficient commitment on the part of the partymembers.

Total supervision and direct interference was exchanged for "pax Kadariensis", bringing prosperity in all spheres of life. Later on it demanded a high price, because only parts of it, not the whole system, was reformed.

Characteristics of the "second society"

The period of these "Quasi" facilities the so-called "shadow society" or second society developed in the socialist countries. But the "Order" has its loopholes. In using them, intellectuals, for the first time, proposed a different form of social collaboration, corroborating and then practising it ideologically.

The leading members in socialism have their ideals about communism and also how to achieve it. There exists a main relation between their motivation and ideas on the one hand, and the ideal and those who act on the other. In this kind of relation society becomes an object, a medium for the realization of ideals. The status of being the object of the society calls urgently for homogeneity, or rather, it forces the ruling members of society to act, as far as possible, in a homogeneous manner, as examples to the "people".

In the sciences for researching ideologies this is known as a "dichotomic way of looking at things". Ideals can be followed or be crucified. In contrast to that, there is a plurality in the second society. Consequently ideals are no longer formulated in a fundamentalist manner, responses to ideals can become multifarious and colorful. In the first period, during decartelization from the first society, negations can still be observed, but in the second period, the beginning autonomy immediately reveals an abundance of nuances.

HORIZONTAL

In the first society, everything is organized in relation to the centre, where the vital decisions are to be made. The centre embodies the ideals of the society, it issues decrees, which are to be accepted as infallible and not to be criticised. It kindly allows the subjects to be "constructive" in criticism, i.e. without touching the basic relations. Incorporation into society happens either towards the centre or away from the centre, i.e. upwards or downwards.

Most relationships in the second society are horizontal. But not all of them, because life is controlled from the centre. In the breaches left by the total supervision a growing, increasingly colourful cross-connection comes to life depending on the real interests of the deprived people. A number of small communities with common interests come to life, supporting one another and giving way to greater independence of, and distance to the centre. This loose, but strong network of groups, movements and initiatives, because of their semi-legal existence, question this verticality, dictated by the centre of power.

NON-NATIONALIZATION

The first society expands its power and sphere of influence by incorporating every possible area of economical, societal and intellectual life, including culture. The second society consists of more or less non-state lobbies. Besides the state sector with its rigidity, especially in terms of service, there appear in the economy those units of production, which can satisfy needs. On that level there exist similar, non-independent groups. Related to these units there are similar groups on the same level, which use decentralized, halfstate or independent initiatives.

NON-POLITICAL FACTORS DOMINATE

The first society is marked by so-called Pan-policity. All activities, relations and interests are politically arranged, controlled and required, even if they seem to be politically neutral at first sight: e.g. sport-achievements, the choice of a foreign language, etc. Politics have an almightiness, even being able to change the reality. In the second society the depoliticizing of any possible relations of human life is strong, so that the factors which really determine life become dominant. This society tries to put politics in their place, so that relations, independent of politics, are able to develop autonomy. The facts, expertise etc. provide the prestige.

NON-TRANSPARENCY

People in power, official bodies and the mass-media form the visible level of social life. They have the right to proclaim, they comment upon the reality, they define the identity of individuals as well as society, and they try to give the impression that they are the only public. This visibility is expected to be tolerated by everybody. Only the alternatives they propose are "valid" and "according to the facts". The second society, on the other hand, is not easy to find. Its manifestations are seldom reported in the official mass media. They are not easily to reach. The second society withdraws itself from the almighty control of the official sphere and forms a largely uncontrollable forum, equipped with much spontaneity and phantasy. Nevertheless it tries to gain influence among the citizens in society, including the first one. That is why it spreads Samizdat and organizes circles and demonstrations on the limits of visibility and underground.

The "second church"

After that short list of the attributes of the second society I should like to draw some conclusions for the catholic church in Hungary. It is accepted that this second society meets the needs of the nation, or of the people better than the first, or at least expresses, in a creative way, the nation's desire for justice. The church has to become aware of this reality and has to relate it to its own organization and thoughts. This parallel is appropriate, because within the church initiatives and movements are to be found, which we can describe, in a way, as a "second church" or shadow church. This interpretation of the church is market by the following characteristics.

DE-IDEOLOGIZING

The second church is aware of the fact that it is on a pilgrim way to the truth, and is by no means the possessor of that truth. It tries to satisfy the real needs of its members. It prefers direct relations. It gives place to expertise from outside the church, e.g. from the so-called social sciences. It provides broad freedom of moment. It facilitates and founds the social activities of individual members and nourishes even politically orientated groups and groupings with its ideals.

HORIZONTALITY

Opposed to the strong verticality of the first church, we find the second church marked by manifold partnership relations, a democracy called in this case "sister- and brotherhood". It will, for example, introduce the habit of addressing a person as "thou"; it recognizes the deep-rooted authority in groups, does not need tutelage in the proclamation of its ideals and acknowledgements, thus enabling the member to become a mature adult. This kind of horizontality also includes the recognition of women in all roles in the second church.

PLURALISM

It might also be called flexibility and a society without taboos. Flexibility means the broad possibility of responding to the most diverse needs of pastoral work, or a natural humanity. Being church in the second church means being less strictly bound to the actual church structures, so that existing groups may change that structure without losing their identity. Without taboos means the same flexibility, but now on the ideal level. The second church tolerates open questions and doubtful answers. This means practical ecumenism and the common search for the truth, even the integration of atheists (who in Hungary seem to be more faith-less than atheist).

INVISIBILITY, UNCONTROLLABILITY

For the existing authorities the second church is invisible and can therefore not be controlled. It is not oriented to the present structures in such a way that it could be observed or even steered. Its collaboration with the first church is autonomous and directed towards action, i.e. new actions, new agreements. As a rule its life does not happen primarily at ecclesiastic levels and places, but rather outside of church-buildings. But the second church would appear in masses at big meetings, like mushrooms in the wood after a rainfall. This would show strength and also its variety. The invisibility also includes its convictions. They grow wildly from a perspective of the established hegemonies. There is little censorship.

186

Consequences

As a result of this parallel it would be wrong to conclude, by way of a short-circuit, that the whole church should transform itself into a "second church". It is a matter of taking the experiences of the phenomenon of "interior" church movements as a mirror for the revival of the whole church. In this mirror, or through it, it is possible, though in a nebulous way, to see the following features:
1 The Hungarian church is subject to the temptation once again to play her half-feudal role in Hungary. Among other things this role will mean, on the one hand assistance in the struggle against the isolation of the citizens, yet on the other hand it means danger. Through the over-emphasise on the role of the hierarchy and the vertical relations, the coming-of-age of the christian in the church will be extinguished. The church has to safeguard her position and function in local society.
2 The official representatives of the church must consider their role as teachers with a great deal of self-criticism. Even in a society in which we can see a general crisis of values, where the reliable and definite teachings of the church are capable of again bringing the christian system of values to light, the teachers of the church will have to be careful not to reject new remarks and teachings, especially those from lay-theologians, out of fear of causing instability or of the queries of the educational authorities.

Ecclesiastical decisions are taken by a rather small circle of people and with no possibility of co-determination. Even in the Bishop's Conference not all members are able to state their opinion. Experts are not chosen for their scientific capacities, but rather for their catholicity. When there is a tendency towards destabilization a firm position can create trust, though not in the case of questionable competence and political integrity where decisions are concerned. In this, the church has to tolerate greater publicity and lay greater stress on the knowledge of specialists.

PART V

ASSESSMENTS

Franciscan spirituality and popular religiosity in context

Andreas Müller OFM, Germany

How can I experience God in concrete every-day life? That is the fundamental question of christian spirituality. Accordingly, Franciscan spirituality is a manner of encountering God and passing this experience on to others in the way that Francis and his brothers did. In what follows, I shall try to point out certain fundamental attitudes of Franciscan spirituality t-which I believe to be essential and indispensable for a liberating mission to popular religiosity.

To be on the side of the poor

Francis has been called the 'father of the poor'. He was a rich merchant's son who gave up his social prerogatives in order to go over to the side of the poor. In them he found Jesus Christ, who became poor for our sake, and in whose footsteps he wanted to follow.
The encounter with the poor leper marked the turning point in his life. Until then, lepers had always been considered an abomination. However, it was the Lord himself who urged Francis to go among them, as he later stated in his testament. From this moment onward, the way he reacted towards people who suffered became to him and his brothers the touchstone of their vocation. He had no doubt whatsoever about his conviction that the appropriate place for Franciscans is among people in distress: "(The friars) should be glad to live among social outcasts, among the poor and helpless, the sick and the lepers, and those who beg by the wayside" (Rule of 1221, 9).

Two spiritual concerns and challenges are in question: the imitation of Jesus Christ, poor and crucified, and the concrete solidarity with the poor who even today discover their dignity as human persons only when they have really and truly experienced that God loves them. For this reason, wherever great misery accumulates in the world, there is the place where Francis would call his sisters and brothers, in order to make it a place of encounter with God and to respond to the needs and profound aspirations of the oppressed people.

For justice and peace

With the whole of his being Francis was a man of peace. He knew himself sent into the world. Mostly he preached in the streets and on the market squares of the towns, always trying to understand and share the distress of the people and making himself understood by using their own language. At the beginning and the end of whatever he said he always invoked peace. This shows us that peace was an issue of immediate concern, even in this time.

In fact, the age when Francis lived was full of tensions, unrest, conflicts and wars. As a youth, he was personally involved in them. After his conversion he understood it to be his task to be a bringer and preserver of peace. There are many exemples, but the most famous is the story about the 'Wolf of Gubbio'. Probably, what legend called a "rapacious wolf" was, in fact, an impoverished knight who lived by robbery and therefore put the townspeople of Gubbio into a state of fear and hostility. The manner in which Francis restored peace between the "Wolf" and the population of Gubbio shows that he knew how to identify the roots of the conflict. He not only recognized the injustice committed by the knight, but also the reason why it had happened. He made the knight renounce violence and persuaded the townsfolk of Gubbio henceforth, to take responsibility for the knight's livelihood. He shows clearly that peace is possible only when nobody is denied what every human being needs and has a right to claim for his or her subsistence.

Justice and peace belong together. This is the political dimension of our christian mission, because concepts such as justice, peace, unjust structures, exploitation, etc. are political categories. This is the point where many of us become insecure, for – as religious – we do not want to become involved with things political. In a narrow sense this may be justified when applied to party politics. However, in a broader sense the word "politics" implies a vision of the coming of the Kingdom of God, and we know ourselves called to prepare God's Kingdom as a utopia of human harmony and as the final goal of God's salvific plans.
This idea has served as a key-note throughout all the talks and discussions of these days. It became apparent that all religious possess some liberating and life-promoting elements, capable of contributing values that prepare the way for the coming of the Lord's Kingdom.

A fraternal church and society

Francis has left us signs and impulses that bring about profound transformations in church and society. By voluntarily embracing poverty, Francis expressed – indirectly but unmistakably – strong criticism against the existing unjust structures of his time which divided society into "maiores" and "minores". By living universal brotherhood, he really revolutionized the hierarchical order that – up to then – existed in church and society. He considered all humans his brothers and sisters; he recognized neither masters nor servants and no class distinctions whatsoever. Probably, here can be found one of reasons why Francis and his Order became so popular among the poorer populations. The exploited and the oppressed felt accepted by him and entitled to dignity and equality. The gospel principle that "all of you are brothers and sisters" (Mt 23,8), accepted by Francis, gave an initial impulse towards a peaceful and non-violent change in society.

This is true in general, but even more so for the church. From pope to beggar, from bishop to leper, all – positively all – should treat one another as brothers and sisters. There is no longer any legitimacy for power structures, least of all in the church, but only for the power of love.

Naturally, we feel how difficult it is to discover such expressions of brotherly and sisterly life in today's church. According to Cardinal Aloísio Lorscheider, this spirit can be found most easily in christian base communities. For this reason, he calls them "the true church", because it is here that people feel united; here the poor may lift their voice; here they are accepted on their own terms and know that whatever they try to express is being taken seriously.

It is the vision of the church willing to listen, ready to give people the necessary time and space to grow. Here confidence is more important than supervision, and creative development more desirable than more obedience. This is a church that renounces its pre-eminence and privileges, its insignia and spiritual power. This is the church Francis dreamt about, and which he wanted us to testify to.

We also recognize such attitudes as necessary for a new approach to popular religiosity. Unfortunately, many recent decisions and church-related events have not been favourable to the hopes and aspirations of christian base communities. There is an increasing danger that they may loose their missionary thrust and commitment because of lack of spiritual support.

Franciscan charisma and the liberating church

Dom Helder Câmara once called Francis "the great symbol of a liberating church of the poor. Thus, it is no coincidence that renowned Franciscans, such as the two Cardinals Paulo Evaristo Arns and Aloísio Lorscheider, the Bishops Adriano Hypolito, Claudio Hummes and many more identified themselves fully with liberation theology and its corresponding practices. Cardinal Lorscheider even inverted the dictum: "Today, religious life in Latin America cannot be understood, unless one contemplates Liberation Theology at the same time, in all its unique originality."

Above all, fundamental concerns of theology are being questioned:
• The option for the poor and against poverty, because this is the will of God, a God of Life who rejects all destructive forces of death.
• Reflection on the salvific truths revealed by God, from the standpoint of the poor and the deprived. In a true sense, this is popular religiosity. It began when BECs instinctively recognized whatever was wholesome in the faith of the people. There is great need for a theology that really concentrates on helping the people; i.e. a theology that takes people seriously in their suffering and leads them to an all-embracing liberation, as God's gift to them.
• Coherency between life and doctrine. Truth must be done, in order to be understood. In holy scripture there is always a link between knowledge of God and religious practice. The question is: How can we profess to be christians in

a world where so much misery is produced by so many unjust structures? The answer is simple enough: We can only be authentic christians in so far as we are determined to commit ourselves to the construction of a more just and more humane world.

In his time, Francis was capable of transmitting to the poor – as well as to the church in general – the liberating effect of the gospel. He achieved this by simply living gospel values in a radical and uncurtained way. Lived in this manner, the gospel is always liberating, and opposes whatever might harm or destroy life.

With prophetic frankness

In Francis of Assisi, the church opened itself to new horizons. It was invited to advance into newly discovered grounds. Similarly, the Franciscan movement has to be ready to dare to take new steps, if it wants to remain faithful to its charism. Of course, there is always the risk of being rejected as "innovators" or "outsiders". Two recent events have made this painfully evident.

CONFLICT WITH SOCIETY

Whoever declared that he desires to live his faith according to the gospel, i.e. for the sake of the weak and the poor of society while questioning unjust structures – exactly what Francis did in his time – inevitably must count on open persecution from two sides. In the first place, it will come from society, bent on maintaining its "status quo" and – for this reason – trying hard to repress evidence of its complicity with the oppressors. Here, the most simple method used by society is to present itself as the guardian of 'orthodoxy', ready to divert any subversive tendencies. This was the centre-piece of the conflict about theology of liberation.

CONFLICT IN THE CHURCH

In the second place, it becomes more difficult when the point in question is a correct understanding of 'orthodoxy', because this touches on the fundamental element of fidelity to the church, a requirement that Francis constantly recommended to his brothers with all his heart.

However, we have to admit that there were moments in the life of our saint when he felt that he could not accept certain obligations imposed by the roman curia. One of the most famous incidents was his open and public rejection of the 5th Crusade (1217-1221). Instead of arming himself like a true crusader, Francis appeared defencelessly before the Sultan of Egypt. With this attitude, he made it clear that he wanted to represent another kind of church; not a church bent on subjecting others to its will, but a church ready "to be subject to every human creature for God's sake" (Rule of 1221, 16). Called by God "to restore his church" (Celano 11/10), Francis made the gospel his "form of life" and preserved "what God has inspired him and his brothers" in the midst of a church that still believed itself authorized to use worldly power.

In all instances, Francis linked fidelity to the church with a corresponding fidelity to the poor. More than once, this two-fold loyalty became the cause of conflict. The example given by Francis shows us that true love for the church does not allow us to recoil from the painful obligation to be critical in a prophetic way. There is no other possibility for the church but to become "semper reformanda", a church that should be ready to renew itself continually, in order to be a trust-worthy sign of God's presence in this world.

Peace with nature

Francis of Assisi cannot be understood without his 'Canticle of Brother Sun', where he calls all creatures his brothers and sisters. To him, nothing was lowly, nothing existed to be dominated and down-trodden. Respect and love for the whole of Creation – in a truly cosmic sense – are attitudes that Francis would constantly recommend us today.
Whatever violence is committed against nature by unlimited exploitation and a squandering of resources, by destruction of the environment through an irresponsible use of technologies and industry, mindless of the ecological equilibrium, is a crime against the unity existing between mankind and nature and helps to destroy the foundations of all life.

The effort to preserve the integrity of creation is an attempt to maintain the vital relationship between man and nature on a non-violent basis and to keep peace with our environment. This is part of the mission we need to proclaim in the church, because even "the universe itself awaits redemption" (Rom 8, 21). For this reason, it is no longer permissible to create an opposition between political and personal responsibility, professional competence and moral obligations. In other words, christians may not simply give in to the slogans of so-called economic or political experts. If such people use their competence to deepen the strangling debt crisis of entire continents, if they permit the destruction and deforestation of whole regions, if they do nothing to prevent a dubious "progress" at the expense of rightful authority, then it is time that we step forward and take over; then our life-style has to exhort people to change their ways and to give up a consumerist mentality.

Fundamental values of Franciscan spirituality can enable us to respond to the just demands for liberation and to the inherent aspirations of the people. In this sense, the Franciscan tradition has always been sensitive to the demands of a sound popular religiosity. This will remain so, as long as we continue to follow the guide-lines established by our Father Francis.

Popular religion, spirituality and liberation

Hadewych Snijdewind, the Netherlands

First, I'll define some concepts which remained ambiguous in our discussions because they lacked adequate formulation. I have some criticisms about the use of the term 'popular religion', because what is meant by many speakers in this congress must, in my opinion, be called "popular religiosity". It characterizes *peculiar* experiences and practices within a given religion. Indeed, each religion has in itself, alongside the official beliefs and practices protected by the religious authorities, a segment of beliefs and practices that can be called "popular religiosity". The question is: do we agree with this notion of "popular religiosity"? Here I make a distinction between "a religion" and "religiosity". When we are speaking about "a religion", we are speaking of a specific religious tradition with its own identity. "Religiosity", on the contrary, is a special way of individually or collectively experiencing and practising that pre-given religious tradition.

The elements of popular religiosity can function in very many ways:
1 they can be implicit criticism of the official and institutional religious elements, which appear unlivable for some religious people; they are in search of salvation in non-official, and in that sense, *peculiar*, devotions; for example: in catholicism, the rosary, pilgrimages;
2 they can function as an affirmation of the status quo, when, for example, in christianity these popular devotions silence the *prophetic criticism* of the gospel;
3 in other circumstances the same non-official *devotional elements* can function as societal criticism, and they can also function as criticism of a byzantine ecclesiastical liturgism.

Popular religiosity, as such, is ambiguous: it can function in a liberating way, and it can function in a enslaving way. Therefore the popular devotions in each religion must be analyzed with regard to their liberating or enslaving functions.

What does it mean: a liberating function? It must be liberating *from* human alienations *to* human freedom and human integrity; and that involves liberation from selfishness to inner freedom – including psychosomatic integrity – to social-political freedom, to corporal health, to save our ecological environment, and so on. And all this borne by the vivid relation to God as the transcendent mystery.

From a theological point of view the concept of the "people of God", which became one of the most important key-concepts of the Second Vatican Council,

196

implicitly criticizes the concept of the so called "service church". The anthropological, and therefore also the theological significance of the concept 'people of
God' lay in the fact that the Council declared that the people of God are *themselves* the subjects of faith and, consequently, also the subject of ecclesial religion.
On the basis of this, the christian religion and the christian churches can be
characterized as a popular religion, but not *per se* in the sense of popular religiosity. Ministerial doctrinal authority and theological doctrinal authority both
make their own contributions to the way in which the religiosity of the people
maintains its biblical roots and direction.

Popular religiosity is characterized by the fact that the everyday world and the religious world – or, to be more precise, religious experience – are closely bound up
together. Bert Hoedemaker argues that missionary work, as intercultural communication, is an attempt to come to a redefinition of the christian message in relation
to the "world": to the socio-historical and socio-political context in which religious
people are embedded. Without this critical reconciliation of the everyday world and
the world of faith christianity cannot become a process of liberation.
Sociologically, we know that popular culture (and popular religion as well) often
functions as an escape through which pressure can be released. The popular
celebration of carnival, for instance, provides relief from the pressures of a society
that is too hard. (Popular culture, here, functions as an affirmation of existing
social conditions). For a short time people escape from the hard, angry world to
live in a world of fantasy, where not only the powerful are ridiculed and criticized
through caricatures, but where even the carnival cities are given different names,
as if they were places where life is happy and easy. The day after, however, we
wake up sober and are back in the old, stressful, everyday routine of the aggressive city.
Yet even in this "relief"-function of popular culture we find silent criticism of
society-as-it-is. Popular culture, and consequently popular religiosity, when they
become more consciously and explicitly aware of the negative contrasts (that are
already latently present in many aspects of popular culture), can develop into a
tradition of protest and resistance and thus contribute towards liberation.
Is not what we have been seeing in the countries of Eastern Europe during the
past months an explosion of resistance of people who rise up and say: "No! Here
and now the boundaries of our humanity have been reached: *as a people* we will
no longer endure this"?
This resistance can be so revealing that even the armed and administrative forces
drop their weapons and take the side of the people. (When a system is extremely
dictatorial and rigid like Rumania, it can come to such violence that it resembles
self-destruction.) Often it is the most innocent, the babies and the children, who
become the victims of this, and their suffering and death open the eyes of those
who previously hesitated and were passive.

Yvette Aklé and Takatso Mofokeng show such a contrast situation in Africa. They
both point out that a religion that is imported and has no roots in popular culture

has no liberating power. On the contrary, it can even be destructive, leaving the neophyte in an emotional, cultural, material and spiritual vacuum, in search of his own African roots, or driven to despair by poverty and exhaustion, not longer even searching. But!... I shall come back to this topic.

In view of all this, I think that the three models proposed by Rob van Kessel[1] are *sociologically* valid for Western Europe and North-America, and, in my opinion, they are also *theologically* valid for the Third World and perhaps also for the Second World, although in the case of these latter regions we cannot reduce the so-called bourgeois model directly to impulses from the 18th century Enlightenment. Van Kessel distinguishes three models:

1 *the traditional model*: devotional belief and devotional behaviour within a service-church, where people go to church and celebrate liturgy at important moments of life – birth, marriage and death – surrounding these moments with "rites de passage";

2 *the bourgeois model*: a church of volunteers who belong to the privileged classes and whose social position ensures their own freedom and their own human rights. This also applies to the so-called "happy few" in the Third World (5% of the 130 million inhabitants of Java/Indonesia, for instance), but hardly to people of the Second World, with the exception of Poland;

3 *the critical and liberating model*. Here popular culture and popular religion mean: finding God's people among the underdogs of society and history, the poor and the oppressed, the people without a curriculum vitae and all those who stand with them, beside them and on their side.

Amando Robles appears to disagree to some extent with this framework. Traditional popular religiosity should disappear and be replaced by a new popular religion based on *ethical-rational* principles. Opting for Rob van Kessel's third model, I feel that I should emphasize – like Johann Baptist Metz and Edward Schillebeeckx – that popular religiosity can only been meaningful, can only be real 'service to God', when it keeps its God-centered and mystical nature and is not reduced to a purely ethical-rational undertaking. Every christian contextual theology that aims at liberation must be borne and consciously directed by a God-orientated spirituality which, while it cannot add up to the solidarity efforts on behalf of fellow human beings, nevertheless has a density and a value of its own. Gustavo Gutiérrez once said: "No one sings and prays like oppressed people who are fighting for liberation". In this spirituality, as a matrix for active solidarity with poor and oppressed people, pentecostalism *can* play a role. But it has to be recognized, on the one hand, that social inequality is caused by our socio-political and economic structures and can therefore be counteracted and, on the other, that the elements of passivity which Francisco Rolim detect in Latin American

---

1 From the congress-paper written by R. van Kessel: 'Theological questions concerning popular religion in Western-Europe' (mimeo).

pentecostalism should be removed to avoid the danger of strengthening precisely those interests that oppress people and keep them down.

Finally, I come back to the topic of Takatso Mofokeng and our guests from Eastern Europe, especially Czechoslovakia. Popular religion in a special sense, namely as a movement in actuality, can be characterized as a certain social practice of people's struggle to be free. And, coming from the basis of the everyday-experiences of the people of God, it links believers and non-believers together, because all, together, are looking forward to an open space, free from oppression, control and bureaucratic institutions devoid of creativity. The basis of this common struggle is the cry for survival and our looking forward to a position – for a short time – beyond the institutions which have trained us by their tools, language, theory and praxis.
The fact that christians of diverse roots, and non-christians as well, work together for a common cause has, as an inner consequence, a very authentic ecumenical dimension which in the long run will overcome confessional doctrinal differences. It is a warning and a challenge to all of us, as we see the indifference, aggressivity and suicide attempts of young people in the west, living in a world of materialism and consumption, to develop, what a Russian woman, Nadjezda Mandelstam, called: "the awareness of the signs of time."

The concept of the 'people of God' dynamizes and empowers a long emotional, practical tradition of sharing our lives, it changes our friend-enemy images and, finally, it will change our ecclesiastical structures of pyramidal patriarchy. Our present political models push the churches, too, towards greater freedom, greater democracy and greater justice. Therefore, we, as subjects of history, have to shift the dominant paradigm, not only for societies but also for the church, because for the sake of the suffering victims within our economic and ideological systems.
The conclusion of this modest reflection is that in the future popular religiosity must emphasize the liberating – mystical and political – aspects of the great religious tradition that we share.

Contextual analysis and unity of perspective
An exercise in missiological method

Bert Hoedemaker, the Netherlands

The importance of context in missiological research is generally accepted, and the concern for contextual analysis does not meet with serious criticism as long as it builds on the traditional concern for legitimate variety within a presupposed unity. It involves, however, more than that. Difficulties arise as soon as contextual self-assertions begin to question and to challenge conceptions of unity and identity that were held to be self-evident. Then the experience of religious pluralism, both within christianity and within humankind as a whole, is no longer innocent, but it begins to disturb the dreams that once inspired the missionary movement (spreading the one faith to the ends of the earth), and to undermine the traditional foundation of missiology as a coherent discipline of analysis and reflection. To be sure, no one doubts that the impressive developments in the study of religion and culture, in the analysis of social and economic relations, and in the awareness of global structures of oppression and liberation enrich our understanding of the religious life of individuals and communities in an essential way; but neither is there any doubt that traditional missiological paradigms are under heavy fire precisely because of these developments.

The fact is: we are no longer dealing merely with local churches exercising their legitimate 'subjectivity' within one visible universal church; we are also dealing with complex religious systems which may have absorbed 'christian' elements but which are sometimes hardly recognizable as christian[1] and we encounter manifestations of religion and theology which seriously criticize the domestication of the so-called universal christian tradition by particular interests exclusive of and destructive in their effect upon others. Looking at all this, it is not enough to conclude that the processes of "mission" and "conversion" are apparently much slower and much more complex than was assumed in traditional missiology. We are challenged to go further and to reconsider some basic presuppositions of traditional missiology. Ultimately we shall have to deal with the theological question, what "unity of perspective" might mean in a vastly differentiated world which nevertheless manifests itself as one because of the problems that engage humankind as a whole.

---

1 See T. Yamamori, C.R. Taber (eds), *Christopaganism or indigenous christianity?*, Pasadena, Yamamori/Taber, 1975.

Implications of the concern for contextuality

BASIC DISTINCTIONS

Definitions of contextuality and contextualization are usually presented in comparison with terms like adaptation, indigenization and inculturation, and there are considerable differences among the various systems of comparison. Common to all approaches is a refined concept of culture. Culture is no longer seen as a static complex of beliefs and practices but as a dynamic system, a structure of communication, geared towards the shaping of individual and collective identity and continually redefining its boundaries and its relation to internal change and external influences.[2] Likewise, tne concept of "translating" or "indigenizing" the gospel is no longer seen as a relatively simple work of using or integrating certain permanent features of a particular culture, but as an effort to sow seeds in such a way that a truly "contextual" expression of the gospel message will grow up. From here on, however, different ways are followed. In the more conservative views of mission, the term 'contextualization' tends to be used as an inclusive concept, designating the various processes by which the gospel message ("text") is integrated into a local culture ("context"). Within this general framework distinctions are made: sometimes between an indigenization typology and a socio-economic typopogy[3], sometimes between a translational, a dialectical and a liberational type.[4] In both cases the "liberational" approaches to contextuality are treated as varieties of missionary adaptation, and the study of culture is used as a tool at the service of a basically unquestioned mission.

We are dealing with a so-called "kernel-and-husk" theory, which, although its takes the concern for contextuality seriously, remains close to the traditional missiological paradigms. A somewhat different position emerges when "inculturation" is held up as the key concept, by which contextualization is to be understood. The focus of attention here is the dialectic between particularity and universality: as the world of cultures consists of inalienable originality and communicable universality, so the local and the universal church are called to mutual enrichment.[5] The term inculturation is not necessarily linked to traditional missionary approaches of "adaptation"; it can be used quite comprehensively and take several concerns of liberation theology into account. Nevertheless, it still presupposes a more or less self-evident and harmonious relationship between the universal and the particular; and it may not be capable, therefore, of dealing constructively with the experiences of discontinuity and incompatibility which also characterize contemporary christianity. Most liberational approaches to contextualization go one step further and very explicitly leave behind the traditional

---

2 See R. J. Schreiter, *Constructing local theologies*, Maryknoll/London, 1985.
3 See J.S. Ukpong, 'What is contextualization?', in: *Neue Zeitschrift für Missionswissenschaft*, 43(1987), 161-168.
4 See L.J. Luzbetak, *The church and cultures*, Maryknoll, 1987.
5 See A.A. Roest Crollius, 'Inculturation and the meaning of culture', in: *Gregorianum*, 61(1980), 253-274.

missionary paradigms. In these approaches the term "contextuality" has necessarily a polemical aspect: here it is the struggle of particular groups against their oppression by larger social and economic powers, and the praxis of faith which is visible in that struggle, that become the starting points for a critical interrogation of so-called universal truth.[6]

It is obvious that the three approaches described above – we may name them 'kernel-and-husk' approach, dialectical approach and polemical approach – cannot always be neatly separated. This is especially true for the second and the third. The dialectical and polemical approach do not necessarily and permanently exclude each other. For instance: in the encounter between African theology and South African black theology the emphasis on culture and the emphasis on the reality of oppression may still lead to different ways of thinking[7]; in recent Asian theology, on the other hand, the two emphases tend to converge.[8] Convergence seems to be possible to the extent that one's concept of culture is comprehensive and dynamic so as to allow for analysis of the internal and external relations of power and the manifold ways in which human beings and communities deal with those relations. Ultimately, the crucial demarcation-line between the two approaches may be constituted by the question whether "universal truth" is regarded as a given framework, to be expanded and enriched and deepened by the various "contexts", or as a hope, newly formulated by the people involved in "contextual" struggles for life, and from there reaching out to the whole of humankind. (It remains to be seen to what extent theologians, who are stigmatized as "inculturationists" and "liberationists" respectively, would be neatly separated by this demarcation-line!). In the first instance, the appropriate theological image of "incarnation" – sometimes "inculturation" and "incarnation" are used almost synonymously – in the second instance it is "God active in history" and the "kingdom of God". The first approach presupposes what we might call a centripetal (synthetic) view of contextuality, the second approach allows for centrifugal (fragmentary) developments without giving up the vision of unity and reconciliation.

ASPECTS OF CONTEXTUAL ANALYSIS

When we put these things together, there seems to be one aspect of the concept of "contextuality" that is decisive for further methodological discussion, even if it is not always made explicit. The term "contextuality" does not refer merely to specific features of particular corners of the human community, or to the cultural or situational self-assertion of individuals and communities. Use of the term presupposes and implies reflection on the relation of those particularities to the

---

6 See S. Torres, V. Fabella (eds), *The emergent gospel. Theology from the underside of history*, Maryknoll, 1978.
7 See various essays in K. Appiah-Kubi, S. Torres (eds), *African theology en route*, Maryknoll, 1979.
8 See C.S. Song, *Theology from the womb of Asia*, Maryknoll, 1986; A. Pieris, *An asian theology of liberation*, Maryknoll, 1988.

whole of global society and to the larger framework of human history. What is brought to attention is not just the "context" as such, in itself, but the context in harmony, in tension, in opposition, in critical communication, in rejection, in continuity, in discontinuity, briefly: in relation to other contexts and to the "whole". "Contextuality", therefore, cannot be dealt with apart from intercontextual and transcontextual realities[9]; some vision of common humanity is always involved. Putting it more strongly: concern for contextuality not only adds more substance or more illustration to what is already given; it also interrupts and disturbs existing concepts of "the whole", for instance, the modern Western concept of "world" and "unity of mankind". In other words, the concern for contextuality raises the question of unity for church and mission in new ways.

It follows from these considerations that analyses of contextual "units" of culture and religion involve more than merely displaying exotic particularities and explaining their background and function; it involves an effort to relate these to the wider field of forces that determine the state of global society, and to explain the way in which the "units" under analysis understand and cope with those forces. "Contextual analysis" means: making a certain situation, a certain configuration of problems, a certain system of beliefs and practices into a "context", that is: into a factor which has its own place and its own role in the whole spectrum of intercontextual and transcontextual realities.

For the study of popular religion this implies, for instance, that the configuration of elements which presents itself as an analyzable unit should be approached as a valid "context", instead of being immediately regarded as an object of purification, reorganization or integration; judgments which, in fact, project the unity and coherence of official institutionalized religion on the forms of popular religion must be suspended. The only relevant question is, to what extent are forms of popular religion capable of maintaining a certain internal cohesion and a consistent pattern of external relations. To that extent they can become mirrors, examples of how human beings organize their symbolic universe, and how this symbolic universe interact with the global field of forces of human society.

The question as to whether popular religion is "liberating" seems to me premature when it implies a measurement based on the unity and coherence of established theology. It is valid, however, if it intends to inquire into how the larger social and economic powers are conceived and how the praxis of faith in the communities under discussion relates to those powers. In that case, the question might stimulate further conscientization among the adherents of the form of popular religion under discussion, but it might also reveal new possibilities of religious strength and resistance which enrich our vision of a common humanity. For behind the question about the liberating potential of popular religion lies a more fundamental question, namely: how do the life-stories of individuals and

---

9 See M.L. Stackhouse, 'Contextualization, contextuality, and contextualism', in: R.O. Costa (ed.), *One faith. Many cultures*, Maryknoll, 1988.

communities reflect the realities and tensions in human society? This is basically what contextual analysis is about: it seeks to elucidate the link between global networks and individual stories.

A final remark about "contextual theology". On the basis of what has been said so far, we should perhaps distinguish between forms of theology that belong to the religious self-expression of particular groups, on the one hand, and on the other, forms of theology that seek explicit dialogue with the "tradition" or with the dominating theological discourse, and which do so on the basis of particular experience and analysis, with the aim of interrogating existing conceptions and introducing new or forgotten aspects of a presupposed common faith. In line with what has been said about contextual analysis, seeking to elucidate the link between global networks and individual stories, perhaps we ought to reserve the designation "contextual theology" only for the second kind.

Missiology: a discipline of hope

THE PREDICAMENT OF MISSIOLOGY
Missiologists have always tried to combine the analysis of the history of the missionary movement with the elucidation of the principles of "mission". The combination never presented real problems as long as the historical and institutional reality of "mission" was unquestioned. As soon as serious questions were raised, however, the two "wings" began to drift apart. Analysis of the history of the missionary movement is being supplemented, if not replaced, by writing church history from the viewpoint of the former "objects" of mission[10], and by describing the mobility and vitality of christianity in the whole of the world history and world society.[11] And in the search for a stronger foundation of the missionary enterprise, the concept of "mission" has been broadened to include all church-world relations or even all God-world relations.[12] In the document of the Second Vatican Council, the priciple of "mission" is presented as a basic ecclesiological category; and in various documents of the World Council of Churches, the term "mission" is connected to divergent enterprises such as humanization, development and dialogue. Compared to earlier times, the reality of "mission" seems to have evaporated in two directions: one is historical and religious pluralism, the other is theolgical generalization. Consequently, much of contemporary missiology can be characterized as an effort to regain some kind of unity: either "from below" (the pluralism) or "from above" (the generalization).

---

10 See L. Vischer (ed.), *Church history in ecumenical perspective*, Bern, 1982; id. (ed.), *Towards a history of the church in the third world*, Bern, 1985.
11 See A. Camps, L.A. Hoedemaker, M.R. Spindler, F. Verstraelen (eds), *Oecumenische inleiding in de missiologie*, Kampen, 1988.
12 See G.F. Vicedom, *Missio Dei*, München, 1958; J.C. Hoekendijk, 'Zur Frage eine Missionarischen Existenz', in: *Kirche und Volk in der Deutschen Missionswissenschaft*, München, 1967, 297-354; H.H. Rosin, *Missio Dei. Term en functie in de zendingstheologische discussie*, Leiden, 1971.

At one end of the spectrum we find approches that begin with plurality and mobility in global society and in the world of religions, in order to discern traces of 'God's mission' leading human beings toward unity and liberation. At the other end theological generalization is transformed into some form of positivism of church or gospel; here it is the unity and the coherence of church institution or biblical truth that over-arches and ultimately judges all plurality. The two ends are hardly on speaking terms, yet they clearly originate in the same perplexity.

This is of course not a very hopeful way of describing the predicament of missiology. Perhaps a more constructive approach is possible, when we take our clue from the fact that systematic reflection on mission has always been developed along two distinct lines, in two distinct styles. The first line or style emphasizes inter-cultural communication as a permanent dynamic movement and seeks to analyze the function and influence of christianity and the christian message in this permanent movement, and the ways in which christianity itself is changed by it.[13] "Mission" is here: engaging in an open process of sharing faith, hope and love in the mobility of human cultural and religious history. The second line or style seeks to define and redefine the essence of the christian message in its relation to and its distinction from "the world": it speaks, for instance, of "the" promise of the kingdom of God and of "humanity" or "world" as a whole, and tries to analyze the various points of confrontation.[14] Here "mission" means: making it very clear where the world and the human being stand in relation to divine judgment and promise. Unlike the first line, this line tends toward global and summary definitions, especially with regard to "world" and "humanity", but also with regard to "God". The two lines or styles distinguished here are both necessary and legitimate, and good missiology will always seek a fruitful relation between them. On the other hand, problems may arise (and may in fact have arisen) from an uncritical combination of the two lines, or, put it in a different way, we can be describe the predicament of missiology by sketching the "spectrum" a little differently.

At the end of the spectrum, where the "communication"-line irrupts into the "definition"-line, the preoccupation with change and variety curtails a clear perception of the points of reference of the christian mission. At the other end, where the irruption takes place in reverse, clear theological definitions may be translated into conceptions of an unchangeable basis or centre of the missionary enterprise, which prevent an adequate appreciation of the processes of intercultural and interreligious communication. Other mixtures of the two lines or styles are conceivable. When, for instance, the concern for communication is governed and limited by ideological conceptions of cultural superiority, of a common

---

13 See H. Balz, *Theologische Modelle der Kommunikation*, Güterloh, 1978; W.J. Hollenweger, *Erfahnrungen der Leibhaftigkeit*, München, 1980. See also R.J. Schreiter, *o.c.*.
14 See K. Barth, *Kirchliche Dogmatik*, IV.3, Zürich, 1959; J.C. Hoedendijk, 'Notes on the meaning of mission(ary)', in: Th. Wieser (ed.), *Planning for mission*, New York, 1966, 37-48; L. Rütti, *Zur Theologie der Mission*, München, 1972.

religion for all of humankind, or of particular socio-economic paradigms, we are in fact dealing with a mixture; and the same is true when "communication" is exclusively modelled after the appeal for individual conversion, which excludes other possible definitions of judgment and promise.

This sketch of the predicament of missiology clearly allows for more flexibility than our first attempt. It becomes a kind of map on which different missiological positions and approaches can be placed and characterized. It would, of course, be tempting to show how this is the case. We should probably be able to observe how the usual classification of contemporary missiology in catholic, ecumenical, evangelical, and liberationist streams[15] is relativized by the fact that all share the same predicament, that each stream comprises several different configurations of responses to this predicament, and that the strong and weak sides of each configuration form part of the same "picture". More important for our present purposes, however, is how to use the sketch for a clear grasp of the major challenge faced by contemporary reflection on mission. The challenge is that of finding a tenable and fruitful interaction between the communication-line and the definition-line. What needs to be brought into interaction (and not merely placed side by side) is, first of all the acknowledgment of human history as an open process of intercultural and interreligious communication, in which christianity maintains its contextual mobility, and, secondly, a theological frame of reference in which human diversity and confusion are related to divine creation, judgment and reconciliation. Good missiology has always attempted this; and we have to attempt it again, yet this time without giving way to the temptation of restoring older, more naïve conceptions of the unity of the discipline.

POSSIBLE POINTS OF VIEW

Missiology is contextual analysis in connection with the theological articulation of the earliest and most essential motive of chistian missionary concern for the "world": faith in the ultimate trustworthiness of God's promises for the whole of humankind. The connection may not produce a new conception for a "missionary movement"; but it can prove a framework for analyzing and evaluating everything that presents itself as "mission". Such a framework is constituted by a number of basic theological points of view which are themselves subject to continuing discussion. What follows is a proposal for two of those "foundation stones".

The first point of view calls to mind the essential correlation between a "universal" conception of God, human kind and the world on the one hand, and a deepening of personal responses in faith commitment and in consciousness of guilt and forgiveness on the other. In a general sense, this correlation of the universal and the personal may be characteristic of all "meta-cosmic" religion in its over-ruling of "cosmic" religion[16]; but in the sources of the christian tradition

---

15 See R.C. Bassham, *Mission theology 1948-1975*, Pasadena, 1979; A.F. Glasser, D.A. McGavran, *Contemporary theologies of mission*, Grand Rapids, 1983.
16 The terminology is from A. Pieris, *o.c.*.

it has been shaped in a specific way. A "revelation" which speaks of the coming of the kingdom of God relevant to the whole world and simultaneously of the 'needle's eye' of conversion, cannot but transcend the boundaries of group-centred conceptions of God, world, sin and redemption.

The consciousness of guilt, especially, gives evidence of a form of faith and religion in which the experience of human life and of the world in general has become universal in scope.[17] It is there that missiology can find a meaningful point of departure. We remind ourselves of the statement made earlier in this paper, that contextual analysis seeks to elucidate the link between global networks and individual stories. It is precisely in this connection between the "global" and the "individual" that basic beliefs about God, world, guilt and reconciliation can be made relevant.

To do this is the business of missiology – rather: of missionary theology. It means relating the faith-dynamic of the universal and the personal to the actual experience of global networks in particular situations. The fact that humankind has come to consist of analyzable social and economic networks, which include realities of oppression and liberation; the fact that human society consists of analyzable entanglements of individual and collective histories (national, racial, cultural and religious) in each other – all this can be brought into relation with basic theological insights.

In this way individuals and communities can be helped to accept inter-contextual communication as a moral aspect of every-day life, and to make sense of the realities of world and history in criticism of all narrow-sighted, ideological and cynical attempts to rationalize evil.

The second point of view suggested here is closely related to the first. It concerns the significance of eschatology for missionary theology.

Without denying the fruitfulness of the image of "incarnation", which remains important for any reflection on the relation of gospel and culture, we must maintain that a weakening of the eschatological dynamic would deprive missiology of its identity. For the ultimate point of reference in "mission" is not the mandate to establish one universal religion which encompasses and transcends all existing cultures and religions, but is a permanent eschatological question which is phrased and re-phrased in the various contexts of the world and which speaks of justice, peace and integrity of creation.

The question originated in ancient Israël and it was renewed and radicalized in the appearance of Jesus. Its points is not a new "religion", but a concretization of the challenges of the "covenant": exodus from slavery, rejection of the gods that seek to domesticate human life, consistent care for the widow, the orphan and the outsider. In the 'Jesus-movement' this question was picked up as a radical question of lostness and faith, of guilt and forgiveness, of death and resurrection – and with that it became a universal question which had to transcend the

---

17 See P. Ricoeur, *La symbolique du mal*, Paris, 1960.

207

boundaries of given cultural, religious and national systems. Because of that it has a uniting power: its unites the various contexts of the world, not in a universal religion but in a movement towards a common point of reference in which the unity of human kind is given as a promise.

Missiology means: interpreting and re-interpreting this permanent question in all contextual analysis.

When the two points of view suggested here are allowed to determine the connection between contextual analysis and theological articulation of basic missionary concern, then missiology can truly be what it always intended to be: a discipline of hope.

Concluding remarks

The discipline of missiology exists by virtue of a faith-hypothesis in which three things are welded together:

first, the original story of the christian gospel – put differently: the permanent covenant-question –;

second, the seemingly endless plurality of human stories produced by basic contextual experience;

and third, the promise of the ultimate realization of "shalom", of salvation, for all humankind.

That these three together finally form one over-arching story, that is the basic hopeful assumption, both of missionary work and missiological reflection.

The question as to how this unity is to become a real and visible unity will have to be left open. For in the open processes of communication in which we live and in the ongoing work of contextual analysis from which we learn, hints of unity can only be provisional. The provisionality is determined by the realities of guilt and reconciliation, and by the fact that the quest for justice, peace and the integrity of creation always stays ahead of any accomplishments reached in these areas.

This is the basic argument for the thesis that mission, in principle, precedes institutional religion, and that missiology is the (eschatological) forerunner of theology.

Contextual analysis and contextual theology are, in that sense, latecomers in the missiological enterprise, and as such they have created quite a disturbance in traditional method. They are, however, basic to the further development of the discipline. The integration of contextual analysis with missiology, as I have attempted to sketch it, will enrich academic theology as a whole and make it truly ecumenical, in other words: make it grow in the framework of world wide intercontextual communication.

The religious plurality which we encounter both within christianity (for instance in the many forms of popular religion) and in the world as a whole – and why should these two forms of religious plurality be essentially different? – can

208

become the point of departure for work on common interpretations of common experience. And when contextual analysis follows the "polemical model", and consequently emphasizes the "centrifugal" dynamics of cultural and religious expression – in other words: when it highlights the guilt-character of human existence and the judgment-character of divine promise – the conflicts can become points of departure for work on a liberating praxis.

The implications of popular religion for liberative contextual theologies

Berma Klein Goldewijk and Jacques Van Nieuwenhove, the Netherlands

In this final contribution we shall not present a textual report of the plenaries and workshop discussions, nor an exhaustive survey of the different approaches, analyses and perspectives that came up during the congress. We shall limit ourselves to some fundamental observations and statements which really were the subject of discussion in the plenary sessions of the meeting. It is our intention to present them and to reflect on them in the light of the problems we were exploring in our introduction paper, taking into account some of the interventions published in this book.

First we shall deal with questions concerning the definition of, and scientific approaches to, popular religion, including questions related to monotheism and 'paganism'. Secondly, we shall reflect on some questions related to the liberative potential of popular religion, including the problem of the politicization and instrumentalization of this religion, especially when a marxist approach to religion is followed. Finally, we shall focus on questions contextual theologies and churches face when confronted with popular religions.

The central problem here remains the question of what resources popular religion offers to liberation and contextual theology and how contextual theology relates to liberation processes. The focus relies on method and contents of analysis.

The concept of popular religion

As we expected, the very concept of popular religion, or religiosity, was a continual subject of discussion. In a provocative manner, Achille Mbembe stated that, strictly speaking, and with all seriousness, there is no such thing as popular religion. In his opinion, the concept of popular religion has to be deconstructed. In the African context, Mbembe argued, the concept of popular religion is burdened by at least three misleading connotations. One of the remarkable misunderstandings is the "confusion" : within the concept of popular religion people tend to include various objects which are vastly different in character and very diverse in their religious procedures which sometimes contradict each other. In this sense – and beyond the legitimate differences between popular catholicism, popular forms of islam and traditional African religions – the concept includes a confusion which arises from the fact that people postulate – yet without demonstrating the fact – that there is a "unity of the religious domain" or "a popular essence of things religious" which exists only in the case of Africa.

Another misunderstanding, according to Mbembe, is the "romantic vision" of things popular; a vision which often assimilates things popular with weakness, with the oppressed and sometimes with revolutionary spontaneity. However, not everything that is popular is necessarily weak, nor is it automatically revolutionary. In the third place, the concept implies the idea of a strict opposition between the popular and the non-popular. Mbembe has a strong objection to the over-emphasized opposition between that which is popular and the contrary. In his opinion, the dominating factor is the interpenetration, the mutual influence between that which is thought to be popular and what is not.

The distinction between popular and non-popular was also the concern of Felix Wilfred. According to Wilfred, a contrast-distinction between popular religiosity and official religion does not really fit in fully with the experience of the peripheral countries of Asia. A religion like hinduism, he argued, does not have systematically organized doctrinal systems and structures to which popular religion can be opposed. Consequently, the widely publicized distinction between, for example, the "great tradition" and the "little tradition" in hinduism, or between the "elites" and the "popular", between "sanskrit" and "non-sanskrit" traditions should not be exaggerated. In popular religion there is a confluence of both the so-called great tradition and the local element, the one flowing into the other. Wilfred also said, however, that the middle classes with their specific economic and political interests must also be taken into account.
We might ask if Wilfred's observations are also valid for christian religious systems in Asia and, at another level of reflection, to what extent relations within a religious system are bound to the economic and socio-political positions of its believers. Wilfred however did not analyze the way in which the economic and political interests of the middle classes intervene in the religious field.

Though no consensus was achieved towards the end of the congress with regard to the determining elements in the concept of popular religion, the conceptual discussion was no mere semantic debate or academic exercise. Because of a difference in understanding of the concept, chiefly shaped by the relevant context itself, the significance and function attributed to popular religion also appeared to be very different. In this sense, one of the workshops concluded that the manifest possibility of a contradictory use of the same notion, according to different contexts, is not a plea for the analytic and explicating meaning of the concept itself. It was precisely this insight which confirmed and strengthened Mbembe's position.

Most of the workshops agreed that popular religion should be defined by its social base, by the people living in a subordinated, dominated and oppressed situation. Mbembe's reluctance to accept the concept of popular religion finally obliged us to relate popular religion, in different contexts, to survival, power-structures and production-processes. There appeared, however, to be less consensus on how the relation between popular religion and power should be articulated. When the relationship with power is decisive, the epithet "popular" requires to be defined more precisely.

Approaches to popular religion

One of the most provocative items which arose in the discussion was the so-called "boom" of new religions, especially in the countries of Africa and Latin America. As Achille Mbembe observed, side by side with the truly ancestral religions a whole series of new religions is springing up in the African religious field. This "boom" challenges the churches and theologies in many ways. How can we understand the move from one religious regime to another? As Mbembe explained, in the African religious context people frequent various milieus at the same time: a person can be baptized, can go to mass in the morning and in the evening consult a soothsayer without sensing a contradiction between these two acts. Similar religious behaviour is to be seen in Brazil, where members of base ecclesial communities also frequent Afro-Brazilian religions and vice versa without experiencing any internal contradiction.

THE DISPUTED IMPORTANCE OF MEMORY
According to Yvette Aklé, this behaviour manifests the extent to which the transmission of European christianity into the African context has left an emotional, cultural and spiritual vacuum and has failed to influence people deeply. Faced with the same problem, Achille Mbembe also developed his point of view. He suggested that what was needed was the restitution of the long-term memory, in other words the rebuilding of an "African memory of that which is religious" which existed prior to the slave trade or the advent of the religions of the Book or even colonization. If we begin to delve into this African memory of the religious we find, first of all, that what constitutes the inherent historicity of the African religious context is the very plurality and the open nature of its religious traditions. At no point in African history – be it prior to, during or after colonization – did African religious traditions resist renewal and change. On the contrary, the African religious areas prior to islamic or christian monotheism were constantly areas of negotiation and barter: the ability to "negotiate" or "barter" religious matters was and remains a characteristic of African religious systems. From this point of view, the circulation or the bartering of rites and cults is a constituent aspect of the African memory of that which is religious. Thirdly, we find that this memory of the religious has not been completely destroyed by the violence of colonization. Colonization, christianization or islamization merely forced indigenous religious dynamisms to change scale and to rebound.[1]

However, the importance attached to "memory" in Mbembe's approach was not uncontroversial. In his reflection on popular religion in the context of Southern Asia, Felix Wilfred confirmed that when dealing with popular religion, it is often said that we must go back to the roots, to recapture, to recover, to return to

---

1 With regard to the strategies or the ruses used by the vanquished peoples (barter) in their relationships to the christianity of the era of colonization, one should see the author's analysis in *Afriques indociles. Christianisme, pouvoir et état en société postcoloniale*, Paris, Karthala, 1988, 75-94.

212

memories. But, he asked, "why should we go back?" According to Wilfred, such an approach results merely in justification, as if cultures and religions in the third world are on trial. Moreover, advocating the image of going back, of excavating memories and recovering the roots, in his opinion, merely raises yet again the same discussion about tradition and modernity. Therefore the whole approach in terms of the past, recovery and memory, says Wilfred, fails to give a proper perspective.

POPULAR MODES OF PRODUCING THE RELIGIOUS

One of Mbembe's central theses maintains that there can be nothing which is popular without a process through which the underclasses rediscover and re-appropriate the rags and the debris of religious traditions. The determining factors in the interpretation of the religious in Africa are the processes of "do it yourself" ("*bricolage*"), of "putting together" ("*assemblage*") and of "*re-invention*", by means of which new religious regimes are manufactured. Such processes can also be seen within the informal economy, in dressing habits, in music and in the practice of medicine. Here it becomes clear again that, for Mbembe, the tradition of barter and negotiation is a constituent element of the African path in the area of religion. If we consider this plasticity as the decisive factor, says the author, it becomes clear, from the analytical point of view, that the concepts of a "religious itinerary" ("*parcours religieux*"), the concept of a "*religious path*" ("trajet religieux") are much more rewarding than that of "popular religion".

The advantage of these concepts of a "religious path" and a "religious itinerary" lies in the fact that they underline the historic and dynamic nature of the processes of the production of the religious and they force us to emphasize the importance of the role played by the actors in these processes; a role which, moreover, changes depending on the contexts, what is at stake, the circumstances, etc. Referring to contemporary African situations, Mbembe points out that the production of that which is religious in Africa today is first and foremost a production of subsistence.

It seems to us that Mbembe's perspective basically agrees with the perspectives of Takatso Mofokeng and Julio de Santa Ana, Francisco Rolim and Amando Robles, to the extent that it sees popular religion as a "*social product*" which emerges within a given society and underlines the fact that people produce what they need. We still have to see whether they agree when it comes to identifying the economic, socio-political, cultural or ideological elements which play a role in the production of the religious.

MONOTHEISM AS A POLITICAL PROBLEM

In a very surprising way, Achille Mbembe introduced the issue of "monotheism" in his analysis of African religions. What happens in this field today, according to Mbembe is to some extent the result of "the way in which the conflict between monotheisms and what has been called 'paganism'" developed and the way in which the conversion of Africans to the religions of the Book was negotiated. This raises two questions: the question of the specific links between monotheism and paganism and the question of the rupture which, according to some people, exists between monotheism and so-called paganism.

In Mbembe's view, the question of monotheism in the African context is a "political" problem. His reasoning can be summed up as follows: "Christian monotheism emerged from an imperial desire for *conquest* which itself was based on a specific image of the *divine*, which was, at the same time, a specific image of the *truth* which – itself – was a specific image of *power*". It is in this sense, according to Mbembe, that in Africa the problem of monotheism is a political problem.

Mbembe considers that this approach to monotheism enables us to examine the issue of "African paganism" from a fresh angle. Indeed, if we consider monotheism as a specific image of the divine, of the truth, of power and of domination, we can conclude that what has been called "African paganism", as such, does not exist. "Paganism" exists merely as an image of monotheistic discourse which excludes that which is different.

This thesis is founded on a highly critical analysis of colonial christianity. To Mbembe's thinking, the christian-inspired monotheist paradigm, in Africa, functioned according to the principle of the exclusiveness, totalization and monopoly, to the extent that the belief in God proclaimed by christianity was only possible if it was accompanied by the suppression of all the other cults which existed prior to it. It defined itself as being totally incompatible with indigenous religions. There where it could, it did not hesitate to use the institutional lever and violence to achieve the subordination of the indigenous peoples. It functioned as an image of domination.

THE OPPOSITION OR THE RELATION BETWEEN MONOTHEISM AND PAGANISM
While it is true that christian monotheism rejected from the outset any form of relationship with indigenous religions, continues Mbembe, we should not, however, conclude that christianity and the so-called paganisms were fundamentally in contradiction. Researchers, analysts and even theologians too readily accepted the thesis that christian monotheism and "paganism" or fetishism were in opposition. They tried to demonstrate that there was a confrontation between two distinct and irreconcilable anthropologies. According to Mbembe, this thesis is not convincing. If we analyze this question from the point of view of the native users we see, according to him, that there is a much closer relationship between christian monotheism and 'paganism' than is generally admitted. How else can we understand that moving from one to the other was much less dramatic than the sociology of African conversion might have led us to believe.

All these factors lead Mbembe to state that if, from the point of view of the users, the difference between the two is not as insurmountable as was thought, and if moves from one to the other are not as catastrophic as was believed, then the only thing which, today, separates them is the capacity of their entrepreneurs

214

to create greater *social validity*. Thus it is from this point of view that we must analyze and interpret the emergence of new religions in Africa.

THE POST-COLONIAL CRISIS
We must now explain why today "paganism" in Africa is more successful in creating social validity than christianity. Mbembe believes that we must first of all reject any explanation which is mechanistic, structuralist or functionalist in character and centre our explanation on the most important event of today's Africa: the post-colonial crisis. We must understand the post-colonial period for what it is – in the same way as the period of colonization itself and the slave trade – as a time of affliction which must be deciphered and made intelligible.

In order to do this, says Mbembe, a critical analysis of the economic and political spheres is essential. It must be stressed – although in this area there is little consensus among Africans – that the economic plans of so-called structural-adjustment implemented in the various countries of Africa substantially undermined the human and social capital; the fact that power in that continent is exercised with brute force is related to a whole economy of death; that the way in which this power is exercised, as a result, raises the problem of the birth of the subject.[2] In his opinion, the majority of popular methods of producing the religious in Africa at the same time define themselves as discourse with regard to the possibility of the subject in the post-colonial context. By the fact that the post-colonial religious economy is an economy of "putting together", it is a discourse which fails adequately to brutalize a logic of the state which – as in communist regimes – defines itself as the absolute subject and works on the principle of non-contradiction.

MONOTHEISM AND POPULAR ATHEISM
In the workshops, Mbembe's questions concerning monotheism were the subject of intense debate. In Marc Spindler's report (missiologist, the Netherlands) it was asked: is it merely a question of the "perverse effects" of this belief when it is used for political ends? Or is judeo-christian monotheism, as such, suspect, as neo-pagan Europe and the New Right claim?

More generally, it was noted that the criticism of official religion, and in particular the repeated condemnation of ecclesiastical authoritarianism during the presentations also leads us to wonder whether the religious and social itinerary of the "people" might not just as easily end up in popular atheism. It has yet to be proved that "the people" are always and everywhere imbued with "religion". The historic experience of the West demonstrates that atheism has been and continues to be "popular". The same report states that no apologetic manoeuverings have

---

2 Readers might be interested to consult *Afriques indociles*, *o.c.*, 127-153, in which Mbembe discusses the "authoritarian principle"; and 153-177, where he considers "politics in a time of death".

been able to disguise the explicit desire on the part of many of our contemporaries to reject all forms of religion.

In the above-mentioned report, another fundamental objection surfaced. Methodological atheism, common in the social sciences and largely adopted in the interventions in our congress, raises the following question: If all religion is purely a "social product" and nothing more, what can we do with a religion without God, without either revelation or transcendence? Open, massive atheism would be much better!

EXPERIENCE AND NON-DUALITY

Other people explained popular religion as a religion of experience, focussing explicitly on cultural patterns and particular modes of knowledge from the point of view of popular religions in non-Western contexts.

Coming from the South-Asian context, Felix Wilfred pointed to "anubhava" as the beginning and foundation of religion. Anubhava, he explained, is not merely connected with a subjectivism nor with a subject, but with a typical hindu understanding of non-duality: neither this nor that; neither the subjective nor the objective. It is like the understanding of God; neither being nor non-being; a non-dual approach to reality. The mode of knowledge Wilfred referred to is a concrete reality-experience that is the symbiosis, the synthesis of what in modern, Western ways of thinking automatically is being split into the subject and the object. It is knowledge through identification rather than differentiation. The anubhava, in that sense, is found at the basis of popular religion and is the foundation and starting point for Asian contextual theologizing.[3]

Popular religion and liberation

With regard to the role of popular religion in liberation processes, the discussion focussed on the liberating potential of popular religions, the politicization, or institutionalizing of popular religion, and the usefulness of marxism as an instrument of analysis.

ITS LIBERATING POTENTIAL FROM THIRD WORLD PERSPECTIVES

From Felix Wilfred's presentation it emerged that historically no social change and transformation – at least as regards South Asia – has been possible without reference to religion and religious symbols. Using some examples from the Indian context, among them the powerful "bhakti movement" Wilfred illustrated that religious resources and religious heritages have been reinterpreted by the people in terms of their liberation. In this line, Wilfred rejected the – albeit often unconscious – underlying presupposition of many of the members of the congress

---

3 To measure the importance which Felix Wilfred accords to this remark one can also turn to an article by this author, 'Inculturation as a hermeneutical question. Reflection in the Asian contexts', *a.c.*, 422-436.

that liberation is the monopoly of christians: christianity can make no claim whatsoever to possess liberation.

On the other hand, Achille Mbembe presented a more critical attitude towards attaching too much reliability to the liberating powers of the people reinterpreting religious heritages. According to him, the processes of the production of religion are ambiguous: the underclasses can produce a religion which, by its content, its functions and its objectives fits perfectly into the very parameter of domination and which ensures the reproduction of the dominations bearing down upon them. They can do so not because they are consciously alienated from themselves (as marxism claims), but because this is the way they choose to articulate their religious interests and this way of articulating such interests is, in their judgement, the most plausible in their particular context. The problem is knowing how it is that a given method of producing religion is seen as being the most plausible in a given context.

In the post-colonial context, he added, the political effectiveness of African "paganism" is ambiguous to the extent that this "paganism" rejects the intervention of evil in the interior life of the native peoples, thus deculpabilizing the state. The post-colonial state does not appear as the central figure in all this economy of conflict. On the contrary, the majority of its procedures call upon the indigenous man or woman to readapt him- of herself in a strictly private manner. Moreover, the production of religion by the popular classes is, according to Mbembe a production of subsistence whose principal aim is to legitimatize the principle of a discourse with regard to non-liberty. The discourse it carries with it is a discourse of non-liberty. In the case of Africa, non-liberty means nothing more and nothing less that what it is: the subjection of the native peoples to an authoritarian principle and the exercise of power by brute force. Independence has not rendered the issue of non-liberty obsolete. And Mbembe concludes: If, therefore, christianity or African theologies are not capable of reflecting theologically on these three elements – the non-subject, power, and brute force, and the advent of the individual – then christianity will remain something rather peripheral in Africa.

A FEMINIST ANALYSIS: A PLEA FOR A NEW PARADIGM

In the discussion, Maria José Nunes (Brazil) stressed the fact that popular religion is basically carried by the spiritual force of women who claim their liberation even when surrounded by oppressive religious structures. In the same line, Mary Grey (Great Britain) pointed out that women's experience has something very specific to contribute to the methodology of liberation. One of the questions prepared by women and put to the plenary – to the men present in particular – was formulated by Maria José Nunes: the theology of liberation developed by using marxism as a scientific tool to approach and analyze poverty. There is, however, a considerable body of feminist tools for analysis. To what extent do you use these feminist scientific theories in formulating your theology?

What contribution comes either from the feminist theology of liberation or from feminist scientific theories?

Here, the response of Luíz Gaiger, a Brazilian sociologist studying in Louvain, was remarkable. According to Gaiger, the challenge facing what is referred to as the woman's question goes beyond the problem of an analytical framework; it raises the problem of an analytical *paradigm*. Marxism's most important and the most basic contribution was to have taken *human practice* as the starting point for any analysis of society. At this level, marxism continues to be valid. Now that a new aspect of this practice has been discovered, we realize that until now – and in most cases unconsciously – we have been working on the basis of a non-gender-specific paradigm, or on the basis of a-sexuality. In concrete analyses, for example of the peasant movements in Brazil, people often talk in generic terms; the position of women always tails along behind the principle analysis. Is there any solution? We could move from the marxist framework to another framework, but there would still be the danger of being trapped in the same paradigm. If we consider the position of woman as one aspect of the differentiation of human praxis – just as Marx introduced the basic variable of the social classes – we could escape from this captivity. This paradigm alters completely our way of experiencing and understanding the situation and how we react to all that is happening before our eyes. It is for this reason, Gaiger insisted, that the challenge requires more than a simple renewal of theory. It calls for quite a different paradigm. To adopt this paradigm would bring about a change in theory.

MARXISM AS A SYSTEM AND AN INSTRUMENT OF ANALYSIS
For the Eastern European participants it was their first opportunity to discuss with liberation theologians from the third world. In recent decades, liberation theology was a difficult issue in the countries of Central and Eastern Europe, particularly because of liberation theology's use of marxism as an instrument of analysis. Yet, reinforced by the failure of aggressive centralism in Eastern Europe, the usefulness of marxist analysis remained a controversial issue.

András Máté-Tóth (Hungary) told of the recent experiences of liberation from real existing socialism, a system that proved to be inhuman when human existence is brought under total control. In his opinion, "existing socialism does not function and a functioning socialism does not exist". Moreover, the distinctions made between e.g. stalinism, post-stalinism and non-stalinism are, in his opinion, mere theoretical distinctions which do not exist in reality.
In this discussion, the sinologist Alvaro Eljach (Colombia) stated that he was perplexed by the fact that the Eastern European participants identified their legitimate rejection of the Communist Party dictatorships with a rejection of marxism-socialism. For Eljach, recognizing that democracy had won over dictatorship did not imply that capitalism had won over socialism. Giving as an example the dollar-corruption of the party-leaders in China, Eljach contested the effects of a limited free-market economy in China. Instead of creating possibilities for

218

greater freedom and democracy it had promoted corruption, child-labour and prostitution.

In the same vein, Gerrit Huizer (Netherlands) warned that developments and democratic expectations in Eastern Europe, especially when orchestrated by Western European countries in a capitalist economic perspective, will also find themselves confronted with the limitations of the capitalist system itself which only works when the third world pays its debts. Here Takatso Mofokeng entered the discussion, congratulating the Eastern Europeans on their recent liberation: "I am happy to taste a freedom that we do not have in South Africa". Mofokeng reinforced Huizer's point of view, asking the Eastern European theologians for an analysis of the roots of Western political economy and Western capitals which went much deeper and which did not merely embrace it as good because it looks better than what there was before.

Reflecting on these observations Máté-Toth stressed that the bitter history of forty years of socialism made it impossible to dream of socialism any longer. Mireille Ryšková (CSSR) also responded to the warnings concerning the move from a marxist to a capitalist system: "Our economies are in a very bad way; the environment has suffered the most damage; the average life span is the shortest in Europe; we do not have enough medicine; food is bad. People are looked upon as workers, not as human beings. Our problem is not the seduction of a Western capitalist system which presents itself as an alternative to the party-dictatorship. We struggle for survival in the midst of an ecological catastrophe in our countries".[4]

Along the same lines, Felix Wilfred's statement was interesting. He argued that the developments in Eastern Europe, in Asia and the world over demonstrate that the ethnic and cultural dimension is coming to the fore and that economics can no longer be the foundation for the unity of humankind and for its transformation. For him, this poses the question of the economic criterion: when confronted with ethnic, racial, sex-specific and popular religious struggles it becomes increasingly clear that economics cannot sustain the world. In his opinion, the economic base, when considered as a guarantee for the unity of the world, is eroding and breaking.

Popular religion and contextual theologies

SHAMANISM AND MINJUNG THEOLOGY

A critical question raised by Edmond Tang (Hong Kong) concerns shamanism as a source for minjung theology: do popular religions, after they have been manipulated by theologians, still remain popular religions? Referring explicitly to shamanism, Tang underlined the fact that most popular religions have a non-

---

4 The same argument was stressed by Svetluse Košíckova in her congress-paper 'Spiritual life and the non-violent revolution in Czechoslovakia'.

linear concept of time, giving importance to the body, to rituals, to that which is unarticulated. However, because of the use made of it by contextual theology, in the case of minjung theology, shamanism has been raised to a rational level. Whereas it was originally presented as being a cultural option for minjung theology to opt for shamanism, the shamanism they encountered was already politicized by the students in the seventies, with strong socio-political connotations, including a linear concept of time.

In this same line, Takatso Mofokeng (South Africa) opened up an interesting debate when he asked if minjung theology contributes anything liberating to shamanism. When Tang answered that the christian reflection above all introduced into shamanism the concept of history and socio-political liberation, the missiologist Georg Evers (Germany) questioned the contextual representativeness of minjung theology in Korea. In Evers' opinion, minjung theology may also be considered a religion of a new urban society, a successful middle-class religion, elitist and the perfect subject for conferences. Tang replied that, indeed, minjung theology cannot be considered characteristic of Korean christianity as such, because of the high socio-political profile of christianity in this theology. Though it is very limited and marginalized and gradually developing into a systematic theology with very little influence among the workers, Tang interprets minjung theology as a legitimate contextual theology. It corresponds at least to the idea that contextual theology needs to have a liberative element.

LINEAR AND NON-LINEAR CONCEPTS OF TIME
With regard to the complex relationships between contextual theology and popular religion, the workshop report presented by Marc Spindler stressed that popular religion can also be recognized by its relation to historic time, or rather by the absence of such a relationship: popular religion functions according to cyclical time, to the rhythm of passage and the circumstances of life and of death. Contextual theologies, on the other hand, integrate "historic time" into their theoretical construction in the sense that they offer an historic project which is worked out within "linear" time. This different time relationship, according to this workshop report, indicates a gulf between popular religion and contextual theology. Even if there can be agreement about the relative nature of the opposition between cyclical time and linear time and even if this gulf is padded, it would seem to be real. Popular religion is not, from the outset, part of an historical project, but it can become part of one a posteriori. This was what happened with minjung theology in South Korea, as Edmond Tang showed.

INTELLECTUALS AND PEOPLE
The role of the intellectual was inevitably discussed in these terms. One of the workshops asked: If we take as our starting point the idea that popular religion is synonymous with a more or less spontaneous "putting together" and "assembling", does the rational ordering put forward and performed by intellectuals and (contextual) theologians not, in itself, mean the calling into question or even the

death of popular religion? "In any case," the members of the workshop stress, "popular religion certainly loses its 'innocence' as soon as it undergoes treatment and processing by intellectuals. And likewise the intellectual who throws himself into popular religion as though into the fountain of youth makes it lose all its properties the moment he throws himself in! It was in this perspective that we discussed Anthony Fernandes' (India) immersion experience (within hinduism). Was that particular kind of immersion not "conserving" rather than "liberating"?

THE CHALLENGE OF MYTHOS AND LOGOS
From his point of view, Felix Wilfred went more deeply into the challenges which popular religion offers to the rationality-criterion of contextual theology. In his opinion, popular religion challenges theological methodology to take the decisive step from the logos to the mythos, from the word to the myth. Because of the fact that the elevated centre and content of christianity – the logos – has become inflated, christianity has become a religion full of words, a diary of words. The centre of theology for Wilfred, however, is myth, which is experienced not as subjectivism, nor as an objective element. Both are transcended. The challenge posed by popular religion is indeed the challenge of recovering the mythos. "Precisely what we do not want is what popular religion wants us to make: are we ready to make the mythos, where the wholeness and totality of reality is embraced, the heart of theology?"

Felix Wilfred's presentation aroused much discussion in several workshops on the rationality of theology. Marc Spindler's report appreciates that, for Wilfred, popular religion calls into question the universal claims of rational theology, a category which also includes "contextual theology" and its social analysis. In the same workshop, the members agreed on the limitations of reason, but they wondered if the reception of mythical material in religious devotion, in the theological formulation and in liberating practice is a principle which is valid for all contexts. In the case of the West, for example, the religious and political myths of the 20th century have been terribly dangerous and evil. Moreover, the revival of myths from deep in the pasts of the Western nations and tribes (the Greek, Roman, Celtic, Scandinavian, Germanic etc. myths) is much more the result of the work of reactionary movements such as the New Right than of liberation movements.
The same workshop admit that agreement would require to be reached about the concept of "mythos". It is nevertheless true that the liberation theologies in Latin America and in the West cannot abandon their critical rational analysis of society: this rationality is a constituent of these theologies and plays a determining role in revealing alienations.

GODDESS-TRADITIONS AND THE IMAGE OF GOD
In this discussion, feminist theologians asked about the liberating potential for women of the goddess-traditions in hinduism. Felix Wilfred replied by asking if the judeo-christian tradition is adequate to reflect the question seriously. He

221

affirmed that there is practically no God in the hindu pantheon who is not connected with both the woman and the man. It is always a couple, the total. Whereas the woman is symbolized as the energy, the very combination of both elements is remarkable: the goddess is the nurturing, mothering goddess as well as the terrifying, gruesome woman. Both aspects are present in the symbol of "kali". In this perspective, Wilfred raised the question of the image of God in the judeo-christian tradition and the way in which the feminist movement deals with it. In the feminist movement, he argued, we find a concern to resource, to find and recover texts from women who lived in the past. In his opinion, however, this is little consolation: the judeo-christian tradition is basically patriarchal. The question must be resolved in the very concept of the divine. Does the judeo-christian tradition not need to be complemented by goddess-traditions from elsewhere?

FEMINIST THEOLOGY AND LIBERATION THEOLOGY

The other question the women brought for plenary debate concerned the contribution of feminist liberation theology to liberation processes. Responding to this question, Felix Wilfred stated that we can legitimately speak about feminist theology as liberation. In his opinion it would, however, be wrong to look at the feminist issue within a general framework of liberation theology. According to Wilfred, no serious argument can be found to explain why some people would like to reduce feminist theology to a general theology of liberation. To his mind, this is quite unacceptable: the general theology of liberation is a rationalistic theology, in which socio-economic analysis is still dominant. The counterpart of this kind of rationalistic theology of liberation is, for him, a holistic theology of liberation, where the wholeness of reality, the fullness, the health, the harmony and the totality are decisive. When this is achieved, liberation takes place. According to Wilfred, feminist theology agrees with this type of holistic theology of liberation. There is therefore need for a constant interaction between this general type of liberation theology and the feminist theology of liberation; feminist theology has a dimension of liberation which the general theology of liberation does not possess.

Mary Grey was, however, firmly opposed to what Wilfred called a "reduction" of feminist theology to a general theology of liberation. In her opinion, feminist theology is a theology of liberation precisely because women start from a position of disadvantage. With regard to the second point, Grey agreed with much that Wilfred said, stressing that feminist theology does start from a *different premise*, moving away from the premises of Western philosophy since Descartes. Feminist theology does not start from a rational, dualistic world-vision, and moves away from a theology in which God is against the world or man is against woman. The subject-object division, which can be found everywhere, in politics and in discourse-construction, must be abandoned. In that sense, the agenda of feminist theology is, according to Grey, much more inclusive than the normal agenda of liberation theology. What unites women the world over is the contribution to a different methodology of theology and a different way of being.

222

The challenge in terms of a different methodology was reinforced by the direct question which Yvette Aklé (Benin) addressed to African male theologians: "I should like to ask those male African theologians present this: for how long will you be silent when your sisters are at work in the field and fight on from day-break with simply the cross of Jesus Christ in their hands and heal and comfort human misery. While in the Vatican – with your complicity – Christ is bureaucratized, Christ is locked in a system of sacraments, while the people live and die in misery. What part do you take, my African brothers, when the female element is pushed away from that heritage which Jesus Christ left to us?"

MISSIOLOGY AND THE CONCERN FOR CONTEXTUALITY

For Bert Hoedemaker (the Netherlands), interpreting contextuality as part of a missiological concept, "contextuality" also refers to raising global issues like cultural pluralism, inter-cultural and inter-contextual communication and secularization. In reaction to Hoedemaker, Georg Evers focussed more specifically on the "global" element in the concept of missiology. Evers contested a supposed, all-encompassing capacity of missiology to answer basic theological questions concerning justice and liberation and stated that Hoedemaker claimed for a single discipline of theology a competence which can not be limited to one discipline alone. To this Hoedemaker replied that indeed his vision is not limited to the discipline of missiology alone and only theology as a whole can reflect these basic questions. However: "As long as theology is not adequate to reflect on what happens with religions and the church in the world of humankind, we need something like missiology to maintain and sustain a vision of humankind. Missiology, albeit in a fragmentary and limited way, is present in the theological faculties as a disturbing element in the community of disciplines. It will continue to remind us of the fact that we are exercising theology in a world that is much larger, much more difficult and much more complex than we usually assume."

CHURCH AS THE AGENT OF CHANGE?

For Georg Evers, however, the "global" element must be related to a "particular" agent of change: "Not so much the global aspect, but the particular aspect of the local church is that of being responsible in the proper context for bringing the Good News with all its implications of justice." In the same vein, Hoedemaker affirmed that for him "church" refers to the communities of people who, to-gether, exercise a form of spirituality, going back to the sources of the tradition, in order to sustain a view of the world as a whole. According to him, it is impossible to have a vision of the church which exceeds the limits of church as a provisional form of unity, which is only there to remind us of a more basic, more encompassing, fuller, much more human form of unity. In this sense church is mid-way between human confusion and ultimate redemption. Therefore for him there are only two basic forms of church which are relevant for theology. It is in the local church that the heart of the christian gospel and the heart of the view of God and the world is lived. But it is in the universal communications between churches from all cultures and sectors of the human community that the hope of humankind is kept alive. These two levels need to be continually related to each other. Thus, for Hoedemaker, the local church is an agent of mission, in as far as it is able to communicate with the universal church and translate that communication in the basic life of the community.

Now that the issue of the agent of change was brought into the discussion Takatso Mofokeng entered the debate. In his opinion, some of the elements, such as peace, women's liberation, the integrity of creation, ecology – issues of great importance in society – which were mentioned in the discussion, in Western Europe are generally taken up outside of the church by people who do not regard themselves as agents working in society on behalf of the church. The question he raised, however, was why theologians working in Western Europe identify the church as a major agent in pursuing such goals. In South Africa, said Mofokeng, the church, the very community which is regarded as a traditional agent for the transformation of society, is a problem. The church is an agent with structures, operating by means of laws and regulations inherited from a Western, liberal tradition. Because the church shares a number of the same goals as the liberal state and society, the above-mentioned goals, strategies and methods will not be realized.

Reflecting on the recent processes in Eastern Europe, also Geert van Dartel (The Netherlands) warned against over-estimating the role which the churches played in the revolutionary movements. "It would be too much honour to the churches," he stated, "to say that they as a whole and only they kept up the valuable standards of the old national and cultural traditions and morality." This does not prevent christians in Middle and Eastern Europe from expecting and hoping to hear from their church leaders a testimony of truth and morality in line with the national tradition and identity. "A moment of such a stand of the church," van Dartel explained, "was the mass religious gathering in Velehrad in 1985 to celebrate the 1,100th anniversary of Methodius, one of the apostles of the Slavs, which immediately turned into a political protest against the totalitarian state in Czechoslovakia." Pastors and christians have braved repression and committed their faith in defence of the right of all to liberty and social justice. "The validity of the christian message and faith was and is judged by the testimony given." Quoting the Czech theologian Josef Zveřina, van Dartel stressed: "For us a theology of liberation should, in the first place, have as its aim liberation from the oppression and the totalitarianism of the communist ideology."[5]

The efficacity of a contextual theology

Anxious to preserve the theological nature of contextual theologies and the theologies of liberation, one of the workshop reports was of the opinion that they

---

5 The quotations are taken from his contribution to the congress 'Popular religion, the churches and liberation in Eastern Europe' (mimeo).

are not theologies to the extent that they provide an analysis of society or of the context, even if this kind of analysis is one of the constituent elements; nor are they theologies because of their ethnic or political commitment or their practice, even if this liberating practice is considered one of the basic conditions for the legitimate exercise of theology (something which we must avoid over-stressing, for sometimes theology can be the antecedent of liberation). Whatever the consequences of this parenthesis, the report regrets that contextual theologies would appear to be exhausting themselves in their historic projects for social change.

This regret carries with it two warnings against some conceptions of the contextualization of theology. On the one hand, according to the report, we could – eventually – say that theology is one of the elements of the social processes and that it forms part of practice. Having said this, the report states that it is only theology to the extent that it is serving the glory of God. Theology has an eschatological horizon which is constantly revealed as long as history is on the move. Theology constantly reminds us that we cannot stand still with our present achievements, be they disappointing or inspiring. On the other hand, the report goes on, it is essential that a theology should be relevant in relation to its context; it does not, however, have to be effective; it is not theology, in itself, which changes the world.

The question of the efficacity of theology gave rise to other points of view. Presenting the work of one of the workshops, Bruno Chenu remarked that the plan to formulate a liberating contextual theology presupposes that theology should be capable of guiding a popular religion. But, he added, can it really do so? This question led Chenu to differentiate between the "historic efficacity" of theology and its "eschatological efficacity".

With regard to its historic efficacity, we must, according to Chenu, examine the roles which theology can play with regard to popular religion. These functions are many. They can be described as legitimation and canonization, judgement or discernment, recuperation or manipulation or enslavement. Other functions could also be identified. While it is necessary to analyze these functions, should we not, nevertheless, recognize that a contextual theology, of necessity, produces a vision of the world, and thus itself becomes one ideology among others?

Reflecting on the question of the eschatological efficacity, Chenu was of the opinion that a critical examination of theological interpretations of eschatology was needed. A theology which reduced eschatology to a so-called "eschatological reserve", the content of which was nothing more than the awareness of a horizon which constantly moves as one goes forward, cannot claim to be truly effective and liberating. Should we not submit that theology should constantly remind us – in the name of eschatology – of the dimension of transcendence within the very heart of the liberating struggle? Moreover, the experience of Eastern Europe attests to the need to safeguard an openness to transcendence; a humanism without transcendence leads to the denial of man. And again, the tension between historical and eschatological efficacity can be maintained when contextual theology succeeds in creating an articulation between – in sociological terms – ideology and utopia, and – in theological terms – love and hope. In this area, we can learn much from Black American popular religion: The two books which are at the centre of all the expressions of this religion are on the one hand Exodus, and the other, Revelation.

In the debate about efficacity and eschatology which followed Chenu's presentation, Felix Wilfred said that he found this framework somewhat dichotomous. It reminded him of the controversy between Latin American liberation theology and political theology with regard to the "eschatological reserve". According to Wilfred, Latin American liberation theologians have been strong in bringing out the fact that transcendence must be found within historical involvement and it must not be postponed. Using the kind of dialectic framework presented by Chenu is, in the opinion of Wilfred, inappropriate; it does not contribute to unity; it divides. Explaining his point of view, Wilfred referred specifically to the challenge of popular religion, bringing a wholeness, appealing to the whole person and to the whole reality in the midst of a dichotomized world. As his central thesis, Wilfred said that if the concern is "transcendence", it cannot be recuperated in terms of eschatology. There are various ways, within the present itself, of contemplating the situation as the fragment, but the fragment which is to be integrated into the perspective of a wholeness yet to be achieved. "Therefore, if we look to the present situation as to the fragment to be overcome, within the present itself the transcendence is present, maybe not by projecting and eschatology. From the hindu world vision you see that we are in a world of illusion, a world that slowly comes to its realization, that would not necessarily call for an eschatology in contrast to the present."
One of the workshops supported Wilfred's observation by relating his statement on eschatology to the conception of liberation. The group argued that the concept of liberation proceeds from an ideology of linear progress which is purely Western and is large nourished by a judeo-christian eschatology foreign both to popular religion and the classic religions of Asia. For this reason, they add, several Asian theologians reject the very concept of a history of salvation.

The suggestion that eschatology is not necessarily thought of in contrast to the present aroused the somewhat polemical comment that the eschatological vision of the universal cannot be abandoned, nor can the hope of universal liberation be rejected. If this were the case, the "contexts" would be completely given over to chauvinisms and nationalisms which would be the sources of new forms of oppression. According to this view, the strongly nationalist forces which some people attribute to popular religion will limit its potential for liberation. Felix Wilfred, for his part, stressed the need to maintain the link between the universal and the particular. For him, the universal cannot be seen as the common ground of all national, ethnic and cultural specificities; according to him, the universal is built into the particular. Because popular religion is a determined experience of a people within a given life-context, it cannot be alienated through the backdoor of the universal. Therefore popular religion poses the question of the concreteness as the in-built totality. Popular religion challenges us to discover the universal and the human at the heart of the particular.

For Wilfred, this has many concrete consequences in a religiously pluralist world. In his opinion, we no longer talk today in terms of dialogue with religious systems in different contexts, or not exclusively at least. "That period is over: requiem eternam. We must say good-bye to the face of that flirting, picking up something here and there, comparing religious systems. What concerns us is the importance of popular religion in terms of participation and the creation of community precisely because the higher systematic religions are divisive". To illustrate this, Wilfred referred to buddhism. When it went to China or to Korea as a religious system it was a divisive force. But buddhism, by becoming a popular religion when it took over the deities of the Chinese, the Burmese, of the Thais and the Japanese became a buddhism which was at home, creating unity which brought people together. In this sense, as various workshops affirmed, contextual theology should not merely reflect the liberative potential of popular religion in political terms or in terms of dialogue between religious systems. Because what would be the relevance of contextual theology if it did not contribute to creating universal community through participation in particular religious universes?

Contributors

Yvette Aklé
She was born in Togo; made her studies at the Ecole d'Administration du Togo. Was Clerk of the Court in Togo and Benin for a period of ten years; took a maîtrise in ethnology with a study on the religious role of African women (1984). During the second half of the eighties she worked in the Communauté Evangélique d'Action Apostolique in Paris. She published 'Des femmes africaines parlent de Jésus', in: *Chemins de la christologie Africaine*, Paris, Desclée, 1986, 289-297.

Anthony B. Fernandes
He was born in Bombay, India; studied and taught philosophy, theology and economy. Since 1974 he is staff-member of CEBEMO (the Netherlands), first as region-responsible for India; then as coordinator and project-evaluator for the Asian section; next he was in charge of a special exchange-programme Third World-Netherlands. At present he is region-responsible in CEBEMO for Colombia/Equador (Latin America). He was co-editor of *Quest*, a magazine covering theological themes brought up by student-theologians.

Jeroom Heyndrickx
Born in Belgium, member of the mission-congregation of the Fathers of Scheut; 1957-1974 he worked in Taiwan and founded the Taiwan Pastoral Institute; 1974-1981 vicar-general of the Scheutist Fathers in Rome; since 1981 he works on the staff of the Ferdinand Verbiest Stichting (Louvain) and is director of the China-Europe Institute of the Catholic University of Louvain. He published on the Chinese church and on intereclesial models of relationship in: *Japan Missionary Bulletin* 39(1985), 40-49 and 40(1986), 180-187, and in: R. Malek/W. Prawdzik (eds), *Zwischen Autonomie und Anlehnung, die Problematik der katholischen Kirche in China*, Nettetal 1988, 19-30.

Bert Hoedemaker
Born in the Netherlands; studied theology in Utrecht (the Netherlands) and at Yale University Divinity School (USA); doctoral dissertation on the theology of H. Richard Niebuhr (1966, Utrecht); taught at the Theological High School Jakarta, Indonesia, from 1967-1972; since 1974 university lecturer missiology at the University of Groningen, where he is professor missiology and ethics since 1984. He is member of the Commission on Faith and Order of the WCC. Published *Met Christus bij anderen. Opmerkingen over dialoog en apostolaat*, Baarn,

1978; and was co-editor with A. Camps M.R. Spindler, F.J. Verstraelen of *Oecumenische Inleiding in de Missiologie, texten en kontexten van het wereld-christendom*, Kampen, Kok, 1988.

Berma Klein Goldewijk

Born in the Netherlands; studied theology and social sciences (development studies); was staff-member of the Grail-project 'Formação de animadoras locais' in Portugal (1979-1980). Since 1984 researcher in the section missiology/Third World theology at the theological faculty Nijmegen; first working on a research concerning the contextuality of the ecclesiology of Leonardo Boff (1984-1988); then researching the relation context-method of Third World theology (1988-1990); at present doing a post-doc research on Afrobrazilian religion-studies and Latinamerican liberation theology (1990-1993). Published several articles on changing social and religious practices in Latin-America; doctoral dissertation *Practice or principle. Base Communities and the ecclesiology of Leonardo Boff* (publ. in Dutch), Kampen, Kok, 1991.

András Máté-Tóth

Born in Hungary. Theologian, active in informal catholic base groups; participating in the Ecumenical Network for Peace and Democracy in Europe. At present working on a doctoral dissertation about liberation theology in Eastern Europe. He published 'Die Idee und Praxis der Gewaltlosigkeit der BUSCH-Bewegung' in: Wilco de Jonge (ed.), *Living in truth. Catholics in Eastern Europe*, Den Haag, Pax Christi, 1989; he is publishing also 'Theologie der Befreiung als Herausforderung für die Christen in der Zweiten Welt' (manuscr. 22p.).

Achille Mbembe

Born in Cameroon; studied history in Yaounde and Paris (Panthéon-Sorbonne) and political sciences at the Institut d'Etudes Politiques in Paris; he is member of the editorial board of *Politique Africaine* and was deputy of the secretary-general of the JEC international. He published *Rome and the African Churches* (Pro Mundi Vita: Africa dossier, 1986, n. 37-38); and *Afriques Indociles. Christianisme, pouvoir et Etat en société postcoloniale*, Paris, Le Centurion, 1987. At present he is university lecturer at the Department of History, Colombia University, New York.

Takatso A. Mofokeng

Born in South-Africa; studied theology at the Theological University Kampen (the Netherlands), where he presented his doctoral dissertation *The Crucified among the Crossbearers. Towards a Black Christology*, Kampen (Kok) 1983; at present lecturer at the University of South Africa (Pretoria) and staff-member at the Institute for Contextual Theology. He also published 'The evolution of the black struggle and the role of black theology' in: I.J. Mosala/B. Thagale (eds), *The unquestionable right to be free*, Maryknoll N.Y., Orbis, 1986, 113-128; and 'A basis for a relevant theology for Botswana', in *Mission Studies* 4(1987)1, 55-64.

230

Andreas Müller
Born in Germany; franciscan; studied philosophy and theology; since 1969 director of the Missionszentrale der Franziskaner in Bonn (Germany). He was editor of *Missionare im Lernprozess. 10 Jahre Seminararbeit der Missionszentrale der Franziskaner*, Mettingen, Brasilienkunde Verlag, 1979; and published 'Blitzlichter auf einen franziskanischen Dialog', in: L. Boff/W. Bühlmann (eds), *Baue meine Kirche auf, Franziskanische Inspirationen aus der Dritten Welt*, Düsseldorf, Patmos, 1983, 141-169.

Maria José F. Rosado Nunes
Born in Brasil; she is post-graduate in sociology at the Pontifícia Universidade Católica in São Paulo; she did research on women and the catholic church and published on women and popular religion in Bahia and the Amazone: *Vida religiosa nos meios populares*, Petrópolis, Vozes, 1985. At the moment she prepares her doctoral dissertation in Paris.

Mercy Amba Oduyoye
Born in Ghana; she is methodist theologian; was lecturer at the University of Ibadan (Nigeria) and visiting professor at the Harvard Divinity School and the Union Theological Seminary in New York; vice-president of the Ecumenical Association of African Theologians, participated at the intercontinental congresses of the EATWOT in Accra, New Dehli en Oaxtepec; she published *Wir Selber Haben Ihn Gehört. Theologische Reflexionen zum Christentum in Afrika*, Freiburg, Exodus, 1988; and was co-editor with Virginia Fabella of *With Passion and Compassion. Third World Women doing Theology*, Maryknoll, N.Y., Orbis Books, 1988. She is director of the women's department of the Ecumenical Council of Churches in Geneva.

Libor Ovečka and Mireille Ryšková
Both were born in Czechoslovakia and live in Prague; Ovečka is theologian, Salesian of Don Bosco; was teaching English during the time of the party dictature; active in base communities of the church; at the moment preparing a doctoral dissertation on moral theology at the Theological Faculty in Passau (Germany). Ryšková worked in a publishing house in Prague; at present she is studying New Testament exegesis and moral theology in Passau (Germany).

Amando J. Robles
Born in Spain; dominican; since 1972 working in Central America; since 1976 living in Costa Rica, where he took his national identity; professor at the Escuela Ecumenia de Ciencias de la Religión, Universidad Nacional, Heredia, Costa Rica and at the Instituto Teológico di America Central, San José, Costa Rica. He published 'Producción de sentido religioso y transformación social en las clases subalternas campesinas de Nicaragua', in: *Senderos*, 1987. At the moment he prepares his doctoral dissertation in Louvain: *Religion et rationalité comme visions*

du monde dans des sociétés du capitalisme dependant en transition de la tradition à la modernité.

Francisco Cartaxo Rolim

Born in Brazil; doctor in sociology of religion (São Paulo); professor at the Universidade Federal Fluminense Rio de Janeiro (Brazil); published *Religião e classes populares*, Petropolis, Vozes, 1980; and *Pentecostais no Brasil. Uma interpretação socio-religiosa*, Petropolis, Vozes, 1985.

Julio de Santa Ana

Born in Montevideo (Uruguay); studied theology in Buenos Aires and Strasbourg; doctor's degree in 1962 in sciences of religion; was director of the Centro de Estudios Cristianos in Rio de la Plata (1963-1968) and secretary-general of ISAL (1962-1970); from 1979-1982 director of the Commission for Participation of Churches in Development of the WCC; since 1983 co-director of CESEP (São Paulo – Brazil). He published *Good News to the Poor. The challenge of the poor in the history of the Church*, Geneva, WCC, 1977; *Towards a church of the poor. The work of an ecumenical group on the church and the poor*, Geneva, WCC, 1979.

Sidbe Semporé

Born in Ouagadougou (Burkina-Faso); dominican; studied theology and exegesis in France, Austria, Israël (École Biblique) and Switzerland; university lecturer in theology and exegesis in Benin, Nigeria en Ivory Coast. Published 'Liberté chrétienne en contexte africain' and 'Afro-christianisme, un courant irréversible', in: *Spiritus* 25(1984)96, 283-292 and 30(1989)115, 193-205; and about African popular religion in Benin in: *Concilium* 22(1986)4, 270-275.

Hadewych Snijdewind

Born in the Netherlands; dominican sister; studied Dutch language and literature, theology and social sciences; former general-secretary of *Concilium* in Nijmegen. She did research on women and the church; is specializing in matters of the Eastern European churches and theology; she published 'Wegen naar niet patriarchale solidariteit', in: *Concilium* 17(1981)3 (Nl), 85-95; and 'Ich weine über meine Kirche die ich liebe', in: N. Sommer (Hrsg.), *Nennt uns nicht Brüder: Frauen in der Kirche durchbrechen das Schweigen*, Stuttgart, Kreuz Verlag, 1985, 121-125.

Edmond Tang

Born in Hong Kong; studied philosophy (Hong Kong) and theology (Louvain); since 1977 researcher for Pro Mundi Vita (Brussels); coordinator of the Ecumenical China Study Liaison Group; editor of *Ministries and Communities* (Pro Mundi Vita) and member of the editorial board of *Voies de l'Orient* (Brussels). He published the results of his research on Taiwan, Cambodia, China, Hong Kong, in: *Pro Mundi Vita Bulletin*. At present he prepares a doctoral dissertation on inculturation in South-East Asia.

232

Jacques Van Nieuwenhove

Born in Belgium; studied philosophy (licence, Rome) and theology (doctorate, Strasbourg, 1973; dissertation on Latin American liberation theology); lecturer at the Seminary of Bujumbura (Burundi), at the Higher Pastoral Institute Lumen Vitae (Brussels), at the Theological Faculty Tilburg. Since 1977 professor actual history of church and theology in Latin America at the Theological Faculty Nijmegen. He was secretary of COCTI (1976-1984) and organized the European preparation (Woudschoten, 1981) for the EATWOT-dialogue with Third World Theologians in Geneva (1983). He published on Latinamerican liberation theology in: *Théologies de la libération en Amérique latine*, Paris, Beauchesne, 1974; and was editor of *Jésus et la Libération en Amérique latine*, Paris, Desclée, 1986. He published on Third World theology in: *Tijdschrift voor Theologie* 23(1983)3, 253-269 and 27(1987)1, 27-36.

Felix Wilfred

Born in India; doctoral dissertation theology in Rome; professor systematic theology at the regional seminary St. Paul in Tiruchiralli (India); president of the Indian Association of Theologians; member of the advisory board for the Asian Bishops Conference (FABC) and for the International Pontifical Commission of Theologians. He published several articles on evangelization an inculturation; also *The Emergent Church in a New India*, Tiruchirapalli, 1988; and was editor of *Verlaß den Tempel. Antyodaya - Indischer Weg zur Befreiung*, Freiburg i.B., 1988.

Allard D. Willemier Westra

Born in the Netherlands, studied anthropology of religion; was researcher on Afrobrazilian religions (candomblé) at the Free University of Amsterdam: doctoral dissertation *Axê, the powers of life. The use of symbols in the social assistance of the candomblé religion in Alagoinhas (Bahia, Brazil)* (publ. in Dutch), Amsterdam, CEDLA, 1987; at present lecturer and researcher in business/industrial anthropology at the Free University Amsterdam. Published several articles on Afrobrazilian religions.

Selected bibliography Arnulf Camps OFM, 1946-1990

Composed by prof. dr. A. Camps and drs. W.A. van den Eerenbeemt

List of abbreviations

AFH   Archivum Franciscanum Historicum (Quaracchi-Grottaferrata, Italy)
ANT   Antonianum (Rome, Italy)
BSMS The Bulletin of the Scottish Institute of Missionary Studies (Edinburgh/Aberdeen, G.B.)
BSNC Bulletin Secretariatus pro non christianis (Città del Vaticano, Italy)
ESA   Everybody's Saint Anthony (Bangalore, India)
HM   Het Missiewerk (Nijmegen, the Netherlands)
IAMS International Association for Mission Studies (Hamburg, Germany)
ID   Informatiedienst, Woord en Wederwoord van Missionarissen (Oegstgeest, the Netherlands)
IIMO Interuniversitair Instituut voor Missiologie en Oecumenica (Leiden-Utrecht, the Nether-
      lands)
MA   Mons Alvernae (Alverna-Wijchen, the Netherlands)
NZM   Neue Zeitschrift für Missionswissenschaft (Immensee, Switzerland)
TvTh Tijdschrift voor Theologie (Nijmegen, the Netherlands)
WZ   Wereld en Zending (Amsterdam, the Netherlands)
ZMR   Zeitschrift für Missionswissenschaft und Religionswissenschaft (Münster, Germany)

Books

Jerome Xavier SJ and the Muslims of the Mogul Empire. Controversial Works and Missionary Activity.
   A dissertation presented to the Faculty of Theology of the University of Fribourg, Switzerland,
   in fulfilment of the requirements for the degree of doctor of theology, 1957, St. Paul's Press
   Fribourg, Switzerland, 1957.
Christendom en godsdiensten der wereld. Nieuwe inzichten en nieuwe activiteiten, Baarn, Bosch en
   Keunig, 1976.
De Weg, de paden en de wegen, De christelijke theologie en de concrete godsdiensten, Baarn, Bosch en
   Keunig, 1977.
Geen doodlopende weg, Lokale kerken in dialoog met hun omgeving, Baarn, Ten Have, 1978.
Partners in Dialogue, Christianity and other World Religions, Maryknoll, N.Y., Orbis Books, 1983.
The Sanskrit grammar and manuscripts of Father Heinrich Roth SJ (1620-1668). Facsimile Edition of
   Biblioteca Nazionale, Rome, MSS. OR. 171 and 172. With Introduction by Arnulf Camps and
   Jean-Claude Muller, Leiden-New York-Kobenhavn-Köln, E.J. Brill, 1988.

Small publications

*An unpublished letter of Father Christoval de Vega SJ. Its importance for the history of the second
   mission to the Mughal Court and for the knowledge of the religion of the Emperor Akbar*, Cairo,
   Centre of Oriental Studies of the Franciscan Custody of the Holy Land, 1956.
In Christus verbonden met de godsdiensten der wereld, Nijmegen-Utrecht, Dekker en v.d. Vegt, 1964.
Christenen in continentaal China vandaag. Inzicht en uitzicht, Kosmos en Oekumene, 15(1981), n.6.
Het Derde Oog. Van een theologie in Azië naar een Aziatische theologie, Nijmegen, Katholieke
   Universiteit, 1990.

Books edited

Camps, A., Cornélis, E., e.a. (eds), *Wie zeggen de mensen dat Ik ben?*, Baarn, Ten Have, 1975.

Camps, A., Hunold, G. (eds), *Erschaffe mir ein neues Volk. Franziskanische Kirchlichkeit und missionarische Kirche*, Mettingen, Brasilienkunde Verlag, 1982.

Camps, A., Hoedemaker, L.A., Spindler, M.R., Verstraelen, F.J. (eds), *Oecumenische inleiding in de missiologie. Texten en kontexten van het wereld-christendom*, Kampen, Kok, 1988.

Camps, A., Houtepen, A., e.a. (eds), *Secularisatie. Noodlot of opdracht. Perspectieven voor zending en oecumene in de context van de secularisatie*, Leiden-Utrecht, IIMO, 1989.

Articles and participation in books

'Metaphysica, geloof en dichtkunst', in: *MA*, 22(1946/47), 26-35.

'Het desiderium naturale bij St.Thomas', in: *MA*, 22(1946/47), 345-365.

'Bij het gedicht "Ballade pour demander la paix van Charles d'Orleans"', in: *MA*, 23(1947/48), 25-30.

'Laymen and the missions. Some data on modern lay-missionary activity', in: *Collectanea Punjabensia* (Lahore), 10(1951), n.22, 371-374; n.23, 382-385.

'Die Schriften der Jesuiten-Missionare Johann Grueber, Heinrich Roth und Antonio Ceschi', in: *NZM*, 13(1957), 231-233.

'Flämische Franziskaner in Konstantinopel, Smyrna und auf der Insel Chios am Ende des 17. Jahrhunderts', in: *Franziskanische Studien*, 40(1958), 239-250.

'Catholicism and Islam in Cairo', in: *Pahana* (Colombo, Ceylon), 9(1958), 20-24.

'The Institute of Oriental Studies. How should it work?', in: *Collationes Lahorenses*, 8(1959), 288-289.

'Franciscan missions to the Mogul Court', in: *NZM*, 15(1959), 259-270.

'Une lettre inédite du P. Valerius Rist OFM, missionaire en Cochinchine', in: *AFH*, 53(1960), 206-209.

'An unpublished Letter of Fr. Jacobus Rzimarz OFM, Prefect Apostolic of Upper Egypt', in: *AFH*, 53(1960), 321-323.

'Schwan Sharif. A city of monks in Sind', in: *Franciscan Echoes* (Karachi), 1(1961), n.3, 20-21; n.4, 26-27.

'Two spurions arabic canons of the Council of Nicea found by the Franciscan missionaries of upper Egypt', in: *Studia Orientalia Christiana*, 1960, n.5, 171-181.

'Possibilities of Lay-Apostolate among the Muslims of West Pakistan', in: J. Speeker SMB, P. W. Bühlmann OFM Cap. (Hrsg.), *Das Laienapostolat in den Missionen. Festschrift Prof. Dr. Johannes Beckmann SMB zum 60. Geburtstag dargeboten von Freunden und Schülern*, Schöneck-Beckenried, 1961, 241-254.

'Rev. Fr. Victor Courtois SJ (1907-1960)', in: *NZM*, 17(1961), 150.

'Christenen in Islamitische landen. Samenwerking tussen missie en zending mogelijk', in: *St. Adelbert* (Utrecht), 1961, n.7, 99-101.

'Pakistan, IV. Religiöse Verhältnisse', in: Görres Gesellschaft (Hrsg.), *Staatslexikon, Recht-Wirtschaft-Gesellschaft*, Band VI, 6.Auflage, Freibourg i.Br., 1961, 5.

'Pir Fazl Shah Jilani Goth, a mental hospital in Sind', in: *Franciscan Echoes*, 1(1961), n.5, 24-25.

'Persian Works of Jerome Xavier, a Jesuit at the Mogul Court', in: *Islamic Culture* (Hyderabad-Deccan, India), 35(1961), 166-176.

'A letter written by Fr. Petrus Franciscus a Saorgio OFM, from an Indian prison (1729)', in: *AFH*, 54(1961), 413-418.

'The cult of Khwaja Khizr in Sind. A legendary Saint', in: *Franciscan Echoes*, 2(1962), n.1, 30-32.

'Oecumenische contacten tussen missie en zending in de laatste jaren', in: *Oecumene*, 1(1962), 31-41.

'De houding van kerk en staat inzake het onderwijs in Pakistan', in: *Rerum Ecclesiae*, 76(1962), 61-63; *Missie*, 21(1962), 61-63.

'De Franciscanen in de huidige republiek van Indonesië een autonome custodie', in: *Neerlandia Serafica*, 32(1962), 199-201.

'Pour un travail d'approche au Pakistan', in: *Le Christ au monde*, 7(1962), 227-243.

'Some aspects of the religious crisis of Islam in West Pakistan', in: *Social Compass*, 9(1962), 221-237.

'Recente contacten tussen missie en zending in West Guinea', in: *Rerum Ecclesiae*, 76(1962), 157-159; *Missie*, 21(1962), 157-159.

'Kerk en négritude', in: *Oecumene*, 1(1962), 270-280.

'De Islam-wereld in ontmoeting met een nieuwe tijd', in: *Rerum Ecclesiae*, 76(1962), 162-167; *Missie*, 21(1962), 162-167.

'Catholic Bishops' Conferences and the World Church', in: G.A. van Winsen, A.G. Bouritius, J. Buys (eds), *Novella Ecclesiae Germina*, Nijmegen-Utrecht, 1963, 244-249.

'Luciano Petech und die Katholische Tibet-Mission im 17. und 18. Jahrhundert', in: *NZM*, 20(1964), 62-64.

'Op zoek naar het rechtgebaande pad. Christelijke visie op de functie van de religieuze leider in de West-Pakistaanse volksislam', in: *Vox theologica*, 34(1964), 189-198.

'Enkele kanttekeningen naar aanleiding van dr. Arend Th. van Leeuwen's boek "Christianity in world history, the meeting of faiths in East and West"', in: *HM*, 44(1965), 45-49.

'De missionerende kerk in haar verhouding tot de niet-christelijke godsdiensten, vroeger en nu', in: *HM*, 44(1965), 141-156.

'Searching after the straight path. The role of the religious leader, the Pir, in the Islam of West Pakistan', in: *Social Compass*, 11(1964), n.6, 23-28.

'Een situatiestudie over preëvangelisatie. Joseph J. Spae CICM, Christian corridors to Japan, Tokyo 1965', in: *Concilium*, 1(1965), n.8, 170-177.

'Korea. Vraag naar Christendom', in: *Rerum Ecclesiae*, 79(1965), 167-170; *Missie*, 24(1965), 167-170.

'Ontmoetingen in Japan', in: *Rerum Ecclesiae*, 80(1966), 37-40; *Missie*, 25(1966), 37-40.

'De consequenties van een christelijke levenshouding voor een daadwerkelijke inzet in de ontwikkelingshulp', in: *Gezondheid in ontwikkeling. De problematiek betreffende de gezondheidszorg in de ontwikkelingslanden*, Verslagboek van het congres te Nijmegen, November 1965, 39-49.

'The missionizing Church in her attitude towards the Non-christian Religions, both in earlier times and today', in: *HM*, 44(1965), 141-156; *Teaching all nations* (Manilla), 4(1967), 198-212.

'De missionaire activiteit van de kerk', in: *Het Concilie in kort bestek*, Roermond, Maaseik, J. Romen en Zonen, 1966, 80-97.

'Mill Hill missionaries in Afghanistan from 1879 until 1881 and their stay in Quetta-Baluchistan until 1883', in: *ZMR*, 51(1967), 13-25, 132-145, 232-245.

'A importância missionária do diálogo ecuménico e da colaboração intereclesial', in: *O Diálogo missionário nos tempos actuais*, Lisboa, 1967, 417-439; 'Het belang van de oecumenische dialoog en interkerkelijke samenwerking voor de missie', in: *Missionaire wegen voor morgen*, Hilversum-Antwerpen, P. Brand, 1967, 258-273.

'Die Wiederentdeckung der ersten abendländischen Sanskrit-Grammatik des P. Heinrich Roth SJ', in: *NZM*, 23(1967), 241-243.

'Présence en proclamation. Het tweede onderwerp van de eerste Europese consultatie van missiologen', in: *De Heerbaan*, 21(1968), 223-232.

'Azione missionaria e dialogo con le religioni. Incontro tra la religioni', in: *Idoc Documenti nuovi*, 4(1968), 125-150.

'De Katholieke kerk en de niet-christelijke godsdiensten', in: A.M. Heidt (ed.), *Catholica. Informatiebron voor het katholieke leven*, Hilversum, 1968, 1891-1897.

'New ways of realizing a christian togetherness in non-western countries', in: *Internationales Jahrbuch für Religionssoziologie*, Band V, Religion, Kultur und sozialer Wandel, Köln und Opladen, 1969, 182-194.

'Father Heinrich Roth SJ (1620-1668) and the history of his Sanskrit manuscripts', in: *ZMR*, 53(1969), 185-195.

'Activité missionaire et structures d'emprunt', in: *Spiritus*, 10(1969), 444-449; 'Missionary activity and borrowed structures', in: Sedos (ed.), *Foundations of mission theology*, Maryknoll, N.Y., 1972, 124-130.

'Coup d'oeil sur la théologie chrétienne non occidentale avec spéciale référence à l'Inde', in: *BSNC*, 5(1970), 69-79 and for the english edition, 5(1970), 67-76.

'De Katholieke Kerk en de niet-christelijke godsdiensten', in: *De Heerbaan*, 23(1970), 442-450.

'De Nijmeegse bijdrage aan de beoefening van de missiologie van 1963-1970', in: *HM*, 50(1971), 5-20.

'De taak van het christendom in Azië in het licht van de problematiek: godsdienst en verandering', in: *De Heerbaan*, 24(1971), 117-127.

'Belangrijke besluiten van de Indonesische Bisschoppenconferentie', in: *HM*, 50(1971), 52-58.

'Religion et développement, quelques implications missiologiques', in: *BSNC*, 6(1971), 7-25 and for the english edition, 6(1971), 7-24.

'Xavier, Jerome', in: St. Neill, G.H. Anderson, J. Goodwin (eds), *Concise Dictionary of the Christian World Mission*, London, 1970, 670-671.

'Nieuwe missionaire structuren voor nieuwe missionaire taken', in: *HM*, 50(1971), 155-166; 'Neue missionarischen Strukturen für neue missionarische Aufgaben', *Thuringia Franciscana*, 1972, n.1, 1-10; en in: *Ordenskorrespondenz*, 13(1972), 378-388; (English) 'New Missionary structures for new missionary tasks', in: *The Japan Missionary Bulletin*, 17(1973), 509-516.

'Le missionaire et les mutations du Sud-Est Asiatique', in: *Quel Missionaire? Rapports, échanges et carrefours de la XLIe semaine de missiologie de Louvain 1971*, Tournai, 1971, 231-241.

'The person and function of Christ in Hinduism and in Hindu-christian theology', in: *BSNC*, 6(1971), 199-211 and for the french edition, 6(1971).

'Missiologie in deze tijd', in: *WZ*, 1(1972), 5-16.

'Dialog der Religionen und Entwicklung: die maieutische Methode', in: *ZMR*, 56(1972), 1-9; *Thuringia Franciscana*, 1972, n.1, 11-16.

'De taak van de christen temidden van drang naar ontwikkeling en religieuze ervaring van de godsdiensten der wereld. Naar een maieutische benadering', in: *Tijdschrift voor geestelijk leven*, 28(1972), 225-244.

'Ter gedachtenis aan Prof. dr. Joh. Beckmann SMB', in: *WZ*, 1(1972), 72-73.

'Catholic Missionary Activities', in: Lowland Highlights, *Church and Oecumene in the Netherlands*, Kampen, Kok, 1972, 108-115.

'Vier sleutelbegrippen voor een meer empirische missiologie', in: *Vox Theologica*, 42(1972), 218-231; 'Four key-notions for a more emperical missiology', in: *NZM*, 29(1973), 133-142; *The Japan Missionary Bulletin*, 27(1973), 583-592.

'Spanning tussen kolonialisme en missie. Las Casas, Lebbe en van Lith', in: *WZ*, 1(1972), 437-448.

'De vele stralen van de waarheid. De derde wereld en het tweede Vaticaans Concilie', in: *25 Jaar wereldgeschiedenis. Onze jaren 45-70*, Amsterdam 1973, 2196-2200; *Omhoog* (Paramaribo), 18 (1973), n.32, 1, 4-5, 8.

'In memoriam voor dr. J.N. van Pinxteren MHM', in: *WZ*, 2(1973), 307-312.

'Christelijke gemeenschappen in Azië en ontwikkeling', in: J. van Lin, *Wereld in verandering*, Den Haag, 1973, 28-40.

'Enige case-studies over de ontmoeting van kerk en verscheidene godsdiensten nu', in: *Kerk aan het werk*, Amsterdam-Brussel, 1973, 1977[2], 88-111.

'Het sekretariaat voor de niet-christenen der R.K. Kerk', in: *Verder dan de Oekumene*, Amsterdam, 1973, 1976[2], 50-52.

'Some Indian theologians on revelation in Hinduism', in: G. Oberhammer (Hrsg.), *Offenbarung. Geistige Realität des Menschen*, Wien, 1974, 221-225.

'Two recent studies on Buddhism and Christianity', in: *Misjonskall ogforskerglede, Festskrift professor O.G. Myklebkst*, Oslo, Bergen, Tromsö, 1975, 36-47.

'Indiase Christologie', in: A. Camps, e.a. (eds), *Wie zeggen de mensen dat Ik ben?*, Baarn, Ten Have, 1975, 125-137.

'Le dialogue interreligieux et la situation concrète de l'humanité', in: *BSNC*, 10(1975), 315-318.

'Ten Geleide', in: R.H. Drummond, *De Boeddha. De leer van Boeddha en het Christendom*, Baarn 1975, 7-10.

'Een bezinning voor "doeners" op het gebied van de ontwikkelingshulp', in: *Een lopende rekening, Kerk en ontwikkeling in de derde wereld*, Tilburg, 1976, 94-106.

'Wereldgodsdiensten erkennen elkaar. Konsekwenties voor missie en zending', in: *Kosmos en Oekumene*, 10(1976), 17-19.

'De bijdrage van het christendom aan de ontwikkeling', in: *ID*, 1976, n.5, 3-5.

'Vorwort', in: W. Bühlmann, *Wandlung zum Wesentlichen. Der Sinn der Evangelisierung*, Münster-schwarzach, Vier Türme-Verlag, 1976, VI-VII.

'Drie dialogen tussen christendom en Islam: Cordova, Tunis en Tripoli', in: *WZ*, 5(1976), 260-268.

'Eine einheimische Theologie aus der Sicht der Missionswissenschaft', in: H. Bettschneider (Hrsg.), *Das Asiatische Gesicht Christi*, St. Augustin, Steyler V., 1976, 69-77.

'Einheit in der Vielfalt. Franziskanische Antwort auf die Herausforderung der "Dritten Kirche"', in: *Bruder aller Menschen, der missionarische Aufbruch in Franziskus von Assisi*, Werl, Dietrich-Celde-Verlag, 1976, 163-182.

'Franciscus ging tijdens de kruistochten in beide linies praten', in: *Franciscus van Assisi. Keuze uit artikelen verschenen in het jubileumjaar 1976*, Utrecht, 1978, 101-107.

'Mit Franziskus ins nächste Jahrhundert. Versuch einer Antwort auf die Zukunfts-fragen der Menschheit', in: *Die Anregung, Seelsorglicher Dienst in der Welt von heute*, Sankt Augustin, 28(1976), 519-523.

'Geschiedschrijving van de missie in de negentiende eeuw', in: *Documentatieblad voor de Nederlandse kerkgeschiedenis van de negentiende eeuw*, 1 februari 1977, 7-12.

'Voorwoord', in: W. Bühlmann OFM Cap, *Er komt een derde kerk*, Hilversum, 1976, 5-7.

'Discurso presidencial para la apertura del IIIo Congresso Internacional de Estudios Missionales (25 de julio 1976)', in: *IAMS News Letter*, 1977, n.10, 2-4; *Ensayos Ocasionales Celep* (San José, Costa Rica), 4(1977), 5-6.

'Van polemiek naar dialoog: noodzakelijke veranderingen in de verhouding Islam en Christendom', in: *WZ*, 6(1977), 319-328.

'Verslag van de Internationale Conferentie over de Islam in Zuid-Oost en Oost-Azië te Jeruzalem, van 18-22 april 1977', in: *WZ*, 7(1978), 159-163.

'Is it necessary to preach the Gospel to men of other faiths?', in: *Zending op weg naar de toekomst. Essays aangeboden aan Prof. dr. J. Verkuyl*, Kampen, Kok, 1978, 128-136.

'Castonaro's "Brevis apparatus et modus agendi ac disputandi cum Mahumetanis" in China', in: H. Waldenfels (Hrsg.) *"Denn Ich bin bei Euch" (Mt 28,20), Perspektiven im christlichen Missions-bewußtsein heute. Festgabe für Josef Glazik und Bernward Willeke zum 65. Geburtstag*, Zürich/Ein-siedeln/Köln, 1978, 155-160.

'Der Heilige, der allen gehört: Franziskus in 6 Kontinenten', in: *Franziskanische Studien*, 60(1978), 275-283.

'Dialogue with Asian religions as condition for total human development', in: *Seminar report: Dialogue with Asian Religions as condition for total human development*, Colombo, 1978, 19-30.

'Aziatisch denken over Christus', in: *Communio*, 4(1979), 101-111.

'Zending en missie: alleen nog in de vorm van dialoog', in: *Rondom het Woord*, 21(1979), n.2, 37-45.

'Die heutige Stellung der Römisch-katholischen Kirche zu den nichtchristlichen Religionen', in: A. Paus (Hrsg.), *Jesus Christus und die Religionen*, Gras-Wien-Köln-Kevelaer, 1980, 233-264.

'Die Notwendigkeit des Dialoges in der Mission', in: Th. Sundermeier (Hrsg.), *Fides pro mundi vita, Missionstheologie heute. Hans-Werner Gensichen zum 65. Geburtstag*, Gütersloh, 1980, 168-172.

'De onderscheiding der goeroes', in: *Communio*, 5(1980), 289-300.

'De Franciscaanse utopie in het missiewerk in Amerika tijdens de 16e en de 17e eeuw', in: *Jaarboekje 1978/1979*, Utrecht, Franciscaanse Academie, 1980, 49-65.

'Prof. dr. Alfons Joannes Maria Mulders, emeritus-hoogleraar missiologie aan de Katholieke Universiteit van Nijmegen, In Memoriam', in: *WZ*, 10(1981), 130-134.

'The spiritual aspects of Hope in various religions', in: *BSNC*, 16(1981), 143-150.

'Säkularisierung in anderen Religionen', in: A. Rotzetter (Hrsg.), *Geist und Welt, politische Aspekte des geistlichen Lebens. Seminar Spiritualität*, Band 3, Zürich-Einsiedeln-Köln, Benziger Verlag, 1981, 107-115.

'In Memory of Mgr. Prof. dr. Alfons Johannes Maria Mulders – January 31, 1893 – April 9, 1981', in: *NZM*, 37(1981), 291-293.

'Een nieuwe uitgave van de handleiding voor de dialoog met moslims', in: *WZ*, 10(1981), 340-346.

'Das franziskanische Missionsverständnis im Laufe der Jahrhunderte', in: A. Camps und G. W. Hunold (Hrsg.), *Erschaffe mir ein neues Volk. Franziskanische Kirchlichkeit und missionarische Kirche*, Mettingen, Brasilienkunde Verlag, 1982, 30-43.

239

'Theologien im "Kontext" der Kulturen: Sergio Torres, Chile', in: H. Waldenfels (Hrsg), *Theologen der Dritten Welt. Elf biographische Skizzen aus Afrika, Asien und Latein-Amerika*, München, H. Beck, 1982, 129-140, 191-192.

'Opening address – Discours inaugural', in: J. Van Nieuwenhove, G. Casalis (eds), *Towards a dialogue with Third World Theologians. Symposium "The Future of Europe: a challenge to theology"*, Woudschoten, 10-14 december 1981, Nijmegen, 1982, 1-5.

'Teilnahme an der Entwicklung: Eine Herausforderung an die Religion', in: *Dokumente internationales Seminar "Die Befriedigung gesellschaftspolitischer Grundbedürfnisse aus christlicher und sozialdemokratischer Sicht"-Bilanz und Ausblick zur 10-jährigen entwicklungspolitischen Zusammenarbeit MZF/FES, Bonn, 16-21. 03-1981*, Bonn, 1982, 77-92.

'Mission in the Franciscan order after the Medellín chapter of 1971', in: D. Dougherty OFM (ed.), *Proceedings of the first International Mission Council of the order of Friars Minor, 6-21 november 1981 Roma*, s.d., 14-22.

'Nieuwe Dialoog met het Hindoeïsme in India', in: *Concilium*; 19(1983), n.1. 82-89.

'Rola dialogu w katechezie Katecheza w Azji', in: Kawalak, W. (ed.), *Rodzina-katecheza-Dialog. Materialyu Sympozjum misjologicznego 1979-1980*, Warzawa, Akademia Teologii katolickiej, 1983, 51-57, 77-81.

'Franziskanischer Dialog mit anderen Religionen', in: L. Boff und W. Bühlmann (Hrsg.), *Baue meine Kirche auf. Franziskanische Inspirationen aus der Dritten Welt*, Düsseldorf, Patmos Verlag, 1983, 88-106.

'Abd-al-Sattar B, Qasem Lahuri', in: Ehsan Yorshater (ed.), *Encyclopaedia iranica*, Vol.1, fasc 2, London, Boston and Henley, Routledge and Regan Paul, 1982, 167.

'Theologische Praxis in einer geteilten Welt, Dialog zwischen Erste-Welt und Dritte-Welt-Theologen, Genf 5-13 Januar 1983, Einführung', in: *Herausgefordert durch die Armen, Dokumente der Ökumenischen Vereinigung von Dritte-Welt-Theologen 1976-1983*, Freiburg-Basel-Wien, Herder, 1983, 137-143.

'Father Felice Zoppi da Cannobio OFM, in Sri Lanka, 1853-1857. Pioneer of Catholic Education in Kandy', in: E.C.T. Candappa en M.S.S. Fernado-pawlle (eds), *Don Peter Felicitation Volume*, Colombo, 1983, 11-17.

'The first Franciscans in the East', in: W.L.A. Don Peter (ed.), *Franciscans and Sri Lanka*, Colombo, 1983, 90-105.

'Dialoog Christendom-Boeddhisme' (co-auteur: Rob Frank), in: C. ten Dorstharst, e.a. (eds), *Verwijlen onder de Bodhi-boom. Een gethematiseerd verslag van een studiereis naar Sri Lanka*, Bolsward, Het Witte Boekhuis, 1985, 77-92.

'Missionstheologie aus interkontinentaler Sicht: der Beitrag Afrikas, Asiens und Lateinamerikas', in: E. Klinger und K. Wittstadt (Hrsg.), *Glaube im Prozess, Christ-sein nach dem II. Vatikanum. Für Karl Rahner*, Freiburg, Basel, Wien, Herder, 1984, 666-678.

'Salvation by Aloysius Pieris SJ, Sri Lanka', in: *Heil voor deze wereld. Studies aangeboden aan Prof. dr. A.G. Honig jr.*, Kampen, Kok, 1984, 63-71.

'Ein grosser Verlust für WCRP: In memoriam Dr. M.A. Lücker', in: *Informationen, Welt-Konferenz der Religionen für den Frieden*, Bonn, 1984, n.16, 3-6.

'Minjung theologie. Een theologie van het volk in Zuid-Korea', in: *Kosmos en Oekumene*, 8(1984), 239-243.

'Het Evangelie daagt ons uit. De invloed van de Latijnsamerikaanse kerk en theologie op de orde der Franciscanen', in: H. Bots, M. Kerkhof (eds), *Forum Litterarum, Miscelânea de estudos literários, linguísticos e históricos oferecida a J.J. van de Besselaar*, Amsterdam-Maarsen, Holland University Press, 1984, 201-210.

'Het testament van bisschop Stephen Neill', in: *WZ*, 14(1985), 183-185.

'A reflection on "Theology by the People"', in: *Ministerial Formation*, 1985, n.29, 3-6.

'Thirteen unknown documents written by Father Zoppi da Canoobio OFM in Sri Lanka from 1953 till 1956', in: *NZM*, 41(1985), 81-101.

'Evangile et inculturation. L'aspect théologique du problème', in: *Eglise et Mission*, 65(1985), n.240, 25-42.

'Ökumenische Initiativen auf internationaler Ebene (IAMS, EATWOT, WCRP)', in: *ZMR*, 70(1986), n.2/3, 248-260.

'Doctoral Dissertations in missiology 1963-1986, Catholic University of Nijmegen, the Netherlands', in: *NZM*, 42(1986), 225-228.

'In memory of Dr. Gregorius van Breda (van den Boom) OFM Cap (1901-1985)', in: *ZMR*, 70(1986), 306-307.

'Ortskirche', in: K. Müller, Th. Sundermeier (Hrsg.), *Lexikon missionstheologischer Grundbegriffe*, Berlin, Dietrich Reimer Verlag, 1987, 360-364.

'De uma Igreja-monólogo para uma Igreja-diálogo', in: *Guia para o diálogo inter-religioso*, São Paulo, Paulinas, 1987, 13-23.

'Dertien eeuwen katholieke missionering in China, 635-1949. Katholieke christenen bleven vreemdeling in eigen land', in: *WZ*, 16(1987), 324-329.

'Was ist auf Weltebene (Weltkirche) in den verschiedenen Kontinenten theologisch, pastoral, menschlich, sozial prägend?', in: *Pastorale und franziskanische Prioritäten im Kontext der Ortskirchen Asiens, Lateinamerikas und Europas*, Bonn, Missionszentrale der Franziskaner, 1988, 5-16, 25-27.

'Celso Costantini, Apostolic Delegate in China (1922-1933). The changing role of the foreign missionary', in: *Tripod* (Hongkong), 44(1988), 9-12 (Chinese) and 40-46 (English).

'WCRP in context: historisch en actueel', in: H. E. Schouten (ed.), *Geloven in Vrede, WCRP en de interreligieuze dialoog over vrede, gerechtigheid en menselijke waardigheid*, Amersfoort/Leuven, De Horstink. 1988, 20-26.

'Dialoog met de Aziatische godsdiensten: eerst nu echt aan de orde', in: *Communio*, 13(1988), 257-259.

'Asien, Burma, Kambodscha, Laos, Thailand, Vietnam', in: V. Drehsen, H. Häring, e.a. (Hrsg.), *Wörterbuch des Christentums*, Gütersloh, Zürich, Gütersloher Verlagshaus Gerd Mohn, Benziger Verlag, 1988, 100, 183-184, 583, 711, 1235, 1326-1327.

'China: van vreemdheid naar kontekstualisatie', in: A. Camps, e.a. (red.), *Oecumenische inleiding in de missiologie*, Kampen, Kok, 1988, 67-80.

'De katholieke missionaire beweging van 1492-1789', in: Id., *o.c.*, 222-229.

'De katholieke missionaire beweging van 1789-1962', in: Id., *o.c.*, 236-243.

'Exporteren wij de secularisatie? Kritische vragen vanuit de Derde Wereld', in: A. Camps, e.a. (eds), *Secularisatie: noodlot of opdracht, o.c.*, 75-89.

'Franciscus leeft overal. M. Kämpchen, Überall lebt Franziskus, seine Brüder in den Weltreligionen, Freiburg i. Br. 1987', in: *Franciskaans Leven*, 72(1989), 94-96.

'De Zaligverklaring van Broeder Junipero Serra', in: *Franciskaans Leven*, 72(1989), 128-133.

'De wereldgodsdiensten en de uniciteit van het christendom', in: C. Cornille en J. Bulckens (eds), *Jodendom en Islam in het vak godsdienst*, Leuven-Amersfoort, Acco, 1989, 199-216.

'Een beeld-studie van de missionaris. De veranderlijkheid van het image van de missionaris', in: *Geest en Leven*, 66(1989), 270-277.

'Two eminent secretaries: Pierre Humbertclaude and Pietro Rossano (1964-1982)', in: *Bulletin Pontificium Consilium pro Dialogo inter Religiones*, 24(1989), 379-382.

'The study of the history of local Churches. Its importance for the development and the future of the Church', in: *Tripod* (Hong Kong), 1989, n.54, 4-9 (Chinese) and 30-38 (English).

'Allocution de bienvenue à Monsieur le Président du CREDIC et aux participants à la neuvième session du Credic', in: *L'Appel à la mission. Formes et évolution, XIX-XXeme siècles. Actes de la IXième session du Credic à l'Université Catholique de Nimègue (14-17 juin 1988)*, Lyon 1989, 6-7 (also 115, 151-152).

'Die Ökumenische Vereinigung von Dritte-Welt-Theologen 1976-1988. Ein komplizierter Bruch', in: G. Collet (Hrsg.), *Theologien der Dritten Welt. EATWOT als Herausforderung westlicher Theologie und Kirche*. Immensee, NZM, 1990, 183-200.

'Dissertation notices from the Catholic University of Nijmegen, the Netherlands, 1969-1989', in: *International Bulletin of Missionary Research*, 14(1990), 45-46.

241

Book reviews

Verslagboek Nederlandse Missiologische Week, gehouden te Nijmegen van 27-30 october 1948 (s.a., s.l., Tilburg), in: *NZM*, 8(1952), 149-150.

Prasad, R., *India Divided*, Bombay, 1947³, in: *NZM*, 8(1952), 318-319.

Jochems, M.J. CM, *De missie in de litteratuur I, van de Middeleeuwen tot de Franse Revolutie*, Bussum, 1952, in: *NZM*, 9(1953), 75.

Sharma, Sri Ram, *Mughal government and administration*, Bombay, 1951, in: *NZM*, 10(1954), 73-74.

Rijckevorsel, L. van SJ, *Pastoor F. van Lith SJ, De Stichter van de Missie in Midden-Java 1863-1926*, Nijmegen, 1952, in: *NZM*, 10(1954), 78-80.

Eerenbeemt, A. van den, *Missieactie en Missieproblemen*, Tilburg, 1953, in: *NZM*, 10(1954), 156.

Missie en Liturgie. Speciaal nummer van het Tijdschrift voor Liturgie, Abdij Affligem, 1954, in: *NZM*, 11(1955), 79.

Wijngaert, A. Van den, Mensaert, G. OFM, *Sinica Franciscana, Volumen V. Relationes et Epistulae Ill. D. Fr. Bernardini Della Chiesa OFM*, Roma, Collegium S. Antonii, 1954, in: *ANT*, 30(1955), 204-205.

The training of converts. Proceedings of the Fordham University Conference of Mission Specialists First annual meeting, January 24-25, 1953, etc. New York, Fordham University Press, 1953, in: *ANT*, 30(1955), 205.

Reding, M. (Hrsg.), *Mohr, Richard, Die christliche Ethik im Lichte der Ethnologie*, Handbuch der Moraltheologie, Band IV, München, 1954, in: *ANT*, 30(1955), 334-335.

Kilger, P.L. OSB, Hiltrup SA (Hrsg.), *Christen und Antichristen. Die Missionen in der religionsfeindlichen und widerchristlichen Welt von heute. Tagung für Missionare zu Münster 25/29-5-1953. Referate und Berichte*, in: *ANT*, 30(1955), 335-336.

Rondelez, V., *Scheut getuigt in China*, Brussel-Leuven, Scheut-Edities-Biblioteca Alphonsiana, s.a. (1954), in: *NZM*, 11(1955), 155.

Köster, H. SVD, *Vom Wesen und Aufbau Katholischer Theologie*, Kaldenkirchen, Hegler Verlagsbuchhandlung, 1954, in: *ANT*, 31(1956) 103-104.

Correia-Afonso, J. SJ, *Jesuit letters and Indian history*, Bombay, 1955, in: *NZM*, 12(1956), 164-155.

Formation religieuse en Afrique noire. Compte rendu de la Semaine d'études de Leopoldville 22-27 d'août 1955, Bruxelles, Lumen Vitae, 1956, in: *ANT*, 32(1957), 82.

Correia-Afonso, J. SJ, *Even unto the Indies. Ignatius of Loyola and the Indian Missions*, Bombay, St. Xavier's High School, 1956, in: *NZM*, 13(1957), 69-70.

Desideri, L.P.I. SJ (ed.), *I Missionari Italiani nel Tibet e nel Nepal*, Parte V, VI, Roma, Libreria delle Stato, 1954/1955, in: *NZM*, 13(1957), 70-71.

Descola, J. *Quand les Jésuites sont au pouvoir*, Paris, Fayard, 1956, in: *NZM*, 13(1957), 71.

Schurhammer, G. SJ, *Franz Xaver. Sein Leben und seine Zeit*, Band I: Europa 1506-1541, Freiburg i.Br., Herder, 1955, in: *ANT*, 32(1957), 453-454.

Hofinger, J. SJ, *Notre message. Thèmes principaux de la prédication chrétienne élaborés spécialement pour les missions*, Bruxelles, Lumen Vitae, 1955, in: *ANT*, 32(1957), 477-478.

Ledit, Ch.J., *Mahomet, Israël et le Christ*, Paris, Ed. du Vieux Colombier, 1956, in: *NZM*, 14(1958), 76-78.

Hawker, E.M.N., *Written and spoken Persian*, London, New York, Toronto, Longmans, Green and Co, 1957³, in: *NZM*, 14(1958), 80.

Meersman, A. OFM, *The Franciscans in Bombay. History of the Franciscans in the territory comprised within the boundaries of the present archdiocese of Bombay*, Bangalore, 1957, in: *The Christian Voice*, 9(1958), n.22, 4.

Löwenstein, F. zu SJ, *Christliche Bilder in altindischer Malerei*, Münster, 1958, in: *NZM*, 15(1959), 226.

Active participation of the faithful in the liturgy of the church. Study week on the liturgy, 9th-12th December 1958, Madras, The Catholic Centre, 1959, in: *ESA*, 26(1960), Jan-Feb., 17-18.

Vincent Cronin, A., *Pearl to India: the Life of Robert de Nobili*, London, Rupert Hart-Davis, 1959, in: *ESA*, 26(1960), March, 19.

Pichler, W., *The Story of God's Kingdom*, Bombay, St. Paul's Publ., 1959, in: *ESA*, 26(1960), March, 19.

Ostra, A.J. (ed.), *Tibet-Hindustan Mission*, Book I, Patna, Ham-Sab Publ., 1959, in: *ESA*, 26(1960), April, 18.

Hofinger, J. SJ, *The art of teaching christian doctrine. The Good News and its proclamation*, Bombay, St. Paul Publ., 1959, in: ESA 26(1960), April, 18-19.

Pereira, A., *Banish Your Blues*, Bombay, St. Paul's Publ., 1959, in: *ESA*, 26(1960), May, 19.

The Novena of St. Anthony of Padua, the Great Wonder Worker, Madras, Good Pastor Dep., 1959, in: *ESA*, 26(1960), May, 19-20.

Chako, M. SJ, *The Drama of the Way of the Cross*, S. India, St.Paul's Seminary, 1960, in: *ESA*, 26(1960), May, 20.

Share in the Sacrifice, The Catechetical Centre. De Nobili College, Poona 6, Bombay, St.Paul's Publ, 1959, in: *ESA*, 26(1960), May, 20.

Maurus, J., *Today is ours, little thoughts for daily life*, Bombay, St.Paul's Publ., 1959, in: *ESA*, 26(1960), June, 18-19.

Catechism for First Communion and Confirmation, Bombay, St.Paul Publ., 1959, in: *ESA*, 26(1960), June, 19.

Royappar, S. SJ, *Family Planning: virtue as vice*, Madras, Good Pastor Dep., 1959, in: *ESA*, 26(1960), July, 18.

A Catholic Catechism. Herder and Herder, Distributors for India, Ceylon, Pakistan and Burma, Bombay, Society of St. Paul, 1959, in: *ESA*, 26(1960), July, 18-19.

Iparraquire, I. SJ, *A Key to the study of the Spiritual Exercises*, 2nd ed., Bombay, St.Paul's Publ., 1960, in: *ESA*, 26(1960), July, 19.

De Decline of Public Morals. A course of addresses by Valerian Cardinal Gracias, Lent 1959, Bombay, St.Paul's Publ., 2nd ed., 1959, in: *ESA*, 26(1960), August, 16 and 23.

Le Christ au foyer. Compte rendu de la semaine d'étude de Bukavu sur la formation religieuse en Afrique Noire, 29 juillet – 3 août 1957, Bruxelles, Lumen Vitae, 1958, in: *ANT* 35(1960), 360.

Most, W.G., *Mary in our life*, Bombay, St.Paul's Publ., 2nd Indian edition, 1960, in: *ESA*, 26(1960), Sept., 8.

Elenjimittam, A., *Saints for young women today*, Bombay, St.Paul's Publ., Revised edit., 1960, in: *ESA*, 26(1960), Sept., 8 and 15.

Mascarenhas, T., *Moral science*, Bombay, St.Paul's Publ., 1959, in: *ESA*, 26(1960), Sept., 1.

O'Brien, J.A., *Happy marriage. A guidance for courtship and after*, Bombay, St.Paul's Publ., 1960, in: *ESA*, 26(1960), Oct., 26.

Lesser, R.H., *What a wonderful world. Course of moral science*, Vol.1, Bombay, St.Paul's Publ., 1960, in: *ESA*, 26(1960), Oct., 26.

Schuster, I., *Illustrated bible history of the Old and New Testaments for the use of Catholic schools*, Bombay, St.Paul's Publ., 1960, in: *ESA*, 26(1960), Nov., 12.

Siekmann, T.C., *Girls, you're important. Instructions for Catholic girls*, Bombay, St.Paul's Publ., 1960, in: *ESA*, 26(1960), Nov., 12.

Caussade, J.P. De SJ, *Surrender to God's love*, Bombay, St.Paul's Publ., 1960, in: *ESA*, 26(1960), Nov., 12 and 20.

Lard, D.A., *The ideal parents*, Bombay, St.Paul's Publ., 1960, in: *ESA*, 26(1960), Dec., 17.

Knecht, F.J., *Child's bible history*, Special Indian Edition, Bombay, St.Paul's Publ., 1960, in: *ESA*, 26(1960), Dec., 18.

Veltrami, A. (servant of God), *Venial sin, its malice, its effects, its punishments*, Bombay, St.Paul's Publ., 1960, in: *ESA*, 26(1960), Dec., 18.

Battista, O.A., *Enjoy work and get fun out of life*, Bombay, St.Paul's Publ., 1960, in: *ESA*, 27(1961), Jan.-Feb., 14.

Maurus, J. (ed.), *Pretty as you please. 365 recipes for young ladies*, Bombay, St.Paul's Publ., 1960, in: *ESA*, 27(1961), Jan.-Feb., 14.

Lard, D.A., *The guidance of youth*, Bombay, St.Paul's Publ., 1960, in: *ESA*, 27(1961), Jan.-Feb., 14 and 23.

Murray T.T., *Islam in India and Pakistan*, Madras, Christian Literature Society, 1959, in: *ESA*, 27(1961), March, 14.

Alberione, J., *Purgatory*, Bombay, St. Paul's Publ., 1959, in: *ESA*, 27(1961), March, 14.

Pereira, A.P., *Success in 30 days*, Bombay, St.Paul's Publ., 1960, in: *ESA*, 27(1961), March, 14-15.

St. Alphonsus Liguori, *Visits to the Most Blessed Sacrament and to the Blessed Virgin Mary for each day of the month*, Bombay, St.Paul's Publ., 1960, in: *ESA*, 27(1961), April, 10.

Siekmann, T.C., *Advice for boys. Instructions for catholic youths*, Bombay, St.Paul's Publ., 1960, in: *ESA*, l.c..

Milani, A., *The great promise or the key of heaven offered by the Sacred Heart of Jesus to all his lovers. Considerations and examples for the nine first Fridays*, Bombay, St.Paul's Publ., 1960, in: *ESA*, l.c..

Gasbarri, Ch., *A saint for the new India. Father Joseph Vaz, Apostle of Kanara and Ceylon*, Bombay, St.Paul's Publ., 1961, in: *ESA*, 27(1961), May, 4.

Ryan, V.J., *Who labour in the Lord. Layfolk in action*, Bombay, St.Paul's Publ., 1960, in: *ESA*, 27(1961), May, 4 and 20.

Glissenaar, J., *Arabieren huilen niet*. Met foto's van Peter Pennarts, Blaricum, 1961, in: *Sint Antonius* 64(Woerden/Weer 1962), 85.

Koren, H.J., *Knaves or knights? A History of the Spiritan missionaries in Acadia and North America, 1732-1893*, Pittsburgh-Leuven-Rhenen U., 1962, in: *Het Missiewerk*, 41(1962), 193-194.

Smet, R.V. De SJ, *Philosophical activity in Pakistan: 1947-1961*, New York-Heverlee-Louvain, International Philosophical Quarterly, 2(1962), in: *NZM*, 19(1963), 71.

Meerman, A. OFM, *The Franciscans in Tamil nad*, Schöneck-Beckenried, NZM, 1962, in: *Het Missiewerk*, 42(1963), 262-263.

Conçalves, J.J., *O Mundo Arabo-Islamica e o Ultramar Português*, Lisboa, 1962, in: *NZM*, 20(1964), 74-75.

Unesco-Pax Romana Meeting at Manilla and First Pax Romana Graduate Conference in Asia, 2nd to 9th Janyary 1960, s.l., s.a., in: *NZM*, 20(1964), 78.

Watt, W. (Montgomery), *Islam and the integration of society*, London, 1961, in: *Social Compass*, 10(1963), 571-572.

Hooper, J.S.M., *Bible translations in India, Pakistan and Ceylon*, London, 1963², in: *NZM* 21(1965), 74-75.

López, G.J. SJ, *El matrimonio de los Japoneses, Problema y soluciones según un MS. inédito de Gil de la Mata SJ (1547-1599)*, Roma, 1964, in: *HM*, 44(1965), 179-180.

Hang, Th., *Grundzüge des Chinesischen Volkscharakters*, Würzburg 1964, in: *HM*, 44(1965), 180.

Enklaar, J.H., *Joseph Kam, "apostel der Molukken"*, 's-Gravenhage 1963, in: *HM*, 44(1965), 180-181.

Gardet, L., *De Islam, Godsdienst en gemeenschap*, Roermond-Maaseik, Romen en Zonen, 1964, in: *Oecumene*, 4(1965), 18.

Growing, P.G., *Mosque and moro, a study of the Muslims in the Philippines*, Manilla, 1964, in: *NZM*, 21(1965), 154.

Spae, J.J. CICM, *Catholicism in Japan, a sociological study*, Tokyo, IRS Press, 1963; *Precatechetics for Japan*, Tokyo, Oriens Institute for Religious Research, 1964; *Christian corridors to Japan*, ibidem 1965, in: *HM*, 44(1965), 262-265.

Deats, R.L., *The story of Methodism in the Philippines*, Manilla, 1964, in: *HM*, 45(1966), 68-69.

Nebreda, A.M. SJ, *Jalones para una preevangelización en Japon*, Estella, 1964, in: *HM*, 45(1966), 69.

Cuttat, J.A., *Le dialogue spirituel orient-occident, avec une lettre du Pandit Nehru*, Leuven, 1964, in: *HM*, 45(1966), 69.

The modern mission apostolate. A symposium, New York, 1965;

Reappraisal: Prelude to change, New York, 1965, in: *HM* 45(1966), 71-72.

Beaureceuil, S. de OP, *Nous avons partagé le pain et le sel*, Paris, 1965, in: *Spiritus*, 27(1966), 223.

Bontinck, F., *La lutte autour de la liturgie chinoise aux XVII et XVIIIe siècles*, Leuven-Paris, Nauwelaerts, 1962, in: *TvTh*, 6(1966), 208.

Bruning, H., *Vormkracht en onmacht der religie*, Arnhem, Missionair Christendom, 1961, in: *TvTh*, 6(1966), 210.

Gramberg, Th.B., *Oecumene in India en Ceylon*, 's-Gravenhage, Boekencentrum, 1962, in: *TvTh*, 6(1966), 217.

244

Italiaander, R. (Hrsg.), *Die Herausforderung des Islams*, Göttingen, Berlin, Frankfurt, Mustreschmidt Verlag, 1965, in: *ZMR*, 51(1967), 189.

Grassi, J.A, *A World to win, the missionary methods of Paul the Apostle*, Maryknoll, N.Y., 1965, in: *HM*, 46(1967), 123.

Anderson, G.H. (ed.), *Sermons to men of other faiths and traditions*, Nashville, N.Y., Abingdon Press, 1966, in: *HM*, 46(1967), 123-124.

Richardson, W.J. (ed.), *Revolution in missionary thinking*, Maryknoll, N.Y., 1966, in: *HM*, 46(1967), 125.

Lopez Gay, J. SJ, *El catecumenado en la misión del Japon del S. XVI*, Roma, Studia Missionalia, Documenta et Opera 2, 1966, in: *HM*, 46(1967), 125-126.

Nieuwe verkondigingsvormen als levensruimte voor de kerk, de Heerbaan n.3/4, 1965, in: *HM*, 46(1967), 126-127.

Anderson, G.H. (ed.), *Christian mission in theological perspective. An inquiry by Methodists*, Nashville-New York, Abingdom Press, 1967, in: *HM*, 47(1968), 119-120.

Meersman, A. OFM, *The Franciscans in the Indonesian archipelago 1300-1775*, Leuven, 1967, in: *HM*, 49(1970), 58-59.

Wicki, J. SJ, *Documenta Indiae X: 1575-1577*, Roma, 1968, in: *ZMR*, 54(1970), 311.

Teukenshuh, Fr., *Profile. A people, a mission, a bishop. Memorial brochure for Most Rev. Alphonse Sowada OSC*, Nebraska, Hastings, 1970, in: *HM*, 50(1971), 131.

Wicki, J. SJ, *Documenta Indica, Vol. XI: 1577-1580*, Roma, 1970, in: *ZMR*, 55(1971), 138-139.

Rommerskirchen, G. OMI, Metzele, G. OMI, Henkel, W. OMI, *Bibliografia Missionaria, Anno XXXIV*, Roma, 1970, 1971, in: *HM*, 50(1971), 283.

Baumgartner, J. SMB (Hrsg.), *Vermittlung zwischenkirchlicher Gemeinschaft*, Schöneck-Beckenried, 1971, in: *HM*, 50(1971), 283-284.

Baumgartner, J. SMB, *Mission und Liturgie in Mexico, erster Band*, Schöneck-Beckenried, 1971, in: *HM*, 50(1971), 284.

Bless, W. SJ, *Vragen rond geloofsverkondiging aan volwassenen, bekeken vanuit de huidige geloofscrisis*, in: *HM*, 50(1971), 285.

Gheddo, P., *Catholiques et Bouddhistes au Vietnam*, Paris, 1970, in: *HM*, 50(1971), 285.

Debruyne, L. CICM, *Le païen? Le salut?*, Louvain, 1971, in: *HM*, 50(1971), 285-286.

Oecumenisme et mission. XLe semaine de missiologie de Louvain, Tournai, 1971, in: *HM*, 50(1971), 286-287.

Hecken, J. van CICM, *Documentatie betreffende de missiegeschiedenis van Oost-Mongolië*, deel 3-5, in: *HM*, 50(1971), 287.

Rzepkowski, H. SVD, *Das Menschenbild bei Daisetz Teitaro Suzuki*, St.Augustin, 1971, in: *HM*, 50(1971), 287-288.

Brown, D., *Christianity and Islam*, dl 1-4; Huelin, G., *o.c.*, dl 5, London, Sheldon Press, 1967-1970, in: *De Heerbaan*, 24(1971), 379-380.

Baumgartner, J. SMB (Hrsg.), *Vermittlung zwischenkirklicher Gemeinschaft*, Schöneck, NZM, 1971, in: *ZMR*, 55(1971), 287-288.

Streit-Dindinger, *Missionsliteratur Indiens 1910-1948*, Rom-Freiburg, Bibliotheca Missionum. Bd. XXVII, 1970, in: *ZMR*, 55(1971), 294-295.

Umanesimo ed evangelizzazione. Atti della nona Settimana di Studi missionari (1968), Milano, 1969, in: *ZMR*, 55(1971), 294-295.

Höffner J., *Kolonialismus und Evangelium. Spanische kolonial-ethik im Goldenen Zeitalter*, Trier, Paulinus Verlag, 2er ed., 1969, in: *BSMS*, 1970, n.8, 106-107.

Hastings, A., *Mission and Ministry*. London, Sheed and Ward, 1971, in: *ZMR*, 56(1972), 63-64; *NZM*, 28(1972), 304-305.

Baeck, L., *De Wereld is ons dorp*, Tielt/Utrecht, Lannoo, 1971, in: *WZ*, 1(1972), 236.

Slomp, J., *Joden, Christenen en Muslims: een driehoeksverhouding?*, Kampen, Kok, 1971, in: *WZ*, 1(1972), 237.

Wicki, J. (ed.), *Documenta Indica*, Vol.XI, Vol.XII, Roma, 1970, 1972, in: *NZM*, 28(1972), 304-305.

Bornemann, F., *Arnold Janssen, der Gründer des Steyler Missionswerkes 1837-1909*, Steyl, 1969, in: *BSMS*, 1971, n. 10, 25.

245

Hallencreutz, C.F., *New approaches to men of other faiths*, Geneva, 1970, in: *Ib.*, 36-37.
Thomas G., *Die Portugiesische Indianerpolitik in Brasilien 1500-1640*, Berlin, 1968, in: *Ib.*, 101-102.
Hollenweger W.J., *Enthusiastes Christentum. Die Pfingstbewegung in Geschichte und Gegenwart*, Zürich, 1969, in: *BSMS*, 1972, n.12, 7-8.
Kähler, M., *Schriften zur Christologie und Mission*, München, in: *Ib.*, 8-9.
Huck, E.R., Moseley E.H., *Militarists, mershants and missionaries, United States expansion in Middle America*, Alabama, 1970, in: *Ib.*, 57.
Baumgartner, *Mission und Liturgie in Mexico, I. Der Gottesdienst in der jungen Kirche neu-Spaniens*, Schöneck-Beckenried, 1971, in: *Ib.*, 67-68.
Martin L., *The intellectual conquest of Peru. The Jesuit college of San Pablo*, 1568-1767, New York, 1968, in: *Ib.*, 71.
Danael, M.L., *Old en new in Southern Shona independent churches*, Vol.I, The Hague-Paris, 1971, in: *NZM*, 29(1973), 75.
Basetti-Sani, G., *Louis Masignon orientalista cristiano*, Milan, Vita e Pensiero, 1971, in: *BSMS*, 1974, n.16, 49.
Noggler, A., *Vierhundert Jahre Arankanermission*, Schöneck-Beckenried, NZM, 1973, in: *Ib*, 1974, n.16, 115-116.
Grichting, W.L., *The value system in Taiwan 1970*, Taipei, Taiwan 1971, in: *WZ*, 4(1975), 142.
Gispert-Sauch, G., *Word among men. Papers in honour of Fr. J. Putz SJ and Frs. J. Bayart, J. Volckaert and P. de Lether SJ*, Dehli, 1975, in: *TvTh*, 15(1975), 347.
Amstutz, J., *Kirche der Völker*, Freiburg-Basel-Wien, 1972, in: *NZM*,31(1975), 227-228.
Kaspar, A., Berger, Pl., *Hwan Gab. 60 Jahre Benedictinermission in Korea und der Mandscharei*, Münsterscharzach, 1973, in: *BSMS*, 1975, n.17, 143-144.
E.V.O. Duc Hauh, *La place du catholicisme dans les relations entre la France et le Vietnam de 1851 à 1870*, Leiden, Brill 1969, in: *Ib.*, 162-163.
Roest-Crollius, A.A., *Thus were they hearing. The Word in the experience of revelation in Qur'an and Hindu scriptures*, Roma, 1974, in: *TvTh*, 16(1976), 466.
Young, W.G., *Patriarch, Shah and Caliph*, Rawalpindi, 1974, in: *NZM*, 32(1976), 70-71.
Vemmelund, L., *The Christian minority in North West Frontier Province of Pakistan*, Rawalpindi, 1972, in: *NZM*, 32(1976), 74-75.
Bühlmann, W., *Wo der Glaube lebt*, Freiburg-Basel-Wien, Herder, 1974[2], in: *WZ*, 4(1975), 240-241.
Verstraelen, F.J., *An African Church in transition: from missionary dependence to mutuality in mission. A case-study on the Roman-Catholic Church in Zambia*, 2 delen, Tilburg/Leiden, 1975, in: *WZ*, 6(1977), 378-380.
Koyama, K., *Creatieve theologie. Het evangelie in Aziatisch perspectief*, Hilversum, 1976, in: *TvTh*, 17(1977), 309-310.
Verkuyl, J., *Inleiding in de nieuwere zendingswetenschap*, Kampen, Kok, 1975, in: *Occasional Bulletin*, 1(1977), 22.
Coffele, G. SDB, *Johannes Christiaan Hoekendijk: da una teologia della missione ad una teologia missionaria*, Roma, 1976, in: *WZ*, 7(1978), 186-188.
Prien, H.-J., *Die Geschichte des Christentums in Lateinamerika*, Göttingen, Vandenhoeck en Ruprecht, 1978, in: *WZ*, 7(1978), 359-360.
Wicki, J. SJ, *Missionskirche im Orient*, Immensee, 1976, in: *NZM*, 34(1978), 153.
Mintjes, H., *Social justice in Islam*, Amsterdam-Leusden, 1977, in: *WZ*, 7(1978), 279.
Young, W.G., *Patriarch, Shah and Caliph. A study of the relationships of the church of the East with the Sassanid Empire and the early caliphates up to 820 A.D. with special reference to available translated syriac sources*, Rawalpindi, 1974, in: *WZ*, 8(1979), 184.
Verkuyl, J., *De onvoltooide taak der wereldzending*, Kampen, 1978, in: *WZ*, 8(1979), 188-189.
Dijk, B., *Moderne poëzie uit Azië*, Amsterdam, 1977, in: *WZ*, 8(1979), 273.
Waardenburg, J.D.J., *Zien met anderman's ogen*, Den Haag, 1975, in: *WZ*, 8(1979), 276-277.
Slomp, J., *Publicaties over het evangelie van Barnabas*, in: *WZ*, 8(1979), 27.
Myklebust, O.G., *Missionskunnskap, en innforing*, Oslo, 1976, in: *WZ*, 8(1979), 278.
Revelation in Christianity and other religions. Révélation dans le christianisme et les autres religions, Roma, Gregorian University Press, 1971, in: *WZ*, 8(1979), 362.

246

La Sacra Congregazione per l'Evangelizzazione dei Populi nel decennio del decreto "Ad gentes", Roma, 1975, in: *WZ*, 8(1979), 362-363.

Wicki, J. SJ, *Missionskirche im Orient. Ausgewählte Beiträge über Portugiesisch-Asien*, Immensee, NZM, 1976, in: *Missiology*, 8(1980), 123-124.

Zeitler, E., e.a., *Women in India and in the church*, Pune, 1978, in: *Missiology*, 8(1980), 369-370.

Kramm, Th., *Analyse und Bewährung theologischer Modelle zur Begründung der Mission*, Aachen, 1979, in: *WZ*, 9(1980), 244-245.

Glazik, J., *Mission. Der stets grössere Auftrag*, Aachen, 1979, in: *WZ*, 9(1980), 245.

Seumois, A., *Théologie missionaire, IV. Eglise missionaire et facteurs socio-culturels*, Roma, 1978, in: *WZ*, 9(1980), 246-247.

Boudens, R., *Catholic missionaries in a British Colony. Successes and failures in Ceylon 1796-1893*, Immensee, 1979, in: *TvTh*, 20(1980), 204.

Glüer, W., *Christliche Theologie in China: T.C. Chao 1918-1956*, Gütersloh, Mohn, 1979, in: *TvTh*, 20(1980), 323.

Strelan, J.G., *Search for salvation. Studies in the history and theology of cargo cults*, Adelaide, Lutheran Publishing House, 1977, in: *WZ*, 9(1980), 367-368.

Religieuze bewegingen in Nederland. Feiten en visies, n.1, Kampen, 1980, in: *WZ*, 10(1981), 281.

Myklebust, O.G., Schreuder, H.P.S., *Kirke og misjon. Land og kirke*, Oslo, Gyldendal Norsk Forlag, 1980, in: *WZ*, 10(1981), 205.

Verkuyl, J., *Preken en preekschetsen in verband met de wereldzending, het werelddiakonaat en de ontwikkelingssamenwerking*, Kampen, Kok, 1980, in: *TvTh*, 21(1981), 218.

Metzeler, J., *Die synoden in China, Japan und Korea: 1570-1931*, Paderborn, Schönrügh, 1980, in: *TvTh*, 21(1981), 328.

Wessels, A., *De renaissance van de Islam*, Baarn, Ten Have, 1980, in: *WZ*, 10(1981), 371-372.

Bühlmann, W., *Wenn Gott zu allen Menschen geht*, Freiburg-Basel-Wien, Herder, 1981, in: *Theologischer Literaturdienst*, 14(1982), n.1, 1-2.

Anderson, G.H., Strausky, F. (eds), *Christ's lordship and religious pluralism*, Maryknoll, N.Y., Orbis Books, 1981, in: *WZ*, 11(1982) 78-79.

Hesselgrave, D.J. (ed.), *Dynamic religious movements. Case studies of rapid growing religious movements around the world*, Grand Rapids, Baker, 1978, in: *WZ*, 11(1982), 283.

Schmidt, W., *Der lange Marsch zurück. Der Weg der Christenheit in Asien*, München, Kaiser, 1980, in: *TvTh*, 22(1982), 328-329.

Anderson, G.H., Strausky, Th. (eds), *Faith meets faith*, New York-Toronto-Grand Rapids, Paulist Press- Ramsey- Eerdmans, 1981, in: *NZM*, 38(1982), 305.

Universales Heil und Mission. Studien über die ekklesial-missionarischen Struktur in der Theologie K. Rahners und im Epheserbrief, St. Augustin, Regina Pacis Meyer, Steyler Verlag, 1979, in: *Missiology*, 10(1982), 119-120.

Rooney, J., *Khabar Gembira (The Good News). A history of the Catholic Church in East Malaysia and Brunei (1880-1976)*, London-Kota Kinabalu, Burns and Gates, 1981, in: *WZ*, 11(1982), 364.

Randwijck, S.C. Graaf van, *Handelen en denken in dienst der zending*, Oegstgeest 1897-1942, I + II, Den Haag, Boekencentrum, 1981, in: *TvTh*, 22(1982), 348.

Bühlmann, W., *Wenn Gott zu allen menschen geht. Für eine neue Erfahrung der Auserwählung*, Freiburg-Basel-Wien, Herder 1981, in: *TvTh*, 22(1982), 446.

Dharampal, G., *La religion des Malabars. Tessier de Quéralay et la contribution des missionaires européens à la naissance de l'Indianisme*, Immensee, NRM, 1982, in: *WZ*, 12(1983), 83.

Jathanna, O.B., *The decisiveness of the Christ-event and the universality of christianity in a world of religious plurality*, Bern-Frankfurt-Las Vegas, Lange, 1981, in: *WZ*, 12(1983), 261-262.

Straelen, H. van, *Ouverture à l'autre, laquelle? L'apostolat missionaire et le monde non chrétien*, Paris, Beauchesne, 1982, in: *TvTh*, 23(1983), 321.

Soetens, Cl., *Recueils des archives Vincent Lebbe. Pour l'Eglise chinoise. La visite apostolique des missions de Chine 1919-20*, Louvain-la-Neuve, Faculté de Théologie, 1982, in: *TvTh*, 23(1983), 440-441.

Torwewsten, H., *Sind wir nur einmal auf Erden? Die Idee der Reinkarnation angesichts des Auferstehungsglaubens*, Freiburg-Basel-Wien, Herder, 1983, in: *ZMR*, 68(1984), 246-248.

247

Cray, M. van, *Kirche im Entkolonisierungskonflikt. Eine Fallstudie zum Krieg um die Entkolonisierung Mosambiks 1964-1974*, München, Mainz, Kaiser, Grünewald, 1981, in: *WZ*, 13(1984), 283-284.

Micksch, J., Mildenberger, M. (Hrsg.), *Christen und Muslims, ein Gespräch, eine Handreichung*, Frankfurt a.M., Otto Lembeck, 1982, in: *WZ*, 13(1984), 285.

The Churches and Islam in Europe (II), Geneva, Conference of European Churches, 1982, in: *WZ*, 13(1984), 286.

Neill, S., *A history of christianity in India. The beginnings to AD 1707*, Cambridge, Cambr. Univ. Press, 1984, in: *TvTh*, 24(1984), 309.

Soetens, Cl., *Inventaire des archives Vincent Lebbe; Receuil des archives Vincent Lebbe. Pour l'Eglise chinoise, I: La visite apostolique des missions de Chine 1919-1920*, II: *Une nonciature à Pékin en 1918*, III: *L'Encyclique Maximum Illud*, Louvain-la-Neuve, Faculté de Théologie, 1982, 1983, 1984, in: *NZM*, 40(1984), 316-317.

Kauffmann, P.E., *China, the emerging challenge. A christian perspective*, Grand Rapids, Baker Book House, 1982, in: *WZ*, 13(1984), 375.

Fulgentius, M., *Een paapjen omtrent het fort. Het apostolisch Vicariaat van Suriname*, Paramaribo, Vaco, 1983, in: *OSO*, 3(1984), 250-253.

Metzeler, J., *Die Synoden in Indochina 1625-1934*, Paderborn-München-Wenen-etc., 1984, in: *TvTh*, 25(1985), 199-200.

Mulrain, G.M., *Theology in folk culture. The theological significance of Haitian folk religion*, Frankfurt a M.-Bern-New York-Nancy, Lang, 1984, in: *ZMR*, 69(1985), 253-254.

Braswell, G.W. Jr., *Understanding world religions*, Nashville, Broadman Press, 1983, in: *WZ*, 14(1985), 276.

Soares-Prabhu, A.M. (Hrsg.), *Wir werden bei ihm wohnen: Das Johannesevangelium in indischer Deutung*, Freiburg-Bazel-Wenen, Herder, 1984, in: *TvTh*, 25(1985), 309.

Soetens, Cl., *Receuil des archives Vincent Lebbe*; Sohier, A., *Un an d'activité du Père Lebbe: 1926*, Louvain-la-Neuve, Faculté de Théologie, 1984, in: *NZM*, 41(1985), 318.

Sundermeier, Th., Wigern, (Hrsg.), *Gensichen, H.W., Mission und Kultur. Gesammelte Aufsätze*, München, Kaiser, 1985, in: *TvTh*, 25(1985), 432.

Neill, S., *A history of christianity in India: 1707-1858*, Cambridge, Cambr. Univ. Press, 1985, in: *TvTh*, 26(1986), 300-301.

Dehm, U.M., *Indische Christen in der Gesellschaftlichen Verantwortung. Eine theologische und religionssoziologische Untersuchung zu politischer Theologie im gegewärtigen Indien*, Frankfurt a/M, 1985, in: *TvTh*, 26(1986), 322-323.

Drummond, R.H., *Toward a new age in Christian theology*, Maryknoll, N.Y., Orbis Books 1985, in: *Missiology*, 14(1986), 509-510.

Wessels, A., *Jezus zien. Hoe Jezus is overgeleverd in andere culturen*, Baarn, Ten Have, 1986, in: *Mission Studies*, 3(1986), n.2, 103-104.

Thekkedath, J. SDB, *History of christianity in India, Vol.II: From the middle of the sixteenth to the end of the seventeenth Century (1542-1700)*, Bangalore, 1982, in: *NZM*, 42(1986), 307-308.

Khoury, A.Th. (Hrsg.), *Buddha für Christen*, Freiburg-Basel-Wien, Herder, 1986, in: *ZMR*, 71(1987), 242-243.

Chemparathy, G., *God en het lijden, een indische theodicee*, Leiden, Brill, 1986, in: *ZMR*, 71(1987), 243-244.

Jongeneel, J.A.B., *Missiologie 1: Zendingswetenschap*, 's-Gravenhage, Boekencentrum 1986, in: *TvTh*, 27(1987), 217.

Stamoolis, J.J., *Eastern Orthodox mission theology today*, Maryknoll N.Y., Orbis Books, 1986; Bria, I. (ed.), *Go Forth in peace, Ortodox perspectives on mission*, Geneva, WCC, 1986, in: *WZ*, 16(1987), 282-283.

Covell, R.R., *Confusius, the Buddha, and Christ. A history of the gospel in chinese*, Maryknoll N.Y., Orbis Books, 1986, in: *WZ*, 16(1987), 372.

Hector Diaz, M.G., *A Korean theology, Chu-Gyo. Yo-Yi: Essentials of the Lord's teaching by Chóng Yak-jong Augustine (1760-1801)*, Immensee, NZM, 1986, in: *WZ*, 15(1987), 372-374.

Takenaka, M., *God Rice, Asian culture and Christian faith*, Geneva, WCC, 1986, in: *WZ*, 16(1987), 374.

248

Jongeneel, J.A.B., Klootwijk, E., *Nederlandse faculteiten der godgeleerdheid, theologische hogescholen en derde wereld. Algemene inleiding en overzichten vanaf 1876*, Leiden/Utrecht, IIMO, in: *NZM*, 44(1988), 57.

Soetens, Cl., *Receuil des archives Vincent Lebbe. La Règle des Petits Frères de Saint-Jean Baptiste*, Louvain-la-Neuve, Faculté de Théologie, 1986, in: *NZM*, 44(1988), 56-57.

Swidler, L. (ed.), *Towards a universal theology of religions*, Maryknoll, N.Y., Orbis Books, 1987, in: *ID*, 1988, 8; *NZM*, 44(1988), 148-149; *WZ*, 18(1989), 177-178.

Amirtham, S., e.a., (eds), *Ministerial formation in a multi-faith milieu*, Geneva, 1986, in: *NZM*, 44(1988), 235.

Spae, J.J., *Mandarijn Paul Splingaerd*, Bruxelles, Académie Royale des Sciences d'Outre-Mer, 1986, in: *NZM*, 44(1988), 235-236.

D'Costa, G., *Theology and religious pluralism. The challenge of other religions*, Oxford, Basil Blackwell, 1986, in: *Missiology*, 16(1988), 228-229.

Kohler, W., Salaquarda, J. (Hrsg.), *Umkehr und Umdenken. Grundzüge einer Theologie der Mission*, Frankfurt a/M-Bern-New York-Paris, Lang, 1988, in: *WZ*, 18(1989), 93.

Spae, J.J., *Scheut in Sinkiang 1878-1922*, Oud-Heverlee, China Update, 1987, in: *NZM*, 45(1989), 63.

Molendijk, A.L., *Getuigen in missionair en oecumenisch verband. Een studie over het begrip "getuigen" in de dokumenten van de Wereldraad van Kerken, de Rooms-Katholieke Kerk en de Evangelikalen in de periode 1948-1985*, Leiden-Utrecht, IIMO, 1986, in: *NZM*, 45(1989), 63-64.

Moritzen, N.-P., *Werkzeug Gottes in der Welt. Leipziger Mission 1836-1936*, Erlangen, Verlag der Ev.-Luth. Mission, 1986, in: *Missiology*, 17(1989), 368-369.

Mensen, B. (Hrsg.), *China, sein neues Gesicht*, Nettetal, Steyler Verlag-Wort und Werk, 1987, in: *WZ*, 18(1989), 391.

Prawdzik, W. (Hrsg.), *Theologie im Dienst der Weltkirche. Festschrift zum 75 jährigen Bestehen des Missionspriesterseminars St. Augustin bei Bonn*, Netetal, Steyler V., 1988, in: *WZ*, 18(1989), 393-394.

249

Tabula gratulatorum

Adroles Adegbola, Centr. for Appl. Rel. and Educ., Ibadan, Nigeria
Prof. dr. Theodor Ahrens, Univ. Hamburg (Fachb. Ev. Theol.), Germany
Oscar Ante, Nijmegen, the Netherlands/Philippines
Theo Beemer, Nijmegen, the Netherlands
C. van den Berg SCJ, Maasbommel, the Netherlands
Stephen Bevans SVD, Cath. Theol. Union Cornell, Chicago, Il, USA
Nils E. Bloch-Hoell, Oslo, Norway
Drs. H.J.W.M. Boelaars OFM Cap., Tilburg, the Netherlands
Drs. Cees Bouma, Arnhem, the Netherlands
Gerben J.F. Bouritius, Tilburg, the Netherlands
J. van Brakel SMA, Nijmegen, the Netherlands
Dr. M.E. Brinkman, De Bilt, the Netherlands
P. Walbert Bühlmann OFM Cap., Arth, Switzerland
Dr. G. Jan Butselaar, Bennebroek, the Netherlands
Jan Camps, Castricum, the Netherlands
H.J.A.M. en R.A. Camps, Geldrop, the Netherlands
M.P.M. Camps, Eindhoven, the Netherlands
Centraal Missionair Beraad Religieuzen, Oegstgeest, the Netherlands
Bruno Chenu, Paris, France
Colegio Olandese, Rome, Italy
Prof. dr. Giancarlo Collet, Everswinkel, Germany
Communiteit Franciscanen Wijchen, the Netherlands
Drs. G.M.M. Cuppen, Broekhuizen, the Netherlands
Geert van Dartel, Oss, the Netherlands
A.J.M. Davids, Nijmegen, the Netherlands
J.G. Donders, Washington DC, USA
Prof. dr. Richard Drummond, Univ. of Dubuque Theol. Sem., USA
Rev. Peder A. Eidberg, Stabekk, Norway
Dr. Marita Estor, International Grail Movement, Bonn, Germany
J. van Eijndhoven, Sint Michielsgestel, the Netherlands
H.J.M. Faazen, Nijmegen, the Netherlands
Robert E. Fulop, Centr. Bapt. Theol. Semin., Kansas, USA
Prof. dr. Michael Fuß, Bonn, Germany
Jacques Gadille, CREDIC, Lyon, France
Prof. D.H.W. Gensichen, Heidelberg, Germany
Henk Geraedts OFM, provinciaal Franciscanen, Utrecht, the Netherlands

Dr. Kenneth Gill, Wheaton College, Wheaton, USA
Josef Glazik MSC, Bergisch Gladbach, Germany
Rev. dr. Jan Górski, Katowice, Poland
Jerald and Donna Gort, Uitgeest, the Netherlands
Dr. Hugald Grafe, Mildesheim, Germany
Mary Grey, Binfield, Bracknell, Berkshire, England
Bert Groen, Nijmegen, the Netherlands
Drs. B.L. de Groot-Kopetzky, Nijmegen, the Netherlands
Dr. R. Haan, Utrecht, the Netherlands
F. Haarsma, Nijmegen, the Netherlands
Maurus de Haas OFM, Wijchen, the Netherlands
Prof. dr. theol. habil. Ludwig Hagemann, Würzburg, Germany
Gordon M. Haliburton, Wolfville, Canada
Hermann Häring, Nijmegen, the Netherlands
Willi Henkel OMI, Pontif. Univ. Urbaniana, Rome, Italy
Dr. Klaus Hock, Bukuru, Plateau St., Nigeria
Bert Hoedemaker, Groningen, the Netherlands
Dr. Marvin D. Hoff, Western Seminary, Holland, Michigan, USA
Bernard Höfte, De Meern, the Netherlands
Prof. dr. P.N. Holtrop, Blokzijl, the Netherlands
Dien en Anton Honig, Kampen, the Netherlands
Dr. George R. Hunsberger, Holland, Michigan, USA
Helma Hurkens, Tilburg, the Netherlands
Marinus Huybreghts, Breda, the Netherlands
Ton van Iersel Oomens, Udenhout, the Netherlands
A.H.M. van Iersel, Amersfoort, the Netherlands
Institut für Missionswissenschaft der Universität Münster, Germany
Paul Jenkins, Basel Mission, Basel, Switzerland
Dr. Kees de Jong SSCC, St. Oedenrode, the Netherlands/Indonesia
A.H. de Jong, Berg en Dal, the Netherlands
Maria C. Jongeling, Leiderdorp, the Netherlands
Prof. dr. J.A.B. Jongeneel, Bunnik, the Netherlands
Jan Kerkhofs SJ, Heverlee-Leuven, Belgium
Prof. dr. Norbert Klaes, Phil. Fakultät, Würzburg, Germany
A.M.J. en B.J. Klein Goldewijk, Oldenzaal, the Netherlands
Berma Klein Goldewijk, Theol. Faculty, Nijmegen, the Netherlands
J.M.G. Kleinpenning, Nijmegen, the Netherlands
Dr. J.A. de Kok OFM, ep. aux, Aartsbisdom Utrecht, the Netherlands
Dr. Fritz Kollbrunner, Luzern, Switzerland
Ben Koolen, Rotterdam, the Netherlands
Dr. Klaus Koschorke, Worb, Switzerland
Drs. Th.M.G.J. Krabbe, Enschede, the Netherlands
Dr. J.N.J. Kritzinger, Pretoria West, South Africa
Sjef Kuppens M. Afr., Nijmegen, the Netherlands
Dr. H. van der Laan, Gorinchem, the Netherlands

Bishop L.S. Ayo Ladigbolu, Methodist Church, Ifaki-Ekiti, Nigeria
Prof. dr. J. van der Lans, Bergharen, the Netherlands
Jan A. (Gerwin) van Leeuwen OFM, Bangalore, India
Ria Lemaire, Amsterdam, the Netherlands
Dr. J. van Lin, Ewijk, the Netherlands
Prof. dr. J.M. van der Linde, Zeist, the Netherlands
Hans Litjens, Nijmegen, the Netherlands
Herman Lombaerts, Brussels, Belgium
Jesús López-Gay SJ, Rome, Italy
András Máté-Tóth, Szeged, Hungary
Atama Matua, Louvain, Belgium
Prof. dr. Gary B. McGee, Theological Semin., Springfield, USA
Priv.-Doz. dr. Johannes Meier, Würzburg, Germany
C.Th.G. Molenkamp SSCC, St. Oedenrode, the Netherlands
P. Andreas Müller, Bonn, Germany
Karl Müller SVD (Steyler Miss. wiss. Inst. e. V.), St. Augustin, Germ.
Martin Muskens, Rome, Italy
Olav G. Myklebust, Oslo, Norway
Valeer Neckebrouck, Korbeek-Dijle, Belgium
Nederlandse Zendingsraad, Amsterdam, the Netherlands
NOVIB-Uitgeverij, Dirk Jan Broertjes, Den Haag, the Netherlands
Alfons van Nunen, Jayapura, Irian Jaya, Indonesia
Hans Oldenhof, Nijmegen, the Netherlands
Rev. dr. Andrews Oyalana, Imm. Coll. of Theol., Ibadan, Nigeria
P. Carlos Pape SVD, Secr. de Misiones svd, Rome, Italy
Prof. dr. J.R.T.M. Peters, Nijmegen, the Netherlands
Els M.C. Pikaar, Nijmegen, the Netherlands
P. dr. Kurt Piskaty SVD, Mödling, Austria
Prof. John S. Pobee, Geneva, Switzerland
Pontificio Collegio Olandese, Rome, Italy
The Rev. Titus Presler, Dedham, USA
The most Rev. Archbishop D. Quatannens, Antwerpen, Belgium
J. van Raalte, Driebergen, the Netherlands
S. Joseph Raj SJ, Vidyajyoti, Delhi, India
Arij Roest Crollius SJ, Rome, Italy
P. Rogmans-Camps, Steensel, the Netherlands
Prof. dr. J. Roldanus, Groningen, the Netherlands
Rogier G. van Rossum SSCC, Valkenburg a/d Geul, the Netherlands
Gert Rüppell, Viittakivi International Centre, Hauho, Finland
Jan van Schaardenburgh, Haaksbergen, the Netherlands
Wilbert R. Schenk, Birmingham, United Kingdom
Lothar Schreiner, Wuppertal, Germany
Prof. dr. R.J. Schreiter, Chicago, USA
Prof. dr. Nico Schreurs, Heumen, the Netherlands
Jur Schuurman, Utrecht, the Netherlands

E.J. Shamatutu, Edinburgh, Great Britain
Prof. Eric J. Sharpe, Dep. of Rel. Stud., Univ. of Sidney, Australia
Luis Ignacio Sierra Gutiérrez, Bogotá, Colombia
Dr. Hans-Dietrich Sitzler, Nettetal, Germany
Drs. Jan Slomp, Leusden, the Netherlands
Prof. Claude Soetens, Louvain-la Neuve, Belgium
Prof. dr. M.R. Spindler, Leiden, the Netherlands
Ph. D. Paul Stadler, St. Gallen, Switzerland
B. Standaert, Institute Gaudium et Spes, Brugge, Belgium
Karel Steenbrink, Leiden, the Netherlands
Alfons S. Suhardi OFM, Jakarta, Indonesia
Edmond Tang, Brussels, Belgium
Saul Kipkosgei Tanui, Limuru, Kenya, Africa
Dr. Sjef Theunis, Fundación El Taller, Reus, Spain
André Truyman, Hilversum, the Netherlands
Dr. E.M. Uka, University of Calabar, Nigeria
Pim Valkenberg, Utrecht, the Netherlands
Drs. Frans Vanderhoff, Breda, the Netherlands
Dr. Charles Van Engen, Fuller Theol. Seminary, Pasadena, USA
Eric Vanhaeghe, Euntes, Kessel-lo, Belgium
Jacques Van Nieuwenhove, Nijmegen, the Netherlands
J. Vernooij, Paramaribo, Suriname
Prof. dr. F.J. Verstraelen, Dep. Rel. Stud., Univ. Harare, Zimbabwe
Rafael Hernandez Villanueva, Quincy, USA
Kees Waaijman, Nijmegen, the Netherlands
Dr. G.J. Wantohi, Nairobi, Kenya
Ludwig Wiedenmann SJ, Bonn, Germany
Dr. Joachim Wietzke, Hamburg, Germany
Frans Wijsen, Maastricht, the Netherlands
Prof. dr. Bernward H. Willeke OFM, Osnabrück, Germany
Dr. A. Wind, Kampen, the Netherlands
Louk de Wit, Enschede, the Netherlands
Rob van der Zwan, Tilburg, the Netherlands
Theo Zweerman OFM, Megen, the Netherlands

KERK EN THEOLOGIE IN CONTEXT (KTC)

In this series the following titles have been published:

Dr. J.F.L.M. Cornelissen
PATER EN PAPOEA
Ontmoeting van de missionarissen van het Heilig Hart met de cultuur der
Papoea's van Nederlands Zuid-Nieuw-Guinea (1905-1963)
ISBN 90 242 3225 2

Berma Klein Goldewijk, Erik Borgman, Fred van Iersel (red.)
BEVRIJDINGSTHEOLOGIE IN WEST-EUROPA
Teksten van het symposium 'Westeuropese bevrijdingstheologie', gehouden op
12-13 november 1987 aan de Theologische Faculteit te Nijmegen
ISBN 90 242 3195 7

Dr. J.N. Breetvelt
DUALISME EN INTEGRATIE
Een studie van de factoren die een rol spelen bij het hervinden van identiteit bij
opgeleide Afrikanen
ISBN 90 242 5019 6

Dr. J.A.G. Gerwin van Leeuwen o.f.m.
FULLY INDIAN - AUTHENTICALLY CHRISTIAN
A study of the first fifteen years of the NBCLC (1967-1982), Bangalore - India, in
the light of the theology of its founder, D.S. Amalorpavadass
ISBN 90 242 4906 6
*Deze studie maakt deel uit van het VF-project 'Contextualiteit in het missiologisch
denken' van de vakgroep Missiologie, Katholieke Universiteit te Nijmegen.*

Dr. C.A.M. de Jong ss.cc.
KOMPAS 1965-1985
Een algemene krant met een katholieke achtergrond binnen het religieus
pluralisme van Indonesië
ISBN 90 242 5415 9

Drs. J.P. Heijke
KAMEROENSE BEVRIJDINGSTHEOLOGIE *JEAN-MARC ELA*
Theologie van onder de boom
ISBN 90 242 5335 7
*Deze studie maakt deel uit van het VF-project 'Contextualiteit in het missiologisch
denken' van de vakgroep Missiologie, Katholieke Universiteit te Nijmegen.*

Erik Borgman
SPOREN VAN DE BEVRIJDENDE GOD
Universitaire theologie in aansluiting op Latijnsamerikaanse bevrijdingstheologie,
zwarte theologie en feministische theologie
ISBN 90 242 6510 X